A Modern Approach to Comparative Law

A Modern Approach to Comparative Law

by *Peter de Cruz, PhD*

Lecturer in Law
University of Keele

1993
Kluwer
Deventer - Boston

Kluwer Law and Taxation Publishers

P.O. Box 23
7400 GA Deventer / The Netherlands
Tel.: +31 5700 47261
Fax: +31 5700 22244
Telex: 40205

6 Bigelow Street
Cambridge MA 02139 / USA
Tel.: +1 617 342 0140
Fax: +1 617 354 8595

Cover: A-graphics design

ISBN 90 6544 662 1

PREFACE

This book has been written as a modern introduction to the comparative study of law and legal systems and to provide a framework for further study by postgraduates or practitioners. The expression 'comparative law' was apparently first used in the nineteenth century and although it is predominantly a method of study, it has also acquired a sufficient number of methodological principles which suggest that it is well on the way to becoming a branch of social science in its own right. But Comparative Law does not have a substantive core content as, for example, contract law or criminal law does in English law. Therefore, once key concepts such as the sources of law, and parent legal families, have been understood, there is a wide range of topics which merit comparative analysis.

The idea for this book grew out of a series of lectures which I gave as part of the Keele University undergraduate Comparative Law course but several concepts and developments have been updated and developed to take into account recent developments. These new trends, such as European and global convergence may therefore be pursued in greater depth at postgraduate level.

As is widely-accepted, Aristotle collected something in the region of a hundred and fifty city-state constitutions in the fourth century B.C. while engaged in devising a model constitution. Similar comparative enterprises have taken place throughout the centuries in most of what is now known as the civilised Western world. The process of codification has a distinguished pedigree, and a distinctive modern meaning in the context of the nineteenth century French and German codes. The method of comparative law is therefore not a modern enterprise. However, several things justify this book assuming a 'modern' appellation. First, all other recent books have assumed that there are three main parent legal systems, namely, civil law, common law and socialist legal systems. This is no longer the case, as a result of the disintegration of the prototype of socialist systems, the former Soviet Union, and the rejection and demise of Communism throughout Eastern Europe and indeed in other parts of the world. We have therefore returned largely to the pre-1917 position of having only two main legal traditions or major legal systems. Socialist systems continue to exist, but are either returning to their civil law roots or developing into another type of hybrid legal system. Secondly, the impact of European Community Law has now to be taken into account as a unique supra-national legal order, and this book addresses its impact and the influence of legal traditions on Community law as it is being developed by the European Court of Justice.

v

Thirdly, existing books on comparative law do not really address adequately the techniques of comparison, except in generalities. I have attempted to provide a blueprint for comparison in Chapter 2.

Fourthly, it is becoming increasingly clear that the common law distinction between contract and tort is somewhat tenuously rooted in the difference between imposed and assumed duties, historical origins and the different rules on remedies. I have attempted to provide at least the basic arguments relating to the analysis of tort and contract as part of the same law of obligations and this dovetails neatly with the civil law approach. Fifthly, as far as I am aware, no other textbook provides an historical and conceptual introduction to the development of civil and common law, as well as their treatment of important topics such as contract, tort, sale of goods, labour law and company law. Sixthly, the latest developments in certain areas are discussed-for example, the rise of the administrative tribunal in England as well as the future of the law in Hong Kong after 1997, when it reverts to China; the implications of German reunification and the latest Russian developments, all of which have inevitably rendered existing texts out-of-date. Finally, there is an overview of the current geopolitical map of global developments and a brief allusion to the phenomenon of convergence of systems, as well as a survey of the possible reasons for the new world order.

As with enterprises of this nature, there are a number of people to whom I have to record my sincere gratitude. In no particular order, I wish to thank Lorna Bomford of the University of Newcastle upon Tyne Library for her generosity in allowing me access to sources and materials unobtainable anywhere else, Margaret Bird, Law Librarian at Keele University, Dr. Klaus Tonner, who provided me excellent notes on his 'German lectures' at Keele and sent me valuable material, Mark Galeotti for sending me the latest Russian legal bulletins and draft constitution; Michael Whincup, Gillian More, Sally Wheeler, Josephine Shaw, Bimbo Olowofoweyeku and John Alder, all of Keele Law Department, as well as to Andrea Jackson; Phil Fisher for helping to set the index and other assorted alignments; and Patricia Clavin for clarifying some of the ideas expressed by Francis Fukuyama in his public lectures and seminars.

As always, all errors and inaccuracies remain the writer's sole responsibility. This book is dedicated to my wife, Lois, and my parents, who were the first persons who introduced me to a multiplicity of cultures, traditions, religions and laws.

Peter de Cruz
Keele
September 1992

TABLE OF CONTENTS

LIST OF ABBREVIATIONS

ABGB	Allgemeines Burgerliches Gesetzbuch fur Osterreich (Austrian General Civil Code)
A.C.	Appeal Cases (English Law Reports)
AG	Aktiengesellschaft (company)
AGBG	Law on General Condtitions of Business (German)
AmJCL	American Journal of Comparative Law
All ER	All England Reports
BGB	Burgerliches Gesetzbuch (German Civil Code)
BGH	Bundesgerichtshof (Supreme Court, Ordinary Jurisdiction)
BGHZ	Reports of civil cases of the German Federal Supreme Court
Civ.	Cour de Cassation, Chambre civile
Camb.LJ	Cambridge Law Journal
DM	Deutsche Mark
ECR	European Court Reports
EJIL	European Journal of International Law
FMSLR	Federated Malay States Law Reports
GG	Grundgesetz of 23 May 1949: Basic Law: West German Constitution
GVG	Constitution of Courts Act 1975 (Germany)
HGB	German Commercial Code
ICLQ	International and Comparative Law Quarterly
JSPTL	Journal of the Society of the Public Teachers of Law
LQR	Law Quarterly Review
MLJ	Malayan Law Journal
ModLR	Modern Law Review
NJW	*Neue Juristische Wochenschrift*: German Periodical
Req.	Cour de Cassation, Chambre de requetes
RGZ	Decisions in Civil matters of the German Imperial Court
Tul.LR	Tulane Law Review
U.Ch.LR	University of Chicago Law Review
U.Pen.LR	University of Pennsylvania Law Review
ZPO	German Code of Civil Procedure (Zivilprozessordnung)

PART ONE: INTRODUCTION

CHAPTER ONE

What is Comparative Law?

A. INTRODUCTION

1.0   As a term of art, 'Comparative Law' must rank as one of the most unique within the scenario of legal research and study. If interpreted as a body of law, it is both potentially all-encompassing in its scope, in the sense of embracing all laws of all legal systems, as well as descriptive of a method of study and research (see Gutteridge (1949) p.1). In their work *Major Legal Systems in the World Today*, David and Brierley proceed on the premise that there is little purpose in pursuing the traditional preliminary questions of defining the purpose of comparative law and emphasing the value of comparative law studies. Accordingly, they merely give a condensed account of these conventional concerns, and stress the more contemporary challenges, namely to emphasise the general utility of comparative law and convince any remaining sceptics thereof; and to provide means of assisting those who wish to use comparative law for their own purposes. (see David and Brierley (1985) pp.3-4). Nevertheless, they also concede that it is 'only natural' that the traditional questions surrounding comparative law should be asked by those first confronted with the phenomenon 'comparative law'. (David and Brierley (1985) p.4)

 The present book assumes that its readers may not necessarily be experienced researchers or seasoned comparatists but may quite possibly be 'first-time' comparatists. It therefore discusses traditional questions and also devotes some attention to reviewing the salient features of the literature dealing with definitional, terminological, methodological and historical questions in the first three chapters. The main reason for this is that there is no up-to-date text that actually provides all this information in one volume. A second reason for this initially traditional approach is that the events of the last twenty years and the last four years in particular in Western and Eastern Europe and the former Soviet Union, have cast considerable uncertainty on the continued viability of the 'socialist tradition' and 'socialist legal system'. But it would be impossible to appraise the current state of the civil law or the future of socialist systems in Europe unless the ground rules for comparison were spelt out very carefully and unless the reader is given a sense of history.

What exactly are the components of comparative law? How did comparative law develop? What are its functions or purposes? How may it be distinguished from the mere study of the law of a foreign jurisdiction? How may be it be distinguished from other legal disciplines? How has it been utilised in practical terms and in scholarly research?

Having examined these questions, we shall then undertake a brief survey of the scope of the notions of the 'common law' and 'civil law' families of legal systems, with reference to typical examples, and will return to this concept of 'parent' legal families in the next chapter. The socialist system, long ranked alongside the common law and civil law as one of the three major legal systems in the world, is now in such decline that it will no longer be analysed in juxtaposition with the other two systems. The writer is aware that Communist China us still very much a superpower and is wedded to the Leninist/Marxist ideology. The different versions of modern Chinese law are discussed in Chapter 6 which also discusses the basic concepts of the Socialist system. It is submitted that, in the light of the continuing decline of forms of socialism, the socialist legal system, while deserving discussion, no longer warrants equal coverage as a major legal system in the 1990s.

Instead, it will be considered predominantly in the context of its contemporary development and in relation to the general decline of socialism in Eastern Europe. A fresh appraisal of the study of parent or major legal families is necessitated by certain trends of convergence between civil law and common law and by the collapse of Communist regimes across Eastern Europe, including the disintegration and demise of the former Soviet Union and its subsequent fragmentation, 'republicanisation' and 'federalism'. A tentative assessment of the current Soviet legal situation will therefore be discussed in Chapter 6.

There is some justification for considering the role of comparison in international law, for it is possible to consider international law as a separate legal system in itself. However, although there is a brief consideration of the international judge's judicial function and the value of the comparative method in providing him with the content of some of the principles he formulates at the international level (see below 1.6.10), it has been decided, at least for the present enquiry, not to pursue this matter in any great depth. There is, of course, the ubiquitous difficulty of the comparability of rules which would have to be constantly overcome. Any domestic rule would have to fit in with the different conditions of the international community. (see 1.6.10)

B. DEFINITIONS AND DERIVATIONS

i. Terminology: Subject or Method?

1.1   The first question that arises is : what is the nature of comparative law? Is it a branch of law, like family law or property law? Further, since law is sometimes defined as a 'body of rules', is there any identifiable body of rules known as 'Comparative Law'? The answer to both these questions is in the negative.

As an academic pursuit, it does not have a core content of subject areas and does not denote a distinct branch of substantive law. On the contrary, as Zweigert and Kotz put it, it describes 'an intellectual activity with law as its object and comparison as its process.' (see Zweigert and Kotz (1977)p.2).

There are no less than forty-two legal systems in the world, and comparison has traditionally focused on three major legal families in the world, namely the civil law system, common law system and socialist system. So 'comparative law' can be said to describe the *systematic study of particular legal traditions and legal rules on a comparative basis*. To qualify as a true comparative law enterprise, it also requires the *comparison of two or more legal systems* (or legal traditions?) or of selected aspects, institutions or branches of two or more *legal systems*. The question of what constitutes a *legal system* or legal tradition is taken up in chapter 2. A legal system may be defined as the legal rules and institutions of a country (as in 'the French legal system') in the narrow sense or, as Winterton (1975) puts it, in the broad sense as the 'juristic philosophy and techniques shared by a number of nations with broadly similar legal systems'(such as the English common law system). (Winterton (1975) p.69-70)

This 'broad sense' is more akin to the concept of a legal family or parent *family of laws*; or a *legal tradition*. Razi argues that a legal system in the wide sense 'is not made of rules alone but is also characterised by its institutions, practices, standards of research and even the mental habits of lawyers, judges, legislators and administrators.' (Razi (1959) 5 Howard LJ 11) This again is much more akin to a legal tradition than to a system as such although it really depends on the context of usage. If one is referring to 'the common law system' or 'civil law system', this one is really using it in the wider or broader sense of a *parent legal family*. Reference to Country X as a civil law system causes no confusion as such and is *prima facie* the use of the narrow meaning. (see Chapter 2 and Merryman (1977),*passim*).

It is therefore *a method of study* rather than a legal body of rules. Accordingly, Edwin Patterson prefers to describe it by its French equivalent-*droit compare*. Other commentators have also labelled it Comparative Jurisprudence or Comparative History of Law or Descriptive Comparative Law or Comparative Legislation. Nevertheless, the method theory has been advocated by such eminent commentators as Pollock, Gutteridge, and David.

However, this has not been the view of a number of other eminent comparatists, such as Saleilles, Rabel, Rheinstein and Hall who have argued that comparative law should be seen as a *social science*, so that the data obtained should be seen not just as part of its method, but forms part of a separate body of knowledge. It would appear that this social science theory has lost ground in more recent times. Yet another view has been to accept both interpretations so that it may be seen both as a science in its own right *and* as a method (see eg, Winterton (1975)p.71).

There is no generally accepted framework for comparison, although most writers appear to assume that the comparative methods which should be employed are obvious. The basic concept, its aims, and its *raison d'etre* as well its methodology have attracted somwhat disparaging critical comment.(We take up the question of comparative techniques in Chapter 2). For present purposes, it should be noted that the subject's intellectual viability has undoubtedly benefited from the ringing endorsements of Professors Ernst

Rabel and Otto Kahn-Freund, both of whom have, over many years, not merely defended but championed its intrinsic worth as an academic and intellectual discipline. Rabel, for instance, declared:'Comparative law can free the kernel of legal phenomena from the husk of their formulae and superstructures and maintain the coherence of a common legal structure.'(cited in Coing *Das Deutsche Schuldrecht und die Rechtvergleichung* (1956) NJW 569, 670; translation by Grossfeld (1990)).

Modern comparative law draws from a range of disciplines, but is eclectic in its selection. It recognises the important relationship between law, history, and culture and operates on the basis that every legal system is a special mixture of the spirit of its people, and is the product of several intertwining and interacting historical events, which have produced a distinctive national character and ambience. Alan Watson, for instance, defines Comparative Law as: 'the study of the relationship between legal systems or between rules of more than one system...in the context of a historical relationship... [a study of] the nature of law and the nature of legal development.' (Watson (1974) pp.6-7). Watson therefore places primary importance on comparative law as the study of the *historical relationship* that exists between legal systems or between rules of more than one system. Legal History and the 'step beyond into Jurisprudence' are what Watson regard as the essential ingredients of Comparative Law as an academic discipline in its own right. Of course, the significance of the legal history behind rules has been acknowledged by long line of luminaries including Dawson, Lawson, Merryman, Rene David, and Kahn-Freund. Fritz Pringsheim (1961) even went so far as to say that 'comparative law without the history of law is an impossible task.'

Hence *mere comparison* of rules *per se*, does *not* constitute comparative law so if one accepts Watson's thesis, the comparison would have to be a study of the *relationship* between the rules of legal systems. What sort of relationships would these have to be? Watson himself suggests there may be three kinds of possible relationships:

(i) The historical relationship.

In this category, it is perhaps most important to note that the private law of societies has nearly always been taken from others, thus tracing the historical background to a given system or rule usually beings insights into the present status of the rule.

(ii) The 'inner relationship' (Pringsheim).

This category, which is so described by Pringsheim, appears to be based on an undeniable similarity between peoples or their development and does not really depend on any actual historical contact, but on a spiritual and psychical relationship between the two different types of peoples, although various forms of 'influence' may well have been experienced by them in the course of historical experience. Watson points to the problems in applying this theory, such as its vagueness, which will make it difficult to define the relationship, and the fact that it will not exist in all areas or at all periods of development. He does, however see its great value 'in the light which it can shed on major legal matters'. He cites the presence or absence of the trust as a good focus for the analysis of reasons why it has or has not developed in English and Roman law, respectively.

(iii) The 'same pattern of development' theory.

This relationship has been suggested by commentators who believe that all legal systems in their early development underwent the same or similar stages of development.

While remaining flexible and open-minded about the possible outcome of a comparative investigation, the comparatist seeks out those key, distinguishing features of a given society which have a common denominator and mirror image in other societies in the world. These features are then organised so as to form a backdrop to the 'black-letter' law of the particular jurisdiction, so as to place it within its historical, social, economic and cultural context.

ii. The Elements of 'Comparative Law'

1.1.1 It would appear that despite the somewhat misleading term 'comparative law' and suggested alternatives such as 'the comparative study of laws' or 'comparison of laws' the appellation is now reasonably well-established. Gutteridge, writing his first edition in 1946, felt that 'comparative law' as a term, although misleading, had become firmly established. It is with some satisfaction that we can confirm this in 1992.

(i) Types of Comparative Studies

1.1.2 What sort of comparative studies would rank as comparative law? Such studies may fall into several categories and Hug (1922) suggests five possible groups of studies: (a) Comparison of foreign systems with the domestic system in order to ascertain similarities and differences; (b) Studies which analyse objectively and systematically solutions which various systems offer for a given legal problem; (c) Studies which investigate the causal relationship between different systems of law; (d) Studies which compare the several stages of various legal systems; and (e) Studies which attempt to discover or examine legal evolution generally according to periods and systems.

C. COMPARATIVE LAW DISTINGUISHED FROM OTHER DISCIPLINES

1.2 Commentators have sometimes attempted to clarify what comparative law is by saying what it does *not* include. For example, Watson (1974) submits that:

(i) Comparative law is not the study of one foreign legal system or part of one legal system, even though there are occasional or even frequent glances at one's own system. A study of one branch of foreign law remains a course on a foreign law, and not comparative law. Zweigert and Kotz (1977) agree with this view.

(ii) It is not an elementary account of various legal systems or various legal families of law. Watson argues that there should be 'the necessary intellectual content';

(iii) Comparative law cannot properly be referring to an enterprise which is primarily a matter of drawing comparisons. Watson regards this as the most contentious of his three propositions, and concedes that, for example, those who disagree with this may argue that they may start from an individual legal problem which they regard as the same in more than one jurisdiction and examine the legal response to it. Watson disagrees on the basis that if the starting point is the problem, the danger is that the main focus of the investigation will be on the comparability of the problem rather than on the comparability of the law, so that it becomes merely a sociological rather than a legal enquiry.

While proposition (i) and (iii) are reasonably well-proved by Watson, proposition (ii) is not so easily acceptable. What is meant by an 'elementary account'? Is it merely an outline? Surely a logical starting point of any course on comparative law would have to be an introduction to the world's major legal systems? The writer cannot really imagine that any teacher on comparative law in any institution, apart from perhaps one teaching it as part of a global study subject in school, would leave the matter to rest after the introduction to the legal systems had been completed. Hence, his proposition stands but its possible applicability must remain fairly unlikely.

1.2.1   Zweigert and Kotz (1977) stress that in order for an intellectual enterprise to be considered as a comparative law enterprise, there must be 'specific comparative reflections on the problem to which the work is devoted' and that this is best done by the comparatist stating the essential of the foreign law, country by country, as a basis for critical comparison, concluding the exercise with suggestions about the proper policy for the law to adopt which may require him to reinterpret his own system. (see Zweigert and Kotz (1977)p.5). They also distinguish comparative law from other areas of law such as private international law and public international law. At this juncture we outline the broad differences between comparative law and these other areas of research and law.

i. Private International Law and Comparative Law

1.2.2   Private International Law is a discrete *body of law* which is also known as the *Conflict of Laws*, or the Laws of Conflicts because it is a form of *private law* which deals with situations involving private individuals in which there is a possible conflict of applicable laws. The function of private international law is to provide a solution as to which of several possible legal systems should be applied to a given case which has a foreign element.

Although it therefore appears quite distinct from comparative law, the two in fact interlink since they both deal with the analysis of the operation of specific rules in several legal systems. The difference is that private international law is much more selective than comparative law, to the extent that the 'choice-of law rules' are very narrow. In practice, every legal system will decide a particular problem according to its own rules and there is still a lack of international consensus on the question of which rules to apply across national frontiers.

6

ii. Public International Law and Comparative Law

1.2.3 Public International Law (often simply 'International law') refers to the *body of law* that governs relationships between States and is thus primarily concerned with the rights and duties of States *inter se*. Comparative law is a *method* of analysing the problems and institutions originating from two or more national laws of legal systems or of comparing entire legal systems in order to acquire a better understanding thereof or provide information and insight into the operation of the system's institutions or the systems themselves.

International law is a distinct body of law, and one of its sources is listed in the Statute of the International Court of Justice as the 'general principles of law recognised by civilised nations' :Article 38(1)(c). The interpretation of this principle can only be rooted in the comparative law method. (see further, 1.6.10).

iii. Legal History, Legal Ethnology and Comparative Law

1.2.4 It has long been recognised that law and history are inextricably linked. Carl Joachim Friedrich called law 'frozen history' and argued that the history of the Western world was inconceivable without law. He went on to say:'From feudalism to capitalism, from Magna Carta to the constitutions of contemporary Europe, the historian encounters law at every turn as a decisive factor.' (see Friedrich *The Philosophy of Law in Historical Perspective* (1963) pp.233-234).

All legal history uses the comparative method, as Maitland (1911) observed: 'History involves comparison and the English lawyer who knew nothing and cared nothing for any system but his own hardly came in sight of legal history' and in a forceful endorsement of the comparative method: 'an isolated system cannot explain itself, still less explain its history.' (Maitland *Collected Papers* (1911) pp. 488-489).

Legal history is a vital precondition to the critical evaluation of the law and an understanding of the operation of legal concepts, which is a primary aim of comparative law. As some jurists have put it, comparative legal history is 'vertical comparative law' and the comparison of modern systems is 'horizontal comparative law.'

Legal ethnology has historically concentrated on those so-called primitive societies which are not yet equipped with the trappings of modern civilisation. Yet it is more correctly regarded as a branch of ethnology and comparative law and it seeks generally to discover 'the origins and early stages of law in relation to particular cultural phenomena' (Adam *'Ethnologische Rechtsforschung'* in Adam/Trimborn, *Lehrbuch der Volkerkunde* (1958)p.192). As Zweigert and Kotz explain, the task of modern legal ethnology is 'to study the changes suffered by societies already observed in adjusting to the intrusion of a higher civilisation.' (Zweigert and Kotz (1977) p.9) Hence legal ethnology is another branch of comparative law which contributes to the task of comparison and analysis through its own unique discipline and techniques of observation.

1.2.5   There are clearly many points of similarity and overlap between the sociology of law and comparative law. In view of its general aims, comparative law needs legal sociology as much as legal history and legal ethnology. Both legal sociology and comparative law are engaged in charting the extent to which to which law influences and determines man's behaviour and the role played by law in the social scheme of things. One fundamental difference between the two is that sociology covers a much wider field than comparative law, and, as Zweigert and Kotz explain, while sociology of law, through field studies and empirical observation, simply observes how the legal institutions operate, comparative law concerns itself with the question of 'how the law ought to be' by studying the rules and institutions of law in relation to each other. (Zweigert and Kotz (1977) pp.9-10) Watson has also emphasised the autonomy of law, legal ideas and legal tradition which transcend purely sociological or socio-historical explantions. (Watson (1974) p.183)

D. A RATIONALE FOR COMPARATIVE LAW

1.3   Why is there any need to look at other societies or other legal cultures? Is it not sufficient to make a detailed and thorough study of one's own culture to gain insights into it?   One set of reasons is admirably put by Ehrmann (1976): '...only the analysis of a variety of legal cultures will recognise what is accidental rather than necessary, what is permanent rather than changeable in legal norms and legal agencies, and what characterises the beliefs underlying both. The law of a single culture will take for granted the ethical theory on which it is grounded.'

E. THE ORIGINS OF COMPARATIVE LAW

i. Early Comparative Law

1.4   Ehrmann's opinion is not a new point of view and can be traced back to the ancient Greeks and Romans. The process of comparative law is believed to have begun in the ancient world, when some of the Greek cities adopted the law of other states, either in whole or in parts. The rationale for this appears to be that the laws or legal institutions of the other state were perceived as superior or more advanced or sophisticated and should therefore be deliberately imitated or adopted. It would seem that this imitation was not seen as an adoption of foreign law but as an adoption of a law that was better than one's own. This process was probably repeated in various other parts of the ancient world.

Sources such as the famous Twelve Tables, the oldest source of Roman law that has been discovered, indicate that the influence of the Greeks on the Roman culture and civilisation is undeniable. Both the writings of Cicero and Gaius appear to suggest that they believed the apparent legend that a legislative committee had been sent to Athens in order to learn from Greek law and legal institutions when Roman laws were being drawn up.

However, it was only in the classical period of Roman law that the further development of the *jus gentium* came to be influenced by comparative enquiries, were therefore denationalised, and turned into a form of 'global law'; this was accomplished by a 'combination of comparative jurisprudence and rational speculation;' (see Mommsen *Romisches Staatsrecht* (1887), p.606 and Muirhead *Historical Introduction to the Private Law of Rome* (1916) p.216). There appears to have been only one comparative attempt to collect diverse laws together dating from the later imperial period of the Roman empire, which was the *Lex Dei*. This was something in the nature of a combination of Roman law and Mosaic principles (the laws of Moses), and is also known as the *Collatio legum Mosaicarum et Romanorum*, which seems to date from c.400 AD. This appears to be one of the earliest known works on comparative law (see Sherman *Roman Law in the Modern Law* (1922) p.111).

In the Middle Ages, after the fall of the Western Roman Empire the principle of 'the personality of law' was applied in Western Europe which meant that each individual was subject to the law peculiar to his nation or tribe. Hence, Roman and Germanic laws were being applied within the same territory. This unique co-existence of different laws suggests that there was familiarity with both Germanic and Roman law, although this did not result in any 'common law' or systematic comparative studies being established. When learning revived in the 900s, the Lombard school was the first secular group to undertake scientific studies on a comparative basis. Feudal law, and canon law, which were already part of the common law of western Europe, were studied, together with fragments of Roman law in the pre-Justinian version. These medieval scholars therefore extended their knowledge to all the major legal systems of their time and civilisation but it was left to the Glossators and their successors to bring about the great renaissance of Roman law which spread from Bologna. (see Chapter 3).

For present purposes, it should be noted that 'the law from Bologna' which was received in nearly all the European countries and achieved well-nigh universal validity as *ratio scripta*, and which was taught in all the university centres of the time, was not really 'Roman law' in its ancient, unadulterated form. It was a combination of ancient law and Roman, and mediaeval and Germanic elements drawn from the Lombardic law and that of the Italian cities (see Gierke *Deutsches Privatrecht (German Private Law)* (1895)p.14). More precisely, it was not the law as derived from the Justinian text but *the law as interpreted by various schools of jurists* (ie the Glossators, Commentators *et al*). This version of Roman law and canon law enjoyed an absolute, unquestioned authority which also accounts for the lack of any interest in comparative study at that time. (Chapter 4 deals with the corresponding development of English law at this time).

In the sixteenth century, a few comparative studies were produced but these only dealt with the laws which were co-existing in the same country. In France, customs were reduced to writing at the beginning of the sixteenth century, but comparative studies were not then undertaken. Roman and Germanic laws were compared in countries like Spain and eventually, Germany.

In the seventeenth and eighteenth centuries, national laws began to burgeon, and jurists on the Continent concentrated on analysis and mastery of their own traditional material rather than on comparative analyses. Nevertheless, although there was no systematic, objective practice of comparative law evident during the seventeenth century, various personages like Bacon emphasised the importance of the lawyer freeing himself from the *vincula* (chains) of his national system in order to make a true assessment of its worth. Leibniz suggested a plan for a 'legal theatre' which could undertake a portrayal of all peoples, places and times on a comparative basis. Subsequent Natural Law exponents such as the Dutchman Grotius (1583-1645) and the Frenchman Montesquieu (1689-1755) used the method of comparative law to place their teachings of natural law on an empirical footing. Indeed, Gutteridge regarded *Montesquieu* as having a claim to being the probable *founder of comparative law* since it was he 'who first realised that a rule of law should not be treated as an abstraction, but must be regarded against a background of its history and the environment in which it is called upon to function.' (Gutteridge (1949) p.12). Kahn-Freund also appears to take the same view on the status of Montesquieu as the pioneer of comparative law. (Kahn-Freund (1974)p.6)

In the nineteenth century, the influence of eighteenth century rationalism which led logically to a codification of laws, took hold so that unification and simplification of laws were the watchwords of the time. Various national codes were drawn up, giving rise to the period also being called the era of the 'Great Codifications' and inevitably jurists turned their main attention on the interpretation and analysis of these codes. Despite all these codifications, interest in foreign and comparative law eventually began to grow in Germany, France, England and the United States.

ii. The Roots of Comparative Law

1.4.1   Although various factors cohered to produce the comparative line of study, *two distinct roots of modern comparative law* may be identified:
(i) Legislative Comparative Law; and (ii)Scholarly Comparative law.

(i) Legislative Comparative Law

1.4.2   This refers to the process whereby foreign laws are invoked in order to draft new national laws. This process was possibly resorted to even in ancient Rome although this has never been definitively established. It apparently occurred in Germany in the middle of the nineteenth century, and grew with the movement for codification and unification of Germany. One may therefore exclude older codes such as the 1794 Prussian General Land Law and the 1811 Austrian General Civil Code, which are predominantly based on Natural Law philosophies. In France, the most influential Code has been its Civil Code of 1804 with its primary aim of producing an amalgamation of the customary Roman laws of Northern France and predominantly Germanic law of Southern France. (see Chapter 3)

Among the notable German law examples are the General German Negotiable Instruments Law of 1848, the General Commercial Code of 1861 (which even included studies of the French Commercial Code), the Company Law reforms of 1870 and 1884, the extended reform process of German criminal law, involving nearly all the well-known teachers of criminal law, which produced fifteen volumes of comparative material. Nearly twenty years elapsed before a draft Criminal Code was produced. The most outstanding example of legislative comparative law, is, of course, the German Civil Code (BGB) which unified the private law of Germany from 1 January 1900. The comparative materials which were consulted in order to produce this work of scholarship include the *Gemeines Recht*, Prussian law, the French Civil Code, Austrian and Swiss law. Ironically, the completion and promulgation of this work gave it an almost encyclopaedic and authoritative aura which meant that no recourse to the empirical and functional methods of comparative law resulted in the interpretation of this Code, and it is usually only in the preparation of legislative material that comparative methods of study are utilised in Germany. (see Chapter 3 on the BGB).

(ii) Scholarly Comparative Law

1.4.3   As an academic discipline, comparative law appears to have taken a long time to achieve recognition. The impetus for the modern methods of comparative law came around the middle of the nineteenth century, when the intellectual movement we now associate with Evolution and Darwinism caught the imagination of intellectuals and scientists across Europe. In the same manner as comparative anatomy, comparative philology and comparative religion, comparative law was swept along in this welter of comparative disciplines engendered by the 'comparative method', hailed by the Victorian author Freeman as 'the greatest intellectual achievement of our time' which signified a stage in the progress of the human mind 'as great and memorable as the revival of Greek and Latin learning.'(Freeman *Comparative Politics* (1873) p.1, 302).

It was, however, only in the second half of the nineteenth century that comparative law appears to have gained definite recognition as a branch of legal study or at least as an approved method for the study of different legal systems. In England, in the nineteenth century, Sir Henry Maine, another contender for the distinction of being the founder of comparative law, published *Ancient Law* (1861) which had applied to the study of the origins of law the process of comparison which Charles Darwin had employed in his *Origin of the Species* (1859). Writing in 1871, Maine declared: 'The chief function of comparative jurisprudence is to facilitate legislation and the practical improvement of the law.' (Maine *Village Communities* (1871)p.4) It was this view that was to have an important influence on the expositions of most of the legal comparatists who succeeded him. (see below for development of comparative law in England).

Various parallel events began to take place in Europe and England. In 1829, in Germany, the German jurists Mittermaier and Zachariae founded a journal for the study of comparative law in collaboration of other foreign jurists. In 1832, a Chair of Comparative Law was founded at the College of France followed in 1846 by the establishment of a Chair of Comparative Criminal Law in the University of Paris. Other similar professorships were established. In 1869, the Corpus Chair of Historical and Comparative Jurisprudence was founded at Oxford, whose first occupant was Maine himself. In the same year, the French Society of Comparative Legislation was formed in Paris, followed in 1873 by the founding of the Institute of International Law which employed the comparative method in the investigation of the problems of private international law. Germany appeared to be content to devote itself primarily to comparative legal history and had to wait until 1894 before founding a society similar to the French Society of Comparative Legislation, but full recognition of comparative law as a scholarly discipline was not achieved until after the First World War.

In 1894, the Quain Professorship of Comparative Law was established at University College, London and in 1895, the English Society of Comparative Legislation was founded, which meant that there were now similar societies on both sides of the Channel.

By the end of the nineteenth century, France, Germany and even the United States had experienced a revival of interest in comparative law, with similar Professorships being established in Columbia and Chicago, and a growing variety of graduate courses in comparative law.

(iii) The Birth of Modern Comparative Law

1.4.4 *Modern* comparative law is usually recognised as having begun in 1900 at the International Congress of Comparative Law held in Paris, where the first serious and organised attempts were made to formulate the functions and aims of comparative law. Although billed as an international conference, only one Englishman, Sir Frederick Pollock, took part as the representative of the English legal tradition. All other participants were from continental Europe. The conference *zeitgeist* was an optimistic faith in progress and a strong desire for mastery of one's fate, and the forging of a common destiny. The Congress' two founders, Lambert and Saleilles, talked of a common law of mankind, a world law created by comparative law. Lambert expressed his vision thus: 'comparative law must resolve the accidental and divisive differences in the laws of peoples at similar stages of cultural and economic development, and reduce the number of divergencies in law, attributable not to the political, moral or social qualities of the different nations but to historical accident or to temporary or contingent circumstances.' (Lambert (1905) *Proces-verbaux des seances et documents*; *Congres international de droit compare*: cited in Zweigert and Kotz (1977) p.2).

A great deal has changed since that time, not least in the cynicism that has replaced the idealistic, optimistic belief in progress but also in the fact that comparatists are more knowledgeable and refined in their methods and now realise that a comparison need not only be carried out between 'peoples at similar stages of cultural and economic development' since it really depends on the aims of the particular comparative investigation. (see Chapter 2)

Another date which is also put forward as the birth of Comparative Law as an academic disciplne is 1869, for reasons that we shall now examine.

F. COMPARATIVE LAW IN ENGLAND

1.5   In England, as in Europe, the first half of the nineteenth century did not see any significant growth in comparative studies but Burge's *Commentaries on Colonial and Foreign Laws*, written for the practising lawyer, published in 1838 and Leone Levi's book comparing the mercantile laws of Britain with Roman law and the Codes, *Commercial Law of the World*, published in 1852, were early attempts to apply the comparative method to practical aspects of law. Burge's work was later praised by Hug (in the United States) and Rabel who declared that the range and quality of the book's treatment made it useful as a substitute for a primer on comparative private law. Levi later proposed the formulation of an international unified code of commercial law and he is thus regarded as the first person to suggest the international unification of an entire area of law through the method of comparative law.

At that time, the Judicial Committee of the Privy Council, sitting in London, was also the highest court of appeal for all countries within the British Empire except Britain. This Court had to apply the law to several different foreign systems, and apart from hearing appeals from common law jurisdictions, had to hear appeals from jurisdictions applying Hindu and Islamic laws (India), Singhalese and Tamil laws (Ceylon), Chinese law (Hong King, the Malay States, Straits Settlements, Sarawak and Borneo), Roman-Dutch law (Ceylon, South Africa and Rhodesia), the French Civil Code (Quebec), Norman customs (The Channel Islands) and African and Asian customary laws. As Burge rightly pointed out, there was a need for 'more ready access to the sources from whence an acquaintance might be derived from those systems of foreign jurisprudence' (Burge *Commentaries on Colonial and Foreign Laws* (1838) p.v). The House of Commons' Select Committee recommended in 1848 that the universities establish Chairs in International, Comparative, Administrative and English law but it was some years before this was implemented.

A seminal publication of the time was Maine's *Ancient Law*, published in 1861, but it is also possible to date the birth of modern Comparative Law *as a separate academic discipline* from the year 1869, when the French founded the Society for Comparative Legislation and Maine took up his Chair of Historical and Comparative Jurisprudence. Sir Frederick Pollock followed in Maine's tradition who, in his pioneering work on English contract law, made it clear that he was simply translating Savigny's work on ancient Rome in his section on 'Intent to Create Legal Relations.' Maitland also showed great interest in Continental legislation and Gutteridge himself became the *doyen* of comparatists of the time. Other great comparatists include Sir Otto Kahn-Freund and F.H. Lawson.

Apart from the establishment of journals, research institutes and a national committee on comparative law, a positive parliamentary step to encourage comparison of laws also occurred. In 1965, *Parliamentary recognition of value of comparative law* was given, with the *enactment of the Law Commissions Act*, which created two reform commissions, an English and Scottish Law Commission whose function *inter alia*, is to obtain information from other legal systems of other countries as appears likely to facilitate their function of *systematically developing and reforming the law of their country*: s.3(1)(f): Law

Commissions Act 1965. The Law Commission enquires into the function of the legal principle, the framework within which it operates, and, by consultation with foreign and local experts, ascertains whether or not the rule has been successful in achieving what it has set out to do.

There have been other instances of English law borrowing from foreign jurisdictions such as the Scots, for example, pleas of diminished responsibility in the criminal trial, the doctrine of the putative marriage and the procedure for the attachment of earnings. The English Ombudsman idea comes from Scandinavia and in 1966, the House of Lords issued a statement through its Lord Chancellor which appeared to imitate the age-old Continental practice of reserving the right not to follow any of its past judgments 'where it appeared right to do so' (see [1966] 3 All ER 77) which essentially indicated that they were prepared to correct any mistakes which had occurred. Although this power has been used sparingly, it represents an important judicial attitude which strengthens the law-making function of the highest appeal court in the United Kingdom and has given it a greater measure of flexibility. Continental courts have long regarded such a right to be part of their judicial duty.

An important stimulus for more comparative studies to take place occurred with Britain's entry into the European Community (EC) on January 1, 1973, which meant that the United Kingdom became a member of three European Communities to which all twelve members belong. Subsequently, the EC Heads of Government then committed themselves to establishing progressively a single market over a period expiring on December 31, 1992. This pledge has been included in a collection of treaty reforms known as the Single European Act 1986, which came into operation on July 1, 1987.

The key to effective comparative analysis is to collect sufficient materials and information which will enable the comparatist to place the particular legal rule or institution or branch of law in context. Norms and patterns of behaviour which one society may deem natural and legal may be categorised as reprehensible and unacceptable in another. In modern times, many of the more important advances have already resulted from 'cross-fertilisation' not just in law, but in science, literature and religion. Comparison enables a strong measure of objective neutrality and critical self-assessment to be applied.

G. THE CONTEMPORARY SIGNIFICANCE OF COMPARATIVE LAW

i. Functions and Purposes of Comparative Law

1.6   Since its recognition as an academic discipline in its own right, in the early twentieth century and indeed since the 1920s, various comparatists have offered several suggestions on the actual and potential uses of comparative law, in the purely intellectual sense, in social science terms, in the domestic law arena and in the context of international law. We have noted Maine's belief in the *legislative function of comparative law* and we have also seen how the *'scholarly' purposes of comparative law* developed in Europe. A fair amount of academic ink has flowed under the bridge and crossed the academic Rubicon since then. Accordingly, let us examine the various functions and purposes of comparative law under the following headings:

 (i) Comparative Law as an Academic Discipline;
 (ii) Comparative Law as an Aid to Legislation and Law Reform;
(iii) Comparative Law as a Tool of Construction;
(iv) Comparative Law as a Means of Understanding Legal Rules
 (v) Comparative Law as a Contribution to the Systematic
     Unification and Harmonisation of Law

(i) Comparative Law as an Academic Discipline

a. Teaching, Studying and Researching Law

1.6.1　　In the era of a crowded and ever-expanding university law curriculum in which many 'black-letter' and 'contextual' optional courses vie for student popularity due to practical value (for example, a Company Law course, which is seen as impressive to employers) rather than academic value, Comparative Law has had somewhat mixed fortunes. In 1936, Professor R.W. Lee in a Presidential address to the Society for Public Teachers of Law deplored the paucity of attention given to comparative law, saying 'what we are doing...for comparative studies in this country [in contrast with] foreign countries is positively shocking'. (Lee (1936) JSPTL 3) Since then, a few more universities have launched courses on the comparative method although it remains confined to a handful of universities even in the 1990s. While many examiners and tutors consider that a PhD thesis should certainly contain some comparative studies covering foreign jurisdictional equivalents, the academic or educational advantages of comparative law has not attracted large numbers of undergraduates.

b. Comparative Law as An Academic Tradition

1.6.2　Yet, as our historical surveys have shown, the comparative method is an essential part of any initial legal education and it has a more recent tradition going back to 1869 in England, when Maine took up his Chair of Historical and Comparative Jurisprudence, and an ancient tradition going back to the Romans and Greeks. Hence, in some form or other, it has formed part of the legal tradition in both the common law and civil law.

Are there any other justifications to include it in present-day undergraduate and postgraduate courses? There are many educational reasons for doing so. Firstly, the comparative method encourages the student to be more critical about the functions and purposes of the rules he is studying and to learn not to accept their validity purely because they belong to his own system of law. In other words, a wider knowledge of the possible range of solutions to legal problems, gleaned from other jurisdictions is thereby made available. Secondly, it will assist in sharpening his analytical skills and methodlogical techniques. Thirdly, it will help to broaden the student's perception of the operation of a legal rule by seeing how it originated and currently operates within different systems, in either similar or different socio-cultural contexts. Fourthly, it gives the student an opportunity to study the interaction of different disciplines and to relate these to the formation and operation of legal rules, for example, when the student sees the interface between law and history. Fifthly, it provides a forum for the cross-fertilisation of experience, ideas, cultures and experience.

c. Using Comparative Law in Research

1.6.3   The other important value of the comparative method lies in what Yntema called 'the constant refinement and extension of our knowledge of law.' (Yntema 'Comparative Legal Research: Some Remarks on 'Looking out of the Cave' (1956) 54 Mich. LR 899,901), which forms an essential component of legal education.

Paton argues that it is impossible to conceive of the existence of jurisprudence without comparative law (Paton *A Textbook of Jurisprudence* (1972) p.41), since all school of jurisprudence, whether historical, philosophical, sociological or analytical, rely on the comparative research methodology. Yntema equated legal research with comparative law, saying the latter was just another name for legal science.

ii. Comparative Law as an Aid to Legislation and Law Reform

1.6.4   Perhaps the earliest example of the use of the comparative method for legislative purposes is when Greeks and Romans visited cities which they felt could provide them with models of laws that were worth enacting in their own country. More modern commentators have even regarded the aiding of the legislator as the prime function of comparative law. Maine's statement to that effect has been oft-quoted and examples of such borrowings can be found in Germany, England, Italy and Greece. Criminal law and Bankruptcy Law reforms in Germany have been based on extensive and comprehensive comparative research. Other examples of private law and commercial law areas include illegitimacy, divorce, personality, privacy, and vicarious liability. Italy and Greece have also enacted codes in various areas, based on the results of their comparative studies.

As we have already noted, statute law requires the English Law Commission to procure information from other legal systems whenever this is seen as facilitating the performance of their function of systematically developing and reforming the law.

Grossfeld (1990) lists many examples of legislators borrowing foreign ideas. For example, the earliest legislation on companies was the French Commercial Code of 1807 which enacted the charter system and formed the basis of the Prussian Company Law of 1843. The notion of income tax, which originated in England, was imitated by German legislators. The doctrine of proper allowances for dealings between connected enterprises, which has also been adopted in Germany, derives from the Internal Revenue Code of the United States (s.482). A number of ideas in the German Civil Code are derived from the Swiss Law of Obligations of 1881 and German civil procedure drew heavily from Austrian law. The anti-trust laws of Austria have also inspired German cartel law. (see Grossfeld (1990) chapter 3).

In addition, many so-called Third World countries have adopted and adapted Western or Socialist laws. One obvious reason has been colonialism and various wars which resulted in hybrid systems co-existing with native customary law. Another has been the ties that have resulted from Western influence which have led to Western academics setting up institutions of learning or helping in the drafting of new laws more suited to the changing social and economic conditions of the particular society.

The American Law Institute was established in 1932 as a national institution which undertakes a wide range of comparative legal studies and research aimed at law reform and general restatment of laws. As set out in its constitution, the Institute's purpose is: 'to promote the clarification and simplication of the law and its better adaptation to social needs, to secure the better administration of justice, and to encourage and carry on scholarly and scientific legal work.'

The leading State agencies which use extensive comparative legal techniques for legislation and law reform are the Louisiana Law Institute and the New York Revision Commission.

iii. A Tool of Construction

1.6.5 The comparative method has frequently been of practical significance to courts and the judicial process, in filling gaps in legislation or in caselaw, in providing the background and origin to legal rules and concepts which have been inherited or transplanted from other jurisdictions, in matters which are not covered by a code provision or statute or caselaw authority. In this way, a variety of solutions to the problem at hand, will present themselves. A current and important example of this is in the practice of the European Court of Justice of the European Communities (the ECJ). By virtue of their legal background and origins, judges of the ECJ are bound to draw upon their own experience as lawyers within the Member States. The court seeks to evaluate and possibly utilise solutions provided by the legal systems from which the judges are drawn. For example, cases indicate that the French Administrative Law doctrine of *Acte Clair* might be followed in order to determine when it is 'necessary' for municipal court to make a 'reference' to the ECJ under Article 177 of the Treaty of Rome.

In *CILFIT Srl* v. *Ministry of Health* [1982] ECR 3415, the European Court of Justice considered the application of Article 177 which requires, *inter alia*, that where a question is raised before a national court of a Member State, that court 'may' request the Court of Justice to give a ruling, 'if it considers that a decision on the question is necessary to enable it to give judgment'. The ECJ stated that 'the correct application of Community law may be so obvious as to leave no scope for any reasonable doubt as to the manner in which the question raised is to be resolved.' (see [1982] ECR at p.3430). This follows the French doctrine of *Acte Clair*, under which the theory is that the obligation to refer does not apply if the highest court concerned is of opinion that there can be no reasonable doubt about the answers to the questions raised-there is no need to interpret a provision if the meaning is clear.

Steiner (1990) suggests that what is clear to one person may not be clear to another. (see Steiner *EEC Law* (1990) p.268) But the ECJ has been very careful to point out that various points should be borne in mind in assessing whether the effect of a provision is clear and obvious: the various linguistic versions of the provision should be compared; comparability of legal concepts must be examined; every Community law provision must be placed in its context and interpreted in the light of the provisions of Community law as a whole, in the light of the objectives of Community law and its state of evolution at the date on which the provision involved is to be applied.

The few cases on this area have indicated that the spirit of cooperation and collaboration has generally prevailed among the Member States and the fears of the ECJ being powerless in requiring a national court to make a 'reference' have so far proved groundless. In other areas as well, the Court often bases its opinions on comparative law. In Chapter 5, we examine how other municipal legal traditions and doctrines have been adapted and adopted by the ECJ in interpreting Community law, a practical and contemporary example of the use of the comparative method in the international and European sphere.

iv. Aid to Understanding Legal Rules

1.6.6   The comparative law method will increasingly be useful in a practical way for the modern and up-to-date practitioner. Recourse to comparative law has been at the heart of private international law (or conflict of laws) and when you consider that so many systems have transplanted and borrowed so many concepts from the major legal systems and adapted them, it is becoming increasingly necessary to be *au fait* with a range of traditions and doctrines, not just because of closer inter-regional cooperation and trade but also because of the setting up of transnational law firms, transnational litigation, the ever-growing influence of American corporations in foreign countries, drafting of trasnational contracts, and international credit arrangements.

International company law is another area where comparative law can make an extremely useful contribution to information, knowledge and understanding. The usual 'groundwork' needed before setting up an international company will usually involve acquiring a good understanding of the legal requirements with which the company will have to comply and the legal framework within which the company will have to transact its business.

Further, in the ascertainment and application of foreign law in national courts, the comparative method is not just a requirement but a necessity in order to resolve anything from domestic disputes across boundaries between American States and Mexico (see *State* v. *Valmont Plantations* (1961) 346 SW2d 853) to the law that governs a drilling accident which occurred on a flagless drilling platform fixed to the continental shelf off the coast of Scotland. Even if one is inclined to set up a foreign tax haven, one needs to have some knowledge of foreign tax law, and who better to turn to than the lawyer who is highly conversant with tax havens around the world?

The time is coming when not just the European law specialist practitioner but the Comparative Law specialist practitioner will be sought after, who will, with a few exceptions, be able to tell his clients dealing in foreign business which legal system they are going to deal with and more importantly, what that means in terms of the legal requirements of that system.

v. Contributing to the Unification and Harmonisation of Law

(i) Early History

1.6.7 The idea of unification of laws is a process that goes back to ancient history. However the first movement for unification has been traced by Professor Gutteridge to King James I, who contemplated the unification of the laws of England and Scotland but did not take it any further as a result of Bacon's discouragement. Unification on a world-wide scale was first proposed by Professor Leon Levi to the Prince Consort in connection with the Exhibition of 1851. The first organised measures taken towards unification occurred simultaneously with the revival of interest in comparative law studies but were at first limited to the field of maritime and commercial law. All this was greatly assisted by the great expansion of international trade in the nineteenth century which produced various unificatory international conventions dealing with private law, commercial law, trade and labour law, copyright and industrial property law, the law of transport by rail, sea and air, parts of procedural law particularly in relation to the recognition of foreign judgments and awards. It is also worth noting the work of the Hague Conference in private international law, and the Rome Institute for the Unification of Law which has worked on the law of sale of goods, which has helped to produce the Hague Conventions on the Uniform Laws on International Sales of Goods (see Chapter 9), and the ongoing work of UNCITRAL which shows the continuing interest in some measure of unification in this century.

(ii) The Paris Congress

1.6.8 In 1900, the Paris International Congress of Comparative Law was held and Lambert stressed the practical function of comparative law as being to provide material for the unification of those national systems of law which have attained the same degree of development or civilisation. The aim would then be to replace those national systems with an international common law.

Of course, the world has changed considerably since great jurists like Roscoe Pound and Hessel Yntema envisaged a world of common institutions, concepts and beliefs shared by all 'civilised' nations. The emergence of Africa, Asia, Russia and Latin America made this ideal a 'pious hope' by their sheer diversity of traditions and ideologies and even with the tremendous fillip for European economic union provided by the Treaties of Rome establishing the European Communities, the current schisms within Europe over the Maastricht treaty illustrate the inherent difficulties surrounding European unification, let alone worldwide unification. Uniting the common and civil law are also in doubt as a result of the current ructions in the European Community, although the creation of the European Community *per se* gives some glimmer of hope to the optimistic unificationist.

Unlike unification which contemplates the substitution of two or more legal systems with one single system, *harmonisation of law* arises exclusively in comparative law literature and especially in conjunction with inter-jurisdictional, private transactions. Harmonisation seeks to 'effect an approximation or co-ordination of different legal provisions or systems by eliminating major differences and creating minimum requirements or standards.' (Kamba (1974) 23 ICLQ 485, at p. 501).

(iii) The African Situation

1.6.9   In the States of sub-Sahara Africa, there is legal pluralism and two or three types of law or legal traditions all operate simultaneously in the same country. But another tradition in West African and East African countries is that of Islamic law. The governments in these countries are therefore grappling with the problems of adapting indigenous customary law to the newly-industrialised states and evolving a single system from the different legal traditions. Comparative legal studies would be extremely useful in the process of unifying, or at least harmonising, the laws of these countries. It is in this context that it is perfectly feasible to look to the experience of countries at a different stage of legal, political, social and economic evolution. If the experience of the West is examined, it will be possible not just to modernise and modify the laws, but also to evaluate it and be highly eclectic in selecting which laws might be adopted and adapted to particular local needs and conditions. In this way, the comparative law method will assist in informing any efforts aimed at improving the laws in these countries so that their people may the ultimate beneficiaries.

(iv) The International Law Dimension

1.6.10   A closely related field of comparative legal research is in the sphere of international law, the law which governs relationships between States. Utilisation of the comparative law method assists in the discovery, elucidation, and application of the 'general principles of law' which international and occasionally national courts are directed to apply. Article 38(1) (c) of the Statute of the International Court of Justice (ICJ) directs the International Court to apply *inter alia*, 'the general principles of law recognised by civilised nations' and Article 215 of the Treaty of Rome 1958 establishing the EEC, provides that the non-contractual liability of the Community is to be governed by 'the general principles common to the laws of the Member States.'

With regard to Article 38(1)(c), Professor Schlesinger has said: "The phrase *'general principles of law recognised by civilised nations'* refers to principles which find expression in the municipal laws of various nations. These principles, therefore, can be ascertained only by the comparative method." (Schlesinger (1988) p.36).

There are, of course, difficulties which confront the international judge in using the comparative law method in the international sphere. Bothe and Ress identify some these problems (see Bothe and Ress (1980)p.61) First, there is the problem of deciding *which legal orders should be compared.* If he selected his principles from only a few legal orders and not others, this would undermine the confidence in the international judicial process of settlement of disputes. Recourse to principles of regional application are on a surer footing, and as we shall see, the recent decisions of the European Court of Justice of the European Communities shows that English, French and German concepts are already making their presence felt. (see Chapter 5) Second, there is the question of *comparability or transferability of concepts* and principles. It is certainly doubtful whether domestic law concepts can be transposed simply into the bases of international law decisions. It will also be misleading to assume that the guarantee of a certain human right in many state constitutions will automatically mean that states are therefore bound to observe that particular right. Nevertheless, there is certainly sufficient material in the internal law of the members of the international community for the international judge to perform a law-creating and lawmaking function. It should always be remembered that the comparative method is not intended to replace the judicial function, only to facilitate, clarify and inform it.

The only reliable method of ascertaining principles of law which can authentically be termed 'general' is through 'comon core research'. This refers to that area of legal research which endeavours to find the 'common core' or highest common factor of an area of substantive law (Schlesinger *Formation of Contracts: A Study of the Common Core of Legal Systems* (1968)) or a legal institution in a number of countries or of laws and institutions of a number of countries within the same legal system. Common core research will assist jurists and others seeking the international or regional unification of law to initally ascertain the extent of similarity and divergence among the legal systems to be unified and to be in a better position to assess these features. Under Article 38 of the Statute of the ICJ, the comparative law method assists the International Court in applying international conventions and treaties and to create new rules or abolish or modify old principles.

The comparative method also assists the international lawyer who requires information on the domestic law of a number of countries. Situations requiring this information might be when regional varieties of international law are sought to be compared(see Green 'Comparative Law as a Source of International Law'(1967) 42 Tul. LR 52, 55) or when the law of a number of countries have to be studied in the course of preparing a draft treaty and when international lawyers are required to advise on whether a country has complied with its international obligations (Hazard 'Comparative Law in Legal Education' (1951) 18 Uni.Chi. LR 264).

Examples may be cited from *international trade law*, where the *preparation of international conventions* has necessitated reference to the laws of many countries, namely: the law of international sale of goods (see chapter Nine), shipping and transport and international bills of exchange.

The European Court of Justice of the European Communities has been utilising the comparative law method, in interpreting Community law and seeking to reach decisions by evaluating solutions provided by various legal systems, for example in *Da Costa en Schaake NV* [1963] ECR 31; *French Republic* v. *Deroche, Cornet et Soc Promatex-France* [1967] CMLR 351. Hence, comparative law is a necessary but neglected element in interpretating the law of international organisations. In addition, national courts are increasingly being required to interpret and apply international law. The comparative legal method will enable this to be done in a systematic, organised and comprehensive manner.

H. KEY CONCEPTS IN THE COMPARATIVE LAW METHOD

i. The Parent Legal Family and Legal Traditions

1.7   Certain key concepts in the comparative law method may be highlighted. We shall assume, for purposes of comparison, that we are using the *'parent legal family'* or major legal family as our basic model for comparison. The notion of *legal family* has served as the organisational linchpin for the analysis of legal systems of the world. This concept did not originate with Professor Rene David, whose masterly exposition of the world's major legal systems in *Les Grands Systemes de Droit Contemporains* in 1950 (see now David and Brierley (1985)) has been regarded as a seminal work. The concept of legal families was certainly outlined by Montesquieu so it is at least as old as the eighteenth century. It is discussed further in Chapter Two. Hence, when we refer to 'civil law countries', we are referring primarily to countries which have inherited the Romano-Germanic traditions (which are part of the *civil law tradition*) which have a distinctive juristic style. Within this civil law tradition we have the French legal tradition and the German legal tradition. Both of these come within the civil law tradition because their legal system originates from Roman law, based on compilations of the Emperor Justinian, as it was interpreted and disseminated by scholars from Bologna in the twelfth century. They also share a tradition of devising systematic, authoritative and comprehensive codifications as their law-making style, working from general concepts and providing solutions to problems. However, apart from differences in the structure of their Codes, they are themselves distinguishable in their separate legal traditions.

The *French legal tradition* is based on a rigid separation between private and criminal law, and 'public' or administrative law on the other; these form in reality *two discrete systems of law*, each with their own courts, their own unique legal concepts and their own commentators and learned authors. It also adopts a deductive method of reasoning, inferring its rules from broad maxims, and deriving solutions from those rules, through a sequence of logically correct deductions. This method is applied to (i) private and criminal law on the basis of the Codes which resulted from the Napoleonic codification, and (ii) to administrative law, elaborated and developed by the administrative courts, particularly the *Conseil d'Etat*, on the basis of the principles of legality.

The *German legal tradition* was greatly influenced by the nineteenth century Pandectist Movement, which was produced from the German Historical School of Law, whose only aim was the dogmatic and systematic study of Roman material. The eventual result was a conceptual, systematic law produced to a high level of abstraction in the German Codes, really very different from the French Codes in their tone, mode of expression and extraordinary precision.

But these two traditions may legitimately be classed together since, for example, they both adopt codifications as their preferred style and both work from the general to the particular in their method of legal reasoning. Similarly, the primacy of legislation is therefore common to both systems, with codes and enacted law being primary sources of law.

The French and German legal systems have influenced a large number of countries where their Codes and codificatory style have served as models of lawmaking and legal philosophy. The civil law tradition, of course, is itself made up of several sub-traditions (see Merryman (1977) p.7).

In contrast, the basic approach of the English common law tradition is a *case-based law*, founded on judicial decisions and the doctrine of judicial precedent (*stare decisis*). In modern times, cases have been heavily supplemented by legislation, which has taken over as the primary method of lawmaking. Indeed, in a reversal of the earlier phases of common law history, judges have frequently been reminded by other more senior or traditional judges that their role is only one of interpretation, not lawmaking when it comes to the *interpretation of statutes*. Within this particular area, the common law frequently resembles the civil law in giving precedence (at least in strict theory, and sometimes in practice) to the 'intention of the legislature' and the 'intention of parliament'.

Accordingly, we shall compare the basic approaches, methodology, and ideology of civil law systems with the common law systems as it functions and operates in present times, as *the* mother system or parent legal family of the 'common law'.

ii. Sources of Law

1.7.1 Another important concept in comparative law is the term 'sources of law'. This can mean different things in different countries and, even in the same country, can mean different things according to different writers. As Professor David points out, however, all the divergent interpretations stem from one single fact: a lack of agreement on the meaning of 'law'. (see David *Sources of Law* International Encyclopedia of Comparative Law, chapter 3 (1981)p.3) This, like sources of law, is partly attributable to the ambiguity of language and the difficulties in obtaining an authentic translation.

Generally speaking, the legislatures of the countries of the world have failed to address this question, presumably to reserve the right to decide what sources of law they will refer to, or change or abolish, according to the needs of the moment. Pragmatically, of course, the legislature of various countries has simply had other more urgent matters to attend to, and usually concern themselves with regulation of a specific practical problem.

Even when statutes set out a hierarchy of sources, irt is still necessary to refer to academic works because the sources often include custom and tradition, which themselves are often undefined and variable.

In reality, 'the subject of sources of law may be governed by different principles, depending on the branch of law.' (David (1981), *ibid*. p.11) Ideally, one would need to examine politics, sociology, psychology and many other areas to seek a definitive answer to the problem of defining a 'source of law'. In purely legal terms, we need only examine the historical background to a particular jurisdiction to see the factual and formal sources and deduce from those sources the current legal position. Hence, nearly every analysis of a legal systems or concept is preceded by a brief *historical examination* thereof.

The *formal sources of law* are legislation, codes, judicial decisions, custom, doctrinal or scholarly writing, and equity. Each legal system has its sources which have a particular hierarchical structure. Thus, the main sources of law in civil law countries are the Codes, enacted law, doctrinal writing, custom and decided cases. It should be noted that the role of cases as a source of law is officially a secondary one of supplementing enacted law or doctrinal sources. There is *no legal doctrine of stare decisis in the civil law tradition*, so that in theory, a case may simply be ignored and need not be followed by a subsequent court. The basic premise is that the legislator, not the judge, creates or makes law. In practice, of course, cases have played a pivotal role in developing the law in civil law countries especially where the Codes or statutes have not provided for novel or difficult situations.

iii. Comparative Law Method

1.7.2   We shall discuss the different techniques that may be utilised in the process of comparison in Chapter Two. Initially, this will be based on the guidelines of Zweigert and Kotz (1977) but not entirely. Despite a number of features which distinguish one legal system from another, perhaps the litmus test of what is the heart and soul of a system, and its quintessential character, is not merely its language or teminology, its organisation, institutions or structure. As G.W. Bartholomew, when speaking about the common law, put it: 'it is in fact no one single thing. It is neither a matter of substantive rules nor a matter of [procedures] in the administration of justice. It resides, it is submitted, in the mental attitudes and habits of legal thought that historically evolved...and which are still used and followed by lawyers and judges...'

By examining a system's history, mode of thought in legal matters, sources of law and legal ideology (collectively called the 'style' of a legal system by Zweigert and Kotz (1977) p.62) we may be better able to understand, appreciate and evaluate our own systems in a systematic and productive way. If used successfully, that understanding, appreciation and evaluation must be the greatest rewards that one may derive from comparative law.

In the 1990s, perhaps more than in nearly any other period in world history, we need to appraise afresh the new world order. The Western and Eastern *blocs* of the world have now entered into various political, economic and cultural co-operative ventures which have presaged the gradual but decisive dis-integration of the Communist *bloc* that has swept across Eastern Europe, fragmenting and replacing the old Soviet Union with new independent republics and one rather tenous 'Commonwealth' which is really more like a *Federation of States*. This has left only Communist China reasonably intact as the last Communist superpower still advocating the 'old' socialism. The catchphrase of the 1980s and early 1990s in the international context has been the 'global village' in which we now live hence it is surely counter-productive for lawyers as much as for anyone else to continue to exist in 'splendid isolation'. As McDougal appropriately expressed it as long ago as 1952:'In a world shrinking at an ever-accelerating rate because of a relent-lessly expanding, uniformity-imposing technology, both opportunity and need for the comparative study of law are unprecedented.'

These words are as apt in the 1990s as they were fifty years ago.

SELECTIVE BIBLIOGRAPHY

Gutteridge COMPARATIVE LAW (1946);(1949); (1971)(reprint)

McDougal 'The Comparative Study of Law for Policy Purposes: Value Clarification as an Instrument of Democratic World Order' (1952) 1 Am. JCL 24

Kahn-Freund 'Comparative Law as an Academic Subject' (1966) 82 LQR 40

Dainow 'The Civil Law and the Common Law: Some Points of
      Comparison (1966-67) Am.JCL 419

Derrett AN INTRODUCTION TO LEGAL SYSTEMS (1968)

Kamba 'Comparative Law: A Theoretical Framework' (1974) 23 ICLQ
      485

Watson LEGAL TRANSPLANTS (1974)

Winterton 'Comparative Law Teaching' (1975) Am.JCL 69

Ehrmann COMPARATIVE LEGAL CULTURES (1976)

Zweigert & Kotz AN INTRODUCTION TO COMPARATIVE
      LAW (1977) Vols.I and II; (1987) (2nd ed.)

de Vries & Schneider: CIVIL LAW AND THE ANGLO-AMERICAN
      LAWYER (1976)

Merryman THE CIVIL LAW TRADITION (1977)

Von Mehren & Gordley THE CIVIL LAW SYSTEM (1977)

David & Brierley MAJOR LEGAL SYSTEMS IN THE WORLD
      TODAY (1985)

Schlesinger et al: COMPARATIVE LAW-CASES-TEXT-MATERIALS
      (1988)

Butler INTERNATIONAL LAW IN COMPARATIVE PERSPECTIVE
      (1980)

Bothe and Ress 'The Comparative Method and International Law'
in INTERNATIONAL LAW IN COMPARATIVE LAW (ed.Butler)

Dutoit 'Comparative Law and Public International Law' *in*
INTERNATIONAL LAW IN COMPARATIVE PERSPECTIVE (ed. Butler)

Markesinis 'Comparative Law-A Subject in Search of an Audience'
      [1990] 53 Mod. LR 1

Grossfeld THE STRENGTH AND WEAKNESS OF
      COMPARATIVE LAW (1990)

PART TWO: MAJOR LEGAL TRADITIONS

CHAPTER TWO

Classification of Legal Systems and Techniques of Comparison

A. TERMINOLOGY

i. Legal Traditions and Legal Families

2.0   It has become established practice to classify the legal systems of the world into three main types of legal families or legal traditions: civil law, common law and socialist law. A *legal tradition* has been defined as a set of 'deeply rooted historically conditioned attitudes about the nature of law, the role of law in the society and the political ideology, the organisation and operation of a legal system.' (see Merryman (1977)). Merryman goes on to suggest that whereas 'a legal system is an operating set of legal institutions, procedures and rules... a legal tradition puts the legal system into cultural perspective.' Hence he makes a clear distinction between a legal system and a legal tradition. On the other hand, David and Brierley prefer to talk of the three main '*legal families*' (ie civil law, common law and socialist law) now regarded as eponymous systems, which they describe as 'certain laws which can be considered typical and representative of a family which groups a number of laws.' (see David & Brierley (1985)). In the same vein, Zweigert and Kotz (1977) also adopt the language of legal families but emphasise at great length the pitfalls and problems that may be encountered in arriving at some sort of consensus among the comparatists as to the set of criteria that should be employed in order to classify the various legal systems into legal families or according to their particular legal tradition. Efforts to achieve consensus on criteria have so far been largely unsuccessful. However, it is submitted that there is at root far more concordance between the ostensibly divergent views because, in a sense, the matter turns on terminology and interpretation and the different approaches are largely consistent with each other. Hence, to say that jurisdiction A belongs to the civil law *tradition* (which includes all the facets mentioned by Merryman) because it conforms to a certain set of civil law criteria, is not inconsistent with saying that jurisdiction A should be classified within the civil law *'legal family'* because it conforms to similar criteria. The point is that jurisdiction A, or indeed Legal System A (if that term is preferred) will, under *either* approach, be classified as a civil law jurisdiction or system. To a certain extent, therefore, some of the academic dialectic represents a distinction without a difference. Real problems and practical difficulties only arise if there is a disagreement over the classificatory criteria which would assist in determining which law to apply to a given situation and it is not possible to decide whether jurisdiction A (assuming it is an obscure country) belongs to a civil law system or tradition or to any other major legal family. It might, for instance, be a 'hybrid' or mixed legal system and knowledge of the laws of that legal system might be required if the conflict of laws rule of a domestic forum points to the internal law of a foreign country as the law that governs the particular case. At this point, as a broad generalization, it may be said, that most legal systems in the world today possess characteristics which are predominantly identified with one or more of the *three major legal traditions or families*, ie civil law, common law and (at least until recently) socialist law. This does not, of course, mean that this trichotomy encompasses every possible legal system existing in the modern world. In places like Asia and Africa and the Islamic countries, powerful elements of customary law (of non-European origin) still remain and are in evidence in varying degrees.

B. CLASSIFICATION OF LEGAL SYSTEMS

2.1 At the beginning of the twentieth century, a groundswell of opinion arose favouring widespread comparative studies and in 1900, the concept of 'families of law' was introduced to comparative law. One of the ultimate aims of the comparative studies was to secure total or at least substantial unification of all civilised legal systems. As mentioned in the first chapter, 1900 was the year of the First International Congress of Comparative Law which was held in Paris. In 1905, Esmein suggested a classification of legal systems into five families of law: (i) Romanistic, Germanic, Anglo-Saxon, Slavic and Islamic. In 1977, Zweigert and Kotz divided legal families into eight groups: Romanistic, Germanic, Nordic, Common Law Family, Socialist, Far Eastern Systems, Islamic Systems and Hindu law. Their criterion-'juristic style'- is discussed in detail below. In 1978, David and Brierley adopted a classificatory system based on ideology and legal technique, so that law families could be classified into Romano-Germanic, Common Law, Socialistic, Islamic, Hindu and Jewish, Far East and Black African.

i. Examples of Each Type of Legal Family

2.1.1 Countries that are usually classified as common law jurisdictions are England and Wales, Australia, Nigeria, Kenya, Zambia, the United States of America, New Zealand, Canada, and various parts of the Far East, such as Singapore, Malaysia and Hong Kong. Civil law countries include France, Germany, Italy, Switzerland, Austria, Latin American countries, Turkey, various Arab States, North Africa and Madagascar. Socialist systems of law included Bulgaria, Yugoslavia and Cuba and, until recently, the former USSR, which has since disintegrated and is now comprised of eleven independent states who have agreed to form the world's second commonwealth known as the Commonwealth of Independent States (CIS) and four of the former soviet republics, who have declared their independence and remain outside the CIS. Examples of hybrid or mixed jurisdictions are The Seychelles, South Africa, Louisiana, the Phillippines, Greece, Quebec in Canada, and Puerto Rico. For these jurisdictions, there is some difficulty in classifying the legal family to which they belong, and even looking to the system to which they most are predominantly similar, will only be helpful up to a point.

2.1.2 The notion of legal families may be variously interpreted. Indeed, there is no consensus among commentators as to whether it is purely heuristic (David), basic and scientific (Knapp), or useless theoretically and descriptively (Friedmann). Even where the concept has been used, there has not been any consensus as to the criteria for classification, for example, Zweigert and Kotz prefer 'juristic style' while Glasson and Sarfatti focus on a system's historical origins as a distinguishing or identifying feature. There is equally no agreement on the groupings of the various legal systems. Undoubtedly, a range of alternative classifications will always be possible depending on the data available and the particular interpretation of that data. It is certainly arguable that each classification will have some merit and in factual terms, there are observable characteristics of each system which place it *predominantly* within one legal family or another (ie the 'predominance principle'). The factual basis or antecedents of Canadian, American, and Australian law are demonstrably English law. Similarly, the French influence on its Eastern neighbours only becomes disputable when one has to decide the boundaries of this influence. Again, the widespread influence of Islam and the Koran is objectively observable in a number of countries. It is only when a comparatist seeks to classify various distinguishing features into groups of systems and attempts to demarcate the parameters of those groups that disagreement inevitably arises. Nevertheless, the question that should be answered with regard to classification is : What is the purpose of the classification? Factual, ideological, and historical characteristics may all be synthesised so as to enable a valid blueprint for comparison (see below). By utilising the 'predominance principle', we move closer to a clearer classification of the various systems. It needs to be remembered, of course, that political, economic, social and moral factors all exert considerable influence on the profile of a legal system and the fact that history is written by victors, suggests that the political fortunes of a country will inevitably be reflected in its postwar or post-crisis legal, economic and social framework.

ii. Criteria used to Classify Legal Systems

2.1.3 Various criteria have been suggested as a means of determining the classification of a particular system, ranging from race and language (Sauser-Hall), culture (Schnitzer), 'substance' (substantive content of laws)

(Arminjon, Nolde and Wolff), ideology, philosophy, conceptions of justice and legal technique (David), historical origins (Glasson and Sarfatti) and juristic style (Zweigert and Kotz). One should remember that the particular stage of development of a given legal system which is selected for comparison will also play a significant part in the process of classification. It is proposed to examine the Zweigert and Kotz approach, with the proviso that the predominance principle should be applied. These two writers suggest that juristic style should be the crucial test which determines the classification of a legal system, which they suggest may be ascertained from: (i) The historical background and development of the system; (ii) Its characteristic (typical) mode of thought; (iii) Its distinctive institutions;(iv) The types of legal sources it acknowledges and its treatment of these; (v) Its ideology.

C. EXAMINATION AND APPLICATION OF THE CRITERIA

i. Historical Development

2.2 As far as historical development is concerned, it is widely accepted that the English common law development was fairly clear-cut, wherein a large body of rules founded on unwritten customary law evolved and developed throughout the centuries, with pragmatism, strong monarchs, an unwritten Constitution and centralised courts being its typical features (see chapter 4). This distinctive development justifies its separate classification. On the other hand, as we already noted, non-common law systems have had a more chequered history and this has caused writers to label civil law systems 'Romano-Germanic' (David and Brierley (1985)). This reflects both the Roman law origins, strong influence of the French Civil Code and the subsequent influence of the German Civil Code. However, more significant has been the influence and reception of Roman law within a particular system. It was Roman law with its notions of codification, systematisation of concepts into concepts, categories, principles and divisions of law which has left its lasting imprint on the French and German Codes. This was in stark contrast to common law adoption of substantive law principles which developed in an *ad hoc* fashion, in response to the need to resolve disputes, whose devlopment was largely dependent on disputants bringing their case to the courts. There was no common law legislative tradition which sought to reform or redress the law by means of the legislature, unlike the civil law. The significant historical fact, therefore, is that common law was developed in and by the courts, giving *judge-made law* considerable 'weight' whereas civil law was formulated, compiled and refined in the universities, later codified and then given statutory force by the legislature. This also explains some of the differences in approach and content. Eastern Europe and the former Soviet Union, of course, have traditionally been labelled 'Socialist' legal systems, reflecting their Marxist-Leninist origins and ideology. It should be reiterated at this point that in the light of the unification of East and West Germany in 1990, the continuing decline of Communist regimes in Eastern European countries and the disintegration of the former Soviet Union in 1991, partly replaced by the new Russian Commonwealth of Independent States (comprising 15 of the former Soviet republics), the whole notion of 'Socialist will eventually adopt (Chapter 6 discusses current Russian developments). Upon reflection, this identifying characteristic is reasonably helpful with the proviso that the non-occurrence of a particular type of historical evolution or historical experience in a given system does not, of course, mean that the particular system is not predominantly a common law, socialist or civil law system. We must therefore consider another significant, more wide-ranging historical phenomenon: *colonialism* of one form or another. For instance, outside Europe, the fact that a given jurisdiction was not dominated by a particular Code or evolved through centralised courts has, in many cases, nothing to do with its legal history and legal evolution. The historical explanation for Far Eastern, Antipodean and American jurisdictions is found in British, French and Dutch colonialism. In the first instance, British, French and Dutch control of places like Malaysia and India, Africa and Indonesia, meant that predominantly common law or civil law was 'received' in these areas. However, in view of the diversity and uncertainty of local customary laws, codifications of laws were introduced into places like India and to a lesser extent, in the Far East, so as to clarify, unify, modernise and adapt the foreign law to local conditions. Hence, the really significant historical devlopment was the occurrence of colonialism which ultimately produced a plurality of laws. So the first criterion is acceptable with the foregoing *caveat*: look to the history but consider other criteria as well.

ii. Mode of Legal Thinking

2.2.1 As a generalisation, civil law or Germanic and Romanistic legal families tend to think in abstract, conceptual and symmetrical terms. Civil law, derived from universities and Roman law, is *rule-based* and constantly seeks *solutions* to a problem before the court. It also thinks in terms of institutions, whereas the English common law is typical for its concrete, court-based approach, seeking pragmatic answers to issues before the court. Where civil law proceeds from general principle to general principle, common law proceeds from case to case. Where cases have formed the primary source of the common law, statutes and codified law have been the civil law counterparts. While common lawyers think in terms of the parties and their particular legal relationship, civil lawyers think in terms of the existing enacted rules, codified or statutory, which may be applied to a given situation. Another consequence of the historical development which is reflected in the mode of legal thinking is the civil law penchant for planning, systematising and regulating everyday matters as comprehensively as possible. In contrast, the classic common law characteristic is to improvise, examining cases for possible precedents which may or may not be 'binding' on the court currently hearing a case and only deciding to legislate in any sort of organised and comprehensive fashion if the particular area of law happens to be confused, obscure or reveals a 'gap' in the law. Even when ostensibly comprehensive statutes are passed, the preceding caselaw is often relevant as a guide to interpretation since the enactment of the statute is generally seen as a consolidation (and possibly clarification) of existing law. The common law statute therefore seeks generally to build or improve on existing caselaw, whereas the civil law equivalent has traditionally sought to enunciate universally applicable principles, clearly set out for either the citizen (as in the French Code) or the specialist (as in the German Code). It frequently sets out to establish new laws, and to do so explicitly. Of course, recent trends have indicated that the common law and civil law systems have been coming closer together in their use of cases and statutes. The UK Children Act 1989, which came into force in October, 1991, while incidentally consolidating and integrating certain existing case-derived rules and statutes, was enacted predominantly to effect 'the most comprehensive and far-reaching reform of English child care law ever introduced' into the UK in the twentieth century (Sir Geoffrey Howe:House of Commons Debates; 26 October 1989, vol 158, col 1071) On the other hand, civil law systems, particularly France and Germany, have begun to rely more and more on cases where, for example, the enacted or codifed law has been found deficient in any way. Socialist law, as developed and based on Marxist-Leninist ideas, has also relied on codification (see explanations of the term, below) from early times and on statutory rules to the exclusion of caselaw and with no doctrine of precedent as such. It had its roots in ancient Roman law and thus uses civil law legal terminology and civil law classifications and conceptualisations (see chapter 6). However, its unique feature was that it simply viewed law as an instrument of State Policy and merely as a vehicle for carrying out Marxist/Leninist ideals. Law was to be used for the purpose of implementing the State Plan in accordance with Marxist philosophy. In contrast to civil law and common law, it has traditionally seen law as created by the State and subordinate to the State. Clearly, therefore, so-called socialist countries have, in many respects, been easily discernible and readily classifiable since, in the former Soviet Union, for example, the supremacy of the State machinery (the Russian Communist Party and the politburo) over any other organisation was manifest. The second criterion is therefore readily applicable at least in the first instance.

iii. Distinctive Legal Institutions

2.2.2 In common law jurisdictions, the typical legal institutions are the trust, agency, tort principles, consideration and estoppel. In the Romanistic family, however, there is a strong tendency towards formalism and 'rules protecting the moral and economic integrity of the legitimate family against outsiders' (Zweigert and Kotz). There is also the direct action, oblique action, and abuse of right, to name but a few unique legal institutions. The Germanic family has institutions such as the abstract real contract, *clausulae generales*, the concept of the legal act, the notion of unjust enrichment, the doctrine of the collapse of the foundations of a transaction and liability based on *culpa in contrahendo*. Typical institutions in socialist legal systems included different types of ownership, unique notions of the role and status of contract in a planned economy, and the 'duty to rescue.' As the new Commonwealth of Independent States (CIS) lurches towards some form of capitalist economy and attempts to introduce social democracy, recent edicts passed suggest that, assuming the CIS survives, there will be radical changes in ownership and the notion of contract for private persons. It is quite conceivable that Western commercial and legal notions will co-exist with more antiquated traditions rooted in civil law, but supported by a quasi-military government traditions rooted in civil law, but supported by a quasi-military government operating as a 'benevolent dictatorship' on the lines of certain Latin American countries. On the other hand, a predominantly social democracy utilising civil law codifications might yet emerge with the threat of military force being used simply to preserve order, peace and security. Changes paving the way for an independent judiciary have already been implemented, (see chapter 6) so that legal conceptions dealing with commercial and private matters will almost certainly change. On balance, therefore, the second criterion appears to be a positive aid to classification.

iv. Choice of Sources of Law

2.2.3 The next identificatory feature suggested by Zweigert and Kotz is the much-discussed topic of sources of law. Basically, the debate has centred on whether cases or statutes are the predominant source of law in any given legal system. Zweigert and Kotz argue that although differences exist with regard to methods of interpretation, court structures and procedures, this topic is really of minor significance in the context of legal families and comparative law as a whole. They would attach far greater significance to the legal institutions of a legal system. It is not entirely clear why Zweigert and Kotz express this view. One obvious reason may be that all systems now use both cases and statutes (and codes) as sources so that mere usage of one or the other is *ipso facto* inconclusive and therefore irrelevant to their classification. Nevertheless, applying the present writer's 'predominance principle' it is still true to say that at the present time, the primary source of law in civil law countries such as France and Germany is still predominantly codified or enacted law whereas in common law countries it is still predominantly caselaw. Exceptions to this general proposition clearly exist but in this case, the exceptions certainly prove the rule. Moreover, it is also true to say that while common law and civil law courts use both cases and statutes as sources of law, their approaches to these sources, methods and techniques of abstraction diverge sufficiently to warrant differentiation. In short, common law and civil law jurisdictions both handle cases and statutes but they do so in different ways. Civil law countries like France and Germany also have written Constitutions unlike the United Kingdom. The United States of America's written Constitution has played a fundamental part in the development of citizen's rights and responsibilities in a similar manner to France and Germany. Thus, mere similarity of sources of law, at least in the context of written or unwritten constitutions, is of limited importance in ascertaining the true 'juristic style' of a legal system. Clearly, other criteria must also be taken into account.

v. Ideology of a Legal System

2.2.4 This is interpreted by Zweigert and Kotz as meaning 'political or economic doctrines or religious belief.' This appears to be the least contentious of all the criteria since it is widely recognised that the legal ideologies of Anglo-Saxon, Germanic, Romanistic and Nordic familes are similar in all

Anglo-Saxon, Germanic, Romanistic and Nordic familes are similar in all important respects. Equally, countries like China, Mongolia, North Vietnam, North Korea, and, until recently, Russia and many countries in Eastern Europe, have adopted a communist theory of law based on Marxist/Leninist philosophy which warrants placing them in a separate category or legal family. Religious legal systems, such as Hindu and Muslim systems, also justify separate categorisation in view of their uniqueness (see chapter 7). However, it is not so easy to classify the legal families of the West since their ideologies are so similar. They may be more readily classifiable according to their history, mode of legal thinking, and distinctive institutions. Sources of law are a distinguishing feature of Hindu and Islamic law and also help to separate the European Continental from the Anglo-Saxon type of legal family. However, as a consequence of recent momentous events in Eastern European and Russian jurisdictions, it has become extremely difficult to say what the eventual ideologies of these countries seeking independence will be. It is possible that some form of social democracy will emerge, although this will arguably be of a species still steeped in civil law legal approaches, and heavily dependent on State Policy and enacted law. Hence, enacted law will continue to enjoy primacy, and only economic growth followed by political maturity and experience will lead to the emergence of a greater reliance on cases. In the case of 'mixed jurisdictions' or 'hybrid' systems of law where civil law and common law co-exist, with or without local customary law, it will be even harder or even impossible to apply the abovenamed criteria.

D. CONVERGENCE THEORY AND LEGAL FAMILIES

2.3 As legal systems continue to resemble each other in their use of sources of law, there may well evolve a situation where both statutes and cases are being used in equal measure and even regarded as authoritative as each other. There may even be increased reliance on opinions of legal or doctrinal writers in common law jurisdictions and possibly a considerable reduction in the weight attributed to local custom in any modern systems of law. Would this mean that a convergence of systems had occurred or would eventually occur? The current debates over the Maastricht Treaty with regard to European cooperation, the ongoing civil war in parts of Eastern Europe, and the uncertainty over the future of the new Russian Commonwealth of Independent States and its uneasy relationship with the West over a range of critical issues suggests that even European unity (between East and West or among Western European countries) at the practical level, is, at present, little more than an ideal. If European economic cooperation is eventually achieved, this will be but one small step towards some form of unity. As far as legal families are concerned, therefore, it is still relevant, useful and accurate to examine common law and civil law systems according to the criteria we have been discussing and to reflect on the identifying characteristics of the few remaining countries which are still avowedly socialist legal systems. The convergence theories will be discussed at various parts of this book, but suffice to say for the moment that although convergence of some description is certainly foreseeable, deep-seated differences in ideology, political attitudes, social and economic policies, not to mention fundamental moral values and philosophies, attitudes to law, and judicial, executive and administrative structures would have to be reconciled with each other.

E. PITFALLS IN COMPARISON

2.4   Before considering the possible techniques of comparative law, we should remind ourselves of some of the potential pitfalls that must be borne in mind by any comparative lawyer: (i) Linguistic and terminological perspectives; (ii) Cultural differences between legal systems;(iii) The potentiality of arbitrariness in selection of objects of study; (iv) Difficulties in achieving 'comparability' in comparison; (v) The desire to see a common legal pattern in legal systems-the theory of a general pattern of development; (vi) The tendency to impose one's own (native) legal conceptions and expectations on the systems being compared; (vii) Dangers of exclusion/ignorance of extra-legal rules.   It is proposed to concentrate on terminological issues and the question of 'comparability' in comparison.

i. Linguistic Terminological and Cultural Issues

2.4.1   Whereas physicians, chemists, economists, mathematicians and musicians have a common vocabulary, legal terminology is fraught with linguistic traps and is a potential minefield of misunderstanding; meanings vary from country to country. There is now a fairly extensive and (and expanding) literature acknowledging the importance of language as a factor in comparative law (see, eg, Grossfeld (1990) especially Chapter 13).

Even in English-speaking countries, homonyms may have different meanings. Hence, even if the basic legal concepts are similar, different terms may be utilised so as to create an impression of divergence and this may occur within the same legal family. Conversely, although the terms used may be identical, their substantive content or actual application in practice may be quite different.

An example of an identical term which is common to two jurisdictions within the same legal family is *stare decisis* (let the decision stand). Both American and English legal systems have adopted a doctrine of stare decisis but their actual operation within their individual jurisdictions are 'markedly different' (see Atiyah and Summers (1987)).   The essential difference between American and English practice is that the lower courts in America are not bound to follow their own decisions, and the authority of a court's own prior decisions depends largely on on the persuasiveness of the reasoning of the earlier courts. Unlike English courts, in America, subsequent judges at all levels have the power to disregard otherwise binding decisions (see Atiyah and Summers (1987) pp.113-34). Thus, a 'binding' decision may not be absolutely binding because the court may believe that the previous ruling was clearly wrong when delivered, or inappropriate to different factual conditions or the composition of the court may have changed so that the majority view has become the minority one.

The doctrine of precedent in America has never acquired the formalistic authority it appears to possess in the English version because of the great volume of decisions, conflicting precedents in different jurisdictions, and the speed of the changes which have taken place in social and economic conditions (see Farnsworth (1987) pp.44-52).

One example of a term used in both civil law and common law jurisdictions is 'equity' (*Aequitas, equite, Billigkeit*) which has a strict technical meaning in English law (rules, maxims and practices of the Courts of Chancery presided over by the Chancellor which remained a separately administered jurisdiction until its fusion with the common law jurisdiction in 1873-5) but which is used by European Continental judges whenever they do not wish to adopt a formal or narrow interpretation of a legal principle. Another example of an identical term used in both common law and civil law jurisdictions but which is by no means identical in meaning or application is the notion/principle of *Good Faith*. This is used as a principle of general application in German commercial law (see chapter 9) and indeed by jurisdictions which have adopted the German-style Code, such as Greece.

2.4.2   In relation to *cultural differences* between the systems, Leon Friedman has highlighted that the cultural elements which the comparatist should seek to discover in a fully developed legal system are the 'values and attitudes which bind the system together and which determine the place of the legal system in the culture of the society as a whole'.

ii. 'Comparability' in Comparison

(i) General Considerations

2.4.3   The comparability of legal systems depends on a number of factors, some constant, many transient. Grossfedl (1990) lists the following determinative factors: the cultural, political and economic components of a society, as well as the particular relationship that exists between the State and its citizens, its value-susyem, and its particular conception of the individual and the world in general. Other general factors include a society's 'cultural climate', a term used by Grossfeld, which he describes as 'that resulting from the people's unconscious axioms, collective feelings, and prevalent ideas of reality.' He also places importance on the 'homogeneity' of the society in question and 'whether it has a cultural consciousness or not.' Other factors he mentions are geographical situation, language and religion and stresses that in order to ascertain the legal effect of legal solutions in different systems, a multi-disciplinary approach is required.

(ii) Comparability of Systems at Similar or Different Stages of Development

2.4.4   It has been argued by many eminent scholars that systems selected for comparison must be those which are a similar stage of development, and these include Gutteridge, Pollock, and Schmitthoff. Nevertheless, it is usually necessary to select systems or institutions which are at a similar stage of legal development, which will then ensure a baseline of similarity. However, it is not necessary that this is followed in every case, because *the choice of legal systems must ultimately depend on the main aims and objectives of the particular comparative investigation.* An example of this sort of comparison is becoming increasingly common in the context of Western input and advice relating to certain African countries where Western organisations and individuals have shared the benefits of their experience with those African countries in order to assist them in adapting their infrastructures to modern technology and a rapdly changing society. Equally, a study of marriage and marital property as it has evolved in the West is illuminating to any society which is considering introducing legislative reforms in these areas.

F. THE COMPARATIVE METHOD

i. Macro-Comparison and Micro-Comparison

2.5 The terms *macro-comparison* and *micro-comparison*, gnerally attributed to Rheinstein, are frequently used to describe the two different species of comparative study that may be undertaken. Macro-comparison refers to the study of *two or more entire legal systems*; micro-comparison refers to the study of *topics or aspects of two or more legal systems*. Among the topics chosen for micro-comparison may be: (i) the institutions or concepts peculiar to the systems; (ii) the sources of law, judicial systems and the judiciary, legal profession or even the structure of the legal system; (iii) the various branches of national or domestic law; (iv) the historical development of legal systems; and (v) the ideological, socio-legal and economic bases of that system. The *purpose of the comparison* will often determine the suitability of selection.

ii. The Test of Functionality

2.5.1 The test of functionality has been suggested by Zweigert and Kotz (1977) who argue that 'every investigation in comparative law begins with the posing of a question or the setting of a working hypothesis-in brief, an idea.' They emphasise that 'The basic methodological principle of all comparative law is that of functionality.' Further, 'the legal system of every society faces essentially the same problems and solves these problems by quite different means though very often with similar results.' It is possible to disagree with this on the basis that certain societies (for example, Eastern ones) may have very different problems because their laws, religions and cultures are different. However, it is equally possible to argree with Zweigert and Kotz on the basis that although different societies have different specific problems, *all* societies have the same basic problems. They therefore need to resolve their particular domestic/local problems and to consider how best 'the law' (whatever that signifies in their society) may deal with these problems. All societies from Alaska to Australia face the basic problem of how best to regulate their society and to resolve and/or avoid conflict.

iii. The Three-Stage Approach

2.5.2 Kamba (1974) has suggested that there are three main stages involved in the process of comparison: (a) *the descriptive phase*: this may involve describing the norms, concepts and institutions of the system concerned; (b) *the identification phase*: identifying differences and similiarities between the systems being compared; (c) the explanatory phase: accounting for the resemblances and dissimiliarities between systems and concepts.

He also stresses that the proper execution of the three phases is greatly influenced by three further factors: (i) the comparatist's *jurisprudential outlook*; (ii) the *social context* of the legal systems under comparison; (iii) the *legal context* of the topics being compared in the case of micro-comparison.

iv. The Method of Comparison: A Blueprint

2.5.3 Bearing in mind the preceding points, a blueprint of comparison may be formulated:

Step One: *identify the problem* and state it as precisely as possible. This follows Zweigert and Kotz's initial step.

Step Two: Assuming that the 'home jurisdiction' is one of the jurisdictions being compared, *identify the foreign jurisdiction, and, if possible, its legal family*. If it is a hybrid system (involving a co-existence of common law and civil law) this should be noted. If it involves a socialist system, this could well pose problems especially if it is a system which is currently engaged in armed conflict. The Russian system is in a state of flux and transition and we can only hazard some idea of its potential future legal development. The People's Republic of China is a unique legal system and we are gradually acquiring more information about its current legal system.

Step Three: *decide which primary sources are going to be needed*. Will you need to examine a civil law code, or a commentary on it? Is the solution contained in a judicial decision or a statute? If there is no obvious answer, move on to the next step.

Step Four: *gather and assemble the material* relevant to the jurisdiction being examined. This should include primary and secondary sources of law. If you do not have strong views on what the legal approach should be (ie sociological, historical), it is suggested that you give equal weight to historical influences and socio-economic factors.

Useful sources are : (a) Bibliographies; (b) any available comparative encyclopedias; (c) introductory works dealing with that particular system or with comparative law generally, if the researcher is a 'first-time comparatist'; (d) codes; commentaries on codes; (e) law reports; (f) commentaries, textbooks, and casebooks; and (g) legal periodicals, wherein updated lists of available legal materials in particular areas of law occasionally appear. If there is any difficulty in procuring these materials, the inter-library loan services are generally very helpful, and a visit to the Institute of Advanced Legal

Studies in London is also recommended. Another useful step is to contact the embassy or consulate of the country in question, especially if it is particularly remote, in order to obtain up-to-date information.

Step Five: *organise the material* in accordance with the legal philosophy and ideology of the legal system being compared. A suggested working outline is: (i) List the main sources of law of the systems being compared-include outlines of general bibliographies; (ii) List the hierarchy of sources: codes, statutes, enactments, edicts, custom, doctrinal writing; commentaries; cases; textbooks; secondary legislation; customs(if any);(iii)Socio-cultural material: -treatises; periodical articles covering the jurisdiction and topic being studied;

Step Six: *Map out the possible answers* to the problem, comparing the different approaches, noting possible cultural differences, different legal interpretations, socio-economic factors and any non-legal factors (such as local customs and conventions) which may have influenced the current legal position in both jurisdictions. The question of how the rule really operates should be posed throughout the investigation.

Step Seven: *Critically analyse the legal principles* in terms of their intrinsic value rather than with any preconceived expectations. What purpose does the rule fulfil? What principle does it support? What practical effect, if any, does or might it have?

Step Eight: *Set out your conclusions* in a balanced manner, with *caveats* if necessary and with critical commentary, wherever relevant, and relate it to the original purpose of the enquiry. It will also be desirable to indicate your method of approach, with your reasons, so that other researchers may not merely read the results of your study but know why you approached it from those angles.

This suggested blueprint strives to integrate a socio-historical approach but comparatists with their own personal interests may focus them accordingly. As with all comparative studies, each successful investigation marks the end of an enquiry but it should also mark the beginning of a fresh outlook on the operation of legal systems, institutions and doctrines.

SELECTIVE BIBLIOGRAPHY

Merryman THE CIVIL LAW TRADITION (1977)

Pringsheim 'The Inner Relationship between English and Roman Law' (1933) Camb.LJ 347

Gutteridge 'The Comparative Aspects of Legal Terminology' (1938) Tul LR 401

Stone 'The End to be served by Comparative Law' (1951) Tul LR 325

Gutteridge COMPARATIVE LAW (1949) Chapter VI

McDougal 'The Comparative Study of Law for Policy Purposes: Value Clarification as an Instrument of Democratic World Order' (1952) 1 Am.JCL 24

Dainow 'The Civil Law and the Common Law' (1966/7) Am. JCL 419

Smith 'The Unique Nature of the Concepts of Western Law' (1968) Canadian Bar Review 191

Friedman 'Legal Culture and Social Development' (1969) 6 Law and Society Review 19

Zweigert & Kotz AN INTRODUCTION TO COMPARATIVE LAW, vol.I

Lawson ONE LAW : European Studies in Law (1977)

Lawson MANY LAWS: European Studies in Law (1977)

Kamba 'Comparative Law: A Theoretical Framework' (1974) ICLQ 485

Lawson 'Comparative Judicial Style' (1977) Am.JCL 364

David & Brierley MAJOR LEGAL SYSTEMS IN THE WORLD TODAY(1985), Part One-Three

Atiyah and Summers FORM AND SUBSTANCE IN ANGLO-AMERICAN LAW (1987)

Schlesinger COMPARATIVE LAW: CASES-TEXT-MATERIALS (1988) pp.1-43; 858-898

Farnsworth INTRODUCTION TO THE LEGAL SYSTEM OF THE UNITED STATES (1987)

Grossfeld THE STRENGTH AND WEAKNESS OF COMPARATIVE LAW (1990), especially Chapters 1,10, 11-13

Weston AN ENGLISH READER'S GUIDE TO THE FRENCH LEGAL SYSTEM (1991)

Varga COMPARATIVE LEGAL CULTURES (1992)

CHAPTER THREE

The Civil Law System

Jus civile

A. TERMINOLOGY

i. Different Meanings of 'Civil Law'

3.0   It is important to clarify the terminology that is used to describe civil
law systems and the civil law tradition, because the very term 'civil law' is susceptible to several different meanings. Civil law, in one sense, refers to *the
entire system of law* that currently applies to most Western European
countries, Latin America, countries of the near East, large parts of Africa,
Indonesia and Japan. It is derived from ancient Roman law, and which
originated in Europe on the basis of the Roman *jus civile*-the *private law*
which was applicable to the citizen, and between citizens, within the boundaries of a State, in a domestic context. It was also called the *jus quiritum*, as
opposed to the *jus gentium*-the law applied internationally, that is, between
States.

In due course, this law was compiled and then 'codified' (see below), and
many commentators often refer to civil law as primarily codified law. Some
writers also prefer to label civil law jurisdictions as belonging to the
Romano-Germanic family (see David and Brierley (1985),p.22) since this
would include both the Roman heritage and the contribution of German
legal science in the development of its juristic style. However, although this
alternative appellation is perfectly acceptable, and will indeed be utilised occasionally in this book, the present writer prefers the terms 'civil law system'
or 'civil law tradition' because they are well-established in content and
generally typify a distinctive juristic style which is widely recognised and accepted. Of course, 'civil law' has many other meanings in other contexts.

(i) Civil Law Countries and Common Law Countries

3.1   We speak of *civil law countries* (in the Roman law sense we have just
described) as distinct from *common law countries*. Civil law countries are
generally those countries which, according to the criteria we examined in the
previous chapter, may be classified as such because of their *sources of law*

(predominantly codes, statutes, and legislation) their characteristic *mode of thought in legal matters*, their distinctive *legal institutions* (and judicial, executive and legislative structures) and their fundamental *legal ideology*. All these elements determine their unique *'juristic style'* (see Chapter 2). Common law countries are broadly those whose juristic style is based on the English common law model, predominantly founded on a system of *caselaw* or *judicial precedent* and for whom legislation has not been traditionally regarded as a primary source of law, but usually regarded as mere consolidations or clarifications of legal rules which are essentially case-based and judge-made.

(ii) Civil law and Criminal Law

3.1.1 Another usage of the term civil law is in connection with the designation of the type of *proceedings* that might be instituted in a court of law, related to the distinct bodies of rules in common law countries, which comprise *civil law*, which provides rules and remedies to regulate disputes *between private individuals*, and *criminal law*, which provides rules, penalties and sanctions for those acts and omissions of individuals which are seen as *offences against the State, public order and society*. In the context of comparative law, this is clearly not the sense in which 'civil law' is being used.

(iii) Civil Law (Private Law) v. Public Law

3.1.2 In civil law systems, there is a fundamental distinction drawn between private law and public law which is much more firmly rooted and more sharply drawn than in common law systems. In conceptual terms, both common law and civil law systems recognise that private law governs relations between private citizens and corporations and public law concerns a dispute in which the State is a party. However, the distinction in civil law systems has far greater practical implications, since flowing from it, there are two different hierarchies of courts dealing with each of these types of law. The distinction between private and public law in English law, has been largely effected for the purposes of academic analysis. The chief consequence of the distinction in English common law is the type of *remedies* that are available to the private individual in a case involving 'public law.' Apart from the specialised orders that are available (*certiorari, mandamus* and *prohibition*) the 1980s has heralded the rise of the public law remedy of *judicial review of administrative action* in England. No separate courts deal with public law disputes in common law jurisdictions which apply the same common law principles which are used for other private law disputes to public law cases as well .

In civil law systems, its substantive body of private law consists principally of civil law (or *droit civil* in French law), which is further subdivided into various divisions of law such as the law of persons, family law, matrimonial property regimes, contractual regimes, property law and the law of obligations (see further, 3.2.22). It should be noted that Commercial Law is not included in this list as it is not considered part of the private civil law in Romano-Germanic legal families.

(iv) Civil law and Commercial Law

3.1.3   The term 'civil law' is also used to describe the substantive body of private law which is based on the French Civil Code of 1804 (as amended), in contradistinction to the body of law known as 'Commercial Law' which is not regulated by the Civil Code. In *common law systems*, there is no distinction drawn between civil law and commercial law, for the simple reason that *in common law systems, 'Commercial Law' is part of their civil (as opposed to criminal) law*. Moreover, as a term of art, 'Commercial Law' is of fairly recent vintage in common law academic thought although its content is traceable to ancient mercantile law (*lex mercatoria*) which was developed by international fairs and mercantile practice. In English law, Commercial Law has been defined as 'that branch of law which is concerned with rights and duties arising from the supply of goods and services in the way of trade.' (Goode: *Commercial Law*,p.35) However, the *content* of the law is largely based on aspects of the *law of contract and property which are relevant to business and commercial practice* and there is no jurisprudential, judicial or statutory recognition of a separate branch of 'Commercial Law' since the law is the same whether between professional traders or between friends.

It therefore contains elements of agency, commercial credit and export sales, but also deals with consumer credit and exemption clauses in contracts the law of which applies equally to all legal persons. The only sense in which Commercial Law is treated differently in English law is in a *separate procedural context* where, for instance, it refers to commercial litigation, and cases involving areas of law mentioned above are usually entered on the 'commercial list' which is allocated to one of the judges of the Queen's Bench Division of the High Court. This judge will sit in what has become known (since 1970) as the Commercial Court where simplified rules of procedure apply. Nevertheless, the substantive rules applied in this court will be identical to the rules that would be applied outside this court.

3.1.4   In *civil law systems*, there are very important reasons for distinguishing between civil and commercial law. *Commercial law in the civil law system is a distinct body of law* which is usually contained in a separate code, such as the French *Code de Commerce* (Commercial Code) of 1807 which is *administered by separate commercial courts at first instance*. It governs, *inter alia*, companies, partnerships, negotiable instruments, trademarks, patents and bankruptcy. (see further, chapter 8) Hence, in France, for example, this branch of law is not covered by the French Civil Code, lies outside the body of private law (known also as civil law) and is part of French Private Law. Thus, yet another meaning of 'civil law' within the Romano-Germanic legal family is the *body of law applicable to ordinary citizens in relations with each other* and *not* the system of law which is generally contrasted with the common law system. Except where otherwise stated, we shall use the term as referring to the system of law, rather than to any other usage.

ii. Meaning of Codification in the Civil Law Context

3.1.5   The meaning of the word 'code' will vary according to whether it is being used by lawyers trained in the   English common law tradition or lawyers brought up in the civil law tradition. In the *civil law system*, a code is an *authoritative, comprehensive and systematic collection of general clauses and legal principles*, divided into Books or Parts dealing in a logical fashion with the law relating thereto. Civil Law Codes are therefore regarded as the *primary source of law*, to which all other sources are subordinate, and often the only source of law on a particular matter.

Confusingly, codes have also been compiled in common law jurisdictions particularly for procedure and in terms of sheer volume, the United States of America have more 'codified' laws than any other country. However, the cardinal feature in a common law code is that it is based on pre-existing law (usually a combination of cases and statutes) and is neither designed nor intended to be formulations of all-inclusive rules.

In other words, common law codes are generally enacted to *consolidate the law on a particular area or to clarify an area of law which has become unsettled, obscure or confused*. It is exceedingly rare for a common law code to attempt to enact new rules or new concepts although a salutary exception in 1991 was the UK Children Act 1989, which, although affirming many of the legal principles already established in the area, has also created new concepts.

Despite the enactment or compilation of various codes in common law jurisdictions, *cases* (or judicial decisions) generally retain their clarificatory significance and will continue to be referred to, *as sources of law*, if there is any ambiguity in the statute or if there is a perceived 'gap' in the legislation which could then be filled by an existing judicial decision. In terms of style and organisation, the format and structure of a typical common law statute is quite different from that of a civil law statute or Code.

B. HISTORICAL DEVELOPMENT OF THE CIVIL LAW TRADITION

i. Roman Law and Western Civilisation

(i) Introduction

3.2   Civil law as an autonomous system of law originated and evolved in continental Europe, and the influence of colonisation, legal science movements, and various key codifications, particularly those of the nineteenth century, have played a part in the formation of this type of law. In addition, this system evolved over more than a thousand years, inevitably undergoing significant changes in substantive content and procedure, and, in the early phase of development, being dominated by the writings of jurists of the classical period, for five centuries.

This type of scholarly pre-eminence was reprised in the eleventh and twelfth centuries in the universities, when the study of Roman law revived, and again in the seventeenth and eighteenth centuries when the Natural Law school exerted its philosophical influence. It is no accident, therefore, that doctrinal writing plays such a significant part even today in countries like France and Germany, since classical jurists actually created the structure within which the practice of law was created and developed.

(ii) The Challenge of Roman Law study

3.2.1   Roman law remains a challenge to modern scholarship and modern-day historians, not least because weaving a tapestry from fragments of evidence and inconclusive evidence has proved an exceedingly speculative enterprise. Buckland pinpoints the problems one encounters when trying to discover what happened in the history of Roman law when he declares that: 'Most ancient monuments and records...perished when Rome was burnt by the Gauls, c. B.C. 390 and what passes for the history of this time is largely a fabrication of later ages, or at best a vague tradition adorned with stories of gods and heroes...[so] we cannot have any exact knowledge of the course of events.'
It is also well-established that there is little direct evidence for Roman law before the time of Cicero. Nevertheless, historians seem to agree that early classical Roman law was *customary law* rather than enacted law, which was probably derived from Romulus or one of the early kings. There also appears to have been a noticeable absence of professional judges during this period.

(iii) The Two Phases of Roman Law in World History

3.2.2   In world history, Roman law appears to have undergone two distinct periods of development, the *first period* dating from the period of the Roman Empire, and ending with the compilation by the Emperor Justinian (A.D. 527-565) of, *inter alia*, the Code and Digest, one bearing the imperialist heritage, the other the fruits of the juristic writing of Rome as it existed, in the pre-Justinian era. The *second period* (sometimes referred to as the *revival* or *Renaissance of Roman law* or the *Second Life of Roman law*(Nicholas)) began with the scholarly study of Justinian's works in the Italian universities in the late eleventh century A.D. The popularity of this intellectual pursuit spread to the rest of Europe and to a certain extent, even to medieval England, leaving a lasting impression on juristic terminology and legal thought as well as on the structure of European legal systems, which continued until the period of the 'great codifications' in the nineteenth century. Before we examine the impact of the great *Corpus Juris Civilis* of Justinian (see below 3.2.13) let us some key features of early Roman law.

(iv) Public law and Private Law in Early Roman Law

3.2.3   The republican constitution protected the common citizen against abuse of power by magistrates, who were from the aristocratic upper class of society. But there were no substantive rights given to the citizen which he could assert against the aristocratic classes or the State. A clear distinction was always drawn between *public law*, which regulated the structures and powers of the State (public authorities) in relation to the individual citizen and *private law*, which governed the relations between citizens.

(v) The Praetor and Iudex in Roman Private Law

3.2.4   In private law disputes, a State official usually officiated or to arranged for a trial to be held after a preliminary hearing. In the conventional civil action, court proceedings commenced with a hearing before a *praetor*, a functionary who was one of a group of magistrates who were elected annually. This hearing identified the *issues* in dispute. The next stage consisted of a separate hearing, in the manner of a *trial* before a *iudex*, an *ad hoc* judge, a private citizen, who was selected by consent of the parties and given authority by the praetor to try the dispute, and to render a binding judgment; no appeal was available. In the majority of cases, neither praetor nor *iudex* had undergone any sort of legal training.

Laymen were also assigned the role of judges in the context of other tribunals and criminal proceedings, where assemblies of laymen (sometimes numbering as many as forty) would sit in judgment. These men found on the facts and also heard and rendered judgment on the whole case, after having heard various alternative arguments on the issues. This form of hearing resembled a form of arbitration before lay judges.

(vi) Case law and Precedent in Classical Roman Law

3.2.5   A system of case-law and precedent developed in ancient Rome under the *praetor-iudex* system. Although praetors had complete freedom to decide each case on an individual basis, and could simply disregard previous rulings on similar cases, a *practice of continuity* began to develop so that new terms which were coined by the Urban Praetor were soon copied for future reference and used in subsequent cases. Clerks attached to the praetor's office kept records of the formulas used and these became available to the public.

From about the middle of the second century B.C., the litigant began to ask the praetor for a *written summary of the claim*, as well as any available defence, addressed to the judge, containing instructions on how to proceed with the case and to dispose of the issue accordingly. The plaintiff would then attempt to persuade the praetor to grant him a 'formula'. The praetor began to give advice to litigants on the conditions under which he would grant the action or allow the defence and the judge would then resolve the case on the basis of this formula.

A *consistent usage* of certain terms and synopses eventually converted them into established formulas (the *formulary system*) and they assumed an air of certainty and predictability which began to serve as guidelines to litigants and legal advisers for future cases. As Allen puts it, 'There could be no more instructive example than this of a whole body of law built up by judicial practice' (Allen, *Law in The Making* (1968)). Remarkably, this system evolved without the publication of judicial opinions, or statement of reasons, or citation of cases and without a theory of precedent.

The praetorian system appears to have evolved through the consistent use of well-tested formulas and pragmatic patterns of action which determined the success or failure of an action and *whether a particular remedy or relief would be granted*. The crucial form of development of the law appeared to be through remedies, very much resembling the development of the early common law in England, where the *system of writs* was the early basis of legal *rights* and *remedies* . In other words, Roman law developed through procedure so that the Roman judge would issue an *actio utilis* in the same way that a common law judge would later issue a writ. Furthermore, the two-stage process and constant mix of officialdom and lay opinion meant that Roman law could respond to the changing needs of a developing society. But it was not the praetors or *iudices* who became the custodians of the Roman law tradition, since their work was both *ad hoc* and temporal. That distinction went to the jurists.

(vii) Jurists, Urban Praetors and Sources of Law

3.2.6 In the absence of legal advisers, the *iudex* eventually turned to a select group of aristocrats, secular *jurists* who came to specialise in giving advice on legal matters. They were, in fact, self-appointed by their interest in the study and interpretation of the law and in *discussing legal problems, both actual and hypothetical, and writing about them*, they established an enduring tradition which, through their writings, was then passed from generation to generation. These jurists advised a number of different persons, ranging from parties to litigation, and lay judges to the *Urban Praetor, who was the most senior magistrate whose primary responsibility was litigation in the city of Rome*. He was therefore chief administrative officer of the judicial system that regulated litigation between Roman citizens, and in the course of his duties, began to *formulate the legal 'issues'* (or matters to be decided/resolved) which were then presented to the trial judges.

During this period, the source of private law was very seldom to be found in legislation, although the Roman assemblies could usually 'amend' private law if they wished to do so. However, the *cardinal source of law proved to be the formal edicts issued by the Urban Praetor*, which also listed the *legal remedies* available, which accorded with the legal opinions of the jurists. The remarkable fact appears to be the manner in which, for many years, these jurists simply assumed the authority to interpret the law without any official authorisation. Throughout the republic, it was the aristocratic upper class of society which controlled and ran the city. In this world of social privilege and personal influence, 'the principal characteristic of Roman legal development was authority: the system was based not on principle as such but on the authority of those who expounded the law' (Smith: 1968). The jurists would therefore have had both wealth, prestige and power to boost their standing in the community. We can only assume that the general public who received this advice from the jurists were satisfied with the quality of the legal advice tendered.

3.2.7   During the course of the first phase of the classical Roman Empire (the Principate), the authority of the jurists was further strengthened. The first emperor, Augustus decided to invoke an obscure law and institute a system ('patenting') which authorised a select group of jurists to give their opinions under his seal so they could 'speak with the leader's authority or imprimatur (*ex auctoritate principis*). This merely validated a system of Roman private law which had already taken root, and the jurists simply continued to give advice as they had done in the past, modifying their advice occasionally to take account of social or economic changes.

From the latter part of the first century, jurists were regularly appointed to be part of the emperor's council (cabinet) and often held top-ranking imperial positions. This became established as a tradition and a thread of continuity began to be woven. The interpreters of the law were always members of the ruling class, whose position encouraged them to ignore public law and to develop private law. This explains in part why public law was not developed or seen to be developing for a considerable period.

Juristic writings included general commentaries, analyses of specific topics, elementary treatises, collections of opinions or problems in which the jurist submitted arguments which eventually led to his particular solution. Their work ranged from the drafting of wills and contracts, advising litigants on forms of action and possible defences, to revising praetorian formulas. As Dawson puts it 'They were problem-solvers, working within [the] system and not called upon to solve the ultimate problems of mankind's needs and destiny.' (Dawson (1968)). The similiarities with English common law techniques of argument based on law and fact may be detected, particularly in the typical style of these jurists of *working on a case-to case basis*. This meant that apart from quoting each other, which they did frequently, they were usually only concerned with *finding the solution to an individual case*, not to formulate a principle for all time and for all societies.

(viii) The Twelve Tables: First Landmark in Roman Legal History

3.2.8   The jurists did not create their rules purely from customary law. They had access to one of the earliest known codes of laws, the Twelve Tables (c.450 B.C.), the first unequivocal landmark in the history of Roman law. These Tables, which were drawn up by specially appointed Commissioners, consisted mainly of Latin custom, with certain borrowings from Greek law, which formed the basis of the law. This was a collection of basic rules, rather than a comprehensive or definitive piece of legislation, yet it came to be regarded by Romans of later ages as the starting point or fountainhead of their legal history. Livy called it 'the fountain of all public and private law.' Nevertheless, even after the Twelve tables, a great deal of the law remained unwritten and it continued to be interpreted by the pontiffs, until the jurists began to interpret the law.

(ix) The Influence of Greece

3.2.9   It is widely believed that another reason for the brilliance of Roman law was the fact that at an important point in its history, during the time of their territorial expansion in the second century B.C. it was enhanced by Greek ideas and philosophy, which the Romans absorbed and modified to bring to near perfection a system that was already adaptable, enduring and pragmatic. From 146 B.C., after the Romans had conquered Greece, Greek culture was assimilated into the Roman Empire and despite being the captive nation, Greek arts, literature and philosophy began to infiltrate into Roman society and indeed wield a dominant influence over it. This was hardly surprising since the Roman intelligentsia had been brought up on Greek philosophy, logic, rhetoric and scientific methods so that the next step was the utilisation of Greek philosophical approaches to bring logic and order to the many collections of Roman court rulings which had accumulated. A considerable fillip to Roman jurists to interpret, clarify and synthesize fully the corpus of the law was given by the Emperor Hadrian (A.D. 118-38) when he commissioned the jurist Julian to consolidate the edict in such a way that once it was published, it could no longer be altered. This, in effect, turned the edict into a permanent statute which could then be generally available and susceptible to varying interpretations.

(x) The First Systematic Collection: The Institutes

3.2.10   Our knowledge of Roman law before the time of Cicero would be so much poorer if not for a remarkable book which was presumably written purely as an elementary introduction to law - the *Institutes* by 'Gaius'. This was the first trace of a systematic compilation of Roman law, a palimpsest of which was discovered in 1819, written by someone who adopted the name of Gaius, a jurist who lived in the third century B.C. and whose *Institutes* appeared around the second century B.C. Roman writers adopted *nom de plumes* just as the English writer who called himself 'Glanvill' did, in medieval England. Gaius' book sets out Roman law in rudimentary terms but in an extrmely well-organised and accessible manner. As one writer puts it, the Institutes offer 'priceless direct testimony to the state of classical law' (Smith (1968)). For example, it tells us that the content and concern of the law is threefold: it deals with persons, or Things or Actions. It then explains the scope of each of these headings, and further sub-divisions or sub-classifications are then given. It would have been extremely difficult to have understood Justinian's later codifications if not for the discovery of this book.

3.2.11   In the third century A.D. Rome experienced severe economic crisis, political instability and disruption. There were something like twenty-five emperors in the first two hundred and sixty-two years of the Roman Empire and a further twenty-one emperors in the next fifty years. These factors, as well as the fact that great writers like Ulpian and Paul had explored Roman law so comprehensively so as to leave very little left for future jurists to analyse, led to the sudden decline of jurisprudence from the third century

A.D. In the later years of the second century the Republican structure began to disintegrate, with the growing gulf between the wealthy landed class and the proletariat, dwindling numbers of citizens to fill the army, and, arguably, by the absorption of Greek morals which were more liberal than that of the Romans of the time and which eventually led to Rome's moral degeneration.

(xi) Collapse of the Western Roman Empire

3.2.12 Once the Roman Empire in the West had collapsed and fragmented, this signalled the end for some considerable time of the only political and cultural power capable of maintaining political and legal unity. The Barbarian Invasion in the fifth century maintained the Mediterranean as the Roman world's chief artery of commerce but the rise of Islam in the seventh century led to Western Europe regressing into a purely agricultural state, becoming a rural civilisation from the eighth century where land became the sole source of subsistence and social existence was founded on property or on the possession of land. This resulted from the closing of the Mediterranean to Western Europe. Law and the political order was therefore fragmented although the Church preserved a great deal of Roman culture and civilisation in its laws.

In the Eastern Roman Empire, the demise of the Western Empire made Emperor Justinian determined not just to recapture it, but to restore Rome to its former glory in the legal context, so that the genius of Roman law and its authors could be a lasting monument to Roman achievement.

(xii) Justinian and the Corpus Juris

3.2.13 In the sixth century, when the Western Empire collapsed, perhaps the most significant single event that took place in the East, where the Roman Empire continued, was the decision taken by the Emperor Justinian (527-565) to enact or re-enact a *comprehensive compilation, systematisation and consolidation of all the existing law, from every source*. The intention was to codify the law based on a selection of the decisions and enactments of the Emperors and from all juristic writings, with all the necessary modifications necessitated by the passage of time and the change in social and economic conditions. This great enterprise produced four compilations which became collectively known as the *Corpus Juris Civilis* or the *Corpus Juris* for short. Various committees of lawyers were appointed, all from the East and probably all Greek speakers. The contents of the *Corpus Juris* are:

(i) The *Institutions* (or *Institutes*)- a systematic treatise, issued as an elementary textbook for first-year law students, based on Gaius' earlier *Institutes*.

(ii) The Digest or *Pandects*- a compilation of edited fragments from Roman juristic writings, arranged according to titles or headings derived from the classical period, but including material from the very late Republic to the middle of the third century. This is the most important part of the *Corpus Juris* and the Classical period writings are still regarded as the most illuminating.

(iii) The *Codex*- a collection of imperial enactments, including edicts and judicial decisions dating from the time of Hadrian, arranged chronologically within each title, so that it is possible to trace the legal evolution of a concept as the facts in a case were distinguished from apparently similar facts in earlier cases.

(iv) The *Novels*- a collection of imperial legislation enacted by Justinian himself, based on private collections, issued subsequent to the publication of the other three parts which were promulgated between 533 and 544. No official edition of the Novels was ever issued.

Since Justinian ordered the compilers to edit the juristic writings and the enactments, the law as presented in the collection is not really representative of either classical Roman law (the Principate) or of the law as it existed in Justinian's era. It is a greatly modified pastiche of legal rules and opinions. However, with the fall of the rest of the Roman Empire, the *Corpus Juris* fell into desuetude and 'vulgarised', crude versions of Roman civil law were applied by the conquerors to the inhabitants of the Italian peninsula. This consisted, in part, of a fusion of Germanic customs and Roman law. Indeed, the German conquerors did not seek to destroy everything Roman in the style of Gaul. Hence a number of *Germanic Codes* emerged, written in Latin, designed for Romans and Germans, drawn from various Roman imperial enactments (eg, *Codex Gregorianus*, and the *Theodosian Code*) but the wording tended to be paraphrases or reconstructions of the original-thus 'vulgarised'.

(xiii) The Revival of Roman Law Studies in the Middle Ages

3.2.14   Over the eleventh and twelfth centuries, in keeping with the Renaissance in philosophy, canon law and theology, Roman law studies also experienced a rebirth and revival, or a 'Second Life' (Nicholas). It is difficult to assign a single reason for this event, but some writers place central importance on the lectures given by Irnerius (c.1055-c.1130), in the late eleventh century, who gave the first university lectures on the *Digest* at Bologna, the first modern European university where law was a major subject. The crucial point is that it was Justinian's *Corpus Juris* that was being studied, not the vulgarised Germanic versions nor customary law derived from the law of the fairs (*lex mercatoria*) nor laws devised by local townships or minor rulers. Various reasons can be found for the success and popularity of Roman law at that time: (i) The political and economic conditions of the time were conducive to the study and acceptance of works like the *Digest*. In political terms, there was a great need for a legal system that could unify and organise the social conditions of that era. Governmental power required centralisation so as to prevent its fragmentation. Economically, a society that saw the emergence of centres of commerce, trade and industry needed a law that could cope with the rapidly changing commercial trade, revival of maritime commerce and the decline of feudalism. Roman law could provide the legal techniques that could promote and strengthen commercial life.

51

(ii) The *Digest* possessed a sense of authority because it was in book form, written in Latin and a relic of the old *imperium romanum*, Rome in its heydey, all-conquering, glorious and supreme and a symbol of unity, offering a hope for a unified law. These images of Rome had never quite left people's minds. A book was a rare entity in the Middle Ages, so that almost any book had an aura of authority, particularly to the average citizen. Latin remained the lingua franca in the civilised world, and had become the language of communication for the Western Church, intelligible to the clergy as well as the language of educated and cultured people.

(iii) The *Corpus Juris* was also the product of Justinian who was regarded by many as a Holy Roman Emperor and therefore his work carried the authority of the Pope and the Emperor and was really a form of imperial legislation. Italian Lawyers therefore almost had a special duty to study the *Digest*.

(iv) The *Digest* was an intellectually challenging compilation to the lawyers of the Middle Ages, difficult to follow in its language, and the order in which it treated various topics as well as in its unfamiliarity of legal treatment, being based on an ancient system of remedies, yet often merely listing decided cases with no guiding concepts. Its study attracted men of high intellectual ability who later became specialists in its study and acquired a professional skill in its interpretation. This ensured that they guarded their knowledge jealously, and trained others only in a professional capacity, but also created a tradition of scholarship.

(v) Roman law as contained in the *Corpus Juris* also provided detailed solutions and approaches to practical problems. It also possessed a conceptually powerful structure, with clear distinctions which could be adapted to almost any situation or problem, with simplicity and clarity. Property and obligation were distinguished, the former being indefeasible against the world, the latter merely a bond between two persons, whose legal effects varied according to whether the parties wished to create rights against one another or on a reciprocal basis.

(vi) Finally, it has been said that it was the 'rational character of Roman law and its freedom from relativity to any particular time or place' (Lawson (1977)) that also accounts for the huge success of Roman law.

(xiv) Growth of Roman Law: Twelfth to Nineteenth Centuries

3.2.15   Irnerius' lectures at Bologna heralded the study of the *Corpus Juris* in Western Europe as a coherent, systematic body of law. By the middle of the twelfth century, there were about 10,000 students in Bologna. The Italian universities became the centre of learning for scholars all over Europe, from whence it spread. There later ensued a succession of schools of thought (most prominently, the groups of scholars known as the *Glossators* and the *Commentators*) about the correct way to study and interpret the *Corpus Juris*. Scholars of Roman law acquired such tremendous prestige that university doctors of law were appointed to the royal councils and were made judges in many local courts. Those who had studied in Bologna returned to their homelands where they promoted the study of the *Corpus Juris* according to the interpretations and approaches of the *Glossators* and subsequently, the *Commentators*. This really laid the foundations for a common law of Europe.

The *Glossators* were a group of scholars who were apparently founded by Irnerius, who initiated the systematic study of Roman law, by analysing the individual texts of the *Corpus Juris* and attempting to reconcile them in a logical manner with other texts. The development of the law from the twelfth century onwards was determined by *the manner in which the Glossators used the Justinian texts*, not Roman law as Justinian might have intended or as it might have existed in classical Rome. Their style is therefore characterised by the short notes or glosses which they appended to particular passages for purposes of comparison with each other in order to pose a question or suggest a solution. As time passed, the work of the later Glossators developed from gloss to commentary.

The Glossators were succeeded in the thirteenth century by scholars known as the *Commentators* (or post-Glossators). Although it is not always easy to distinguish where the late Glossators ended and the early Commentators began, it is true to say that as a general proposition, the Commentators could be identified by their systematic commentaries and synthesis on the law.

This approach was required because (i) the *Corpus Juris* was no longer the only set of texts on which the academic study of law was based. *Canon law* gained ascendancy and became a university subject in its own right. This was followed by theologians and philosophers turning to systematic analyses of the writings of Aristotle. The study of his *Ethics* and *Politics* eventually produced a systematic philosophy of Natural Law and what later became known as the *Natural Law Movement* (see below); and (ii) By 1200, Roman law had actually been 'received' into Italy as binding law, applicable in the absence of any local custom or contrary statute. It was therefore necessary to bring it up to date and to adapt it to local conditions and practical matters and to reconcile it with the medieval legal tapestry. Several 'receptions' of Roman law took place, which resulted in its authoritative acceptance in court practice in most of Western Europe.

A third group of writers, the *Humanists*, emerged during the sixteenth and seventeenth centuries, based in the French University of Bourges. They were opposed to both the Glossators and Commentators' approaches to the study of Roman law, and advocated the *return to the original Roman texts and sources*. They believed that the only authentic method of studying Roman law was to scrutinise the classical Roman texts unadulterated by commentary or gloss. Their approach did not, however, convince the practising lawyers who needed a living law which was practice-oriented, and this particular philosophy never gained any widespread popularity or acceptance.

Eventually, through the Bologna lectures and the dissemination of Roman law through its scholars, filtering through to the courts and legal practice, Roman civil law as interpreted by the Glossators and Commentators became the basis of a *common body of law and legal commentaries, a common legal language and a common approach to teaching and scholarship*. This is often called the *common law of Europe* or the *jus commune*. Hence, from the twelfth to about the sixteenth century, the *Corpus Juris* became the basis for legal science throughout Europe. Judges could apply Roman law and not local laws or customs to cases that came before them because of the existence, of a *'pluralism of legal sources'* (Coing (1973)) which meant that courts were free to apply the law from *a number of possible sources*, and thus from any book of authority, not being confined to local customs if they were found lacking. Roman law was later accepted in the Italian courts as part of the custom of the courts.

As far as other 'Receptions' of Roman law were concerned, large-scale instruction in Roman law in France only took place in the thirteenth century (see further on development of French law, below). Of course, in Italy, Spain and southern France Roman law had never completely disappeared. In northern Europe, only customary law remained, which varied from place to place. In northern France, the Reception began much earlier than in Germany, but was less widespread and happened somewhat gradually. The German courts did not receive Roman law until the end of the Middle Ages, around 1495. (see further on history of German law, below). By all accounts, the Reception was completed in the course of the sixteenth century.

The common law of Europe that eventually emerged towards the end of the Middle Ages was therefore a mixture of local statutes and customs, a form of Roman law as interpreted by the various schools of thought and Canon Law. The unity achieved by the reception of Roman law into the Civil Law was further reinforced by Canon law, which had become the universal law of the Western Church and which remained in use even in the darkest days of Roman law. English courts, on the other hand, never received Roman law at all, despite the fact that it was early known and taught, due to centralisation of courts at an early stage, powerful monarchs and the pragmatic character of early English law.

During the sixteenth, seventeenth and eighteenth centuries, despite the intervening revival of classical learning led by the school of Humanists the influence of the Natural Law Movement gained ascendancy and played a significant part in the development of the civil law by:

(i) posing a challenge to the authority of the *Corpus Juris* as the only authoritative statement of definitive legal rules. It did so on the basis of rationality and reason, which it claimed had to be satisfied, and although frequently following the Roman solution, argued that there was no obligation to do so. The members of this School were highly conversant with Roman law and preferred to rely on the orginal wording of the unannotated Roman text to solve a particular problem. They clearly overlapped with the Humanist thinkers though not in all matters; and

(ii) transforming the methods of systematisation of the civil law. By utilising a deuctive method, they started with a small number of very general concepts, which were then deductively developed in successive ranges of fewer and fewer general abstractions, categories and principles until the lowest level of abstraction was reached, whereupon specific rules were enunciated which were applied to actual factual situations.

The Natural Law Movement represented an upsurge of rationalism, and the belief that 'the law for any society could by the use of reason be derived from principles inherent in the nature of man and society.' (Nicholas (1962)). The Dutchman Grotius (1583-1645) was the first great Natural Law exponent, and he applied it to the formation of a body of international law. However, his treatise on the jurisprudence of Holland considerably influenced the course of Roman-Dutch law. But it was in the international law field that the school of natural law was most influential although it led to the elimination of the more irrational or 'authentically Roman' features of the law which were replaced by liberal doses of 'logic' in the law.

The Natural Law Movement gave rise to a renewed interest in codification, which appeared to be the best way of preserving a logically consistent set of principles and rules. In retrospect, (i) it was responsible for the revival of public law, the division of law that regulated the relations between government and citizen but which, in practical terms, had remained relatively dormant in Roman law for many centuries; (ii) it led to codification, bringing to fruition and consolidation many centuries of learning in Roman law, which was then actually transformed from the theoretical taught law of the universities into the living law of the land. This was thus a watershed in civil law history; (iii) through the phenomenon of codification, a fusion of practical and theoretical law was created as well as a unified set of laws, from a sometimes confusing diversity of customs and practices; (iv) through codification, a set of systematic expositions of the law was formulated to suit the conditions of eighteenth century society; (v) the Natural Law Movement also reaffirmed the power of the soverign to play a major part in defining and reforming law-thus, a form of legislative Positivism was also revived by the natural law ideas.

Some early codes were compiled in 1756 and 1794 but *the most important codificatory event was the enactment of the French Napoleonic Civil Code in 1804*. This proved to be a momentous event, not just because it meant France had a single system of law but because many countries adopted, adapted or copied the Code throughout the world. Although its adoption was partly the result of Napoleon's victories, its enduring attraction survived long after his final defeat. This was partly because of the clarity and cohesion of the Code and partly because of France's status and prestige in the nineteenth century. Jurisdictions such as Belgium, Italy, Spain, Holland, Louisiana, Quebec, Egypt and parts of South America adopted the Code in one form or another.

In Germany, the French Code was not adopted primarily because of the jurist Savigny (1779-1861) but also because conditions were then not quite right for the Code's acceptance.(see History of German Law, below).

ii. History of French Law

(i) Pre-Revolutionary French Law

a. Multiplicity of Customs

3.2.16   For several centuries, France consisted of a multiplicity of customs, existing in over sixty separate areas, each with its own rules. When Gaul was part of the Roman empire, Roman law prevailed in it, but it appears likely that, in accordance with the practice of the time, certain local customs were allowed to subsist. There was certainly *no common law in France* in its *early Roman period* either dealing comprehensively with private law matters or administered with the imprimatur of a sovereign. In the fourth century A.D. the sources of French law were the Codes of Gregorius and Hermogenius, the *Institutes* of Gaius and Paul's Sentences. By the fifth century, the Code of Theodosius had been compiled, but by this time, part of Gaul had already been occupied.

Despite the collapse of the Western Roman Empire in 476, Roman law survived (as the law for peoples of non-Germanic origin) in the Germanic states which succeeded it and continued to do so in the course of the fifth century, particularly in the kingdoms of the Visigoths, Burgandians and Franks. A key factor that contributed to the continued existence of Roman law was the enactment of a statute-*Lex Romana Visigothorum*-passed by the Visigoth King, Alaric II, which contained a summary both of the *Leges* and of the *Jus* and, *inter alia*, a summary and commentary of the Code of Theodosius.

The *Lex* consisted of the various documents called *constitutiones*-which were opinions, enactments and decisions which had been handed down directly from the various emperors. The *Jus* consisted of the writings of the jurists-their interpretation and development of the older legal sources, extending back to the middle of the third century A.D. The terminology (*lex* and *jus*) appears to have originated in the fifth century and the terms corresponded to the English distinction between statute and common law. (see Amos and Walton (1967)p.26).

b. System of Personal Laws

3.2.17 During the sixth century, the Franks secured control and dominion over the whole country, but instead of removing Roman law from the newly acquired Roman subjects, adopted a system of personal laws. The Franks, Visigoths and Burgandians lived each according to his own law and permitted the Roman Provincials to live by theirs. For some five hundred years, in this *Frankish period*, the main source of law for the conquered Gauls, was the *Lex Romana Visigothorum*. In the south of France, therefore, Roman law continued to survive, unlike the case in northern France, where the Franks chose to apply their own customary laws of Germanic origin, which were later consolidated into statutes.

c. Feudal System

3.2.18 In the course of the ninth century, this personal system of laws began to disintegrate, giving way to a *feudal system* which then engaged in a struggle with local, seigneural judges and the emerging royal, central power. While the great lay and ecclesiastic lords enjoyed widespread privileges, their 'inferiors' suffered ever diminishing loss of powers and privileges. A form of 'territoriality of law'(Amos and Walton (1967)) started to develop, with different laws in different localities, the population dividied into different classes of people (nobles, middle class, serfs) with correspondingly different legal status.

A further conflict also developed between the power of the Church and that of the developing State. On this particular conflict, as Von Mehren and Gordley (1977) at p.14, put it:'Jurisdictions overlapped. The administration of justice was notoriously slow, complicated and expensive. No institution existed with a sufficiently general and exclusive jurisdiction to permit the development of a body of common law.'

d. Two Geographical Zones

3.2.19 It was during the course of the thirteenth century that the law of France became the law of *two geographical zones*:
(a) The area of *droit ecrit* (written law) in the South;
    or *pays de droit ecrit*; and
(b) The area of *droit coutumier* (law of customs) in the North;
    or *pays de coutumes*.
 In the Southern Provinces (the *Midi*), the Land of Written Law, Roman civilisation and Roman law were paramount. Roman law was the common law of the country so that when the renaissance or the Second Life of Roman Law took hold, and the *Corpus Juris* came to be studied, there was a relatively easy reception of that law which came to be accepted as the practical, living law of the land.
 In the Northern Provinces, local customs based on Germanic customs were in force. This was a larger area than the Southern Provinces, covering three-fifths of the country. The customs were varied, some applying to a whole province or large territory (*coutume generale*) numbering about sixty or so; others were in force only in a city or village (*coutumes locales*) numbering about three hundred.
 There was, however, no complete division since the *pays de droit ecrit* had, at least in the earlier periods, written customs influenced by Roman law, but containing Germanic elements. Eventually, all other local customs died out and Roman law was the only governing law. Similarly, in the North, although the *coutumes* were the common law, the law of contracts and obligations used Roman law as a supplementary law since the *coutumes* were silent on these matters. Similarly, Roman law was invoked if the *coutumes* were ambiguous or had nothing to say on other areas of law. In both zones, any matters which fell under the jurisdiction of the Church, such as marriage, were governed by canon law.

e. The Monarchical Period

3.2.20 Four main events took place in the period 1500-1789, during which, even by the end of the fifteenth century, royal power had been consolidated and became more dominant:
(i) The compilation of customs;
(ii) The passing of royal ordinances and the grand ordinances;
(iii) The Custom of Paris; and
(iv) The emergence of a common law.

In view of the multiplicity of customs, Charles VII ordered the official compilation of all customs in his Ordinance, *Montils-les-Tours* of 1453. Hence, by the end of the sixteenth century most of French customary law which was officially recognised had been reduced to written law. But uniformity had by no means been achieved.

During the course of the fourteenth to the seventeenth centuries, many royal ordinances were passed, mostly dealing with administration or with civil or criminal procedure but these must be distinguished from a series of *grand* ordinances, such as the Code of Commerce and Code of Civil Procedure, which were codifications of a branch of law. However, these royal ordinances eventually regulated substantive private law as well.

Two major legal figures in the era of Louis XIV (1643-1715) were *Jean Baptiste Colbert* (1619-83), his chief minister, and *Guillame de Lamoignon* (1617-77) who was the first president of the *Parlement de Paris*, the judicial branch of the king's court. In 1665, on Colbert's advice, Louis set up a special commission, the *Conseil de Justice* which consisted of eminent jurists and members of the King's Council, requesting memoranda from the provincial *parlements* and various legal experts suggesting areas of law that required reforming and possible remedies. The jurists on the Commission were aware that Lamoignon had already produced an outline for a code. The Ordinance of 1667 on civil procedure, produced as a result of the Commission's work, intended to provide a complete and detailed systematic codification of civil procedure but supplementary edicts were later found to be necessary. In 1670, another Ordinance on Criminal Law and Procedure was produced, with the co-operation of the *Parlement* throughout the preparatory sessions, which owed much of the drafting to Lamoignon. His book, outlining a scheme for a single code based on customary law, was extremely influential, being used by jurists of the eighteenth century and relied upon by Louis XV's chancellor, Daguesseau (1668-1751) in the compilation and issue of various royal ordinances which were really mini-codes on donations, wills, and entails. These ordinances were later incorporated into the Civil Code.

The *Custom of Paris* was a collection of laws laid down by the judges of the various courts of justice, emanating from the *Parlement de Paris*, which had become independent towards the end of the thirteenth century. Various provincial courts (*parlements*), were established between 1443 and 1775 which covered a wide area, the influence of the capital city, their intrinsic merits, and the eminence of their commentators combined to give these laws a pre-eminent position. They were regarded by many as the common law of France since judges were applying a braod range of customs and tended to develop unitary rules.

The publication of the various customs made them more accessible and led to a more detailed study of them. General principles were discerned which were seen to be readily applicable to the whole of France. But it was really the work of great jurists such as Dumoulin, Coquille, Loysel and Pothier (1699-1772) who provided the draftsmen of the Code with both material and a format. Pothier's elegant and lucid style was so impressive that some parts of the Code are really mere summaries of his statements.

Hence, despite the multiplicity of customs, the royal ordinances exercised a certain unifying force and they were generally in force throughout the kingdom. As in early English law, canon law also played its part in providing a common source of law and indeed influenced certain branches of French law such as family law. It was a combination of all these factors that led to the emergence of a common French law, but it is equally important to realise that the 'tradition of local independence', retained its force in the provinces (see Von Mehren and Gordley (1977) p.48). Each particular province appeared to regard its particular law as a heritage guaranteed by the pact that had incorporated it into France. (Von Mehren and Gordley, *ibid*).

f. The Revolutionary Period

3.2.21   The Revolution of 1789 ended the *ancien regime* or period of ancient law and also marked the beginning of the transitional period usually called the period of 'intermediary law'. Reform was directed at the fields of public law and the law of political institutions. The old institutional structures were destroyed and political power and the machinery of government were now centralised as never before in France. Feudal laws were abolished, as were ancient privileges, Frenchmen were declared to have equal rights under the law, 21 was made the age of majority, marriage was secularised, divorce introduced, individual liberty was guaranteed and the protection of private property was reinforced.

Codification attempts began with the vote by the Constitutent Assembly on 5 July 1790 'that the civil laws be reviewed and reformed by the legislators and that there would be made a general code of laws simple, clear and appropriate to the constitution.' The First Title of the Constitution of 1791 therefore concluded with the promise that 'a Code of civil laws common to the whole Kingdom will be enacted.' Nevertheless, actual work on codification only began under the Convention (1792-95). Various drafts were formulated until Napoleon appointed a commission of four to prepare yet another. By 'consolidation, moderation and compromise', Napoleon, working with a small team of lawyers, 'transformed the laws of the Revolution into a workable system of codes.' (Schlesinger *et al* (1988), fn.(c), p.267) and after several political wrangles with the various organs of the legislative body, the Civil Code was eventually enacted in 1804.

The task of the Code was 'to fix, in broad perspective, the general maxims of the law; to lay down principles rich in consequencesm and not to descend into the details of questions which may arise on each topic' (see Portalis *Discours Preliminaire* cited in Rudden (1974) p.1011)

The Civil Code presented the law in clear, concise and readily understandable language, addressed to the average citizen of France. It is a novel piece of substantive law which fused the *droit ecrit* and the *coutumes* and created a unified law for the whole country without any unnecessary destruction of existing law. The Code is a collection of rules of civil law in that it derives from Roman law *as it was practised in France*-a *ius commune*-a modernised form of Roman law.

In his *Discours preliminaire*, Portalis explains the thoughts of the drafters of the Code:(i) A code ought to be complete in its field; (ii) it ought to be drafted in relatively general principles rather than in detailed rules; and (iii) it ought at the same time to fit together logically as a coherent whole and to be based on experience.(cited in Tunc 'Methodology of the Civil Law in France' [1976] Tul.LR 459-60) In practice, however, it has not been possible to adhere absolutely to these aims and objectives.

By 1811, four additional codes had come into force: the Code of Civil Procedure, the Code of Commerce, the Code of Criminal Procedure, and the Penal Code. These Codes were all subsequently amended or replaced with more modern provisions and today only the Civil Code remains in much the same state it was in when first enacted.

The Civil Code has, however, been amended in relation to status, family law, matrimonial property and security interests. Several attempts have been made to produce a more fundamental revision of it but a comprehensive revision has never materialised. It has dominated the Prussian Rhine provinces for a hundred years, been imitated by the codes of Belgium and Luxembourg, greatly influenced the Codes of Italy, Spain, Portugal and the Netherlands as well as Egypt, South America and Louisiana.

iii. Structure and Overview of French Civil Code

3.2.22   The Civil Code is composed of three 'Books' or Divisions, following Gaius' *Institutes* and commences with a Preliminary Title, which really seems to introduce the purpose of the Code, namely to implement the 'publication, effects and the application of the laws in general'. Book One is headed 'Of Persons', Book Two 'Of Property and Different Kinds of Ownership' and Book Three 'Of the Different Ways of Acquiring Property'. Each Book is divided into Titles such as Enjoyment and Loss of Civil Rights, Marriage, Divorce, Domicile, and Adoption. These are again divided into chapters and in several instances, these chapters are divided into sections. The ultimate units are the articles and there were originally 2,281 of these. These are typically short, not exceeding more than eight or ten words.

Book One deals with matters such as marriage, divorce, the status of minors, guardianship, and domicile. Book Two deals with property, usufruct and servitudes. Book Three consists of twenty titles and deals with a rather odd assortment of topics: gits, wills and intestate succession but also obligations in general, including contract, quasi-contract and tort. In addition, it covers marriage settlements, sale, lease, partnership and other special contracts as well as mortgages, liens and pledges and prescription.

Book One has been heavily revised, from about 1965. Title I of Book One used to contain particular rules as to the acquisition and loss of French nationality but these rules were subsequently extracted and placed in a special, frequently amended statute called the Code of French Nationality. Civil law countries tend to treat citizenship as a public law subject which should not therefore be covered in a civil code. In France, the question of nationality assumes a considerable significance because it has an impact on the jurisdiction of courts, and to a certain extent, on choice of law. French and European commercial publishers therefore tend to include excerpts from the Nationality Code in the light of its special significance in French law.

One in three of the Articles in the Civil Code has been repealed, amended or enlarged. More than half the Articles in the Code deal with the organisation of the family, and over half the Articles have been considered by the legislators at some stage. The strong preoccupation with the family is particularly noticeable. The reforms that have been made have dealt with removal of restrictions upon the capacity of married women, modernisation of the matrimonial regimes, facilitation of marriage, and augmentation of the rights of illegitimate children. The continuing influence of religion and its tension with more secular philosophies is evident in the fluctuating fortunes of French divorce law and is reflected in Code amendments relating to the family.

The Code proceeded on the basis that judicial decisions shall have no authority beyond the cases in which they are rendered and that there shall be no authoritative interpretation by anyone except the legislature itself. If the Codes did not cover a particular matter, a judge was directed where to turn in order to decide the case.

The following Code provisions emphasise the obligation of the judge in a French Court to resolve a dispute that comes before the court. Article 4 of the Civil Code states that: 'If he refuses to adjudicate a case for the alleged reason that there are no provisions in the law applying to this case or that the provisions to be found in the law are obscure or insufficient, a judge may be prosecuted as guilty of the criminal offence of refusal to administer justice.'

But in Article 5 it states: 'Judges are forbidden, when giving judgment in the cases brought before them, to lay down general rules of conduct amounting to a regulation.' This prohibition stemmed from the separation of powers' doctrine and the underlying purpose seemed to be the limitation of the power of the judiciary associated with the power of the *Parlements*.

After a century of experience, French jurists conceded that it has not been possible to keep to the letter of Article 5 and that judges are in fact making law, even though this may never be expressly acknowledged as a matter of strict theory.

A strong moral and ethical core of values also runs through the Code, as illustrated by Articles 6 and 1134. Article 6 states that 'No derogation is allowed, by way of private conventions, from statutes which affect public order or good morals.' Article 1134 states that 'Agreements legally entered into have the force of laws for the parties thereto. They may be revoked by the mutual consent of such parties only, or for the causes allowed by the law. They shall be performed according to good faith.'

After a hundred and eighty-eight years of the French Civil Code, the words of Portalis when he was writing about the role of courts in a codified system of law, bear reiterating. He singled out three main tasks of the judges in those circumstances: (i) To clarify the meaning of the rules in the various circumstances which are submitted to the judge; (ii) to clarify what is obscure in the law and to fill in its gaps; (iii) to adjust law to the evolution of the society and, to the extent possible based on the existing texts, to provide against the inadequacy of the law in the face of contemporary problems. (see Tunc (1976) p.463-4)

In a more recent appraisal of civil law codes in a 1987 article, which includes a reference to the 'tort provisions' of the French Civil Code, Professor Hein Kotz illustrates the many similarities that actually exist between civil codes and English law and stresses that 'the legislative style adopted in each country is the result of the particular political, historical and social circumstances existing where and when the codes were drafted.' He continues, in relation to the French Civil Code, that 'a code can hardly be more inventive and sophisticated than the collected legal experience existing at the time it is drafted.' (Kotz (1987) 50 Mod. LR,p.7). He emphasises that a Code is a child of its time, and must be judged in its true historical context. Although the Civil Code has undergone several revisions and amendments, and its has been overtaken in many areas by supplementary legislation it has certainly stood the test of time as a model codification, as a result of the clarity of its concepts and the accessibility of its language to the ordinary citizen and the fact that it was, in Portalis' words 'grounded in experience.' It remains the prototype of civil codes.

iv. Sources of Law

3.2.23   The sources of French law are: (i) *Primary Sources of Law*: enacted law-statutes, constitutional law (which is at the very top of the hierarchy of sources), Regulations, (*reglements* and *arretes*) the five Napoleonic Codes, General Principles of Law and Custom; and (ii) *Secondary Sources of Law*: the judge, court decisions (*jurisprudence*), learned annotations of academic writers (*doctrine*), textbooks, commentaries, monographs by experts and writers of repute and decisions of foreign courts applying a similar legal system.

a. Doctrine

3.2.24   *Doctrine*, a term in use in French law since the nineteenth century, signifies: 'the *body of opinions on legal matters expressed in books and articles..* (and) is also used to characterise collectively *the persons* engaged in this analysis, synthesis and evaluation of legal source material, members of the legal professions who devote substantial attention to scholarly work and acquire reputations as authorities.' (David and de Vries (1958)p.122). The word is thus a *faux ami*, as is *jurisprudence* and is therefore best translated as legal writers/scholars or the writing of legal scholars.
In modern times, as a result of the impersonal and terse style of French judgements, which are generally devoid of any argumentative threads, the function of explaining and developing the law through argument and counter-argument is peformed in France by legal scholars and those who are responsible for drawing up reasoned proposals for a decision in any given case. These scholars include not just professional lawyers but also the members of State Counsel's Office in their submissions to the courts.
It would appear that it is these submissions of State Counsel that most closely resemble English-style judgments, because of their 'personal, argumentative, discursive style' (Weston (1991) p.116) and it is only because of the learned annotations by some distinguished legal scholar that it is at all clear whether a given decision 'affirms, modifies or departs from case-law.' (weston (1991) *ibid.*)
Thus, as in Italy and Germany, it is the leading law professors and lecturers who are accorded a much more prestigious position in the legal profession than either their counterparts in England or judges in France. Admittedly,

legal textbooks are being cited more in the England of the late 1980s and early 1990s, but the prestige of docrinal writers in France is greater and of much older vintage.

Modern doctrine places court decision in their proper perspective and indicates the policies underlying legislation. However, it is not binding authority on the courts, not a binding guide to decision. It merely has *persuasive authority* much in the style of early English common law which accorded a certain status to old and established treatises but did not regard them as sources of law *strictu sensu*. (see Chapter 4) In a system that is rooted in codes and codification, doctrine can only assist in the interpretation and guidance of legal development within the established legal framework.

b. Status of Judicial Decisions (*Jurisprudence*) in French Law

3.2.25   What exactly is the current *position of case law in modern French law*? Judicial decisions are not *per se* binding. However, as Blanc-Jouvan and Boulouis express it 'Without having binding authority *de jure* they at least have *de facto* authority. This authority varies according to circumstances.' (Blanc-Jouvan and Boulouis in *International Encyclopedia of Comparative Law* (1972) p.F-61). They give further useful pointers of the factors which are especially relevant: (i) the number of similar decisions which can be invoked; (ii) the importance of the court which rendered the decision; and (iii) the way in which the judge has expressed himself.

It would appear that when a harmonious line of cases has accumulated, in which a single authoritative principle consistently emerges, this phenomenon is characterised in French law as *la jurisprudence constante*. If such a consistent line of caselaw has built up, French courts will tend to follow them, albeit as illustrations of a general principle. The single decision of a first instance court is given less weight than that of the Court of Cassation (particularly if this is given by the Plenary Assembly). A decision which expressly confines itself to the facts of the particular case will be less authoritative than a decision firmly based on principle.

There has never been a prohibition against reference to judicial precedent during the course of litigation. Thus, despite the absence of any formal doctrine of *stare decisis* there is a strong tendency on the part of French judges to follow precedents, particularly those of the higher courts. The reasons for this have been conveniently summarised by David and de Vries (1958): (i) the maintenance of professional dignity; (ii) the sharing of responsibility for decisions within the judiciary as a whole; (iii) the saving of time and research for attention to other matters where no precedent exists; (iv) the fulfilment of the expectations of parties who have relied upon previous decisions of the courts, and (vi) the avoidance of excessive or prolonged litigation where a uniform line of decisions clarifies doubtful issues. (see David and de Vries (1958) p.117) In other words, the reasons for the common law practice have resulted in a similar pattern of predictable judicial behaviour in France.

Ever since the famous speech by Ballot-Beaupre (1836-1917) delivered in 1904, in his capacity as president of the French Supreme Court (*Cour de cassation*) there has been a 'no less than spectacular development' (David and

Brierley (1985) p.120) since 1900 in the law of liability for civil wrongs which corresponds to the sentiments expressed therein, by giving *new interpretations to the provision dealing with civil responsibility* or delictual liability of persons, namely the words of Article 1384 of the French Civil Code-that a person is responsible not only for the damage caused by his own actions and for those caused by the actions of persons for whom he must answer but also for damage ' *caused by things under his care*' to develop a new law on delictual liability. This is an area where judicial decisions have filled a gap in the legislation to adapt to the changing conditions of French society but it has to be viewed as exceptional in the context of areas of law governed by Code or legislative provisions, since it must be noted that the *Code provisions remain central to the judicial process* and albeit expanded, provide the legal authority *strictu sensu* for the law regulating this area.

v. Key Features of the French Legal System

3.2.26   The basic notion of law under the French legal system is different from that which is typical of common law countries. As David puts it 'The law is not a restricted domain. It is not the business of judges and practitioners alone, because the law is not limited to litigation. The law is seen as a method of social organisation, always changing, and is thus of primary interest to statesmen and in fact to all citizens.' (David *French Law. Its Structure, Sources, and Methodology* (1972) trans. M. Kindred,p.viii). Hence, a Frenchman and French lawyers have a much broader view of law than the typical English lawyer, who sees it as mainly linked to the possibility of a court action. The French conception of law comprises '*all* the rules devised to establish the structures of society and to regulate people's conduct, and these include many which cannot give rise to an action in the courts but are none the less basic to the organisation of the State.' (Weston *An English Reader's Guide to the French Legal System* (1991) p.46).

There are also different words that are used for different senses of 'law': 'a law' (or statute) is *une loi*; 'the law' is *la loi* or '*la justice*' as 'to fall foul of the law'; but the law as an academic discipline is *le droit* as it is for legal systems of different countries (*le droit anglais*) and for different branches of the law (*le droit penal* etc) (see Weston (ibid)).

French law, being derived from the Romans, is based on Roman law, *as interpreted by the Glossators and post-Glossators*, and as practised in France. It is not, therefore, based on ancient Roman law. Its primary legal methodogy is codification and its primary source of law is therefore legislation. Another point we need to bear in mind, as ever, is that the French approach to law is different from that of the common law tradition in its *legal categories* or *classifications of areas of law*, in its form and approach to legislation and caselaw and in its heavy reliance on *doctrinal material* as a source of law. It is also based on a rigid separation between (i) *private law* and *criminal law*; and (ii) '*public*' or *administrative law*. There has never been a distinction between law and equity in the sense of the common law distinction and the concept of the 'trust' does not exist in French law.

There are *distinctive legal institutions* in France such as special administrative courts and special doctrines such as the *abuse of rights, direct action* and *oblique action*. There is also an important distinction between the ordinary courts and the administrative courts.

(i) The Court System

3.2.27   There are two words available in English meaning 'court' namely a general term 'court' and a narrower term 'tribunal' which refer to panels and bodies which exercise administrative or (more usually) judicial functions, but with limited or special jurisdiction. In France, it is as well to remember that French judges are not supposed to perform a law-making function as a result of the doctrine of the separation of powers between the legislature, executive and judiciary. French courts are organised on the basis of general and limited jurisdiction. Weston makes several linguistic points on the comparative problems regarding an understanding of 'courts' in French law and English law (see Weston (1991) Chapter 6 *passim*), the more significant of which we summarise here.

The higher courts are mostly called *cours*, and all deliver *arrets*, while the lower ones are mostly called *tribunaux* and all deliver *jugements*. There is a third term in French law , *juridiction*, which appears to be superordinate to the other two. Any *cour* or *tribunal* (or an individual judge) may be described as a *juridiction*, whereas some juridictions are *cours* and others *tribunaux*.

Juridiction must be translated as court though in the plural, as in *les juridictions francaises*, where it would refer to 'courts and tribunals'. If, however, the special division of the Criminal Court of Appeal (the *chambre d'accusation*) and the investigating judge of the Criminal Division of the Tribunal de Grande Instance, the *juge d'instruction*, are referred to together as *juridictions d'instruction*, the term will then be best translated as 'judicial authority'. Hence, as Weston points out, 'the three French terms are in practice generally to be translated by a single English word because the distinctions between cour, tribunal and juridiction, in so far as they correspond to distinctions in the English language at all, are not reflected in the English language system.' (Weston (1991) p.67).

The French court system has a dual system of courts, ordinary courts (the *ordre judiciaire*) and administrative courts (*ordre administratif*). The ordinary courts , which are divided into civil and criminal jurisdiction, have jurisdiction unless a case involves the State or a State employee or corporation as a party, in which case the administrative courts will have exclusive jurisdiction. All English courts have jurisdiction to decide cases in administrative matters and to exercise control over administrative bodies and tribunals.

Another conceptual point to note is that the administrative courts really belong to the executive arm of the State and are seen as part of the administrative machinery. Hence, to the French legal mind, only the ordinary courts strictly belong to the judiciary (or, in the French appellation-*autorite judiciaire*- 'judicial power'). It is only these courts that a French lawyer thinks about when discussing the 'judicial' system. The distinction between ordinary and administrative courts is therefore far more significant in French law than the one they also have between civil and criminal courts.

The court system has *three tiers*, but there are only a few similarities with the English legal framework. In the lower tier, there are four hundred and eighty-five *tribunaux d'instance*, which is roughly equivalent to the English magistrates' courts and county courts, that is, limited primary jurisdiction. This is the only court in France presided over by a single judge, and all other courts have a Bench of judges. There are also a number of ordinary courts of first instance, which are specialised or special courts, only the first of which is a 'court' rather than a tribunal.

They are (i) the *tribunaux de commerce*, of which there are nearly 230, consisting of three lay commercial judges, with a minimum of five years' experience, elected by their peers in the form of an electoral college comprised of traders' delegates. The English Commercial Court set up within the Queen's Bench Division of the High Court in 1970 has a similar jurisdiction. (ii) Social security tribunals, with lay assessors, of which there are a hundred and ten; (iii) Employment tribunals: there is at least one in each *departement* and numbering over two hundred and eighty, which are further subdivided into five divisions, corresponding to different sectors of employment. (iv) Landlord and tenant tribunals, numbering around four hundred.

At the next level, in the second tier, so to speak, though not in an appellate sense, are the *tribunaux de grande instance*. These deal with civil actions involving sums higher than thirty-thousand francs, or with more serious criminal offences. There are a hundred and eighty-one of these, exercising an unlimited jurisdiction, a hundred and seventy-five of which are in metropolitan France. This *regional court* has several chambers or divisions and is often likened to the High Court of Justice in England but there are several differences: (i) it is the normal court of first instance in civil matters (apart from the small claims dealt with by the *tribunaux d'instance*); they are therefore closer to the English county court but they have a criminal jurisdiction. (ii) The English High Court jurisdiction is primarily civil and it has appellate jurisdiction in both civil and criminal cases. The *tribunaux de grande instance* do not have any appellate jurisdiction; (iii) The English High Court is represented in large provincial cities by a district registrar, has the right to statutorily sit anywhere in England and Wales, although based in London. The *tribunaux de grande instance* is really a regional court.

In the second tier, there are thirty-three courts of appeal (*cours d'appel*), which are again decentralised and regional courts. They can hear appeals from each of the *tribunaux* of one or more *departements*. Each court of appeal has several divisions. Within its civil divisions, it hears appeals from the civil division of the *tribunaux de grande instance* , from the agricultural land tribunals, and the industrial conciliation tribunals.

A Social Division hears appeals from the social security appeal tribunals and a Commercial Division hears appeals from the commercial courts. Within its criminal jurisdiction, appeals are usually heard by a Criminal Division, except for those involving a minor, which will be heard by the Juvenile Division.

There is a crucial difference between the English Court of Appeal and the French version. The French *cour d'appel* conducts a re-examination and re-hearing of the whole case and can therefore substitute its own view of the facts or the law for that of the original court that heard the case. The English Appeal Court has the power to do this but very rarely disagrees with the trial judge's view of the primary facts, since he had the opportunity to see and hear the witnesses, and evaluate the evidence first-hand. The normal practice has been for the Appeal Court to overturn the original court's view only if new or fresh evidence comes to light (as in the spate of recent English criminal cases involving alleged terrorist activities) or forensic evidence proves the original verdict was not 'safe' and could no longer be upheld. In addition, the English Appeal Court will overrule a lower court decision if it is proved that the original court acted in such a way that no reasonable judge would have acted, either excluding evidence that should have been included, or misinterpreting the evidence which he did take into account.

Another notable difference between the French and English appellate courts is that in England there is predominant reliance on oral evidence gleaned from the adversarial process in one continuous hearing. The facts in a French case are obtained through a rigorous investigation of the court itself, the results of which are then complied in a written *dossier*. It is obviously easier to review this *dossier* at the appellate stage.

The Supreme Court with jurisdiction over the whole of France is the *Cour de cassation*. This consists of five civil chambers and one criminal chamber. The first three are called the first, second and third civil Divisions, the remaining two the Commercial and Financial Division and the other the Social Division.

A minimum of three (and usually five) judges hear a case from a single division and there are more than a hundred judges in all. The first three Divisions or chambers deal with litigation arising out of general private law; the Commercial and Financial Division deals with trade and economic law cases and the Social Division deals with litigation arising out of labour and social security matters. There is no civil jury, but there is one for criminal cases.

The *Cour de cassation* is known as a court of error which means that it only deals with cases that appeal on a point of law, such an appeal being known as a *pourvoi en cassation* (or sometimes known as a *recours en cassation*) which is an appeal on points of law, a form of application to have a judgment set aside purely on legal grounds. It does not appear to have any direct equivalent in English law although the nearest would seem to be the English *application for judicial review*, which asks the court to review not the merits of the case but the legality of an administrative decision.

However, this court does not fulfil the same function as the House of Lords. If it finds the *pourvoi* justified, it has no power to substitute its own decision but merely to quash it. The case will then be remitted for further consideration to another court of equal jurisdiction to the first court that heard the case. If this lower court takes the same view as that of the original court, the matter will be referred to the *Assemblee pleniere* (Plenary Assembly) of the *Cour de cassation* on which all five divisions are represented, with twenty five judges presiding. If the *Assemblee pleniere* again quashes the lower court's decision on the same grounds as before, the *Assemblee pleniere* will then remit the matter to a third court, which is then obliged to follow the view taken by the *Assemblee*. Recent time-saving reforms have made it possible for either the Division which which has dealt with the first *pourvoi* or the *Assemblee pleniere* to enter a final judgment if its decision on the particular point of law in question leaves nothing further for the court below to consider.

Cases may be referred direct to the full court by a joint bench or even by an ordinary bench. If this is done and the lower court's decision is quashed, the Assemblee's decision will be binding on the court to which the case has been remitted.

The primary function of the *Cour de cassation* is to secure uniformity of interpretation, a task which, in England, is carried out by the Court of Appeal. The whole ethos of the Cour de Cassation is different from the House of Lords, which, as stated by the former Lord Chancellor, is not a court you should usually appeal to unless the case is one which is not covered by the law. The *Cour de cassation*'s philosophy is that there should be unrestricted access to the courts for every litigant who wishes to argue a particular issue in law. In pursuance of this, there is no filter division such as the Appeals Committee of the House of Lords, and there are one hundred and twenty-seven judges in the *Cour de cassation*.

The House of Lords only hears something like seventy cases a year as opposed to the fifteen thousand that the *Cour de cassation*'s five civil chambers hear per year. The number of cases that go to the *Cour de cassation* have tripled in the last ten years and it is currently facing a severe overloading problem with an increasing backlog. The *Procureur-general* and the *Premier President* of the Court have drawn attention to this crisis last year and the latter suggested having a filter to vet cases that were appealing to the *Cour de cassation*.

Finally, all courts, except for the *tribunaux d'instance*, are collegial in that they act as a Bench of at least three judges, or at least seven in the Cour de Cassation, but that they are seen to act as one body. At the end of a case, they issue one judgment, there are no published reports of dissenting judgments. Moreover, the actual judgment tends to be exceedingly terse and laconic by English law standards, as little as one sentence if thought appropriate. Thus, reliance has to be placed on the opinions of doctrinal or academic writers who produce what French law calls *doctrine* (see below). While the English judge is often a public figure, whose views and even physical features may be relayed and displayed on a television screen or 'tabloid' newspaper in an important case, the typical French judge remains anonymous.

(ii) Public and Private Law

a. Introduction

3.2.28 English law has devoted relatively little attention to the problem of classification in the law, primarily because of the late development in legal science in England. However, the distinction between *public law* and *private law* 'seems to many Continental European lawyers to be fundamental, necessary and, on the whole, evident. Institutional works, student manuals and treatises contain discussions of the dichotomy, often in confidently dogmatic terms that put to rest incipient doubts' (Merryman 'The Public Law-Private Law Distinction in European and American Law (1968) 17 J.Pub.Law 3. The distinction itself is traceable to the Roman jurist Ulpian who drew the distinction (usually placed at around AD 200). His statement appears near the beginning of the Digest and is repeated on the first page of Justinian's *Institutes*: 'There are two aspects of this subject: public and private law. Public law deals with the state...private law with the well-being of individuals.' (quoted in Kahn-Freund, Levy and Rudden (1991) p.10).

As we have seen, there is one Supreme Court (*Cour de cassation*) which deals with private law matters and another (the *Conseil d'Etat*) for public law matters. There is also the *Conseil constitutionnel*, created by the 1958 Constitution, and the closest equivalent to a constitutional court that France possesses although its powers are much more restricted than those of the United States Supreme Court. It has a dual function: adjudicative and advisory. It vets all election cases, parliamentary standing orders, and parliamentary legislation. This has become more closely approximated to a contitutional court, since its decisions are binding on the *Cour de cassation*, the *Conseil d'Etat*, the legislator and government and it has a very strong influence on other juducial authorities.

However, it cannot declare an Act of Parliament unconstitutional once it has been promulgated, nor can it review the constitutionality of regulations and it is not a supreme appellate court such as the US Supreme Court. The question will remai as to whether it can properly be called a court.

b. Content of Public and Private Law

3.2.29   Public law (*droit public*) governs relations to which the State (or a subdivision of it such as a *departement*, or a State-owned enterprise or a public authority) is a party, (this means relations between public bodies *inter se* and between public bodies and private persons) while private law (*droit prive*) governs the rights and duties of private persons and corporations. Public law administers State-run bodies that provide public services, schools, hospitals and municipalities as well as regulates the legal position of persons who serve the State (such as civil servants or soldiers).

It is important to note that the divisions of the law are firmly fixed in the minds of civil lawyers but the divisions themselves are by no means immutable as a result of at least two factors. First, the existence in many countries (including France) of a *special hierarchy of courts dealing with administrative matters* and secondly, the *involvement of the State in certain cases where the central parties are private persons*.

On the first point, it would be incorrect to assume that there the scope of the administrative courts' jurisdiction is the scope of public law. Many disputes to which the State is a party and which would belong to the province of public law, are within the domain of the ordinary Courts of law.

On the second point, in many cases, although the parties to a given relationship are private citizens (or companies), the State is not indifferent to this relationship. Rules are accordingly provided to regulate such relationships, to which the parties are obliged to submit. A typical example is the area of marriage and divorce. Parties are bound to abide by most rules formulated dealing with the marriage ceremony or of its effects or its dissolution. The point is that the essential, feature of marriage is that it is a private relationship between persons, but it is one in which the State (or society) has particular intercsts, such as the protection and security of the vulnerable party (generally the wife) and children of the relationship. Accordingly, these rules are imposed as a result of what English law would call 'public policy'. It may, of course, be provided that private law rules shall apply to a given relation although the State is a party to such a relationship.

c. The Separate Hierarchy of Administrative Courts

3.2.30   As a result of the separation of powers, the French executive is not subject to the jurisdiction of the ordinary courts but it is subject to the control of the central organ of the executive, the *Conseil d'Etat*, created in 1799 by Napoleon, which, in this capacity, performs a function very much like a court. Thus, the executive can only be 'kept in check', so to speak, by a court that is part of the executive system itself. The *Conseil d'Etat* (literally: 'Council of State') has been supplemented by a number of other lower-level administrative courts, and together with these courts, forms a self-contained hierarchy of courts with three tiers as well. The *Conseil d'Etat* is the supreme administrative court at the top of this hierarchy.

The *lowest tier* of the administrative court structure consists of the *tribunaux administratifs* (administrative courts), which are regional courts, numbering twenty-six in metropolitan France, and, since 1989, by virtue of an Act of 31 December 1987, there is now an *intermediate tier* of appellate administrative court: the *cour administrative d'appel*(Admnistrative Court of Appeal). This system is a regional set-up, with five courts having been established at Paris, Bordeaux, Lyon, Nantes and Nancy. From these courts, appeal lies to the *Conseil d'Etat* in the form of a *recours en cassation* ('appeal on points of law'). it is worth noting that the law that is applied by these administrative courts is almost entirely caselaw, and is found in the decisions of the *Conseil d'Etat* and there is now a voluminous literature which informs this area of law.

These administrative courts have a dual jurisdiction: (i) they exercise a review jurisdiction, called the '*annulment jurisdiction*' from which even statutes are not necessarily immune, ever since a 1975 decision of the *Cour de cassation* which held that a treaty took precedence over a later Act of Parliament; and (ii) they exercise a *pleine jurisdiction* (full jurisdiction) which allows them to award damages to those who have suffered injury or damage as a result of a wrongful act on the part of a public servant acting in the course of his duties. This entitles the court to substitute the administrative decision which is being challenged.

Two categories of executive or administrative acts which are not subject to review by the the administrative courts are (i) those 'connected directly with, or forming part of, the legislative process and parliamentary proceedings'; and (ii) 'those concerning the government's relations with foreign countries or with international organisations.' (see Weston (1991) p.87)

d. Current Status of the Distinction

3.2.31 The whole question of the dichotomy has been under scrutiny and undergone criticism over the last ten to fifteen years, but it has remained at least in its basic structure. The problem is that there are occasions when a civil or criminal court will have to apply administrative law, for example when a person charged with an offence created by an administrative regulation wishes to challenge the legality of the regulation. Or an administrative court has had to take cognisance of private law on several occasions. It is also a moot point as to whether criminal law should be classified as public or private law. In the context of crime prevention, it seems to fall within public law but criminal cases are brought before the private law courts. The fundamental distinction really seems to be between administrative law and private law, since public law encompasses constitutional law, which lies outside the jurisdiction of the administrative courts. As a preliminary proposition, it appears that the distinction between public and private in the strict, concentional sense, is breaking down as the frontiers of State intervention begin to encroach into private law matters.

e. Conflict of Jurisdiction

3.2.32 There is also the *Tribunal des conflits*, a sort of Jurisdiction Disputes Court, dealing with matters such as whether a case should be heard in the ordinary courts or in the administrative courts. The main area of conflict has been the case where a private citizen sues a public servant in the ordinary courts and the administrative courts wish to argue that the matter belongs properly to the realm of public law. If the local prefect enters a plea of no jurisdiction arguing that the ordinary court in question has no jurisdiction to hear the case and the court rejects this plea, the prefect may apply to the Jurisdiction Disputes Court for a final ruling. This ruling must be given within three months. if the original court accepts the plea, the plaintiff must either sue in the administrative courts or else appeal to a higher ordinary court. A final point is that conflicts of jurisdiction between the civil and criminal ordinary courts are decided by the *Cour de cassation*.

(iii) Distinctive French Legal Doctrines and Concepts

a. Abuse of Right

3.2.33 Among the distinctive doctrines of French law is the notion of the *abuse of right*. This is a kind of fault-based action which consists in the abusive (ie wrongful) exercise of a right motivated by the desire to cause harm. The reported cases dealing with this type of situation suggest they occur most often in the context of the law of property. The basis of the action appears to be *quasi-delictual* rather than delictual. The closest English law analogy is the English *tort of nuisance*. (see Chapter 7).

b. Direct Action (*action directe*)

3.2.34   In French law and indeed, in the Romanistic legal family, the *action directe* (direct action) makes it possible for a person who is only indirectly represented, to intervene in a contract concluded on his behalf by a middleman. Thus, in a few specified instances, the French Civil Code gives a person an independent right of suit if that person has a special interest in a contract concluded between two other parties (see Articles 1759, 1798, and 1994).

English law only allows such actions as an exception to their general rule of privity of contract-that only parties to the original contract may sue-unless one of the many exceptions may be successfully invoked (such as trusts, agency or assignment).

Examples of this action in French law are: (i) where a landlord can proceed against a subtenant if the tenant is in arrears with the rent; or (ii) where a principal may claim directly against a third party to whom his agent has delegated the performance of the authorised task; and (iii) in the realm of the law of insurance. If a tortfeasor is covered in respect of an accident by a policy of insurance, the victim can sue the insurer direct. In the case of the *action directe*, it is the legislator who decides on the basis of an abstract balancing of the interests involved, that the third party should have a right to intervene, regardless of whether this accords with the intention of the parties or not.

c. Oblique Action

3.2.35   This is an action whereby a suing creditor is empowered to exercise, in the insolvent debtor's name, all the latter's rights and actions, except those which are purely personal. This, in terms is what is stated by Article 1166 of the Civil Code. Thus, the creditor is allowed to stand in the place of the debtor but can only exercise the right belonging to the debtor by bringing an action. The personal rights and actions may be either (a) ones which are not primarily of a pecuniary nature, or (b) ones which the debtor may decline to exercise for conscientious or other personal reasons: (Amos and Walton (1967) p.241).

In order to bring the action the creditor or creditors must have a 'personal interest' in bringing the action. (see Civ. 11.7.1951.586;). The debt has to be certain, due and liquidated (see Req.25.3.1924, D.H. 1924.282,S.1924.1.67) and there will not be no such 'personal interest' if the debtor is solvent or if he is already prosecuting the claim in question himself (see Amos and Walton (1967)p.242). The main purpose of the oblique action is to prevent the debtor from negligently allowing his rights to be lost.

A practice that has developed outside the Code is that the creditor bringing the oblique action usually joins the debtor as a party to the action.

Any defence which would be good against the debtor is good against the creditors because the action belongs to the debtor, but is simply brought by the creditors in his name. This will apply to defences which have become available after the bringing of the action.

72

The creditors instituting the oblique action do not obtain any priority or charge with regard to what is recovered. If the action is successful, the property recovered will simply be included in the general estate of the debtor. Indeed, if the other creditors wish to do so, they can prevent the creditor who filed the action from applying the proceeds to his own claim. (Amos and Walton (1967) p.243).

All in all, there is little incentive for a creditor to institute the oblique action and its use is relatively rare, because there is the more effective remedy of attachment (*saisie-arret*) under the Civil Procedure Code (see Article 557 *et seq.*).

v. History of German Law

(i) Early German Law

3.2.36   In the Middle Ages, the law of Germany consisted mainly of customs and traditions, as did medieval law generally. The private law of the German territories before 1400 thus took the form of local custom. Although originating in common Germanic ideas, they were locally developed in each part of the territories of Central Europe which were part of the 'Holy Roman Empire of the Germanic Nation.' Some of these customs were applied in a single city, some over large stretches of territory, yet others were confined to a single village or manor or to a special group of persons. The revival of the title of Roman emperor and its assumption by German kings did not result in the rules of the *Corpus Juris* being applied, either as legislation or to fill in gaps where local custom was silent.

Roman law was taught in cathedral and convent schools but some Germans travelled to Bologna while others began to attend Italian and French law schools. These private law rules were highly localised, 'orally transmitted and immensely diversified.' (Dawson (1968) p.153)

However, many of these customary rules were privately collected and expanded in law books, some of which eventually attained high status as works of authority, rather like the early books of English law by Bracton and Glanvill, such as the *Mirror of Saxon Law* by Eike von Repgow (*Sachsenspiegel*) produced around 1225, which predates Bracton. The central power in the Empire did not, however, attempt to implement Roman law to all German territories as a form of common law to supplant local customs.

Nevertheless, in the 1450s till nearly the end of the fifteenth century, a great deal of factional strife, frequent anarchy and the lack of a strong central authority were factors which convinced all reformers that there should be an end to private warfare. Emperor Maximillan (1493-1519) sought to restore the power of the monarchy and to secure lasting peace and unity.

In 1495, for reasons which remain mysterious, and which have never obtained consensus from various historians, Roman law was adopted by the newly-established imperial court, the *Reichskammergericht*, the operative ordinance stating that judges were ordered to decide cases coming before them 'according to the Common Law of the Empire' which meant according to Roman law. The ordinance of 1495 placed 'statutes' and 'customs' on an equal footing.

(ii) Reasons for Non-Reception of Roman Law

3.2.37 Many reasons have been adduced for the 'reception' of Roman law, bearing in mind that there was no complete displacement of German law by Roman law. Von Mehren and Gordley (1977), in reliance on various researchers' findings, suggest *six reasons*: (i) Lack of legal unity within Germany; (ii) Lack of written law often made it difficult to ascertain the rules; (iii) Lack of written law was seen as a major cause for the unsystematic nature and lack of rational structure of the Germanic law. (iv) As a result of the highly fragmented nature of the legal order, neither a strong legal profession nor one with extensive knowledge of Germanic laws had been produced. In England, for instance, the legal profession fought to prevent any takeover by Roman law. (v) Legally skilled administrative personnel were increasingly needed to replace the 'unlearned, noble administrator' and the only source of such personnel was students trained in Roman law at the Italian and other other universities.

The Roman law received was not the 'unadulterated' sixth-century *Corpus Juris* but the version that had been modified by the Glossators and Commentators. Some parts were actually ignored and Germanic Commercial Law, for example, remained intact. The degree of reception was also far from uniform with the more northerly regions retaining their Germanic law, and when some cities reformed their legal systems in the fourteenth and fifteenth centuries, they again retained many of the original Germanic elements.

Hence, instead of having a sophisticated university-derived Roman law and Canon law which co-existed with local customary law, by the middle of the sixteenth century, there was a reasonably homogeneous common law based on post-classical Roman law principles, adapted and 'harmonised' to suit daily life, but which co-existed with a mixture of Germanic principles (see Forrester, Goren and Ilgen *The German Civil Code* (1975), p.xxiii). This brand of 'common law' or *Usus Modernus Pandectarum* continued to exist in certain parts of Germany, subject to many local variations, until 1900. A great disadvantage with these laws was their sheer bulk, so that even commentaries on them could not ensure legal uniformity or legal certainty.

(iii) The Pandectists

3.2.38 During the sixteenth, seventeenth and eighteenth centuries, Roman lawyers in Germany and elsewhere were producing syntheses of modern Roman law in the name of the Law of Nature and the Law of Reason. The whole style and characteristic philosophy of these Movements was to present this adapted Roman law in a logical and orderly progression of concepts. It was out of this Natural Law and Law of reason that the German branch of the Movement, so to speak, emerged-the *Pandectists*. They sought to promote the dogmatic and systematic study of Roman law. Their plan was to study all historical sources which had shaped German legal history, and they viewed law as a closed system of ideas, principles and institutions derived from Roman law. Their methodology was a scientific, logical approach to the solution of legal problems. Law was therefore approached outside any ethical, moral or religious considerations, and , at least for the resolution of problems, was a mathematical process determined by a 'conceptual calculus'. The German Civil Code (BGB) is a product of the Pandectist School, in its abstraction, precision and logical symmetry. Ethical and moral considerations were not, by any means, irrelevant, but law's basic methodology did not, *prima facie*, utilise such concepts.

(iv) Diversity of Political Entities

3.2.39   The situation was not helped by there not really being a united political entity which could be called Germany, but rather hundreds of independent political entities varying enormously in size and influence, each with its own judges and courts and all steadfastly clinging to their own customs as far as they could. This was despite the fact that there was an Emperor and the German territory was meant to be part of the Empire. Natural law philosophy, and the merging of various smaller states into larger political units and the rise of an absolute monarchy led to territorial codifications which partly preserved the pre-existing law as a residual source which would be applied in the absence of statute. With the formal dissolution of the Empire in 1806, state legislation had reigned supreme for some time.

(v) Political Unification: 1871

3.2.40   In the early nineteenth century, at the Congress of Vienna 1815, the German Confederation was established. This was a loose association of states which included Austria, Bavaria and Prussia. It lasted until 1866, when Prusso-Austrian rivalry led to a conflict which Prussia and her allies from the North German states won. After Austria's defeat, a new North German Confederation was set up but there was no final coalition between the northern and southern states until nearly five years had passed. In 1870, a war broke out between France and an alliance of German states. The German alliance won, which saw the French army surrender at Sedan in September 1870 and Paris fall in early 1871. Bismarck, the Prussian Chancellor accordingly proclaimed the new German Empire or *Reich* at Versailles in 1871.

(vi) Legal Codification

3.2.41   For most of the nineteenth century, after the establishment of the Congress of Vienna in 1815, various attempts were made to achieve codification. Several German States had already adopted national codes such as Prussia (1794) and the French Code had been adopted by certain Rhineland states during the Napoleonic wars. These wars strengthened the feeling for national unity, but one of the major obstacles to German codification was the celebrated dispute between two distinguished German scholars, Carl von Savigny (1779-1861), leader of the Historical School of Jurisprudence and Professor Thibaut of Heidelberg, the leading spokesman for the Natural Law school of jurisprudence, who argued for codification. This powerful conflict of learned opinion set back the success of codification for several decades. Some have portrayed this opposition as a conflict between the Romanists (such as Savigny) and the Germanists (such as Thibaut).

Thibaut's views ultimately won the day and natural law elements have been integrated into the German Civil Code (BGB), but the sharp disgareement between two such prominent thinkers deprived the codification movement of considerable impetus for some time.

Nevertheless, several discussions did take place between members of the Confederation to achieve uniform laws governing bills of exchange and to work to produce a uniform commercial code. A number of states also proceeded to draft civil codes which all remained unadopted in 1871, except for Saxony which produced a Code of Civil Law in 1863, which, in its Pandectist approach and structure, was a forerunner of the BGB.

In 1871, an extraordinary constitutional and legislative situation existed. As one set of commentators put it, 'There were more than twenty kingdoms, grand-duchies, duchies, free cities, principalities, and one imperial territory.' (Forrester *et al*, (1975) p.xiii). As these writers go on to explain, 'each of these had their own hierarchies of courts and their own laws, or at least their own particular combination of ancient codifications, Rom-German law, modern codifications and local custom.' (Forrester *et al*, *ibid*). In fact, more than ten codifications were in force, but the point was, they did not necessarily apply if they contradicted local custom. Even more confusingly, different texts applied in different areas within individual states.

Of course, a fairly uniform law merchant, or commercial law, did exist and it was mainly in the field of family law and succession that the greatest uncertainty existed, as a result of the diversity of laws.

Upon establishment of the German Empire in 1871, the new Constitution gave the federal government power in a variety of fields, including civil procedure, organisation of courts, criminal law and criminal procedure and bankruptcy. The first law enacted by the new German Empire in 1871, was the Criminal Code, which was most easily achieved because the Northern German League had adopted a Criminal Code in 1870 which the Reich took over.

(vii) The System of Courts

3.2.42   There are five different sets of courts in Germany, apart from the Federal Constitutional Court. there are civil courts, general and administrative courts and labour courts. Each set of courts is three-tiered, in that there are courts of first instance, courts of appeal, and a federal supreme court. The first instance courts and the courts of appeal are courts of the several regions (*Lander*) so it is up to the individual region/district to staff, maintain and equip these courts which will involve employing, paying, promoting and pensioning judges who sit in them. Only the courts of last resort are federal courts whose judges are federal judges.

The jurisdiction of these courts is determined by federal legislation. Although the Basic Law (article 74, paragraph 1) provides that the constitution of the courts and court procedure fall within the area of concurrent legislative competence, the federal parliament has legislated so comprehensively in this area that it utterly dominates this area of law leaving little scope for the *Lander*.

It is the ordinary jurisdiction courts with which the average citizen has most contact, which has more judges than any other jurisdiction and hears nearly all matters of civil and criminal law. At first instance, small claims are brought to the lowest civil court, the *Amtsgericht* but claims exceeding DM 6,000 must be brought in the regional court, the *Landgericht*, where each party has to be reprepresented by a German lawyer who has *locus standi* at that court. The *Amtsgericht* is also the forum for the enforcement of judgments, and handles non-contentious business such as the maintenance of the land register and the commercial register, the supervision of guardians, testamentary administrators, and trustees in bankruptcy. Civil cases in the *Amtsgericht* are heard by a single judge which is also the case for criminal cases, unless serious crimes are involved. In that sort of case, two lay judges sit on the bench with a professional judge. The *Landgericht* also sits as a trial court in cases unsuitable for the *Amtsgericht* in which event the case is heard by a special division of the *Landgericht* called the *Schwurgericht*.

This consists of three professional judges and two lay judges who have the same voting power as the presiding professional judges and have the right to consider issues of fact and law in the case. Both the sentence and the verdict must be approved by a two-thirds majority of the judges.

Most of the work of the Court of Appeal consists of civil matters since appeals from criminal convictions rendered by the *Landgericht* usually go direct to the federal court. The Appeal Court hears appeals from decisions of the *Landgericht* sitting as a court of first instance and from decisions of the *Amtsgericht* sitting as a Family Court. The Appeal Court judges sit in divisions called senates which comprise three judges each, one of whom has a higher rank and presides.

Civil cases falling outside the jurisdiction of the *Amtsgericht* start in the *Landgericht* or district court. The *Landgericht* also hears appeals from first-instance decisions of the *Amtsgericht*. But if the *Amtsgericht* was sitting as a family court, the appeal goes directly to the Appeal Court (*Oberlandesgericht*). In principle, decisions of the *Landgericht* are made by a panel of three professional judges but it is quite common for a single judge to be delegated to hear straightforward cases.

The *Landgericht* has a special chamber for commercial cases (as defined in Article 95: GVG) which is usually dealt with by a panle of three judges-two experienced commercial men, acting as honorary commercial judges and one presiding professional judge.

Appeals can be made against both the decisions of the *Amtsgericht* and the *Landgericht* but in civil matters, the amount has to be at least DM 1,200 in order to obtain leave to appeal. A further appeal to the Federal Court on points of law is possible against the decisions of the Court of Appeal in cases involving amounts greater than DM 60,000 or in disputes involving matters of fundamental importance. (see Bocker *et al* Germany: Practical Commercial Law (1992)p.3).

In criminal cases, the *Landgericht* hears appeals from convictions from decisions handed down by the *Amtsgericht*.

The highest of the courts of ordinary jurisdiction is the Federal Supreme Court (*Bundesgerichtshof*), which sits in Karlsruhe and consists of fifteen senates, ten for civil matters and five for criminal matters. There are five federal judges in each senate, one of whom presides. Appeals from the decisions of the Appeal Court are heard by the criminal senates. As the matter stands, an appeal is available to the Federal Supreme Court only if the Appeal Court has given its permission or if the case is one which it believes concerns a matter of principle, or that its decision deviates from a decision of the Appeal Court. (Article 546 ZPO (Code of Civil Procedure).

Labour courts have jurisdiction over disputes concerning labour law, such as matters involving employment contracts, collective bargaining agreements and works agreements. The appeal system is three-tiered with two regional courts in every German district and a Federal Court which has jurisdiction over the whole country to determine appeals on points of law.

Administrative courts deal with disputes relating to the actsof public authorities. Cases start in the Administrative Court, then proceed up on appeal to the Administrative Appeal Court, and finally, to the Federal Administrative Court in Berlin which must be on a point of law.

There is also a special branch of social courts, the Courts on Social Matters, which deal with social insurance and allied matters, which contains two lay judges at each of the three levels. There is, however, one professional judge in the first instance court.

Disputes of revenue law are heard by a special set of tax courts but there are only two levels of court in this context because complaints against decisions of the tax authorities first come before special committees.

In addition to these five systems, there is the Federal Constitutional Court, to which anyone can bring a formal case lodging a 'complaint', alleging an infringement of his constitutional rights through an act of public authorities. There is always a possibility to challenge a new law or a final judgment as unconstitutional if it is case of human rights. This court has built up a store of cases. The Constitutional Court may declare any law or judgment null and void.

vi. Enactment of the BGB

3.2.43   After a long period of drafting, discussion, and more redrafting, the final draft was submitted to the German legislature in June 1896 for debate. No less than a hundred and twenty-five speeches were made on the draft code, and over a third of these dealt with rights and liabilities related to game and domestic animals! This illustrates the predominant outlook of the legislators to the draft. Speakers also spoke on habitual drunkenness as a ground for placing a person under guardianship, divorce on the ground for insanity, civil marriage, parental consent to marriage, holograph wills and parental authority.

The *Burgerliches Gesetzbuch* (BGB)-Civil Code-was officially promulgated on 18 August, 1896, and entered into effect on 1 January 1900, and effectively unified the private law in the German Empire. It regulates the relations between private persons who are regarded as equals rather than as subordinate to the State, as under public law.

Its main objectives were clarification and consistency in the law, and it is represents a harmonisation of pre-existing law in the various parts of the Reich. The political values of nineteenth-century liberalism appear to have set the agenda for the contents of the rules of the Code. Its key themes are the individual and his need for freedom. The BGB thus gives parties great freedom in contracting and in the realm of property, reflecting the view that equal freedom for all individuals would ensure the smooth functioning of social justice.

The BGB is not written for the laymen, unlike the French Civil Code. It is *addressed to the legal profession*, giving precedence to precise solutions, and predictability of outcome. It looks to the economy, not the law, to secure social justice. Some commentators like Bochmer (1965) have therefore said that it reflects the end rather than the beginning of an era, because its structures, the choice of approach, and the code's values all come from the nineteenth century. As Von Mehren and Gordley point out, although Romanist in inspiration, the influence of the Germanic tradition is seen in a number of its paragraphs, for example, dealing with: joint ownership (paras. 705, 1416, 2032), the contract of inheritance (para. 2281), the law applicable to executors of wills (para. 2197), the concept of acquisition in good faith from unauthorised persons (para. 932), the introduction of the land register (para. 873), the concept of contracts for the benefit of a third party (para. 328) and the assumption of debt (para. 414). (Von Mehren and Gordley (1977) p.79)

The BGB has been used as a model for codes in many countries: the Japanese Civil Code (1898), the Swiss Civil Code (1907) and the Swiss Code of Obligations (1911), as well as the revisions for the Austrian Code in the 1910s, and indirectly, the Turkish Code of Obligations (1926). In the light of strong legal ties between Italy and Germany, the drafters of the Italian Code have also been influenced by the BGB.

vii. Structure of the BGB

3.2.44 The format adopted by Justinian's Institutes was to divide the codes into self-contained chapters, subdivided into sections which are called 'paragraphs' dealing with different topics such as persons, obligations, property and succession, though by no means in that order. The BGB does not actually follow this tradition and calls its Book One the 'General Part' followed by the words 'Book One', which is followed by 'Books' or chapters on obligations, property, family law and succession.

Thus Book One (The General Part) contains paragraphs 1 to 240, Book Two (Law of Obligations)-paragraphs 241 to 853, Book Three (Law of Property)-paragraphs 854 to 1296, Book Four (Family Law)-paragraphs 1297 to 1921, and Book Five (Law of Succession) paragraphs 1922-2385. The paragraphs are equivalent to an English statute's 'sections'.

This format is similar to the method adopted by Roman scholars, such as the judge and scholar, Professor Heise of Heidelberg, who adopted a similar style of analysis. He divided his teaching of Roman law into five sections, the first dealing with the basic principles of legal behaviour and the methods of creation of legal relationships. (see Forrester, Goren and Ilgen (1975) p.xiv)

Book One fundamentally provides the definitions and legal vocabulary which govern the remaining four books. It commences by describing the types of persons, (who may be physical or juristic) who can have rights and obligations. It also defines the different types of property, and outlines the principles underlying the creation and dissolution of legal obligations. Book Two starts off with 200 paragraphs containing general principles relevant to all obligations and the next 400 deal with thirty specific types of obligations, which illustrates the approach of commencing with the general concepts then moving to the specific examples, but in order to ascertain the scope of a particular obligation, you would have to refer to Book One, the first part of Book Two and the specific provisions pertaining thereto, in Book Two.

Using the Code therefore requires a high degree of familiarity with its contents, since it constantly requires cross-referencing from the specific Title to the relevant provisions of the General Part. Accordingly, in modern practice, there is now a 2,000 page book, printed on extra-thin paper, which is called a Short Commentary on the BGB (*Kommentar zum BGB* (1974), edited by judges of the imperial and federal courts, which contains a collection of *cases*-judicial decisions on the various paragraphs- which no practising German lawyer is ever seen without, when engaged in interpretation of the BGB. There is also a Commentary on the BGB which is a seven-volume collection commentating on the BGB but which also gives a great deal of coverage to the views of academic writers (see *Munchener Kommentar zum BGB* (1978))

viii. Amendments to the BGB

3.2.45   The BGB has undergone alternations and amendments in the course of its long history which spans nearly a hundred years. Some of its sections were repealed during the Nazi era, and the practice developed of enacting special laws outside it. Accordingly, it is necessary from time to time to refer to legislation which supplements the BGB. New social legislation, either included within the Code's framework or through supplementary legislation, has been the trend for several decades, and has accelerated apace in the 1980s and early 1990s.

By the 1970s, there had already been nearly sixty statutory modifications of the Code, and more than 800 of its 2,385 paragraphs have been repealed, modified, renewed, undergone insertions, and even declared unconstitutional by the Federal Constitutional Court.

Some of the more important alterations to the Code have occurred in relation to family law, particularly in respect of matrimonial property (implementing a new marital property regime), celebration and dissolution of marriage, the status of illegitimate children, and a number of provisions dealing with the welfare of children in need of protection by the Guardianship Court. Other changes have occurred in the field of property law, and employment law.

ix. Style of the BGB

3.2.46   The legal language of the BGB is generally seen as being rather abstract and complex but it is precise in what it says about the particular area of law. But the main difficulties lie in the need to be familiar with the various concepts, as interpreted by the courts and in practice, a knowledge of technical language and the need to cross-reference. For example, paragraph 157 states 'Contracts shall be interpreted according to the requirements of good faith, giving consideration to common usage.' and paragraph 242 states 'The debtor is bound to effect performance according to the requirements of good faith, giving consideration to common usage.' (see translations in Forrester *et al* (1975) p.xvi). It will be noticed that key phrases such as 'good faith' and 'common usage' are not defined and you would therefore need to consult the caselaw on the subject. In fact, paragraph 242 is the most utilised section in the whole BGB, having been used by the courts to create a whole corpus of law, to vary and supplement contracts, using 'implied' terms much in the same way as in English law, thereby creating flexibility within formalism.

Paragraph 242 has become a controlling statutory enactment of the general principle of 'Good Faith' which dominates the entire legal system. (see Horn, Kotz and Leser (1982) pp.135-145; and Chapter 13 of this book, for a comparative study of Good Faith).

The significant point that this illustrates is that despite the key civil law principle that gives supremacy to legislation (and, of course, has ultimate allegiance to the Constitution), no civil lawyer is able to answer or resolve questions and issues of law without some recourse to caselaw. Further, in accordance with the civil law ideology, the opinions and writings of doctrinal or academic writers have to be consulted, as in the French system, in order to obtain a considered view on a particular provision. General and abstract statements of principle clearly have to be elaborated upon in order to be applied to specific circumstances not covered by the Code. Paragraph 133 provides that in construing legal texts, the underlying intention and not the literal meaning of the words should prevail This is sometimes referred to as the *teleological approach* or *purposive method of interpretation*.

Another point worth noting is that the BGB does not have any 'foreign' non-German terms in it, eschewing Latin for German translations. Terms such as bona fides, or conduct contra bonos mores have been translated as *Treu und Glauben* and legal transactions *gegen die guten Sitten*, respectively. This was the result of its nineteenth century background, in that the BGB is a national and strongly German code with a powerful strain of nationalism and patriotism running through it. Again, the caselaw is the only way in which it is possible to know what these particular terms will mean in a given context.

Bearing in mind the importance of cases to the Code's interpretation, what is the legal method employed to accommodate the legislative supremacy principle?

x. Interpretation of the BGB

3.2.47   The basic point to note about the *judicial style in Germany* is that the judge is not permitted to simply cite a case as an authoritative source of a legal principle. Some legislative provision or Code provision has to be cited, or some well-established general legal principle, for example, the notion of *culpa in contrahendo* (liability due to fault existed before contracting) which does not appear in the BGB, but which has been cited by the courts. Thus the courts would have to say: 'According to paragraph XYZ of the BGB (or: according to the general principle of...) as interpreted by the BGH (the Supreme Court), we find that the legal position is...' To emphasise the point, although an English court does the same in cases turning on the interpretation of a statute, usually citing the need to ascertain 'the intention of Parliament', this general approach in German law is applicable to *all cases*, not just those involving statutory interpretation.

Thus, the BGB is accordingly interpreted in the manner illustrated above, and, as has been stressed, by consulting the caselaw on a particular provision. Another important point to note is that since there is *no doctrine of precedent in German law*, the cases on the provision need not be followed. However, cases of the Supreme Court tend to be followed, but will be departed from if seen as out-of-date or inappropriate.

xi. Application of the BGB

3.2.48   A sixth 'Book' or Chapter was included in the 1895 Draft of the BGB which dealt with the relationship between imperial and state laws and other private international law problems. Although removed from the Code itself, it was enacted separately, after modifications, as the Introductory Law (*Einfuhrungsgesetz zum Burgerlichen Gesetzbuch*) (EGBGB) at the same time as the BGB and is still in force, but it is of far less utility today than it might have been in the early twentieth century. The EGBGB has a long list of the fields in which the laws of the states may survive and in which they lapse, but there are now far fewer civil law (private law) areas which are regulated by state legislation than there used to be. Some remaining areas are forestry, water rights and mining.

The EGBGB also contains rules which govern conflicts between the BGB and foreign law. They also cover situations where the BGB and the *lex locus delicti* (law of the place of commission of the act) differ in the extent of available remedies. These provisions of the EGBGB would need to be consulted in cases where a foreign element is involved.

Of course, the BGB does not and cannot, govern all legal disputes or controversies, but is only meant to provide an authoritative guide to disputes of a civil (private law) nature between citizens. Its delict provisions, for example, have no penal significance. It has no application to questions of public law involving the federal government or the states. Commercial law is regulated by a separate Commercial Code (HGB), which deals with merchants and their commercial transactions. There are also Codes dealing with employment, tax, patents and copyright and other public law topics. There are also separate hierarchies of courts dealing with tax, social security, and administrative law.

Local District courts (*Amtsgerichte*) are the greatest users of the BGB, and these are spread all over the country. Not all these courts perform full judicial functions, however, as they often deal with very small cases. Higher up the hierarchy, the Code is also referred to but not with such frequency particularly because of the increasing supplementary legislation that has been passed in the last two decades or so.

xii. Other Important Legislation Affecting the BGB

3.2.49   Finally, there is also a collection of laws known as the *Basic Law*, which was a form of Constitution adopted in 1949, while Germany was still under military occupation, by the states now comprising the Federal Republic of Germany. This document was not the Constitution of a unified Germany but only the expression of the will of a number of German states. Accordingly, it was called a Basic Law rather than a Constitution. It lays down certain directly enforceable fundamental human rights and citizen's rights, which are recognised in all constitutional states in the West, and which is covered by the European Convention for the Protection of Human Rights. Thus it contains, *inter alia*, the following principles: that everyone has a right to life, corporeal integrity and the unhampered development of his personality (Article 2); that everyone is equal before the law (Article 3); that freedom of belief, conscience, religion and ideology is inviolable (Article 4); and that everyone has the right to express himself freely in speech, writing, or pictures (Article 5).

It is worth noting that Article 3 has already had a far-reaching impact on the law relating to rights over marital property as laid down in Book Four of the BGB and this was confirmed by subsequent legislation.

xiii. Evaluation of the BGB in the Modern World

3.2.50   The BGB has certainly proved its durability over a period spanning two world wars, political, economic and military upheavals and, in the last two years, the re-unification of East and West Germany. Although it is written in an abstract style and requires frequent cross-referencing, it has withstood amendments and alterations, and been supplemented by two Short Commentaries, caselaw and the Basic Law, not to mention the opinions of learned commentators. It remains an impressive testament to the Pandectist school of thought, but in the modern world, will provide a basic law of another sort, namely, one with basic concepts, principles and fundamental values which will continue to require adaptation and modernisation in order to cope not just with a new Germany but with a new European order.

3.2.51 We have seen therefore that German law, as influenced by their particular legal heritage, has developed in a systematic, logical, abstract and conceptual manner. This is traceable to the Pandectists and their philosophy. German law thinks in terms of *general principles* rather than in pragmatic terms, conceptualising problems rather than working from case to case. The legal terminology and central method of lawmaking-to *codify* laws in a comprehensive, authoritative and precise manner-distinguish it from the common law approach. Flowing from this, the primacy given to enacted law and specific statutory provision, is at once typical of the Continental style of law. Further, although cases have grown in importance in interpreting the Codes and statutes, they are still primarily considered to be illustrations of general principles which are universally acknowledged or illuminations of statutory provisions which embody such principles. However, there is no doubt that the last twenty years has seen a significant rise in recourse to caselaw in the interpretation of the BGB and as these develop a consistent pattern, some notion of precedent might be followed in practice, though not in strict theory. As the United States experience has shown, once caselaw reaches unwieldy proportions, it becomes necessary to systematise, abstract and collate them in an organised fashion. Hence, the American Restatements resemble the Continental Codes at least in their structured and systematic approach to legal topics wherein they commence with the general principle, and in their technique of providing illustrations to the general principles. The difference is that the American compilations are not statutes and are at best, secondary sources of law.(see further, Chapter 4). In Constitutional terms, Germany now accepts its Constitution as being at the apex of laws, having priority over all other law, and it as it is written, German constitutional law has closer affinity in some senses to the United States than the United Kingdom which has no written constitution. Indeed, in the German Constitutional Court, if a Constitutional Court holds any law as being incompatible with the Constitution (ie the Basic Law) that law will henceforth be applied no longer. Court decisions are therefore regarded as being authoritative pronouncements of the law, which is certainly an unusual feature in a civil law system. Of course, caselaw is also the main source of law in the special administrative courts in France (see above).

xv. Political Unification of Germany

3.2.52 The Unification of the two German States, East and West Germany, which took effect on 3 October, 1990, was the culmination of a process of change exemplified by the opening of the Berlin Wall on 10 November 1989. It occurred with a speed that surprised most commentators and citizens, both German and non-German. It is not intended here to discuss the many legal implications of this dramatic and undoubtedly historic event. This section is by way of a Coda to our discussion on German law, and seeks to highlight the brief background to the division of Germany and to identify some of the more salient implications of German reunification.

(i) The 1945 Position

3.2.53   Following the defeat of Germany in 1945, the Four Powers (the United Kingdom, United States, Soviet Union and France) assumed authority over Germany, including the right to decide its status and frontiers. It was expressly emphasised by them that this was not an annexation. Hence Germany retained her status as a State. The original intention was to prepare Germany for a peace settlement with its former adversaries but unfortunately, co-operation broke down among the Western powers and the Soviet Union, and in 1949, two new States, the Federal Republic of Germany (FRG), and the German Democratic Republic (GDR), which would be effectively under the control and administration of the USSR. On 23 May 1949, the Basic Law (Federal Constitution) (see also,3.5.12 above) came into force in the FRG, according to which the FRG is a democratic, social and federal state based on the rule of law. It is characterised by its separation of powers. The Constitution controls the exercise of all the State's powers.

However, the Four Powers at every critical stage, maintained the existence of rights and responsibilities with regard to Germany as a whole. This continuous assertion of rights over Germany 'as a whole' has caused some writers to think that there was in fact a third German State in addition to East and West Germany, over which all the Four Powers retained certain rights and responsibilities (see, eg, Piotrowicz (1991)p.636).

(ii) The Road to Unification

3.2.54   By 1989, there were two German States which existed relatively independently but not without several wrangles over the true status of each of these States in relation to each other. Nevertheless, West and East Germany entered into negotiations that their mutual relations had to be resolved and the Four Powers were also involved in seeking to establish the place of the sinlge German State in Europe. Two major Treaties were concluded between the FRG and the GDR on the road to political unification. *First*, there was the Treaty of 18 May 1990 establishing a Monetary, Economic and Social Union. It, *inter alia*, recognised the introduction of the social market economy in the GER as the basis for further economic and social development. In addition, the monetary, economic and social union was seen as 'an initial significant step...towards national unity'.

The Preamble to the Treaty provides that the parties are moving towards national unity 'in accordance with Article 23 of the Basic Law ' (Constitution) of the FRG. Article 23 thereof provides that the Basic Law is to apply in all parts of Germany under West german control plus West Berlin. It then declares that 'In other parts of Germany it shall be put into force on their accession.' Of course, this was drafted in 1949 and the feeling in the FRG seems to be that it was the 'real' Germany. By agreeing to this, the East Germans almost appeared to be saying that they agreed with this view. The GDR has, in fact, acceded to the West German Constitution and has become a part of the FRG. As one writer sees it, 'No new State has been created; one has ceased to exist, having been incorporated into the other, which has consequently expanded its territory.' (Piotrowicz (1991) p.639-40)

Secondly, the Treaty on the Establishment of the Unity of Germany was signed on 31 August 1990 and entered into force on 3 October 1990. This agreement actuallly established the unity of the two States and brought about the end of the GDR. It *also* mentions Article 23 of the Basic Law.

This Treaty deals, *inter alia*, with the coming into force of the Basic Law in the former GDR, the amendment of the Basic Law, the harmonisation of laws and the application of treaties of the two States. Piotrowicz and Hailbronner see the accession by the GDR to the FRG as an instance of State succession or universal succession, since this is a case where one State, with its consent, is absorbed by another, 'thereby forfeiting its own separate legal identity' (Piotrowicz (1991) p.640) and where 'with regard to the Federal Republic's treaties only an enlargement of territory has taken place'. (Hailbronner (1991) p.32)

(iii) The Moscow Treaty: Final Settlement

3.2.55   A third Treaty, the Final Settlement with Respect to Germany, also known as the Moscow Treaty, was concluded, after the six countries had met in Bonn, Paris and finally Moscow. These negotiations towards a final settlement were known as the Two-plus-Four Agreements-the two Germanies and the Four Powers. It signifies the final acceptance by Germany that it has an obligation to live within its borders. Article 1(1) states:'The united Germany shall comprise the territory of the Federal Republic of Germany, the German Democratic Republic and the whole of Berlin. Its external borders shall be the borders of the Federal Republic of Germany and the German Democratic Republic and shall be definitive from the date on which the present treaty comes into force. The confirmation of the definitive nature of the borders of the united Germany is an essential element of the peaceful order in Europe.'

This Treaty resolves the controversial question that surrounded the nature of Poland's tenure over the Oder-Neisse territories: they are conclusively Polish territories. Hence, no other State may have any claim to them. The most important point that this Treaty settles is that all the States which might possibly have had any claim to any rights in this matter, have now accepted the border question as definitively resolved under the unification arrangements.

Article 7 of this Treaty also terminates the rights and responsibilities of the Four Powers over Berlin and Germany as a whole; this effectively dissolved all corresponding agreements, decisions, practices and institutions which the related Four Powers were involved in.

On 4 March, 1991, with the deposit of the last ratification of the Treaty by the Soviet Union, Germany became a full sovereign State.

xvi. Unification-Two Years On

3.2.56   A postscript to unification would seem to indicate that the new united Germany has experienced a great deal of problems in coping with the transformation of the former GDR territory of the FRG from a State-run economy to that of a market economy. Two years after the 'unification' there has been a total breakdown in the East German economy, which has also seen rising unemployment, and the continous flow of migration from east to West has not abated, all of which have given rise to even more problems ranging from racial tensions to neo-fascist demonstrations.

All these points are mentioned because one of the central themes of the comparative law methodology is that an understanding of the societal and ideological conditions of a particular jurisdiction is essential if the legal landscape that one is attempting to put together is to be put into its true perspective. No comparatist should therefore be surprised if State intervention does increase if only to establish some semblance of order, organisation and economic progress to the whole of Germany.

xvii. Application of EEC Law in the Former GDR

3.2.57 As a result of the accession of the former GDR to the Basic Law of the FRG, the territory of the former GDR automatically necame part of the EEC without any amendment of the Treaty of Rome. Indeed, the European Council has confirmed the legal integration of the GDR as an enlargement of the territory of an existing Member State and the integration became effective as soon as the unification had been legally established, subject to the necessary transitional arrangements. (European Council Doc/90/1 of 28 April 1990. By virtue of Article 227 of the EEC Treaty, EEC law takes immediate effect in the new German *Lander*, since it provides that the EEC Treaty is applicable to the Member States in their respective territories unless special provisions like Article 227, paragraph 2, apply. Hence, as Hailbronner points out, the principle of 'moving treaty frontiers' may be applied to supranational organisations like the European Community in the same way as it does to States (Hailbronner (1991) p.37).

C. OVERVIEW OF THE CIVIL LAW TRADITION

3.3 Although the oldest extant legal tradition in the Western world, the civil law tradition continues to go from strength to strength, while continuing to adapt to changed and changing social, economic, and political situations. It has developed different sub-traditions and, seen as a broad church, encompasses both the French and German legal traditions. It has exported its ideology and legal ideas throughout the world and spawned many imitators and acquired many admirers. It proceeds from principles and thinks in concepts and, in German law, in sophisticated abstractions. Yet its caselaw has been invaluable to its need to adapt to different conditions and to develop progressive legal concepts. It has influenced the law of the European Community in structure, style of judgment and ethos and it will have to be seen how much it will form of the new European law that is at the crossroads and, in the view of some, on the brink of being subsumed under a 'European Law' banner which will eventually destroy its inherent beauty and priceless heritage.

It is undoubtedly 'converging' with the common law in various ways, not least in its increased reliance on caselaw, albeit still citing cases as illustrations of general principles. However, in many ways, it remains very much a tradition in its own right, in its Constitutional protection of the individual, in vigorous moral and ethical principles, separate and specialised courts, attitudes towards access to justice and of course, in the pre-eminence it accords to individual liberty.

SELECTIVE BIBLIOGRAPHY

Pringsheim 'The Inner Relationship between English and Roman Law'
    (1933) Camb. LJ 347

Lawson   A COMMON LAWYER LOOKS AT THE CIVIL LAW (1950)

Buckland   ROMAN LAW AND COMMON LAW (1953)

David and de Vries THE FRENCH LEGAL SYSTEM (1958)

Amos and Walton INTRODUCTION TO FRENCH LAW (1967)
        (Lawson/Anton/Brown)

Smith 'Roman Law' in AN INTRODUCTION TO LEGAL SYSTEMS (1968) (ed. Derrett)

Dawson   THE ORACLES OF THE LAW (1968)

Rudden 'Courts and Codes in England, France and Soviet Russia'
[1974] 48 Tul. LR 1010

De Vries and Schneider CIVIL LAW AND THE ANGLO-AMERICAN LAWYER (1976)

Lawson   THE COMPARISON:(1977)Vol. II in European Studies in Law

Merryman THE CIVIL LAW TRADITION (1977)

Mehren and Gordley THE CIVIL LAW SYSTEM (1977)

David   ENGLISH AND FRENCH LAW (1980)

David and Brierley MAJOR LEGAL SYSTEMS IN THE WORLD TODAY (1985)

Zweigert and Kotz AN INTRODUCTION TO COMPARATIVE LAW (1987) vol I

Robinson, Fergus and Gordon AN INTRODUCTION TO EUROPEAN LEGAL   HISTORY (1987)

Piotrowicz 'The Arithmetic of German Unification: Three into One Does Go' [1991] ICLQ 635

Hailbronner 'Legal Aspects of the Unification of the Two German States' (1991) EJIL 18

Varga COMPARATIVE LEGAL CULTURES (1992)

International Encyclopedia of Comparative Law: vols. I and II

CHAPTER FOUR

The English Common Law Tradition

A. INTRODUCTION

4.0   The English common law system, with its characteristic traditions, is rightly regarded as one of the two major legal systems in the world, as well as one of the two most influential. Although not the oldest legal system in existence, it is the oldest national law in existence, common to a whole kingdom. It is also comparable to the oldest, the civil law system, in the extent of its spread throughout the world, and in its remarkable influence, having been adopted by a wide range of countries and cultures, even in their post-colonial era. As with the civil law system, the English legal system has been spawned from a particular sequence of historical events, a set of distinctive legal sources, ideologies, doctrines, institutions, and a distinctive mode of legal thought which collectively constitute an English common *legal tradition*. This legal tradition was successfully 'transplanted' in many countries throughout the world which are culturally as well as geographically and linguistically different from England and English culture. This legal transplantation (Watson) is a testimony to its genius and its adaptability, particularly where the 'reception' of English law was not legislatively imposed but voluntarily adopted.

Initially, reception of English law was the result of British colonisation, trade missions, and the dominance of the British empire during vital periods in world history. However, several former colonies, well into their post-colonial era, and after their 'nationalist' stage of development, continue to use the common law approach and legal philosophy in their legal system.

Key events which shaped English legal history were the early *centralisation of courts*, mainly brought about by Henry II, wherein the royal courts (the common law courts) became the main source of the law common to the whole country, the *writ system* which ensured a particular style of development geared to existing writs, which were later supplemented by the creation of the Courts of Chancery, which developed a separate body of law (known as 'Equity'), both of which gave rise to a remedy-orientated, pragmatic approach which had no need for scholarly input or advice. Therefore English law developed through judicial decisions (or 'caselaw') and 'Equity' could, up to the late nineteenth century, only be administered by the Courts of Chancery. Equity and the common law were eventually 'fused' by the Supreme Court of Judicature Acts of 1873-5 in their jurisdictional application but continue to exist as separate bodies of law, which may now be utilised by one and the same court.

English law never 'received' Roman law in the way that it was received in civil law countries. The rigidity of the common law procedures, the need to conform to the framework that had been created, and the centralised courts, all helped to mould a diversity of local customs and primitive Anglo-Saxon practices into a law that was followed by the whole country, which thus became a common, unified law.

It has been said that the common law 'dates from time immemorial' but it really dates from about the middle to the late twelfth century when *a* common law was identifiable and could be said to be in place. Furthermore, at the time of the twelfth and thirteenth century, when there was a *frisson* of Roman law 'intellectualism' running through continental Europe, consisting of learned treatises on the *Corpus Juris*, Romano-Canonical treatises on procedure, customary law and royal legislation, all of which had undergone a massive absorption of Roman law, English law had already experienced its era of 'modernisation'. The English common law tradition and the common law courts were already established and were, by that time, impervious to any 'reception' of Roman law or indeed, any foreign law.

English law also created *prerogative writs* (*certiorari*, *mandamus* and prohibition) which enabled administrative decisions of State organs and officials to be challenged, which therefore rendered unnecessary any separate administrative courts such as those that developed in civil law countries.

Examples of common law jurisdictions are Australia, the United States, Singapore, Malaysia, New Zealand, large parts of Africa, India, Pakistan, South East Asia, and North America. Despite acquiring independence, several Commonwealth nations have maintained links with the United Kingdom and although they have adopted written Constitutions, their judges have continued to interpret these in accordance with typical English legal methods, doctrines and legal conventions.

B. TERMINOLOGY

4.1   A *legal tradition* is not the same thing as a legal system although the legal system inevitably forms part of the legal tradition and *vice versa*. A legal system (unless it is a *parent legal system* or distinctive *legal family*) usually consists of an operational set of legal rules, procedures, and institutions which may belong to a so-called major legal system (ie parent legal system) such as the civil law or common law systems. However, a *legal tradition* suggests certain forms of legal practice, or legal rules or norms, substantive or procedural, which have been established over a period of time and whose origins are not of recent vintage. It also suggests a well-defined, consistent, and reasonably well-established, 'historically conditioned set of attitudes'

(Merryman (1977)) about the relationship between legal rules, law and society. The term 'legal tradition' will be used particularly, but not exclusively, in referring to those legal systems which are not the parent legal system or family, because this is precisely the type of context in which the term is most appropriate.

The term *'common law'* may refer to: (i) the English legal system developed in, applicable to, and common to England (and Wales, but not Scotland); (ii) that part of English law which was created by the king's courts, or *common law courts* (ie and developed as caselaw) in England from about the twelfth century , rather than 'statute law' or the law enacted by parliament *as opposed to* the body of rules and principles of *equity*, as established by decisions of the Courts of Equity (ie or, as they were otherwise known, courts of Chancery) which began to be develop from around the fourteenth century; (iii) the modern usage which includes English cases and statutes, *including* principles developed and established by common law courts and the Courts of courts of equity; and (iv) that part of English law which has been 'received' by a given jurisdiction and which applies therein either through colonisation or *via* unilateral and voluntary enactment by that jurisdiction.

The common law should also be distinguished from international law, which applies between States, and canon or ecclesiastical law, which derived from the Church and was administered by the church courts. Although the common law is not derived from Roman law, it is, in many respects, closer to ancient Roman law in some of its jurisprudential content and procedural practices than the modern civil law systems.

If the law on a particular topic happens to be identical under English law and in American jurisdictions, it is frequently referred to as the *Anglo-American* legal position. Despite the radical 'Americanisation' of the law in the United States, English law continues to be a major source of law or at least still represents the primary source of law in relation to several major areas of law in the United States. It may be argued, with some justification, that in many cases, it is no longer accurate to use the term 'Anglo-American' law in the way that has been done since about the early twentieth century since American law has now developed a character of its own and diverges from the English common law in so many different ways (see Atiyah and Summers in *Form and Substance in Anglo-American Law* (1987), an Anglo-American academic enterprise).

C. THE ENGLISH COMMON LAW TRADITION

4.2   The key features of the common law tradition are: (i) a case-based system of law which functions through analogical reasoning; (ii) an hierarchical doctrine of precedent; (iii) sources of law which include statutes as well as cases;(iv) typical institutions like the trust, tort law, estoppel, and agency. Although some of these institutions appear in one form or another in other legal systems, the 'trust' concept is unique to the common law system. Civil law jurisdictions have utilised a general notion of *unjustified enrichment* (see Zweigert and Kotz ((1977) vol.II,pp.208ff.) to cope with situations where English law has utilised a 'trust' concept; (v) a distinctive improvisatory and pragmatic legal style; (vi) categories of law such as contract and tort as separate bodies of law as well as two main bodies of law: common law and equity, which may nevertheless be administered by the same court. Remarkably, in classical Roman law there also existed two bodies of law that bore a remarkable resemblance to English common law and courts of equity, but the fact that modern civil law, as embodied in its codes, is a product of the last two centuries, and was able to combine precise general rules and equitable principles, rendered an 'equitable' jurisdiction unnecessary in civil law countries; and (vii) no substantive or structural public/private law distinction as that which exists in civil law systems.

The common law tradition is typically identified with a *case-based system*, but although cases play a dominant role, the primary sources of English law include not just *caselaw*, which is a body of principles derived from *court decisions* regulated by the *doctrine of precedent* (*stare decisis*); but also *statutes*, which is the law contained in legislative enactments. In more recent times in England, legislation has become not just an authoritative source of law, but sometimes *the* primary source of law where no cases are relevant to the issue at hand, or even where decided cases do exist. The law applicable may depend on the particular facts of the case and/or the interpretation of the 'intention of the legislature' in the statute concerned.

The *doctrine of precedent* governs this caselaw system. Thus, *decisions of higher courts are generally binding on lower courts*, a practice which probably originated around 1800 when law reports acquired a degree of reliability sufficient to sustain the consistent application of such a doctrine. That part of the case which is considered binding on a subsequent court is the *ratio decidendi* (the reason for the decision) which is broadly the principle established by the case. Any other comments of the judge are *prima facie*, classified as *obiter dicta* or comments uttered in passing which are *not* strictly binding on the court. However, depending on the particular area of law, the ultimate status of a judicial pronouncement may depend on what a *subsequent* higher court says about it.

The English Court of Appeal generally disposes of between 800 to 900 cases a year and the House of Lords hears between 50 to 70 appeals. This may be contrasted with the thousands of cases (25,000 cases in 1987) which the French Court of Cassation handles per year. However, the courts in France are regionalised, they have far more judges generally and particularly in the *Cour de cassation*, and are more specialist. There is, it would seem, a very different attitude between civil and common law to the right of appeal.

The typical *common law style* may be called *pragmatic* and improvisatory, *primarily geared to the adjudication and resolution of disputes*. One reason for this is that English law is not codified, in the civil law sense of being contained in enacted collections of authoritative and *prima facie* exhaustive rules of law. Civil law, *ex facie*, is codified in the authoritative sense. Countries like France, Germany, Italy, Spain and Portugal all possess a collection of Codes, including a Civil Code, a Commercial Code, a Code of Civil Procedure, a Penal Code and a Code of Criminal Procedure, but England has not, by tradition, enacted any code on the lines of the Continental codes, and the only area in which it has attempted to 'codify' the law is in commercial law, and, to a certain extent, company law. Unlike France and Germany, England has no written Constitution or any comparable, comprehensive piece of constitutional legislation.

Although statutes are an authoritative and burgeoning source of law in English law, the typical English legal attitude towards statutes, with some rare exceptions, is that statutes are passed to consolidate or clarify existing law, and are intended to build on existing caselaw, which may legitimately be invoked to interpret any ambiguities or uncertain meanings in a statute. Hence, while civil law codes (and therefore judges) think in terms of *solutions* to problems, derived from systematic and authoritative expositions of the law and work towards solutions, from general clauses and principles, English law judges see their primary function as the arbiters of disputes and that their task is to *resolve disputes*. They therefore pay special attention to the particular *facts of a case*, examine the legal question to be decided (the '*issue*'), and make a ruling based on a careful study of whether that case 'fits' into any previously decided case whose facts happened to be similar. If they found that there was a similar case decided by a higher court (such as the Court of Appeal or the House of Lords), they would usually apply the *ratio* of that case to the present one.

If an English judge did not wish to follow a previous decision, he has the option of '*distinguishing*' it (ie decide it is not applicable), on the basis of its facts or law or both. If there is a statute that appears to govern the instant case which is in conflict with a judicial decision, the rule is that the statute would prevail.

Another source of law in Britain today is the *law of the European Communities*, which is supposed to take direct effect in the United Kingdom without the need for implementing legislation to be passed. This is the result of Britain's accession to the Treaties establishing the European Communities and the UK European Communities Act 1972.

Academic or scholarly writings are cited occasionally in English courts but not usually in a favourable light. Doctrinal writing in common law countries does not have the status of authoritative sources of law as in Continental countries, but the situation may well change, though probably not in the immediate future.

4.2.1   The public law/ private law distinction was recognised in England at least by the late nineteenth century. In civil law countries, it is crucial to the *process of allocation of the court which has jurisdiction to hear the case*, whereas English common law makes a distinction between the *procedure to be used* depending on whether the purpose of the case is to enforce the *public duties of a state agency or state body*, or the *private rights of a citizen*. English academic writers have used the term '*Public Law*' to cover both constitutional and adminstrative law. When English lawyers think of public law, it is thought of *primarily in terms of the application for judicial review*.

The practical importance of the distinction in English law is that if a private citizen wishes to question the exercise of a public law function by an administrative body, the special procedure for doing so is known as an *application for judicial review*. This will not be heard by any special administrative court, since there is no separate administrative court system *within the 'ordinary' civil courts' system*. However, there are *specialist administrative tribunals*, but these are still subject to the normal review and appeal powers of the ordinary courts of judicature and have never really caught the imagination of the general English public.

Judicial Review is similar to the Court of Cassation's powers which merely pronounces on the legality of actions, and the court has no power to substitute the original decision with its own. There are no English public law rules separate from the general principles of common law. Contracts between private citizens and the State will be subject to the same principles as those which govern contracts between citizens. The English judiciary do not generally see a sharp and clear dividing line between public and private law. This was confirmed by two House of Lords cases, *Davy* v. *Spelthorne* [1983] 3 All ER 278 and *Roy* v. *Kensington and Chelsea and Westminster Family Practitioner Committee* [1992] 1 All ER 705.

However, in most continental legal systems, apart from criminal matters, the jurisdiction of the ordinary courts is generally limited to disputes governed by private law. When the ordinary courts found it difficult to cope with the increasing volume of public law disputes, special administrative courts were set up in France, headed by its *Conseil d'Etat* and this was then imitated in other Continental countries.

4.2.2   The existence of *special prerogative orders* (formerly prerogative writs) as well as *tort actions against public officials* who would be sued in their individual capacity, meant that there were legal devices available for dealing with alleged abuses of power by government agencies and officials. No immunity attaches to public officials simply because of their status. *Certiorari* prohibits a tribunal from exceeding its jurisdiction and *mandamus* compels a government official to carry out his duty. The writ of *prohibition* can prevent a tribunal from exceeding or abusing its jurisdiction.

4.2.3 Although the ordinary courts have jurisdiction over matters of public and private law alike, there are many hundreds of *specialist administrative courts*, called *tribunals*, of which there are seventy different types. The law established and developed by these administrative, industrial, and domestic *tribunals*, often consisting of professional and lay assessors, which deal primarily with small cases, has been growing very rapidly and is notable for its sheer volume. These have been created to determine claims by citizens against public authorities or *vice versa* and deal *solely* with public law matters. They exercise administrative and/or judicial functions but have limited or special jurisdiction and were created to provide a means of settling disputes efficiently and speedily, without the formalities of a court of law. Tribunals hear about six times the number of contested disputes heard by the High Court and county courts courts of law. Their proliferation has been a distinctive feature of the development of judicial administration in Britain over recent decades and the workload of these tribunals greatly exceeds that of the High Court and county courts. (*The Royal Commission on Legal Services* (1979) Cmnd 7648, para. 15.1, Tables 2.1. and 2.2). Their main defects are the lack or limitations of rights of appeal, the limited efficacy of claimants' remedies and preclusion of legal representation by certain administrative tribunals.

The French *tribunal* does not correspond to the English term 'tribunal' in its narrow sense and none of the French terms (*cour, juridiction* and *tribunal*) are reflected in the English language. The French *Conseil d'Etat*, and the hierarchy of administrative courts represent the deluxe model of administrative courts on the Continent and has earned deserved admiration from most countries in continental Europe. The Councillors of State are legally trained and are competent to adjudicate on all conflicts in which public authorities at whatever level are involved. These courts have built up an imposing body of caselaw, and have generally succeeded in protecting the citizens' civil rights and pecuniary interests against the errors of bureaucracy and officialdom. They have the right to *annul* administrative acts, decisions and regulations and have the right to award damages to those who have suffered injury or damage as a result of a wrongful act on the part of a public servant acting in the course of his duties.

In the United States there is a multiplicity of administrative tribunals and regulatory agencies which deal with most areas of social and economic life. Access to these bodies is, as in Britain, easier and cheaper than to the ordinary courts. A major preoccupation of the US Supreme Court has been the review of administrative actions. Around one-third of its full-opinion cases generally deals with such issues whereas only a quarter of the Supreme Court's cases have adjudicated on constitutional law issues proper.

4.2.4   The Civil law and Commercial law distinction, common in civil law systems, does not have a great deal of significance in English law. In English law, the subject may be fragmented into subjects such as Agency, Bailments, and Sale of Goods. Commercial law, having developed separately from Common Law, is now part of the English Common Law and 'consists in an extension of the general principles of contract law to special transactions of a mercantile character' (Gutteridge 'Contract and Commercial Law' (1935) 51 LQR 91). For the most part, common lawyers do not draw a sharp distinction between civil law and commercial law and most textbooks indicate that such a distinction is either not perceived or, by not being mentioned, is actually obscured (see Weir *International Encyclopedia of Comparative Law* (1971) p.111 and books cited therein).

D. THE COMMON LAW IN THE UNITED STATES

i. Preliminary Observations

4.3   When we look at how the English common law has fared in the United States, several points should be borne in mind. Firstly, the law of the United States comprises Federal and State laws as well as Constitutional law. It is therefore an example of English law being transplanted into a legal and constitutional set-up which is radically different from the common law homeland. Secondly, both English law and the laws of the United States have now reached a stage in legal evolution when a long, hard look needs to be taken to decide if it is any longer legitimate to maintain this 'Anglo-American' unity of appellation. Thirdly, by virtue of the first point, given the complexity of the territory, its unique cocktail of foreign influences, systems within systems, as in Louisiana, and its immense size and pace of development, it is very rarely possible to state what the 'American law' is on a particular subject. Clearly, this often varies from State to State, but it might also depend on whether there is a possible conflict between State law, Federal law or Constitutional law. Clearly, all these factors make meaningful comparisons difficult.

The United States has undergone profound changes not just in technology, economics and culture but in its development of concepts and principles of law which have transformed its legal scenario, with themes like individual liberty, checks against abuse of power and the pre-eminence of the Constitution. Many articles and tomes have been written about these far-reaching and significant developments. The following section merely presents an overview of a selection of areas for comparison.

ii. Linguistic Issues

4.3.1   The famous observation by the English playwright, George Bernard Shaw, that England and America were 'separated by a common language' rings true today even more than it did nearly fifty years ago. At the most basic level, there are problems of translation-not least because there is 'American English' and also 'American legal language' which is not always equivalent to English legal language. For example, in American usage, 'High Court' refers to the United States Supreme Court whereas in England it refers to the only court of first instance with unlimited jurisdiction. Another striking example is the term 'Judicial Review' which we have examined earlier with regard to English law where it refers to the power of the English High Court to scrutinise the legality (but not the merits) of a decision taken by an inferior court or a public body. In America, judicial review is 'the power of any court to hold unconstitutional and hence unenforceable any law, any official action based upon it and any illegal action by a public official that it deems to be in conflict with the ...United States Constitution' (Abraham (1952) p.251). On a broader comparative note, it is a power that *ordinary* courts possess in Australia, Brazil, Burma, Canada, India, Pakistan and Japan.

iii. History of American Law: Some Observations

(i) Early Legal Development

4.3.2   The story of the development of American law in the fifty different States, has been told elsewhere and it is not my intention here to recount it in any sort of detail. However, certain historical events may be highlighted which may give some insights into the way it has developed since that first English settlement occurred in 1607 at Jamestown, Virginia.

Legal development in the original thirteen colonies occurred at different stages, since the colonies were established at different times and each had its own separate charter, being separate units under the English Crown. As with other British charters of this nature, most of the colonies' charters provided for limited local autonomy. But there was diversity as to the extent of Crown control, and the dates of settlement.

English settlers brought with them the law with which they were most familiar. Thus, if they came from provincial towns and villages the law they were most conversant with was really that of local customs as they existed in their boroughs, manors and villages, not the 'common law' administered by the royal courts of Westminster. But the English common law was increasingly utilised when society became more complex, which was inevitable when the population grew, and shipping, commerce and industry also developed. Appeals from the colonial courts were still directed to London, but ecclesiastical courts were never established in the colonies. Significantly, the institution of trial by jury in both crminal and civil cases was adopted with great enthusiasm and one of the key grievances of the colonists in their struggle with England was their resistance to any attempts by the British Government to shift political cases to vice-admiralty courts where there were no juries.

(ii) The First Continental Congress

4.3.3   In 1774, the First Continental Congress was formed and met in Philadelphia and this comprised about fifty-five delegates from almost all the colonies. This was one of the first concrete signs of union among the colonies and war against England. There was strong feeling among the colonists that the individual rights of the English and the Bill of Rights of 1689 should be followed and introduced into the American colonies.

(iii) Post-Revolutionary Status of English Law

4.3.4   Once independence was won in 1776, it was clear that the English common law had become the basis of the legal systems in each of the thirteen colonies. By that time, English law had come to be highly regarded and indeed essential to the needs of increasing commercial enterprise and to support effectively grievances that were expressed to the Crown. Each colony had a Bar of trained, able and respected professionals, capable of working with a technical and refined system of rules. The colonial legal profession had also achieved considerable economic success and social standing. Twenty-five of the fifty-six signatories of the Declaration of Independence were lawyers. (see Farnsworth (1987) p.8).

But different 'cut-off' dates (as to when English law would cease to apply) were statutorily enacted by different colonies. Indeed, after the Revolution, some colonies exhibited a *reaction against the application of English law* and their legislatures prohibited the citation of English decisions which had been rendered after independence. The adoption of a written constitution was seen as a break with English tradition, Louisiana, when purchased from the French in 1803, and admitted to the Federation in 1812, continued to maintain the French law tradition, and indeed traces of its period of Spanish rule. Louisiana adopted several codifications based on the French model, including the French Civil Code.

Around this time, there was a period of uncertainty caused by anti-British sentiment, since there was no adequate body of American caselaw to replace the 'banned' English decisions, the American Bar lost a number of their most able lawyers and despite the fact that law reports began to be published at the end of the eighteenth century, they were too few in number to be used effectively. French and Roman law were considered as possibilities to replace the gap left in the law, and European writers were cited as authorities especially in the field of conflict of laws and commercial law. But civil law failed to make its way into the United States primarily because there were insufficient numbers of judges who were conversant with foreign languages, English reports and treatises were still available and the French Civil Code did not appear until the beginning of the nineteenth century.

In early American legal history, English common law principles were applicable only insofar as they did not contradict the constitutional, political, or geographic conditions of the new States (see Rheinstein: Int.Enc.CL: vol.I p.U-137). However, the law actually administered was apparently a 'simplified version of the law of England' (Rheinstein, ibid.) The law that was being relied upon was gleaned from books such as Blackstone's *Commentaries of the Common Law of England*, which first appeared in America in 1803 and acquired a wide American readership. This ensured that legal language, legal methodology and basic concepts of private law in America were to remain firmly rooted in the English legal tradition.

But there was no formal or organised system of legal education in mid-eighteenth century America and it was not until the beginning of the nineteenth century that the American law school and scholarly writing tradition began, with the establishment in 1829 of the Harvard Law School by Justice Joseph Story who wrote a set of treatises on the main branches of the law. A steady flow and ever-burgeoning number of textbooks, many written by professors of the increasing number of law schools, marked the cooperation that was to distinguish the special relationship between legal practice and scholarship, which has played a dominant part in shaping the development of the law in the United States.

The early part of the nineteenth century witnessed a revival of interest and a return to the English tradition with the publication of the works of James Kent and Joseph Story which eventually replaced Blackstone. The growth of agriculture and trade began to dominate the economy as efforts were directed to shaping English law to fit the westward expansion that had gathered momentum. The foundations of contracts, torts, sale of goods, real property and conflict of laws were laid during this period, mainly by a reappraisal of pre-Revolutionary English law but sometimes the law was derived simply from local customs and usages. This occurred in the case of farmers and gold miners, and cattle-raising where English principles were adapted to suit the different conditions.

Codification was seen as an important issue in the nineteenth century and while English common law was seen as unwieldy, the French Code was considered an impressive model. Codification first took root in Massachusetts, which was followed by New York. The famous Field Code of Civil Procedure drafted by David Dudley Field, a lawyer, was accepted by New York in 1848, and codification started to gain impetus. But by 1865, Field's Civil Law Code was greeted less enthusiastically because the codification movement had begun to lose its popularity.

(iv) Diversity of American Cultural Influences

4.3.5 The diversity of religions, nationalities and economic groups gives some idea of the range of cultural, religious and linguistic influences America was enriched by. Although the English were in the majority, there were also Dutch, French, German, Irish, Scots, and Swedish settlers. Of course, several States were under Spanish rule and so there is also a trace of this heritage in the law of marital property and the law relating to Spanish-Mexican land grants. But all the community property states (such as Louisiana, Texas, New Mexico, Arizona, California, Washington, Idaho and Nevada) have experienced modification and modernisation of the old laws. The Spanish tradition continues to play a dominant role in the Commonwealth of Puerto Rico which was acquired from Spain after the Spanish-American War in 1898. Spanish remains the predominant language in Puerto Rico but Common Law concepts govern most private law fields of endeavour, the law of procedure and a large area of public law matters.

(v) Constitutional Developments

4.3.6 There was no official reception of English statute law since 1776 and English Common law developments after that date were not considered as having to form part of American law. In 1776, state constitutions began to be adopted, but not without considerable political debates and bitter inter-state hostilities. A movement away from the loose Confederation gathered momentum among the delegates at the Constitutional Convention in 1787 who were seeking to preserve the union. A vitally important decision taken at the Convention was that there should be a central government with extended powers designed to have control over individuals, not States.

In September 1787, the Federal Constitution was signed and submitted to Congress. It become effective with a two-thirds majority of the states in July 1788 and the first President, George Washington, was inaugurated in April 1789. It contains the notion that the people are sovereign and that their government is based on a social contract. However, there was no guarantee of basic human rights. This was soon introduced under ten amendments to the Constitution which were proposed by Congress in 1789, and ratified in 1791.

(vi) Separation of Powers

4.3.7 Three Articles in the Constitution expressly delineated the three major governmental powers: legislative, judicial and executive which represented the concept of the doctrine of 'checks and balances', or *separation of* *powers* between these three limbs. Americans were undoubtedly familiar with the writings of Locke and Montesquieu and they had long experienced the proactical operation of the doctrine in their own governments in the colonial period. Although the distribution of governmental powers was contained in the Constitution, it was only in 1803, with the landmark case of *Marbury* v. *Madison* (1803) 5 US (1 Cranch) 137, that the scope of judicial review of these powers was clarified. In 1789 Congress had passed the First Judiciary Act which appeared to contemplate federal judicial review of of state court decisions in certain cases. The Act implemented the judiciary Article of the Constitution by creating lower federal courts and by defining their jurisdiction together with that of the Supreme Court. The new federal courts began to declare state legislation as contrary to the federal Constitution itself.

In the famous case of *Marbury* v. *Madison* (above), the Supreme Court refused to give effect to a section of a federal statute, on the ground that Congress had exceeded the powers granted it by the Constitution when it enacted that statute. The Court held that its review powers under the First Judiciary Act 1789 was not limited to the review of State law for its constitutionality but included examination and review of federal legislation. Federal government had limitations on its powers as defined under the Constitution and thus federal legislation would be subject to *judicial review* in the federal courts. This decision was not based on any express provision in the Constitution but was derived from the basic philosophical approach of the Americans honed by colonial experience of the problems caused by excess of powers and from Constitutional tradition. It gave effect to the principle of separation of powers. *Fletcher* v. *Peck* (1810) 10 US (6 Cranch) 87 was subsequently decided by the Supreme Court in 1810, which confirmed the authority of the federal court under the Federal Constitution to review the constitutionality of state legislation. These decisions helped to unify the law in this area, making the principle of separation of powers an actionable claim for the observance of the 'rule of law' in the United States. Equally, a state court can also refuse to enforce a state or federal statute on the grounds that it violates the federal Constitution but its interpretation is subject to review by the US Supreme Court.

(vii) State Law and the Federal Courts

4.3.8   Another important matter is the scope of powers of the federal courts. The essential point is that federal law is supreme only in limited areas. In either a state or federal court, an action based on a right derived from state law may be met by a defence based on federal law. Alternatively, a case based on state law may be met by a defence based on federal law. Hence federal courts frequently apply state law but the role of state law in the federal courts should be noted briefly.

The landmark case of *Swift* v. *Tyson* (1842) 41 US (16 Pet.) 1, saw the US Supreme Court recognising the duty of the federal courts to give effect, on questions within the law-making competence of the states, to State law that was 'local' in character, for example, State statutes and decisions which interpreted these. However, where the State law was regarded as part of the 'general law' or general provisions of the common law, the federal courts were under a duty to ascertain the relevant legal principles independently and to apply them irrespective of what the courts of the particular state would have done.

The Supreme Court therefore declared that the federal courts have developed a 'federal common law' that was uniform throughout the United States, which finds its ultimate expression in US Supreme Court decisions. This federal common law was therefore binding on federal courts but not on state courts. The outcome of litigation might therefore depend upon which court, state or federal, heard the case and many felt that this would cause uncertainty, injustice due to 'forum shopping', and the frustration of state policies.

Swift v. *Tyson* was eventually overruled by the US Supreme Court in *Erie Railroad Co.* v. *Tompkins* (1938) 304 US 64, which held that that the Constitution of the United States did not empower the federal courts to create any common law of their own, that the common law was entirely state law and that in in areas reserved by the Constitution to the states, the federal courts were bound to apply state law just as they were bound to apply the statute law of states. Subsequent cases have established that the exclusive state law character applied not only to the substantive common law but also to the branch of the common law known as the Conflict of Laws. A nationally uniform law of Conflict of Laws thus exists only in relation to those matters which belong to the sphere of federal regulation, as indicated under the Constitution.

In cases involving choice of law, in order to determine what foreign law to apply, the federal court must, in cases where it is giving effect to state law, follow the choice of law principles of the state in which it sits. In cases involving a diversity of jurisdiction, therefore, a federal court adjudicating claims arising from state law must arrive at substantially the same outcome as would a court of the state in which it sits. The law in this area appears to be unnecessarily complex and could probably be resolved by legislation. It will not, however, be a simple matter to reconcile the difficult jurisdictional and Constitutional issues which bedevil this area.

The demands of a rapidly increasing industrial society led to the need for a stable system of law which could cope with the developments in corporations, public service companies, railroads and insurance. During the final quarter of the nineteenth century, the judge's role changed from a law-creator to a systematic applicator and interpreter of the law. It is therefore only in the 1800s that it is possible to speak of any sort of distinctive 'American law' existing as such.

By the end of the nineteenth century, the general consensus was that the system of judicial decision on a case-by-case basis had failed to match the speed of political and economic change. Legislation began to come into its own as an instrument of change, consolidation and adaptation and was used extensively to cope with the needs of a newly emergent society.

(viii) Reception of Equity

4.3.9   The move to integrate law and equity began in 1848 with the adoption of the Field Code in New York. This provided for a single civil action and laid down that 'the distinction between actions at law and suits in equity, and the forms of all such actions and suits heretofore existing are abolished.' Fusion of the two systems was accomplished for the federal courts in 1838 and in 1947, New Jersey reorganised its court system, and retained a Chancery Division. The only states which still administer law and equity separately are Alabama, Arkansas, Delaware, Mississippi and Tennessee.

iv. Uniformity and Diversity in American Law

(i) Continuing Differences

4.3.10   There is no common Supreme Court of Law and Equity, since the Supreme Court has limited itself to matters of constitutional importance which involve the Constitution of the United States and to federal legislation, including international treaties. For most States, the supreme courts' decisions are final. But there is a considerable diversity among the various States in: (i) their matrimonial property regimes, where the majority of states have separation of assets (as in English law) but eight States of the South and West(as well as Puerto Rico) have community property regimes; (ii) the law of real property; (iii) the laws of divorce.

However, the state laws have all been built on the basis of the English common law, with the same conceptual and institutional framework are all applied by the judiciary who follow the same basic approach, and procedure.

A simplification of procedure has taken place so that there is far less formality in court proceedings, and a number of changes were made to abolish professional monopolies, and to make the criminal law more humane. Judges are publicly elected in the United States for set periods ranging from ten to twenty years and have to justify their re-election. The judge has been characterised by Roscoe Pound as a 'social engineer' who can only perform his job effectively if he understands the full circumstances of each case and the full consequences of his decision. Hence a notable difference in American court judgments, apart from the single judge delivering the main judgment in appellate cases, is the court's approach to medical information, psychiatric information, economic considerations and criminological facts. English courts also refer to medical and psychiatric information but the significant difference is that all the experts called in an American court are seen as participating in a joint exercise to assist the court to ascertain the 'best' decision to be made in any individual case. A somewhat wider range of experts may be called in than in a comparable English court.

Finally, legal education in the United States is often conducted not just by law teachers but jointly with political scientists, sociologists and doctors, which indicate a far more multi-disciplinary approach to law.

(ii) Unifying Influences

4.3.11   Three influences may be identified as unifying factors which have served to preserve the fundamental unity of of the laws of the United States. First, the National Conference of Commissioners on Uniform State Laws (NCCUSL); secondly, the American Law Institute and thirdly, the legal scholars or doctrinal writers.

The NCCUSL has specialist commissioners who prepare draft statutes which, when approved by the Conference, are then recommended for adoption by all states. These commissioners are appointed by the governors of all the states in pursuance of the original objective of the American Bar Association, to promote 'uniformity of legislation throughout the Union'. This organisation can only recommend adoption to national legislatures, which they may or may not adopt, with or without amendment. It has been most successful in the area of commercial law where, in conjunction with the American Law Institute, it produced a Uniform Commercial Code which has been adopted in 1967 by all states except Louisiana, which has only adopted parts thereof. Revision of the Code has also been effected. The Code has four hundred sections, is divided into nine major substantive articles which correspond to the 'Books' of the Civil Law and these are divided into 'parts' which correspond to 'titles' in civil law codes and these are further divided into 'sections' which correspond to 'articles'. It fills over seven hundred pages containing comments and took over a decade to prepare. It is perhaps the most modern collection of commercial law concepts currently available.

The second organisation which assists in unifying American law is the American Law Institute, which was organised in 1923 to overcome the uncertainty of American law, and consists of a group of about eighteen hundred lawyers, judges and law teachers. They have worked on a wide variety of projects, each under the supervision of a prominent scholar in the field, but their most outstanding achievement has been the Restatement of Law, which is an extensive collection of laws covering the following fields: Agency, Conflict of Laws, Contracts, Foreign Relations of the US, Judgments, property, Restitution, Security, Torts and Trusts. The Restatement also resembles civil law-type codes. The common law rules are stated in a systematic and precise style. Each section is followed by explanatory comments and illustrations. The drafts of these Laws were subjected to scrutiny by several bodies before being published under the name and auspices of the Institute.

The Restatement does not possess official authority and does not have the status of legislation. On questions on which there is no universally accepted legal principle or rule, the Restaters selected the one which they considered most accurate in reflecting the common law tradition and current policy. Nevertheless, it has been cited to many judges over many years who, in accepting the validity of many of its rules, have contributed to the unification of 'American principles'. It is regarded as representing the considered opinion of some of the leading American scholars and although it is not followed as a Code, it appears to enjoy a stronger 'weighting' than a doctrinal treatise. The American Codes now far outnumber the civil law Codes. Nevertheless, it is still true to say that despite superficial similarity, the American Code *cannot* be equated with civil law codes and really represent a half-way house between a full-blown authoritative and binding source of law and a mere source of reference. They are certainly closer to English style legislation in their intention to clarify and consolidate the law. The rate of citation of the Restatements to appellate courts-4,000 times a year-suggests that they exercise an appreciable influence towards unification of the law.

These Restatements are guides to the law particularly for foreign lawyers but there is no guarantee that a stated legal principle is the current principle governing an area of law. The usual recourse to caselaw and statutes still needs to be made to ensure its accuracy.

The final unifying influence is that of legal scholars who have stamped their academic influence of the shape of American law in its formative years. It is well-known that Professor Christopher Columbus Langdell (1826-96), a New York lawyer introduced, through his casebooks, the *case method of instruction* into American Law Schools, and it is clear that brilliant scholars such as Corbin, Williston and Kent and Story have played a major part on unifying the law and guiding the courts in its application. Unlike the English tradition, treatises and articles of the leading professors of law are often cited with approval in American appellate courts.

On a comparative note, we may reiterate the powerful influence of doctrinal writers in the civil law and their continued influence in the modern Continental setting.

(iii) The American Judge v. English Judge

4.3.12   Atiyah and Summers (1991) chapter 12) have noted certain divergencies and similarities between English judges and their American counterparts and this section is based on their main observations. *Firstly*, apart from their different backgrounds and mode of training and selection, they note that the system of written briefs and a more 'office' like procedures of American appellate courts, makes an American appellate judge more politically and socially oriented than his English colleague, which he needs to be to perform satisfactorily within the American system. *Secondly*, as a result of different pay scales, English judges are invariably drawn from the leaders of the practising profession whereas American judges are not, being far less well-paid than their colleagues in private practice. *Thirdly*, English judges may be characterised by their formal, pragmatic and professional attitude to the resolution of disputes, born of many years' experience as a barrister in writing briefs which tend to identify the law and apply it to fact, expressed in neutral terms. American judgeships are far more political, they usually have to attract attention in some way, and often have to align themselves with a political party, and are not seen as lifelong jobs unless they become federal judges, so that the 'American lawyer is sometimes less interested in impressing other judges or practising lawyers, and more interested in impressing scholars, law reviews, and the academic community generally.' (Atiyah and Summers (1991) p.351). *Fourthly*, the English judge is far more homogeneous than his American counterpart, with the vast majority coming from the same upper middle-class background. All English professional full-time judges come from the Bar, whereas there is a wide range of ethnic and educational backgrounds represented in the American judiciary. There is no such thing as a single legal culture in America. Accordingly, Atiyah and Summers also make the important point that, contrary to the opinion in certain quarters, the 'indeterminacy of rules' in the English legal system is far less pronounced than it is in the United States. There is, in fact 'wider agreement about the criteria for determining the validity of rules'. English law is formulated in terms of formal rules which are usually applied strictly in accord with their terms, giving them a 'high mandatory formality.'

The 'background factor'appears to explain the greater willingness of the American judge, when compared to the English judge, to cite academic literature in his opinions and to pursue theoretical and intellectual issues.

Finally, the American judge appears to be dealing with a different set of sources, different types of legislation, and cases. As Atiyah and Summers point out, among the many questions an American State supreme court judge may have to face is whether his court should follow a prior decision when most of the state supreme courts have pursued a different line. This is the sort of question which no English judge has to consider. (see Atiyah and Summers (1991) p.358). Despite all these differences, the basic American judicial approach most closely resembles the English common law tradition than any other.

v. Comparative Overview

4.3.13   Both England and America had similar sources of law in their formative phases of development and both use similar divisions of law and approaches to law, but, as Atiyah and Summers put it, 'these two legal systems embrace very different *conceptions* of law.' (Atiyah and Summers (1991) p.417) This also applies to legislation, where it is not surprising that the American conceptions of legislation as a form of law are also different from the English conception.

Certain fundamental American approaches in terms of legal vocabulary, basic philosophy and principles and concept have generally not deviated greatly from their original English roots. Farnsworth isolates three main English law ideas which he argues still dominate American legal thought: (i) the concept of supremacy of law, best illustrated by the notion that the state is subject to judicial review; (ii) the tradition of precedent; and (iii) the notion of a trial as an adversarial, contentious proceeding, in the American context, usually before the jury, 'in which the adversarial parties take the initiative and in which the role of the judge is that of umpire rather than that of inquisitor'. (see Farnsworth, (1987)pp.11-12) It should be noted that the American version of judicial precedent is very different from the English notion. (see Farnsworth (1987) pp.45-52).

Differences between the American legal scenario and the English one may be explained by divergencies in their historical experience, in their constitutional structure, the different political and social conditions, the diverse geographical and climatic conditions, in their remarkable technological advancement, and by the distinctive judicial and academic personnel who have played a major role in shaping the destiny and substantive content of its current legal scenario. However, in Rheinstein's view, 'in spite of all its local variations and differences, the United States constitutes one single nation, economically, politically and socially. Everyone regards himself as an American first, an Illinoisian or New Yorker, Californian or Louisianan second.' It is perhaps this nationalist fervour that best unites the vast American continent.

E. THE COMMON LAW TRADITION IN SOUTH-EAST ASIA

4.4   The countries covered by the term 'South-east Asia' (SE Asia) include Burma, Thailand, Cambodia, Laos and Vietnam, the Phillipines, Malaysia, Singapore, and Indonesia. However, since our discussion is concerned only with the countries that may be classified as predominantly 'common law countries', we shall only be looking at the representative legal systems of Malaysia and Singapore, which are within the group of countries Professor Hooker has labelled as 'The English Legal World'.

i. Historical Introduction to the English Legal World in SE Asia

4.4.1   The colonial territories in which English law eventually became the general law of application were the Straits Settlements, the Federated and Unfederated Malay States, the British Borneo Territories and Burma. The Straits Settlements comprised Penang, Malacca, and Singapore: the last has been an independent republic since 1965. Penang and Malacca were incorporated into the Federated and Unfederated Malay States and the Borneo Territories (British North Borneo and Sarawak) and became part of the State of Malaysia. Burma is now an independent republic. These countries all share a common *reception* (see 4.12.1 below) *of English law* in which all had the following features: English law was made the *general applicable law* and the *English courts were courts of general jurisdiction*. Hence, once reception of English law had taken place, even when native courts had been established, native law was applied, *subject to English legal principles and to the overriding jurisdiction of the general courts*. Reception of English law did not, however, take place at the same time, and general reception in Malaya only occurred in 1951-6.

As Hooker puts it, 'the history of the English legal world in South-East Asia is a history of the accommodation between English principles and the indigenous laws, resulting in the latter being absorbed within the English legal system by way of both statute and case law' (Hooker (1978) p.123). The term 'indigenous' as applied in older works refers to native, religious, customary or tribal laws. Hooker continues, 'The legal history of the area is not so much a history of institutions as of the formation of special precedents giving effect to local laws.' (Hooker (1978)). These special precedents therefore became *part of the whole body of the English common law which was applicable in the territories concerned*.

The prevalent and characteristic legal methodology in this English legal world in South-East Asia, from about the eighteenth century was a *case-law method*, and the substantive law consisted of the English common law as it existed at the time (ie English court decisions and statutes) and local customs were usually given effect, but not without inevitable uncertainty and confusion in all quarters.

In 1807, a Charter of Justice was granted by the Crown establishing a Court of Judicature in Penang, with the jurisdiction and powers of an English superior court, which had several justices and judges, and the powers of an ecclesiastical court, so far as the several religions, manners and customs of the inhabitants would admit. The law which the court was to apply was the law of England with the necessary modifications, that is, subject to local customs, religions and local legislation.

British colonisation of the Malay Peninsula began in 1786 when the English East India Company acquired the virtually uninhabited island of Penang from the Sultan of Kedah. The British had occupied Dutch Malacca since 1795, but returned it to the Dutch in 1818 under the Treaty of Vienna of 1814. Having lost Malacca, the British turned to Singapore, which was also virtually uninhabited except for 150 Malay fishermen and a few Chinese. Under a treaty of friendship and alliance concluded with an official of the Malay Sultanate, the English East India Company obtained permission to establish a trading post on the island and in 1819, the British Crown acquired full sovereignty over the island of Singapore. In 1824, Malacca was ceded to the British under the Anglo-Dutch Treaty of the same year.

The Dutch later formally transferred Malacca to the English East India Company in 1825, following the cession of Malacca. Subsequently, the courts were required to apply English law to all three Straits Settlements with due regard for 'native customs, usages and law' under their Charters (the Charter of Justice 1826) which applied to Penang, Malacca and Singapore. It was generally accepted that the Charter of Justice of 1826 introduced English law into the Straits settlements but doubts existed over the definitive extent of the modifications necessary to take into account religion and local custom. In 1858, *R*. v. *Willans* (1858) 3 Ky. 16 defined a local custom within the meaning of the Charter as excluding a pre-existing European law. The rule was eventually settled that the Charter did not sanction local law but merely admitted it as an exception: see also *In the Goods of Abdullah* (1835) 2 KY. Ecc.Rs.8 and *R.v. Willans* (above).

The subsequent history of English law in the Straits Settlements is predominantly a history of an accommodation of the law to local circumstances, given the variety of races (Malay, Chinese, Indian) and of religions (Islam, Hinduism and a *potpourri* of Chinese religious customs). A regime of 'personal laws' sprang up, rather in the way it did in the interregnum between the first and second Life of Roman law. Laws were applied to persons of a named religion or race as part of the general common law of the territories. From 1942 to 1945, British Malaya was occupied by the Japanese in the course of World War Two, but after the Japanese surrender, the British resumed control. By then, the spirit of nationalism had begun to grow, and indeed, after the war, the movement for independence started to grow in European colonies throughout the region.

In 1957, independence was proclaimed and what was then the Federation of Malaya became a sovereign state within the British Commonwealth. Singapore won internal self-government in 1959, was briefly merged with Malaysia in 1963, but in 1965, political differences between the two countries led to her secession and she remains an independent republic.

ii. Reception of English Law in Singapore and Malaysia

(i) Meaning of 'Reception' of Law

4.4.2   The phenomenon of reception appears to be a universal one. It appears to have been used as a technical term in connection with the introduction of Roman law into Western Europe and also refers to the spread of law of the metropolitan countries into their colonies.

The common law interpretation of the term appears to date from the early seventeenth century (*Calvin's case* (1608) 7 Co. Rep. 1a; 77 ER 377), acknowledged through the eighteenth century and reaffirmed in the classic case of *Campbell* v. *Hall* (1774) 1 Cowp. 204; 98 ER 1045).

A distinction was drawn between *settled* and *ceded (or conquered) colonies.* For settled colonies which were either uninhabited prior to the settlement or only inhabited by a nomadic population without the arts of cultivation, the settlers carried with them, as their birthright, the law of England. (see Bartholomew (1985) p.6) In the case of ceded (or conquered) colonies the law existing prior to the conquest continued in force 'until the royal pleasure was known' (Bartholomew, (1985) *ibid*).

The effect of subsequent Letters Patent was to declare that, to a lesser or greater extent, English law should be applied. English law thereby spread throughout the territories of the British Empire, but was subject to a number of qualifications and restrictions. Blackstone, in writing of settled colonies, agreed that in uninhabited territory which was discovered by English subjects, all the English laws which are then in being are immediately there in force but added:'[T]his must be understood with very many and very great restrictions. Such colonists carry with them only so much of the English law as is applicable to the condition of an infant colony....The artificial requirements and distinctions incident to the property of a great and commercial people...are neither necessary not convenient for them, and therefore are not in force...'(see Blackstone *Commentaries*, vi,p.107).

The accepted view is that the same restriction applies to ceded (or conquered) colonies in which English law applies by virtue of the royal will.

However, to have stated the rule did not settle the question of which laws were applicable to the various colonies, and to what extent.

(ii) Reception of English Law in Singapore

4.4.3   The reception of English law in Singapore appears to have been settled in the following way. Despite the passing of a Third Charter of Justice in 1855, this was not regarded as effecting a re-introduction of English law as it stood at that date. Unlike the Second Charter of 1826, which created a new court for Singapore, the Third Charter had been passed to reorganise the structure of the existing court(see Sir Benson Maxwell,R in *R.* v. *Willans* (1858) 3 Ky. 16 at p.37). Thus, through the Second Charter of Justice 1826, Singapore received (i) a *court system* based on the prevailing English structure; and (ii) as a result of judicial interpretation of the language of the Second Charter of Justice 1826, it received *English law* 'as it existed in England' on the date of the Charter, 27 November 1826. So any English statute passed after that date is not applicable in Singapore. Arguably, there was no 'cut-off' point but the matter has never been definitively resolved. This *dual reception* is known as the *'general reception of English law'*. Hence, the foundations of the infant Singapore legal system were laid, which place it unequivocally within the English common law family or tradition.

Moreover, only English law of general policy and application was to be received (*Choa Choon Neo* v. *Spottiswoode* (1869) 12 Ky. 216 at 221, per Sir Benson Maxwell, CJ and *Yeap Cheah Neo* v. *Ong Cheong Neo* (1875) L.R. 6 PC 381 at p.384), and such English law was to be applied subject to local customs and religions and local legislation.

(iii) Reception of English Law in Malaysia

4.4.4   Malaysia was initially divided into the Federated and Unfederated Malay States. A feudal system existed in Malaysia and in a purely formalistic sense, still does. Each of the States had a king (the Sultan) who was an independent monarch in his own right. When Malaya became a federation, all these sultans retained their sovereignty except to the extent that they would owe primary obedience to the Head of State, the *Yang di-Pertuan Agong*, the Chief Sultan, who by tradition, resides in the capital, Kuala Lumpur.

Unlike the Straits Settlements, the Malay states were not colonies in the formal sense but really *protectorates* whose rulers continued to exercise power in most formal matters of administration but effective and ultimate power was exercised by the British Resident, a sort of governor who was a representative of the British Government.

The position established by a number of cases is that the Sultan retains his independent sovereign status, despite the fact that they had bound themselves by treaty not to exercise some of the attributes of sovereignty (see *Mighell* v. *Sultan of Johore* [1894] 1 QB 149; *Duff Development Company* v. *Kelantan Government* [1924] AC 797 and *Pahang Consolidated Co. Ltd* v. *State of Pahang* [1933] MLJ 247).

Even after the Residency system had taken effect, and up to the early twentieth century, English law was not applicable *simpliciter* in these Malay states. As far as Malays were concerned, they were subject to Islamic law and Malay *adat*, a form of customary law. Islamic law was not a foreign law but a local law of which the courts were obliged to take judicial notice (*Ramah* v. *Laton* (1927) 6 FMSLR 128). Each of the FMS had legislation regulating the administration of Islamic law.

There was also legislative recognition of Chinese family law and Hindu law was considered on a par with Chinese law, since the courts recognised Hindu law, and local variations thereof, on substantially the same grounds as Chinese law. Since the higher ranks of the judicial hierarchy were filled with

English lawyers, trained in English common law, some English rules were certainly starting to appear in the nineteenth century. Recourse to English law appeared to be necessary to fill *lacunae* that appeared since in certain cases, it was not possible to ascertain what law, if any, applied.

In 1937 English law was legislatively introduced into the FMS by the Civil Law Enactment No.3 of 1937 and extended to the Unfederated Malay States by the Civil Law (Extension) ordinance of 1951. This was later repealed in 1956 by the Civil Law Ordinance of the same year, section 3(1) which repeats the provision appearing in the earlier Acts providing for the application of English law 'subject to such qualification as local circumstances render necessary'. This was therefore merely according legislative recognition to *de jure* judicial practice. Judicial precedent from each state jurisdiction may be freely cited in modern Malaysia, and this will only be subject to later legislative amendment.

Malaya is now known as West Malaysia and the law that applies to all its States is a mixture of English Common law, English rules of equity, local legislation, imperial legislation, and group personal (customary/religious) law (ie the law that is applicable by virtue of membership of a defined racial, religious or ethnic group).

Unlike England, both Singapore and Malaysia have written Constitutions but in Singapore, in particular, the Constitution does not dominate the availability of legal rights and remedies in the way that it does, to a great extent, in the United States, France and Germany. The Privy Council remains the highest court of appeal for Singapore but not for Malaysia. This refers to the Judicial Committee of the English Privy Council, and the origin of this practice is traceable to the days when the English Sovereign ruled by and with the advice of the Privy Council. Orders from the Privy Council are still issued from the Privy Council today.

By virtue of the Judicial Committee Act 1833, (as amended in 1844) a committee was set up within the Privy Council to hear appeals from overseas either under the Act or under the customary jurisdiction of the Privy Council. Until 1966, only single opinions were given but dissenting opinions are now permissible.

In criminal cases, the jury system was abolished in Singapore by the Criminal Procedure Code (Amendment) Act 1969. This is certainly not in keeping with other major common law jurisdictions.

It can be seen, therefore, that where Portuguese and Dutch influence centred on Malacca for predominantly trade motives, English influence eventually extended over the whole peninsula and was to leave a permanent legacy to the political and legal institutions of the country. Of course, Indian culture and religion were transplanted through the Indian immigrants who settled in Malaya, bringing with them Hindu law and Hindu customs as was the Islamic religion and law of the Muslims. However, the *adat*, or native Malay customary law, prevailed and indeed, has a direct link with the feudal set-up. Thus, the influence of customary law was allowed to flourish despite the 'general applicability' of the English common law but the ethos of English law and philosophy is still very much in evidence in Singapore and Malaysia.

F. THE COMMON LAW IN THE FAR EAST: HONG KONG

4.5   Early Hong Kong was apparently inhabited by some peasants and fishermen who lived there under Chinese rule and custom. The law to which they were subject at the time was that of the Qing dynasty, partly codified by the Qing codes. The colony of Hong Kong was acquired by the British in three stages in 1842, 1860 and 1898. Hong Kong was not, however, acquired for settlement or territorial expansion but as a base in the Far East to advance the commercial, diplomatic, and military interests of Great Britain (see Endacott *A History of Hong Kong* (1973) p.38).

The legal system that existed in Hong Kong in the 1840s, such as it was, was not suitable for these purposes. On 5 April 1843, Hong Kong received a local legislature and *English law was to be received into the colony* but not in cases where it was considered not suitable for its inhabitants or to the circumstances of Hong Kong. Although there was no differentiation in the types of English law, there was in practice, a distinction drawn between statutes and cases. The 'cut-off date' for Acts was 5 April 1843: all Acts contained in the English statute book on that day, provided they were general and not purely local in character, and not unsuitable to the circumstances of Hong Kong or its inhabitants, were automatically applicable to Hong Kong. All English Acts passed after that date, were not applicable to the colony unless they necessarily applied by their own terms or were specifically imported by prerogative legislation or local ordinance. Common law, in the sense of caselaw, was considered unchanging, and therefore remained applicable even after the cut-off date, since these cases were seen as merely declaratory of the law that had always been applicable. This quaint concept has been discarded, but the continued reception of contemporaneous judicial decisions meant that there was possibility of Hong Kong being left with a set of ossified legal decisions.

However, it became increasingly problematic to ascertain which English Acts were in force in 1843 and to discover accurate texts. Hong Kong's own legislature nevertheless continued to produce statute law specifically adapted to the colony so that a voluminous collection of English law was rendered nugatory.

i. New Legislative Formula

4.5.1   In 1966, a new legislative formula was introduced through the Application of English Law Ordinance 1966. It divided English law into two types :(i) enactments; and (ii) common law and equity, dealt with each separately and abolished the cut-off date. Under s.3(1) thereof, English common law and the rules of equity shall be in force so far as they are applicable to the circumstances of Hong Kong or its inhabitants and subject to such modifications as such circumstances may require. Common law and equity may be amended by legislation but their operation in the territory is only to be affected by statutes which themselves have effect in Hong Kong. Thus Acts of Parliament apply if extended by their own terms or by other legislation, including the schedule to the Application of English Law Ordinance itself(s.4).

Various anomalies resulted from this Ordinance, since it applies some English Acts to Hong Kong (for example, the Justices of the Peace Act 1361 and the Distress of Rent Act 1689) but not others. Caselaw then established that the effect of the Ordinance would seem to be that if a common law rule was affected by English legislation it was the *amended common law which applied*, irrespective of whether the amending Act of Parliament took effect in Hong Kong or not. Hence, an Act passed in England, though without reference to conditions in Hong Kong or the wishes of the Hong Kong government, and not itself directly in force in Hong Kong, would, if it impinged upon the common law, indirectly affect the law that was applicable in the colony. (see Wesley-Smith *An Introduction to the Hong Kong Legal System* (1987)p.37)

The local legislature therefore amended the Ordinance so that it was made clear that the common law and equity are to be applicable in the colony notwithstanding amendment of them as part of the law of England made at any time by legislation not in force in Hong Kong. This did not resolve other potential anomalies but the current position appears to be that 'the common law imported into Hong Kong can be affected by legislation made as part of the law of England which does not apply to Hong Kong, provided that such legislation was formerly in force under the old formula'(Wesley-Smith (1987) p.38). Ironically, therefore, the cut-off date retains its significance because all statutes which were part of English law on 5 April 1843 and which abolished common law or equity, continue to have that effect. Section 3 will only apply to English legislation passed after 5 April 1843 to earlier legislation which was never in force in the colony.

iii. Preparing for 1997

4.5.2   In 1997, Hong Kong will once again come within the sphere of China's control. In order to ensure that by then, Hong Kong will possess a comprehensive body of law which owes its authority to the Legislature of Hong Kong, it will be necessary to replace British legislation by local legislation on the same topics. A legislative programme has been adopted to achieve this. The Hong Kong Act 1985 provides for the Hong Kong legislature in specified fields with Hong Kong ordinances, and the Hong Kong (Legislative Powers) Order 1986 specified the fields of civil aviation, merchant shipping and admiralty jurisdiction. A further Order was made in 1989 which confers similar powers to enact legislation to give effect to international agreements which are applicable to Hong Kong. At the basic level of compatibility of laws, Hong Kong's caselaw will have to be codified if there is any hope of the two systems being harmonised with each other.

At midnight on 30 June 1997, Hong Kong will become a Special Administrative Region (SAR) under the direct authority of the Central People's Government (CPG) of the People's Republic of China(PRC) and according to the promise of Deng Xiaoping in 1982, there will be 'one country, two systems'. The National People's Congress (NPC) of the PRC will enact a Basic Law for the Hong Kong SAR pursuant to Article 31 of the Constitution of the PRC. The second draft of the Basic Law, published in February

1989, is a sort of mini-constitution for the future Hong Kong SAR designed to provide a constitutional framework for the maintenance of Hong Kong's present legal and economic system after 1997.

Article 5 of the Basic Law draft states that: 'The socialist system and policies shall not be practised in the Hong Kong Spcial Administrative Region and the previous capitalist system and way of life shall remain unchanged for 50 years.' Article 8 goes on to provide:'The laws previously in force in Hong Kong, that is, the common law, rules of equity, ordinances, subordinate legislation and customary law shall be maintained, except for those that are inconsistent with this Law or have been amended by the legislature of the Hong Kong Special Administrative Region'.

Thus, problems of integration of policy, culture, ideology and politics apart, Hong Kong will continue to receive for 50 years *after* 1997, the *English common law*. Hence it will continue to apply the doctrine of precedent, and appeals from its Court of Appeal will still lie to the Privy Council. Article 83 allows the courts to refer to precedents from other common law jurisdictions. Hong Kong's Court of Appeal held in 1973 that any relevant decision of the Privy Council is binding on the Hong Kong courts. Hence decisions of Chinese courts will have no impact on Hong Kong until 2047.

Judges are meant to be appointed from within Hong Kong and Articles 81 and 91 of the Draft Basic Law permit the appointment of judges from other common law jurisdictions to sit on the Court of Final Appeal and other courts respectively. A continuing problem has been the difficulty in procuring judges of sufficient calibre and experience to sit on the Bench.

iv. Can Socialism and Capitalism Co-exist?

4.5.3   The study of Puerto Rico's legal history by J.A. Morales, which illustrated how American common law transformed the fragmented Puerto Rico's Spanish civil law tradition, has suggested that the domination of a law in a country which already had an indigenous law or which has already been ruled by another law for many years may be due to a several factors: the choice of legal language, the content and style of legal education and the type of legal personnel it produced (Morales 'Puerto Rico: Two Roads to Justice' (1981) 79 *Revista de Derecho Puertorriqueno*, p.293, cited by Epstein in 'China and Hong Kong' in *The Future of the Law in Hong Kong* (ed. Wacks) pp.60-1). If common law and socialist law begin to co-exist after 2047, experience in other jursidictions suggests that one of the systems will prevail. Given the obvious military might of China, that system might arguably be imposed from across the sea, from the Mainland.

China falls into the category of a socialist legal system since it shares with the few remaining socialist countries common economic, ideological and political foundations. China has primarily looked to civil law codes and indeed codification as a preferred style of legalism, but socilist law was not created in a vacuum. It was in 1927 when the 'Chinese Soviets' were established in Jiangxi and Hunan that Soviet law began to make a lasting impression on China and the Mainland Chinese leaders. The policy of the Chinese Communist Party (CCP) at the time, clearly played no small part in China's eventual 'conversion'. True to Marxist/Leninist ideology, Chinese Marxist orthodoxy views all law as an extension of the economic system and the system of ownership which determines the mode of production. Law is an integral part of the political structure but is also merely the instrument of the political will of the ruling class.

A new form of *'preliminary socialism'* has entered into China's official ideology relatively recently and this argues that because socialist China emerged from a semi-colonial, semi-feudal period without passing through a stage of highly developed capitalism, its productive forces have lagged far behind those of developed capitalist countries. China would first have to undergo a long period of preliminary socialism wherein the private economy will be allowed to co-exist with the socialist public economy and by allowing mixed economic forms, the CCP has been given the latitude and discretion to reform China's economic and social systems without undermining their leadership or their socialist ideology. The capitalist productive forces of Hong Kong are seen as a means to an end of 'preliminary socialism'. The question that must lurk in the back of one's mind, therefore, is when will the period be seen to have served its purpose so that the socialist state can move on to the next stage of development? Can China's economic and ideological systems co-exist with Hong Kong's capitalist system?

v. The Future of the Common Law in Hong Kong

4.5.4   As far as Hong Kong and China are concerned, there are fundamental ideological, institutional, philosophical and economic differences between them which need to be resolved before any sort of successful integration and co-existence will be possible. It should be remembered that the system proposed for the post-1997 Hong Kong is not a federal system of power-sharing and that Hong Kong's lawmaking competence will derive from the NPC and ultimately from Article 31 of the Constitution. Hence the Basic Law is not really a mini-constitution in the way that one would expect. It will be an NPC law which can extend or restrict the application of the Chinese legal system to Hong Kong as the NPC thinks fit, subject to amendement or repeal like any other NPC legislation. However, as long as it remains in force, it will be constitute a fetter or check on the application of Chinese law in Hong Kong.

In essence, China's legal system remains incompatible with that of Hong Kong. Mainland China's historical roots are overwhelmingly rooted in civil law and their predominant socialist law ideology means that they give very little recognition to private rights, since everything is generally geared to the State Plan and the best economic interests of the State. Mainland China retains a legislative jurisdiction in defence, foreign affairs, and other matters outside the limits of Hong Kong's 'high degree of autonomy'. Other factors which will influence the shape of things to come will be the Mainland's control of legal language, personnel and the weight and popular appeal accorded to public policy and morality, counterbalanced by Hong Kong's devotion not just to the money market and prosperity but also to its own sense of justice, human rights and democracy. At present, most legal proceedings in Hong Kong are conducted in, and nearly all law is published in, English, a language which is not the mother tongue of 98 per cent of the inhabitants. Its District and Supreme Courts, and Lands Tribunal function only in English. Interpreters are provided for non-English speakers. However, the government has committed large resources to translating the entire statute book into Chinese and to draft new ordinances and subsidiary legislation into both languages, with both languages to be equally authentic. Legal education, on the other hand, will continue to be in English only but some secondary literature in Chinese is beginning to emerge. These elements may all be irrelevant if Mainland China were to exercise their military powers or play their public order card, and simply take over the island and rule it as they deem fit. In a very real sense, the survival of the common law in Hong Kong might also ensure the survival of a democratic society and greater freedom for the citizen of Hong Kong in the twenty-first century.

G. COMPARATIVE OVERVIEW

4.6   As with the civil law system, the Common Law tradition has inevitably undergone notable changes over its nine centuries of existence. In its parent country, where legislation was once regarded as a necessary evil and occasional inconvenience, a remarkable proliferation of legislation has taken place particularly in the latter half of the twentieth century. Its basic philosophy has remained the resolution of disputes, rather than the provider or vehicle for, universal truths and general solutions. However, it has, both explicitly and implicitly, been ready to posit principles, based on standards of morality, social policy and commercial probity. In this, it has many parallels with civil law systems.

Its basic legal technique remains firmly rooted in a process of abstraction, operating at different levels of generality, and reasoning by analogy and by precedent, in reliance on decisional law, or judicial precedent, rather than primarily in adherence and interpretation of statutes. A crucial difference with the civil law approach, is that, with some exceptions, in order to determine a point of law, instead of consulting a code or statute, the common lawyer and judge will consult cases and textbooks of cases, *before* looking at statutes, and primarily in order to resolve a dispute.

The vast proportion of cases in more recent times have been decided by the lower courts and specialist tribunals, the latter presided over by judges and arbitrators outside the ordinary courts' structure. But the appeal courts and the House of Lords continue to exercise control and influence over the shape and progress of legal development. There is still very little evidence of English law being subsumed within or markedly influenced by European Community law although the highest court of appeal for English domestic courts is now the European Court of Justice of the European Communities, and EC Law is applicable to Britain under the European Communities Act 1972.

The doctrine of precedent, despite its flaws, inherent rigidity, and inability to play a pro-active role in law reform, has, at least in England, been assisted by the expedient of legislation, particularly in the area of company law, commercial law and family law. Farther afield, it has been adapted considerably, so as to acquire different characteristics and features in countries like

America to accommodate rapidly changing social and economic conditions. It has thrived in the former colonies of Britain and has managed to co-exist quite successfully alongside indigenous customary law.

In England, there has also been a remarkable increase in the number of cases of judicial review, especially over the last decade and questions must be raised over the efficacy of the ancient prerogative writs to secure for the citizen, acceptable standards of justice and to provide sufficently strong protection against governmental power and control. There appears to be a discernible trend in common law jurisprudence to broaden the juristic base for the articulation and enforceability of the rights of the individual, particularly against the State and State interests and the potential removal of any remaining distinction between public and private law in England, except in a small proportion of cases.

Judges remain in the forefront of the common law legal tradition, both at home and abroad, and it is their role and function that is currently undergoing closer scrutiny than ever before.

Caselaw has also been steadily acquiring a higher profile in civil law countries like France and Germany, whereas in England, the so-called law-making function has been carried out in far greater measure in the last decade by the legislature than in the past. But, as far as convergence of legal systems is concerned, judgment has to be reserved. The preceding survey will have at least indicated that although several similarities exist between common and civil law countries, several more ideological, jurisprudential, institutional and procedural dissimilarities will first have to be reconciled before any sort of true 'harmonisation of laws' can occur.

SELECTIVE BIBLIOGRAPHY

Levy-Ulmann THE ENGLISH LEGAL TRADITION (1935)

Pound 'The Development of American Law and its deviation from English Law' (1951) 67 LQR 49

Buckland & McNair ROMAN LAW AND COMMON LAW (1952)

David & Brierley MAJOR LEGAL SYSTEMS IN THE WORLD TODAY (1985) Pt.III

Hay AN INTRODUCTION TO U.S. LAW (1976)

Hooker LEGAL PLURALISMS (1975)

Hooker A CONCISE LEGAL HISTORY OF SOUTH-EAST ASIA (1978)

Harlow "Public" and "Private" Law: Definition without
    Distinction" (1980) 43 Mod.LR 241

Manchester MODERN LEGAL HISTORY OF ENGLAND AND WALES (1980)

Tunc 'The Not So Common Law of England and the United States, or Precedent in England and the United States, A Field Study by an Outsider' (1984) 47 Mod.LR 150

Farnsworth AN INTRODUCTION TO THE LEGAL SYSTEM OF THE
    U.S. (1987)

International Encyclopaedia of Comparative Law: Vols. I and II

Bartholomew, Chapter 1 in THE COMMON LAW IN SINGAPORE AND MALAYSIA (1985)
    (ed. Harding)

Zweigert & Kotz: AN INTRODUCTION TO COMPARATIVE LAW
    (1987): vol.I

Schlesinger et al: COMPARATIVE LAW: CASES-TEXT-MATERIALS (1988)

Van Caenegem THE BIRTH OF THE ENGLISH COMMON LAW (1988)

116

Chan AN INTRODUCTION TO THE SINGAPORE LEGAL SYSTEM (1986)

Wacks (ed.) THE FUTURE OF THE LAW IN HONG KONG (1989)

Rheinstein: International Encyclopedia of Comparative Law: Vol. I

Horwitz THE TRANSFORMATION OF AMERICAN LAW (1977)

Hurst LAW AND THE CONDITIONS OF FREEDOM IN THE
    19TH CENTURY IN THE UNITED STATES (1975)

Hohmann 'The Nature of the Common Law and the Comparative Study of Legal Reasoning' (1990) 38 Am.JCL 143.

Ingman THE ENGLISH LEGAL PROCESS (1992)

117

CHAPTER FIVE

European Community Law

A. INTRODUCTION

5.0 We now consider the law of a special, single political entity, the 'European Community'-a unique legal system, at once *sui generis*, separate from either civil or common law parent families, yet 'supra-national', a *regional system* and a *distinctive legal order* in its own right. As 1993 approaches, and with it the planned implementation of the European Single Market, it becomes increasingly important to recognise the importance of the law of the European Community as a legal order, in the sense of 'an organised and structured system of legal rules, with its own sources, and its own institutions and procedures for making, interpreting and enforcing those rules'(Isaac, *Droit communautaire*, (Masson) (1983)p.111). In some respects, of course, it is a particular kind of 'hybrid' legal system, but the term hybrid is not usually associated with this sort of legal system.

'The European Community, founded on the Treaties of Paris and Rome, is governed by a quadripartite institutional system-novel in its conception, unique in its assignment of powers, different from all previous national and international systems, a Community system in letter and in spirit.' This is how the European Documentation on the Court of Justice of the European Communities describes the three European Communities, generally referred to as 'the European Community' or the 'EC' which usually refers to the Economic Community. Although it is *in law three communities* (see below) there is only *one set of institutions for all three*. Thus it has become generally acceptable to refer to the three Communities as *the* European Community.

It is widely recognised that the Treaty of Paris (1951), and Treaties of Rome (1957) have had an unprecedented effect and impact on the major European countries by virtue of their creation of the European Communities: the European Coal and Steel Community (ECSC), the European Economic Community (EEC) and the European Atomic Energy Community (Euratom).

Just as there developed a 'common law' in England, the Treaty of Rome appears to have laid the foundations for the evolution of *a common European law* which is implemented both by the institutions setting up the treaty and by law-making and law-enforcing agencies of the member states. This law is also capable of being invoked by *individuals* of those member states.

B. SCOPE OF CHAPTER

5.1   There is now a vast and ever-burgeoning body of literature on the European Community (EC) and its law, and caselaw continues to grow dealing with topics ranging from human rights to agricultural policy but the purpose of this chapter is to place EC law in its contemporary and comparative legal context, outlining its key characteristics and comparing them with those of the legal systems which we have already analysed. We shall also examine the sources of EC law, and its relationship to national laws, the influence of French, German and common law traditions on its structure and development, and speculate on its future directions, and potential role and development as a unique from of European law. This chapter is therefore highly selective, and will examine Community Law primarily within a conceptual and comparative framework.

C. MONISM, DUALISM AND THE ACCESSION OF BRITAIN

5.2   An international treaty such as the Treaty of Rome will usually come into force when it has been signed and ratified by its signatories. However, since treaties are governed by international law, the implementation of the Treaty into the domestic laws of the Member State depends on whether that State has a *monist* or *dualist* form of constitution. Broadly speaking, a monist constitution accepts that international law obligations are of the same nature or are even superior to, national law obligations. According to this constitutional approach, a rule of customary international law or a rule established by an international treaty to which that State is a party, is automatically part of that State's national law. Hence, once a State has concluded a Treaty guaranteeing certain rights for its nationals, those rights are automatically protected by national law. For example, it may be said that both the French and Dutch Constitutions are monist constitutions.

A *dualist* constitution, which is the category into which the British Consitution broadly falls, is one under which only limited status is given to rules of international law, until and unless they have been transformed (ie implemented) into national law by some method of national enactment, for example by an Act of Parliament.

However, it is inaccurate to categorise a State as being wholly monist or dualist, and it is more correct to say that in the first instance, a State is governed by its monist or dualist tradition. This is because a State with a monist constitution may retain the power in its courts to decide *which* provisions of a Treaty are binding (as under the Dutch regime) and a 'dualist State' may have a general judicial presumption that its parliament does not intend to legislate contrary to international law and this will extend to obligations imposed by treaties as well as by general principles of international law (as in the UK). As far as Britain was concerned, therefore, Community law was not automatically applicable when it ratified the EC Treaties.

Britain's attitude to membership of the Community has been characterised by some as antipathy and disdain throughout the many years of the Community's genesis but this attitude changed in the 1960s and eventually, having signed the Treaty of Accession on 22 January 1972, on 1 January, 1973, Britain joined the Community. English, Danish and Irish became official Community languages and the translations into these languages of the EEC and Euratom Treaties were declared to be authentic texts. (see below: Legal Styles; Legal Language of the Community).

As a result of Britain's accession, the European Court of Justice (ECJ) ranks above the House of Lords as the ultimate court. However, this is only so in disputes involving Community law and Community-generated law. Thus the ECJ is, for the most part, a 'court of reference' rather than a court of appeal, which means that it deals *primarily* with questions relating to the interpretation and validity of Community law. It will therefore still be up to the national courts and tribunals to apply the interpretations handed down by the ECJ. The House of Lords remains the final court of appeal in Britain in internal, domestic cases.

By virtue of the UK European Communities Act 1972 (the Act), Britain has adopted the provisions of the Community Treaties but has not adopted either a strict monist approach (leaving the courts and administration to work out the exact implications of the treaties) or a highly specific dualist one (ie by detailing precisely the changes that will take place in UK law under the Treaties). It has chosen a middle line, and opted for flexibility rather than rigidity.

Generally, under s.2(1) of the Act, European Community law, whether arising from the treaties or from Community regulations, and whether such law has already been made or is to be made in the future, is to take direct effect in the UK without the need for the UK parliament to pass a statute each time. Hence, it recognises the principle that the Treaties should determine the extent of these rights in the UK and permits the direct enforcement of these rights in the UK.

In addition, under s.2(4) of the Act, 'any enactment' (and this is wide enough to include a statutory instrument as well as a statute) passed or to be passed in the UK must be construed with directly applicable Community law in mind. Hence, there appears to be a presumption that UK statute law is to be read subject to European Community law. Hence, if there is a conflict between European Community law and domestic English law, Community law will override domestic law wherever the former is directly applicable. Recent cases appear to confirm the supremacy of Community law over domestic or municipal law: *Duke* v. *GEC Reliance Ltd* [1988] 1 All ER 626; *Factortame Ltd* v. *Secretary of State for Transport (No.1)* [1989] 2 All ER 692; *Factortame Ltd* v. *Secretary for Transport (No.2)* [1991] 1 All ER 70; *Kirkless Borough Council* v. *Wickes Building Supplies Ltd* [1991] 4 All ER 240.

It should be noted that all these above-cited cases are House of Lords decisions apart form the last which is a Court of Appeal decision. In *Duke* v. *GEC Reliance Ltd* (above), the House of Lords affirmed their previous position that they will not deliberatcly misconstrue the meaning of a UK statute

121

in order to enforce against an individual a Community directive which has no direct effect between individuals. Section 2(4), in the words of Lord Templeman (at p.636), with whom the other Law Lords expressly agreed: 'Section 2(4) applies and only applies where Community provisions are directly applicable.'

The European Communities Act 1972 does not expressly forbid Parliament from amending or repealing that Act itself and indeed under the constitutional doctrine of constitutional supremacy, the 1972 Act could be repealed. Until that happens, the 1972 Act provides a legislative bridge which links Community law to English law so that those provisions of Community law which it requires to become part of the national legal system automatically become part of the UK legal system in accordance with the definition of its meaning and effect laid down by Community law.

Recently, the European Court gave an affirmative answer to the question which the House of Lords referred to it, which was: 'Under Community law, must a national court ignore its own national law and provide interim relief for a person with directly enforceable Community law rights who would otherwise suffer irreversible damage because of delay in having those rights determined?'

In *Factortame Ltd* v. *Secretary of State for Transport (No.2)* [1991] 1 ALL ER 70, the ECJ not only replied in the affirmative but further stressed that under Community law a national law(whether legislative, judicial or adminstrative in character) must be set aside by a national court if it prevents the application of Community law.

Since these decision, Lord Denning, who has now retired from the Bench, has criticised the impact of Community law upon English law, departing considerably from his famous 1974 dictum of the 'incoming tide' of Community law which could not be held back, by describing it as a 'tidal wave bringing down sea walls and flowing inland' over British fields and houses, 'to everyone's dismay'. (*The Independent* (1990) 16 July). he now calls for the amendment of the 1972 Act and suggests that European Court decisions and Community directives should only be binding if they are approved by , respectively, the House of Lords and the relevant British government minister.

However, in *The Factortame case* (No.2) (pp. 107-8) (above), Lord Bridge said criticisms of the European Court were based on a 'misconception' and that 'there was nothing novel in according supremacy to rules of Community law in those areas to which they apply and to insist that, in the protection of rights under Community law, national courts must not be inhibited by rules of national law from granting interim relief in appropriate cases' (which is what was done in the case itself because of the two-year wait which had to be undergone before an ECJ ruling could be procured) 'is no more than a logical recognition of that supremacy.'

In the light of these recent developments, Community law, for the moment, retains its primacy over domestic legislation and ony time will tell if it is eventually truly integrated into English law.

D. THE SINGLE EUROPEAN ACT 1986

5.3   Various other treaties and amendments have been agreed upon and passed but proposals to move towards this 'ever closer union' have had a stormy reception. The 1980s experienced further attempts to revive the sense of excitement and adventure which existed in the 1960s and despite attempts to devise a throughgoing reform of the original Rome Treaty, in fact the EC heads of Government met in Luxembourg and agreed only to various amendments to the Rome Treaty, which constituted the Single European Act 1986. Under this Act, which came into force on 1 July, 1987, its signatories pledge themselves to establishing progressively a single market (ie a complete free internal market between Member States) over a period expiring on 31 December 1992. The Act defines a single market as 'an area without internal frontiers in which the free movement of goods, persons, services and capital is ensured in accordance with the provisions of this Treaty.'

The Act also seeks to assist the free movement of goods by *inter alia*, breaking down technical barriers (for example, different national product standards), national restrictions, and subsidy policies. It also aims to expedite EC decision-making by extending majority voting to most major areas of the single market programme, which replaces the unanimous voting requirements which applied before the Act took effect. It therefore amends the EEC Treaty so as to provide a clear legal authority for Community programmes on economic and monetary policy, social policy, research and technical development and the environment. It further states as an aim of the Treaty the achievement of a common foreign policy and encompasses the political cooperation procedures within the scope of the Treaty, which is another innovation.

The Single European Act (SEA) represents an important commitment to the achievement of a single market but it is clear that its future success is by no means assured. Apart from nationalistic antipathy, the drafters of the SEA did not appear to have given a great deal of thought to the implications of grafting amendments onto a dynamic and living legal system which has already been shaped and formed by caselaw from the European Court of Justice. This, in itself, will conceivably pose not inconsiderable problems of interpretation for Member States and European Community administrative and judicial bodies.

E. THE INSTITUTIONAL FRAMEWORK OF THE COMMUNITY

5.4   The legislative and judicial machinery of the EC consists of *four main 'institutions'* which are: the Council of Ministers, the Commission, the European Parliament (EP) and the European Court of Justice (ECJ). These have been set up under the following Treaties: ECSC (Article 7), EEC (Article 3) Euratom (Articles 1 and 9), the Merger Treaty and the Convention on Certain   Institutions Common to the European Communities (Articles 1, 2(1), 3 and 4(1). The first three are political institutions. These four institutions carry out political, legislative, executive and judicial functions of the Community and have jurisdiction over all the Member States. They are autonomous, and independent of Member States. So are they really different from traditional international organisations?

i. EC Institutions and Traditional International Organisations

5.4.1 At first glance, the EC institutions appear to be very similar to a traditional international organisation, such as the Organisation for Economic Cooperation and Development (OECD) or the North Atlantic Treaty Organisation (NATO). For example, those sorts of bodies have also been created by multilateral treaties, possess a distinct legal personality and act through the agency of institutions created and regulated in accordance with the terms of the parent treaty. However, several comparative comments may be made on the general nature of EC institutions. First, they do not correspond to the classic 'separation of powers' format, because, for instance, the EP (formerly 'the Assembly') as it has been known since 1962, is primarily a consultative body and has no power to affect the content of legislation, merely to be *consulted* on proposed legisaltion in many but not all cases. The EP's powers of consultation were increased by the co-operation procedure introduced by the Single European Act (see below). In practice, *the Council is the dominant force in the Community* and the progress of the Community is usually determined by the speed at which the Member States thereof act to pursue or promote proposals or resolve difficulties.

Secondly, another unique feature of the institutions is that they are involved with, and often exert a considerable degree of regulatory control over matters which have traditionally been within the exclusive jurisdiction of individual States. Their capacity to make rules which are directly and automatically binding not just on the Member States but also on individuals and corporate bodies within those States make them *sui generis*, and endowed with a supra-national character since in so doing, they are unlike any conventional institutional organisation.

Thirdly, the EC institutions were conceived of as a collaborative enterprise and must therefore be analysed in their 'team' context.

Finally, it should be noted that unlike other international institutions, they were created with the primary goal of European political integration and as such, the European Court of Justice even makes its decisions with the goal of European integration in mind.

ii. The Council of Ministers

5.4.2 This is composed of Ministers from the Member States' governments (Article 2 of the Merger Treaty), and is a collegiate body of the Community which advises and supervises the Commission on many important areas of decision-making under the ECSC Treaty. It has been described as the Community's 'decision-making body', which takes the final decision on most EEC legislation, concludes agreements with foreign countries and, in conjunction with the Parliament, decides on the Community budget.

However, the Council does not possess the requisite administrative machinery to put these decisions into practice. The actual *implementation of decisions is therefore carried out by the Commission.*

The minister who usually represents a Member State is its Foreign Minister, but this may be varied and specialist ministers frequently represent their countries depending on the subject-matter being discussed. The Council possesses legislative powers under the EEC and Euratom Treaties and has responsibility for the co-ordination of Member States' economic policies, but it basically agrees legislation based on the proposals put forward by the Commission.

The office of President of the Council is held on a strict rota basis and determined alphabetically and it is only held for six months per presidency. This means that each state will hold the presidency at least once every six years.

The Treaty prescribes three methods of decision-making:(i) Simple majority: Article 148: EEC Treaty, which states this as the norm; at least seven Members must vote in favour; (ii) Qualified majority: Article 148(2) sets out a system of weighted voting based on the population of Member States; the largest countries, UK, France, Germany and Italy have ten votes each, Soain has eight and so on; and (iii) Unanimity, which is presribed by a large number of Articles, for example in relation to admission of new members, and the provisions dealing with supplementary legislative powers. Despite this elaborate voting procedure, the vast majority of decisions are taken by consensus.

The Single European Act extended the applicability of the qualified majority voting procedure, especially with regard to matters dealing with the internal market and this has expedited decision-making.

The heads of government of the Member States have met regularly for a number of years as 'the European Council' but this body must *not* be confused with the Council of Ministers, which we have just been discussing. This European Council had no formal recognition in the original Treaty but has always had a wide agenda which did not confine itself to matters within the scope of the Treaty but dealt with matters of general policy, and left its conclusions to be concretised by the Commission and the Council of Ministers via the normal legislative process. It has evolved into 'the most politically authoritative institution' of the Community (Bulmer and Wessels *The European Council* (1987) p.2). Article 2 of the Single European Act 1986 gave official recognition to the existence of the European Council but did not make it an official institution as was envisaged by the draft of the EP. Article 2 also describes neither the functions nor the powers of the Council, and this perhaps emphasises the informal nature of the Council and its flexibility.

Each Council meeting deals with a particular area of policy, and since 1975, the Council has met on average three times a year, primarily to break deadlocks in negotiations, which it has done several times. Article 2 of the Single European Act stipulates that the Council shall meet at least twice a year and and in the view of some commentators this indicates the intention of the parties to return the responsibility for taking important decisions to the other major institutions. The deliberations of this Council are specifically excluded from the jurisdiction of the ECJ (Article 30) which means their decision will not be legally enforceable under Community law.

iii. The European Commission

5.4.3   This is the body that proposes EC policy and legislation, and consists of seventeen members. All must be nationals of a Member State, one at least from each State. It carries out decisions taken by the Council and supervises the day-to-day implementation of Community policies. It also negotiates agreements between the EC and non-EC countries. Of the seventeen, there are two each from France, Germany, Italy, Spain, and the UK, one each from Belgium, Denmark, Greece, Ireland, Luxembourg, the netherlands and Portugal. Commissioners are appointed unanimously by the Council for four-year terms. Each Commissioner, upon appointment, renounces national allegiance and gives a solemn undertaking to be completely independent in the performance of duties and not to seek or take instructions from any government or any other body. As such, they are appointed to act not as national delegates but in the interests of the Community as a whole. Each Commissioner is in charge of an area of Community policy and formulates proposals within that area aimed at implementing the Treaties.

The powers and functions of the Commission are set out in fairly broad terms in Article 155: (i) The Commission shall ensure that the treaty provisions and the measures taken by the institutions pursuant thereto are applied.

This is the *policing function of the Commission*, which involves detecting breaches of Community law (Article 213 gives supervisory powers to collect necessary information and to carry out necessary checks). It also gives the Commission primary responsibility for taking legal action against Member States in breach of the Treaty, the most common procedure being under Article 169. Under this provision, a Member State is given maximum opportunity to remedy an infringement before being taken to court by the Commission. The other key area where EC policy 'bites' is in the *enforcement of its rules against individuals and corporations in competition policy*, where violations of the Treaty's competition provisions under Articles 85 and 86 may be punished by substantial fines. Article 86 deals with 'abuse of dominant position'.

(ii) The Commission shall formulate recommendations and deliver opinions on matters dealt with by the Treaty, if it expressly so provides or if the Commission considers it necessary.

Although recommendations and opinions have no binding force, this forms a major part of the Commission's work, to sustain the spirit of integration and provide institutional relations.

(iii) The Commission shall have its own power of decision and participate in the shaping of measures taken by the Council and the Assembly (now the EP) in the manner provided for by the Treaty.

It should be remembered that the main method of legislation is for the Council to act on a proposal of the Commission. However, the right of participation in the legislative process, and to be physically present at meetings of the EP, is possibly the most important feature of the Commission's role as promoter of integration. The Commission has the right to amend its proposals at any time before they are adopted   by the Council. The Commission's view must also be sought formally by the Council before the latter may be allowed to act on the issue in question.

(iv) The Commission shall exercise the powers conferred upon it by the Council for the implementation of the rules laid down by the Council.

As has been pointed out (see 5.2.2), although the Council is styled as the primary decision-making body, it lacks the administrative machinery to transform decisions into practice. hence this particular function is the task of the Commission, which braodly carries out (i) *administrative* tasks; and (ii) *legislative tasks*.

Included under administrative functions will be the supervision of policies, the power to grant exemptions, investigate complaints and impose fines, a chief example of which is in the area of competition law. Within the second category of tasks, is the detailed implementation of policy by secondary or subordinate legislation, particularly in relation to agriculture policy.

iv. The European Parliament

5.4.4   This was orginally called the Assembly, and is a directly elected body with 518 members, which exercises political control over the   Community. There are 81 members from the UK. It possesses consultative and advisory functions. Its name was officially changed by Article 3(1) of the Single European Act. The Commission is accountable to the European Parliament (EP). As mentioned above, this Parliament does not have any legislative functions as such but three relatively recent innovations have improved its position.

(i) A new conciliation procedure may now be initiated at the request of the EP in order to reach agreement between itself and the Council if the Council intends to depart from the opinion of the EP.

(ii) Articles 6 and 7 of the Single European Act, provides for a '*co-operation procedure*' between Council and the EP in the passage of certain types of legislation and requires the assent of Parliament, by an absolute majority of its members, to the admission of new Member States and to association agreements with non-member countries.

The co-operation procedure applies to legislation under ten articles including Article 7 (elimination of discrimination on grounds of nationality); Article 49 (free movement of workers); and Article 118a (protection of the working environment). When it applies, the legislative procedure will proceed in the usual way (and include the consultation of Parliament) until the stage when the Council would normally be ready to accept the act in question. At this point, instead of doing so, the Council will adopt by qualified (ie weighted) majority a 'common position'. This common position will then be communicated to the EP together with a full statement of reasons which led the Council to adopt it and a statement of the Commission's position. The EP will then have three months to decide how to act. It can approve or reject the common position, or propose amendments to it. If the EP approves the common position, or fails to make a decision, the Council will adopt the act in accordance with the common position.

However, if the EP rejects the common position, the Council must be unanimous in order to pass the legislation at its second reading. The Council must act within three months or the proposal is deemed not to have been adopted.

If the EP proposes amendments, the Commisssion has one month within which to re-examine its proposal in the light of the proposed amendments. It has the option of adopting some or all of the amendments but is not obliged to do so. The Commission then sends the proposal to the Council, whether or not it has agreed to adopt the EP's amendments.

The Council may then either accept the proposal as amended by the Commission for which a qualified majority will be sufficient, or it can amend it, either by accepting amendments proposed by the parliament but rejected by the Commission; or by adopting amendments of its own. In the latter two cases, the Council must be unanimous if it wishes to pass the legislation.

Ultimately, the new procedure merely charges the Commission with a legal obligation to consider the EP's proposals and to give reasons if it rejects them. The centre of power and decision-making has not really shifted.

v. The European Court of Justice

5.4.5 The Court of Justice of the European Communities, which is the full title of the European Court of Justice (ECJ), was set up by the ECSC Treaty to ensure that the law would be observed in the interpretation and application of the Treaties: Article 164: EEC Treaty. It is the fourth institution of the Community, and has a number of functions to fulfil. It is required to act as an international court (Article 170), an administrative court (Article 173-76, 178, 184), a civil court (Article 215), an administrative tribunal (Article 179) and as a transnational constitutional court (Article 177).

(i) Composition and Organisation

5.4.6 There are thirteen judges in the ECJ, and six advocates-general, who are appointed by 'common accord' which means they are unanimously elected by the governments of the Member States. That procedure strongly affirms the concept that the Court is one of the institutions of the Community. The judges hold office for a renewable term of six terms and three advocates-general are replaced or re-elected every three years. The independence of the judges is guaranteed by the Treaty and the rules of procedure contained in the Statute of the Court (which is a protocol to the original Treaties). It is based on three procedural principles: (i) their deliberations are secret; (ii) judgments are reached by majority vote; and (iii) judgments are signed by all the judges who have taken part in the proceedings although dissenting opinions are not published. This is certainly unlike most national courts (in the common law jurisdictions) and other international courts.

The President of the Court, who holds office for a three-year renewable period, is appointed by the judges themselves by an absolute majority vote in a secret ballot.

According to Article 166 of the EEC Treaty, the function of the advocates-general is to act 'with complete impartiality and independence, to make, in open court, reasoned submissions on cases brought before the Court, in order to assist the Court in the performance of the tasks assigned to it'. These legal officers have no direct counterpart either in common or civil law, and their duties should not be equated with those of a public prosecutor or similar kind of functionary in a French court. The Government Commissioners (*commissaires du gouvernement*) of the French *Conseil d'Etat* is the closest civil law analogy but they are not allowed to act independently, and are specifically obliged to confer and deliberate with the *conseillers*(*d'Etat*) or senior ranking members of the *Conseil d'Etat*.

Several weeks after the lawyers have addressed the court, there is a separate hearing in which the advocate-general will comment on the salient points of the case, weigh up the provisions of Community law, compare the case with previous ruling and propose a legal solution to the dispute. Thus, there is the influence of both civil and common law traditions (see further, 5.6.1-3, below). The court is not bound to follow the advice or opinion of the advocate-general and has been known to even reject them explicitly. In any event, the advocate-general does not participate in the deliberations of the Court and the opinions of the advocates-general have been an important source of the ECJ's *jurisprudence*.

(ii) The Court's Powers

5.4.7   All the Treaties establishing the European Communities use the same formula to define the specific responsibilities of the ECJ, namely to 'ensure that in the interpretation and application of this Treaty the law is observed'. Thus, the Court interprets and applies the whole body of Community law from the basic Treaties to the various implementing regulations, directives and decisions issued by the Council and the Commission. However, the Court only has the power to interpret or rule on the validity of provisions of national law when an individual case arises concerning the failure of a Member State to fulfil an obligation. In this type of case, it will rule on the relationship of national law to Community law. On rare occasions, the Court may also be asked to apply and interpret national law in disputes involving contracts to which the Community is a party.

The ECJ is the Community's supreme judicial authority. Since the Treaties establishing the various Communities could not possibly cover every possible eventuality, the gaps that have appeared in the legal framework have been ably and aptly filled by the ECJ. However, it has also had a heavy workload and so the Single European Act has made provision for the establishment of a court of first instance to be attached to the ECJ, which will have jurisdiction over a limited range of cases. A point that has been commented upon with regard to the ECJ is that there is no appeal from its judgments. Once the Court of First Instance is established, there will be a right of appeal on points of law to the European Court from the First instance court.

The ECJ does not have any inherent jurisdiction but only such jurisdiction as has been conferred on it by the Treaties. Caselaw has indicated that any attribution to the ECJ of jurisdiction outside the Treaties will fail. A case would need to be brought within one of the specified heads of jurisdiction before the Court could hear it. Recourse to the court is relatively simple, but a fundamental distinction is drawn between (a)judgments and (b) advisory opinions and rulings.

As far as *judgments* are concerned, there are two types of basic actions which may be initiated: (i) A *direct action*, which involves disputes between parties and which begins in the European court; and (ii) *Requests to the European Court for preliminary rulings* which are actions begun in a national court, which takes the form of questions put to the ECJ by national judges.

If an action is begun in the European court, it will end in the European Court, so that the Court's judgment will represent a final determination of the dispute between the parties, the Court will grant any appropriate remedies and the judgment (at least, until the First Instance Court is established) will not be subject to appeal. But if a national court commences the action, it will, accordingly, end in a national court because the ruling of the ECJ will be transmitted to that court which will then itself decide the case.

Direct actions may be divided into two main categories: (i) those in which there is an *agreement between the parties* which gives the Court jurisdiction; and (ii) those in which the Court has jurisdiction *by operation of law*. Applications in the first category are uncommon in practice and mainly concern actions arising out of a contract concluded by the Community which contains a clause that gives the ECJ jurisdiction.

In the second category, actions may be further subdivided into cases in which:(i) the action is against the Community; or (ii) the action is against a Member State.

Actions *against the Community* include: (a) Proceedings for 'annulment' (judicial review); (b) Plenary jurisdiction proceedings, which include: (i) actions for damages for non-contractual liability (tort); (ii)appeals against penalties imposed on private individuals for violations of Community law; and (iii)actions brought by Community officials against the institution employing them.

The EEC Treaty adopts the philosophy that neither the legislature nor the executive are above the law of the Treaty and has made the ECJ the supreme arbiter of the law. It has therefore introduced Article 173 and 174 which are a form of *judicial review*. These Articles allow the ECJ, in specified circumstances, to review the legality of and declare void an act of the Council or Commission. As Brown and Jacobs (1983) have noted, the 'decisions of the Court of Justice cannot be reversed by an act of the Council; on the contrary, any measure of the Council having legal effect can be annulled by the court if contrary to the Treaties'. (Brown and Jacobs *The Court of Justice of the European Communities* (1983) p.32-4) Of course, the Treaties also set out the limits of the powers of review of the ECJ.

The Treaty therefore talks in terms of *'review'* and *'annulment'* rather than 'judicial review' or declarations or injunctions. Actions may be brought for review of (i) *Community acts*; and (ii) *Failure to act* or to fulfil obligations. (iii) Actions may also be brought to dispute the *legality* of a Community regulation.

Article 173(1) describes the *four grounds* on which an act (other than recommendations and opinions) may be annulled: (a) *lack of competence*, which corresponds to the English legal concept of substantive *ultra vires*, alleging the Council or Commission have acted outside their authority;

(b) *infringement of essential procedural requirements*, which is similar to the English concept of procedural *ultra vires*, but the ECJ appear to take a much more active role than English courts in striking down decisions, for instance on the ground of failure to give reasons for EC decisions.

(c) *infringement of this Treaty or any rule of law relating to its application*, which constitutes the most important ground, and somewhat overlaps with the previous two grounds. Its generality has made it the most used gound in annulment actions. Apart from procedural and substantive irregularity in procedure, the *'rule of law'* limb of this ground has been used by the ECJ to develop a unique blend of *European administrative law*, on the basis that caselaw has established that there are certain *'general principles of law'* which are widely recognised and which underpin the Community legal order and against which the legality of Community acts must be measured: see *Stauder v. City of Ulm*, Case 29/69 [1969] ECR 419. This particular legal method is discussed further, in our subsequent consideration of the Community legal order as a whole and its legal techniques (see , below). A highly topical an important area of development has been in the field of *human rights*.

In the *Stauder Case* itself (above), it was clearly stated by the ECJ that although the EEC Treaty made no specific mention of human rights, there were 'fundamental human rights enshrined in the general principles of Community law and protected by the Court'. This was echoed in *Internationale Handelsgesellschaft* v. *Einfuhr und Vorratsstelle fur Getriede und Futtermittel* [1970] ECR 1125, when the ECJ reiterated that there was a guarantee of human rights inherent in Community law and that respect for human rights is 'an integral part of the general principles of law protected by the Court of Justice'. The principles which English law refers to as 'rules of natural justice', namely the need for an absence of bias and *audi alterem partem* (hear the other side), have also been culled by the ECJ and used in other cases.

(d) *Misuse of powers*: this ground derives from the French detournement de pouvoir, for which there is no precise analogy in English law, and involves the use of a legitimate power in an illegitimate manner or for an illegitimate purpose. It has now been overtaken by ground (c) above, in contrast to its early days when it used to be the sole ground for complaint in the ECSC Treaty.

Article 175 grants a remedy for a wrongful *failure to act*, 'in infringement of [the] Treaty' on the part of the Council or the Commission, but there are at least two differences between this Article and Article 173, which it appears to resemble. First, proceedings cannot be brought under Article 175 unless a request for action has been sent by the complainant to the defendant. The defendant then has two months to comply and the action may then be brought within the following two months. Secondly, there is only one ground of complaint here whereas there are four under Article 173. However, although it seems clear that there must have been an infringement of a provision which imposed an obligation to act, it is not clear whether Article 175 can be extended to 'any rule of law relating to the application of the Treaty' which could apply to Community legislation or indeed, whether it might further be extended to include infringement of a 'general principle of law'. These matters may well need to be resolved by the ECJ in the not too distant future.

Actions for damages may be brought by either a *Member State* or a *private individual* and the applicant is required to prove that he has suffered loss as a result of Community action. In the case of contractual liability, where it is alleged that the Community is in *breach of contractual obligations*, the applicable law will be the law governing the contract, and the case may be heard by the national court or by the ECJ if the parties so decide.

In actions for *non-contractual liability*, which have a five-year time bar from the date the damage was suffered, the Community must 'make good any damage caused by its institutions or by its servants in the performance of their duties' in accordance with 'the general principles common to the laws of the Member States'. Caselaw in this area suggests that before the Community will be liable for damages there must be a *sufficiently serious* ('manifest and grave') *violation* of a superior rule of law intended for the protection of the individual. (see *Zuckerfabrik Schoppenstedt* v. *Council* [1971] ECR 175) There has been some controversy over the meaning of what is 'manifest and grave' but the current position appears to require that the complainant prove that both the extent of the loss and the dgree of the Community's violation were manifest and grave, in other words, sufficiently serious to warrant compensation. (see *Amylum* v. *Council and Commission*, Cases 116 and 124/77 [1979] ECR 3497; and *Koninklijke Scholten-Honig* v. *Council and Commission* [1979] ECR 3583).

With regard to actions against Member States, there are *two methods* whereby such actions may be taken against any Member State 'which fails to fulfil an obligation under [the] Treaty'. Article 169 of the EEC Treaty, allows the *Commission* to initiate such an action or a *Member State* may do so under Article 170 of the EEC Treaty. Thus, the Commission, as guardian of the Treaties and of the decisions taken by the institutions, may initiate proceedings for dailre to fulfil an obligation. If it considers that a member State, in some aspect of its administration, has not honoured a Community obligation, it will ask the Member State to make its comments on that view; after receiving that State's observations, or even if it has not received them, it will then issue a 'reasoned opinion', which will set out the reasons for the allegation, and set a time-limit for the rectification of the situation, which is usually six months but which may be shorter in more urgent cases. If the State does not act on the opinion within the stipulated time, the Commission may take the matter to the ECJ.

A Member State may also initiate this procedure after notifying the Commission and again, the Commission will ask the Member State against which the breach is alleged, to respond after which it will issue its reasoned opinion. If the Commission does not produce the opinion within three months from the date of the request, the matter may be directly referred to the Court.

The ECJ may, if it agrees that the case is well-founded, it will make a *declaratory judgment* stating that the obligation has not been fulfilled, which appears to be the only sanction although Article 171 of the EEC Treaty states that the State is 'required to take the necessary measures to comply with the judgment'. There are no penalties available to enforce the ECJ ruling. In practice, it appears that Member States generally comply with the Commission opinions either before the proceedings are commenced or during the course of proceedings and the Commission tends to withdraw the case once the State has complied with the opinion. It would appear that the majority of Member States regard the declaratory judgment as a sufficient public and recorded blemish against them and seek to avoid it. In the unusual event that a State refuses to comply, the Com mission has the power to initiate a second action based on Article 171, and a declaration should be obtained stating that the first decision has not been complied with. Among the subjects of the actions, which have been taken against most of the Member States at some stage or other, have been customs duties and charges and the ongoing Anglo-French saga involving fishery legislation.

The ECJ's role is somewhat limited in the context of the *preliminary reference procedure* since it merely seems to rule on an abstract point of law, leaving the national court to decide relevant issues of fact and to apply the law-albeit as interpreted by the ECJ-to those facts.

Nevertheless, this particular procedure (provided by Article 177) maintains an extremely important link between Community and Member State because it affects the relationship between Community law and national law. By determining the scope of rights and obligations of private citizens in Member States *as laid down and interpreted under Community law*, the ECJ is directly applying Community law within the Member States. Through this procedure, similar to the civil law practice of referring to the national constitutional court to ensure uniformity and conformity with the constitution, the Treaty seeks to ensure uniformity of application of Community law in all the national legal systems. Article 177 references were expressly stated to be heard by a full Court in plenary session and not by a Chamber of the Court (Article 165(2)) but the sheer volume of applications invoking this procedure has forced the ECJ to abandon the initial requirement and hear such cases in Chambers.

Article 177 has therefore been called 'an instrument of transnational law' (Pescatore in *Legal problems of an Enlarged European Community* (1972) (eds. Bathurst et al) and the ECJ has also been called a 'transnational constitutional court' drawing an analogy between the EEC Treaty and a written constitution (see Stein 'Lawyers, Judges and the Making of a Transnational Constitution' [1981] 81 AJIL 1).

The role of the ECJ in this context is to provide an *interpretation of the law*, not apply it, since the latter function is the task of the national court although Article 177 also permits the ECJ to rule on the validity of Community legislation. In certain cases, the ECJ has found it difficult not to transgress into the area of application of Community law. In such cases, the Court has managed to reformulate the question asked so as to bring it within their jurisdictional competence. Hence it is through this preliminary reference procedure that the ECJ has established the twin doctrines of direct effect and the supremacy of Community law over national law. (see below).

F. DIFFICULTIES IN COMPARISON

5.5   In the light of its complex institutional structure, and its unique legal character, it is not easy to find a ready basis for comparison of the European Community with other political or legal entities. The Community contains features of other ordinary international organisations and of course, the Treaty is an agreement governed by international law. However, the Community structure also contains features of *federalism*, which are most prominent with regard to the judicial and legal system but rather weak in matters such as legislative and executive powers, taxation, defence and monetary issues. The reasons for this are rooted in history and the objective of creating a United States of Europe consisting of some form of European federation. Hence the Community has hybrid features which must be kept in mind when examining its legal configuration. Its political organs, the Council, the Commission and the Parliament each contain international and 'federalist' features. (see Hartley (1986)) A typical international organisation is a form of inter-governmental cooperation which operates on the basis of consent, so that no Member State may be bound without its consent.

Yet Community law is said to be binding on the Member States as well as on individuals, in many cases and applicable by national or domestic courts. Further, Community decisions derive their force from the fact that they are taken by organs which have been given the power by the the Community's constitution-the Treaties.

They do not therefore derive their power from the fact of consent by the Member States. This is why the Community legal order is sometimes described as *supra-national*. However, caselaw from the European Court of Justice suggests that individual Member States are not necessarily bound by Community law unless various implementation measures are enacted, and it will also depend on the nature of the legislation involved and its date of implementation. In practical terms, the UK, have generally proceeded to amend the legislation or law in question so as to be in accord with the European court's rulings whenever national legislation has been called into question, on questions of discrimination at work or human rights issues involving access to children in care.

Community Law has, of course, emanated from the civil law systems. As such, it has adopted some of the typically civil law judicial, administrative and legislative styles. It is on the basis of comparing the particular 'juristic style' of Community Law with that of common law and civil law parent systems that the discussion now proceeds.

G. COMPARISON OF LEGAL STYLE OF COMMUNITY LAW
   WITH OTHER SYSTEMS

5.6   As we have seen in Chapter 2, the juristic style of a particular legal system, (as suggested by writers like Zweigert and Kotz) may be determined by an examination of the following factors: (i) its historical background and development; (ii) its characteristic mode of thought in legal matters; (iii) its distinctive institutions; (iv) the types of sources it acknowledges and its treatment of these; (v) its ideology.

When we examine the historical antecedents of Community law we see that its modern beginnings may be traced to the post-war sense of helplessness and fear of survival which was felt by European nations involved in the two global conflicts, coupled with the rise of power of America on whom the West was growing increasingly dependent, and the rise of the Soviet Union and China as Communist superpowers. However, as we have seen, the common law of England was shaped by the powerful centralisation of courts and its visionary kings, judges and statesmen; and the legal configuration of the modern civil law, although initially derived from Roman law and customary law, in France and Germany, was determined by its rebirth in the Italian universities, the French Revolution and the German Pandectists.

Since civil law was the legacy of the European nations that first entered into the EEC Treaty of Rome, it is the European 'continental' legal style, specifically the French tradition, that the Community has adopted in its court structure, and administration of justice, and, before the German and common law tradition made themselves felt, in the interpretation of codes, statutes and rules of procedure. In the 1980s, however, two further influences have started to make their way into Community law via the judgments of the European Court of Justice: the German legal approach and the English legal style. (see below)

As has been stated time and again, history and law are generally inseparable and history clearly leaves its footprints in the shifting sands of legal opinions, legal literature and legal discourse.

Unlike common law jurisdictions which have a caselaw-oriented system, despite its increasingly reliance on statutory law, many civil law countries, particularly France and Germany, approach legal problems in terms of *general concepts and principles*, which are predominantly but not exclusively *contained in its codes and statutes*. European Community law has adopted and adapted *a number of different legal styles*, beginning with the French style, then the German approach, in its earlier phase when there were only Six in the Community, then, with the enlargement of the Community, it has slowly started to rely on previously decided caselaw in the style of the common law and has even begun to develop its own version of *stare decisis* (see Koopmans (1991)).

i. The Influence of French Law

5.6.1 In the modern period, a great deal of the Continental and predominantly French legal ethos, ranging from sitting as a group or team of judges and delivering a collegial or collective judgment, to being permitted to consult *travaux preparatoires* and other extraneous aids to statutory or legislative interpretation, is evident in the judgments of the European Court of Justice (ECJ). However, one need not have looked far to see the initial influence of French administrative law, particularly in the period when there was only a Community of Six.

For instance, take Article 173 of the EEC Treaty, dealing with provisions on *actions for the annulment of Community decisions*. This Article, *inter alia*, permits a natural or legal person to institute proceedings against a decision addressed to him. It confers jurisdiction on the Court to review the legality of acts of the Council and the Commission, other than 'recommendations' or 'opinions' and Article 173(1) enables parties to attack a Community act on any one of *four grounds*: Lack of competence; infringement of an essential procedural requirement; infringement of the Treaty or of any rule of law relating to its application; or misuse of powers.

These four terms are borrowed from French administrative law, and the *grounds of annulment* are similar to those developed by the French *Conseil d'Etat* as forms of *'excess de pouvoir'* which leads to annulment in French administrative law. However, caselaw from the ECJ suggests that despite their origin, and the fact that they are terms of art with definite meanings, they are now terms of Community law and must be taken in that context alone: [1957-58] ECR 133. Indeed, the ECJ has developed these terms far beyond the parameters of the French concepts.

Even more historically illuminating, is the influence of the French administrative legal tradition generally on even the basic structure and legal philosophy of the Community Institutions. For instance, among the draftsmen of the first Treaty of Paris, was M. Maurice Legrange, who was one of the first Advocates-General at the Euroepan Court. In a very real sense, one can see the link between the development of the French *Conseil d'Etat* and its pre-eminent position in France and the creation of the ECJ. It was in Article 12 of the Law of August 1790 that it was stated that 'Judicial functions are distinct and will always remain separate from administrative functions. Judges in the civil courts may not...concern themselves in any manner whatsoever with the operation of the administration.' Read within the context of the history of the ancien regime, we then see a clear recognition of the necessity for a check on the unlimited power of the administrator. To this end, the *Conseil d'Etat* was set up in 1799, and through a body of caselaw, has established rules by which the executive must regulate their affairs so as to promote effective administration and protect the individual. If one bears in mind the fundamental division between public and private law in civil law countries and in the first Six Community countries, one sees that the whole concept of judicial control over administration unites the laws of civil law countries within the Community since 'from an ideological standpoint, all have been powerfully influenced by the French Revolution and Empire and by the *liberlisme bourgeois* of the nineteenth century.' (Auby et Fromont *Les Recours contre les Actes Administratifs* (1971) p.449, cited and translated by Mackenzie Stuart in *The European Communities and the Rule of Law* (1977)).

Another sign of the French influence, apart from the concise single collective judgment, was the *individual advisory opinion* of the *advocate-general* which precedes the judgment, which finds its provenance in French law, in the *Cour de cassation*, the supreme court in private law and criminal court. A similar function is performed in the *Conseil d'Etat* by the *commissaire du gouvernement* (Government Commissioners) although unlike his counterpart with the same appellation in the other administrative courts, this official is *not* a member of the *Conseil d'Etat* at all, but is a senior civil servant who represents governments and is responsible for putting forward government views and projects. In France, at that level, he is a ministerial spokesman.

Of course, the fact that other members of the Six included Belgium and Luxembourg who have legal systems very similar to the French, and the Italian system which is closer to the French style than any other, explains why the French influence was so dominant, and this was also noticeable in the style of legal reasoning, which was deductive and pitched at a high level of abstraction. (Koopmans (1991)

ii. The Influence of German Law

5.6.2   However, the impact of the German legal tradition soon began to appear in the ECJ's caselaw. In accordance with the Court's attempts to identify general legal principles, one of the principles so earmarked was the *principle of proportionality*, derived from German administrative law, which is that administrative action should be proportionate to the ends that it seeks to achieve (*Verhaltnismassigkeit*). This had been fully developed in German law but has now become an established part of Community Law: see Article 30, EEC Treaty. The principle was illustrated in the famous German beer case: *Commission* v. *FRG*, Case 178/84 [1987] ECR 1227, which dealt with sixteenth century German legislation on beer purity. This legislation required beer to be made from a limited number of natural ingredients, and had the incidental effect of preventing beers made in other Member States which contained various additives or preservatives from being sold in Germany. The basic issue was whether the German legislation could be regarded as fulfilling the mandatory requirements of protection of health or protection of consumers. On the first question, the Commission could show that all the preservatives or additives at issue were permitted under German law to be used in other foodstuffs. Thus, despite the German government's arguments that beer was consumed on a large scale by German drinkers, the Court held that these preservatives and additives did not constitute a threat to health in beer. Another illustration is the *Italian vinegar case*: see *Commission* v. *Italian Republic*, Case 193/80, [1981] ECR 3019. The principle from these cases is that while national legislation may limit free movement of goods for reasons of public health, such restrictions can only be permitted so far as they were indispensable for ensuring public health.

Another concept borrowed from German law has been the concept of respect for legitimate expectations (*Vertrauensschutz*). Further evidence of the German influence can be seen it the way in which the ECJ's judgments have become 'less deductive and apodictic' (Koopmans (1991)p.502) and an examination of judgments in the 1960s and 1980s will reveal differences in the breadth of the Court's judgments, and the tendency to be more discursive in its judicial style.

iii. The Influence of the Common Law Tradition

5.6.3   With the accession of the United Kingdom, Ireland and Denmark new tradtions entered the Community. However, it was the common law that gradually wielded an influence on the character of Community Law. This took some time, but during the 1980s, for example, a greater awareness of procedural problems developed in two ways: (i) The Court showed a willingness to reopen a case for oral argument when it felt that it was possible to expedite a decision on the basis of arguments which had not yet been addressed by the parties: see *A.M. & S Europe*, Case 155/79 [1982] ECR 1575; *Lancome*, Case 99.79 [1980] ECR 2511, 2526-2528; *Commission* v. *UK* [1983] ECR 2265, 2268-2270; The adversarial approach derived from the common law, was clearly being encouraged where the Court felt it would expedite matters to do so.

(ii) The Court began to recognise a company's right to a fair hearing in the decision-making process before an administrative body or agency. This right was acknowledged even when the relevant Community provisions did not mention it: see *Transocean Marine Paint Association*, Case 17/74 [1974] ECR 1063. In this case, the English rule of *audi alterem partem* was utilised to strike down a Commission decision which had varied the legal position of the applicants without giving them an opportunity to be heard, that is, to submit their views on the matter.

Commentators have also pointed out that the Court's judgments in anti-trust cases, shifted from focussing on the effectiveness of competition rules and the scope of Community Law, to the rights of companies accused of anti-competitive behaviour. (see Korse *EEC Antitrust Procedure* (1988)ch.3-4; and Korah (1980) Current Legal Problems 73).

It was during the eighties that the Court began to rely on previously decided caselaw. But more significantly, it also began to develop the practice of declaring that it would follow a previous precedent because no new arguments had been advanced. It has repeatedly held that in the system of preliminary rulings, national courts should never feel obliged to refer questions to the Court when a ruling on the matter has already been given. The Court has also emphasised that national courts are at liberty to submit new questions on the issue for the Court to consider when they believe that these have not yet been determined by the Court: see *CILFIT* v. *Ministero della Sanita*, Case 283/81 [1982] ECR 3415. Hence, the ECJ appears to be developing a form of *stare decisis* which is broadly in accordance with English common law tradition, but which is not exercised in exactly the same manner as in contemporary English common law. Previously decided cases are relied upon in later cases, but the scope of their applicability may be extended or restricted in accordance with the particular circumstances.

Another indication of the influence of the common law tradition is the fact that the Court's proceedings have now assumed a less formal atmosphere, in the context of the encouragement of some sort of dialogue between judges and lawyers. This is very much in the spirit of the English common law tradition. When it works, it appears to work very well indeed, but when it is hampered or hindered by translation problems, for example when the Court has to listen to oral interpreters who may not appreciate fully the vital nuance in the particular statement or give a *literal* but *not* an *accurate* translation. This brings us to the tricky question of the 'language of Community Law'.

iv. The Language of Community Law

5.6.4   The difficulties of comparison of Community Law with other legal systems are compounded when we look at *the language of Community Law*. Indeed, a preliminary point to clarify is that what is referred to in this section is: the actual different languages used which require accurate translations to render them intelligible and meaningful to national systems and, if necessary, to the Courts, *not* the legal terminology *per se*. In the present context, therefore, it will be evident that there are several languages used to express Treaties and other enabling provisions.

Although the ECSC Treaty is in one authentic version in French, the other Treaties have been drawn up in a single document in several European languages, including German, French, Italian and Dutch, Danish, English, Irish, and Norwegian, all said to be 'equally authentic'. Of course this is an accepted form for a multilateral, multi-lingual treaty. The 'equally authentic' formula ensures that all texts, having an equal status, can be cited as the authoritative statement of the law and no one text may therefore take precedence over another. The EC Commission has 1,000 staff who are employed in translating the mountain of documents, an enormous task necessitated by the nine official languages and authenticity approach.

However, it is now becoming more widely recognised than ever before, that translation of a legal text is much more than simply providing mere synonyms or literal equivalents for terms, and translators need to be very conversant not just with the operation of 'registers' (different levels, 'pitches' and contexts), legal registers and legal terms *per se*, but with the overall legal system into which the concepts fit. To use the title of an article on this matter, difficulties in giving *accurate* translations is a problem which no EC directive can eliminate. (see Reeves '1992 Languages: the barrier no EC directive can eliminate' (1989) *Linguist*, p.5).

An additional linguistic difficulty is that Community law has now developed several distinctive concepts whose meaning and application are far removed from their original or derivative meanings. Consequently, the Member State may well be unwittingly misled by the superficial similarity of terms. Finally, Community law must be interpreted in the light of its overall matrix, in the light of its objectives, its particular evolutionary stage and according to the contemporaneity of the issue. Thus, something decided in 1973 might not necessarily be interpreted or decided in the same way in 1992, if conditions have rendered the earlier decision obsolete or inappropriate.

As 1993 approaches, it might well be essential for linguists who are also trained lawyers to work as interpreters and perhaps for many more 'exchange programmes' to be set up which could ensure a constant flow of cultural and legal ideas on both sides of the Channel and across Western (and indeed, eventually, Eastern) Europe.

The Community Regulations are drawn up in the nine official languages of the Community and published in the EC official gazette (Official Journal of the European Communities). As far as the ECJ is concerned, the official languages of the Court are: Danish, English, French, German, Italian and Dutch but Irish (although not official) may be used. Generally, only one of the official languages may be used as the procedural language, but there is a certain amount of flexibility allowed to participants in the court process. The applicant has a choice of language, and if the defendant is a member state or a person or corporation subject to a member state the procedural language will be the official language of that state. If so desired, the parties may jointly request the use of another official language as the procedural language, which the Court may allow, and in exceptional circumstances, the court may authorise the total or partial use of another official procedural language if one of the parties so requests.

v. Legislation as Language

5.6.5   At another level,the characteristic mode of thought in Community Law is in fact derived from its secondary sources of law, which we discuss further, below. In other words. if one were to ask a European Community lawyer what his typical legal language is when he deals with Community law, his answer, at the basic level of generality, will be : in terms of *regulations*, *directives* and *decisions*. As we shall see in our discussion on Community Law sources, each of these have a special, unique meaning and each of these, in the European context, are almost instantly associated with the legal language of the European Community. In the company law field, in particular, there has been a series of directives emanating from the EC, some of which have already been implemented in national legal systems. Thus, the types of legislation that has been enacted within and by the Community has become part of the legal order and legal language of the Community and is now identifiable as such.

H. THE COMMUNITY'S LEGAL ORDER/REGIME

i. Nature of Community Law

5.7   Community law has been described as a body of law that is 'at once hierarchical and autonomous' (Valee (1983) *Le droit des Communautes europeennes 'Que sais-je?'* No.2067, p.90). In considering what Community law represents, we might first say what it is not. It is not a superstate, nor a quasi-state nor a federal state. (Dagtoglou [1973] CLJ 259). The Treaty of Rome is *not a federal constitution*, although there may be some who would wish it were. However, Community law is a *separate legal system*, distinct from, though closely linked to, both international law and the legal systems of the Member States: *Van Gend en Loos* [1963] ECR 1. As the ECJ has put it, in creating the European Community the member states have 'limited their sovereign rights, albeit within limited fields, and have ...created a body of law which binds both their nationals and themselves' (*Costa* v. *Ente Nazionale Per L'Energia Elettrica*(ENEL) [1964] ECR 585). The *Van Gend en Loos* case also emphasised that the Community treaties are more than mere international agreements. They also form the constitution of the Community (*Les Vertis-Parti Ecologiste* v. *European Parliament*, Case 294/83 [1987] 2 CMLR 343) and the rules of law derived from them constitute the internal law of the Community (*Federation Charbonniere de Belgique* v. *High Authority*, case 8/55 [1956] ECR 245 at 277.

 In addition, it has been pointed out that although it has been 'engendered by international law, it does not share all its characteristics, having more in common with branches of national law such as constitutional and administrative law' (Hartley (1988)). But national legislatures do not have the power to repeal or amend it and it will override any national law with which it comes into conflict. Its interpretation, in the final analysis, comes within the exclusive jurisdiction of the ECJ: *Van Gend en Loos* (above).

Community law has therefore been conceived not simply as a supra-national body of law but was intended to be an integral part of the legal orders of the Member States and be enforced by the national courts as well as by the ECJ. As far as the UK was concerned, upon its accession to the Communities, the effect of the new legal order was clear. In the much-quoted words of Lord Denning: '[W]hen we come to matters with a European element, the Treaty is like an incoming tide. It flows into the estuaries and up the rivers. It cannot be held back. Parliament has decreed that the Treaty is henceforward part of our law. It is equal in force to any statute...Any rights or obligations created by the Treaty are to be given legal effect in England without more ado. Any remedies or procedures provided by the Treaty are to be made available here without being open to question. In future, in transactions which cross the frontiers, we must no longer speak or think of English law as something on its own. We must speak and think of community law, of community rights and obligations and we must give effect to them.'

Although this was uttered in the context of the UK, the impact of Community law on other European Member States is no less significant.

ii. Direct Applicability and Direct Effect

5.7.1 The first point to note about the so-called principle of 'direct effect' is that it is nowhere explicitly mentioned in the treaty. It is therefore a creation of the ECJ which was first established in the case of *Van Gend en Loos* [1963] ECR 1, for a number of reasons which we shall explore presently. A more accurate term might therefore be 'direct applicability' which has been defined as denoting 'the ability of a provision of Community law to become part of the domestic legal system of a Member State without the need for formal enactment by national means'. (Freestone and Davidson (1988) p.28) In other words, it is a concept that suggests that in the appropriate case, Community law is directly applicable in national law and can thereby create rights in favour of individuals which national courts must protect.

The next point to note about this concept is that the concept of direct applicability is found in Article 189 (EEC Treaty) with regard to the effect of Regulations. That Article declares that a Regulation has general application and 'It shall be binding in its entirety and directly applicable in all Member States'.

The question of the direct applicability of Community rules first arose in the case of *Van Gend en Loos* (above). In September 1960, the plaintiff Dutch haulage company van Gend en Loos, imported an aqueous emulsion of ureaformaldehyde from Germany for use in the manufacture of glue. It received a claim from the Dutch customs authorities for duty at a rate higher than the rate current for the product at the time when the Treaty of Rome entered into force. As a result of an agreement consluded between the Benelux countries in July 1958, aqueous emulsions had been transferred from a category of products taxed at 3% to another category taxed at 8%. The glue manufacturer protested to the national authorities on the grounds that Article 12 of the Treaty prohibited the common market countries from increasing the customs duties that they applied as between themselves on 1 January 1958, when the Treaty entered into force.

In turn, the authorities concerned, the Dutch revenue appeals tribunal (*Tariefcommissie*), using the procedure of Article 177 of the Treaty, put the following question to the ECJ: 'Whether Article 12 of the EEC Treaty has direct application'-as argued by the plaintiffs in the action-'in other words, whether nationals of Member States can, on the basis of the Article in question, lay claims to individual rights which the courts must protect?'

The German, Belgian and Dutch governments submitted their observations to the Court. In their opinion, only member States or the Commission could bring any alleged infringements of the Treaty before the Court. The Treaty, they submitted, conferred rights and imposed obligations only on the signatory States and certainly not on private individuals who must remain subject to their national law. The Advocate General agreed, giving his reasons for his view.

However, the Court thought differently, and in another well-known passage, said: 'The objective of the EEC Treaty, which is to establish a Common Market, the functioning of which is of direct concern to interested parties in the Community, implies that this Treaty is more than an agreement which merely creates mutual obligations between the contracting states. This view is confirmed by the preamble to the treaty which refers not only to governments but to peoples. It is also confirmed more specifically by the establishment of institutions endowed with sovereign rights, the exercise of which affects Member States and also their citizens.'

From these propositions, the Court could therefore declare that: '[t]he Community constitutes a new legal order of international law for the benefit of which the states have limited their sovereign rights, albeir within limited fields, and the subjects of which comprise not only member States but also their nationals. Independently of the legislation of Member States, Community law therefore not only imposes obligations on individuals but is also intended to confer upon them rights which become part of their legal heritage. These rights arise not only where they are expressly granted by the Treaty, but also by reason of obligations which the Treaty imposes in a clearly defined way upon individuals as well as upon the Member States and upon the institutions of the Community.'

Hence, the Treaty has created in each of the Member States, whose constitutional law relating to the internal effect of international obligations differs widely, rules of substantive law which were enforceable by private individuals. In the instant case, the importer was therefore to be placed on the same footing as if there had been full observance of the Treaty.

It was perfectly possible for the Court to have reached its final conclusion by confining itself to a discussion of Article 12. However, it has been argued that it chose not to do so, because : (i) it wished to rebut the suggestions from the governments that direct effect was an exception; (ii) it felt that there was a need to defend the system created by the Treaties against the tendency to apply Community law purely in accordance with the subjective wishes of the parties rather than as a system that stood on its own and functioned independently of the parties' wishes; (iii) it seemed to wish to promote the individual as the beneficiary of Community law and thereby be an effective instrument for enforcing a Member State's obligations: (see Louis (1990)p.109)

Since that famous case was decided, the ECJ has built up a large body of caselaw elaborating on the tests to be applied but this is not the place to pursue the many ramifications which arise from the principle. Suffice to say that, to be directly applicable, a provision must itself be legally self-sufficient (Freestone and Davidson (1988) p.31) and according to statements made in cases like *Reyners* v. *Belgian State*, Case 2/74 [1974] ECR 631, the tests to apply in deciding whether a provision meets this requirement are: (i) the obligation it establishes must be clear and precise;(ii) the obligation must be unconditional; (iii) the obligation must not be dependent upon further action by either the Community or national authorities.

iii. Supremacy of Community Law

5.7.2 Several months after the judgment in *Van Gend en Loos*, a Milan judge brought before the Court a request for interpretation of the Treaty in a case which required clarification of the situation in the event of a conflict between Community law and national law. In the famous case of *Costa* v. *Enel* [1964] ECR 585, Mr. Costa, a shareholder in Edison Volta, argued that he had suffered injury through the nationalisation of the facilties for the production and distribution of electricity in the country. he refused to pay a bill for a few hundred lira presented by the new nationalised company ENEL. When summoned before a court in Milan, he submitted in his defence that the nationalisation law was contrary to the Treaty of Rome. The judge hearing the case therefore approached the ECJ. Meanwhile, the Italian constitutional court had intervened in connection with the law establishing ENEL. In its opinion, the situation was: since the Rome Treaty had been ratified by an ordinary law, the provisions of a later conflicting law would have to take precedence over those of the Treaty.

But the ECJ disagreed and in its judgment, pointed out that: 'By creating a Community of unlimited duration, having its own institutions, its own personality, its own legal capacity of representation on the international plane and, more particularly, real powers stemming from a limitation of sovereignty or a transfer of powers from the States to the Community, the Member States have limited their sovereign rights, albeit within limited fields, and have thus created a body of law which binds both their nationals and themselves.

The integration into the laws of each Member State of provisions which derive from the Community, and more generally the terms and the spirit of the Treaty, make it impossible for the States, as a corollary, to accord precedence to a unilateral and subsequent measure over a legal system accepted by them on a basis of reciprocity.'

As if this were not forceful enough, they went on to add that 'The executive force of Community law cannot vary from one State to another in deference to subsequent domestic laws, without jeopardising the attainment of the objectives of the Treaty...The obligations undertaken under the Treaty establishing thc Community would not be unconditional but merely contingent if they could be called in question by subsequent legislative acts of the signatories.' As in *Van Gend en Loos*, the Court then affirmed the precedence of Commmunity law as laid down in Article 189, which, it added, is subject to no reservation and would be 'meaningless' if a State could unilaterally nullify its effects by means of a legislative measure which could prevail over Community law. Accordingly, the ECJ concluded that 'the law, stemming from the Treaty, an independent source of law, could not, because of its special ...nature, be overridden by domestic legal provisions, however framed, without being deprived of its character as Community law and without the legal basis of the Community itself being called into question.'

This approach was confirmed in subsequent cases like *Minister of Finance* v. *Simmenthal* [1978] ECR 629, where the ECJ confirmed that in cases where national law and directly effective Community law came into conflict, national courts are under a duty to give effect to Community law, which would even override incompatible rules of national law which were passed subsequently. It stressed that Community law provisions are a direct source of rights and duties for all those affected thereby, whether Member States or individuals and that national courts were under a duty to give full effect to Community law provisions.

iv. Community Techniques of Legal Interpretation

5.7.3   A reading of the caselaw decided by the ECJ reveals the particular legal approach or techniques of legal interpretation which it applies when dealing with Community law. First of all, it considers the issue or dispute which has been brought to its attention in the light of any relevant Treaty provision, or piece of secondary legislation. If these are clear and unambiguous, it adopts the *literal interpretation*, very much as most legal systems do, whether common or civil law, unless there are good reasons for not doing so. Cases also indicate that the ECJ is conscious that the same standard of draftsmanship found in national legislation cannot be expected in treaties. The next interpretative principle is the *logical interpretation* of the text, wherein the Court will consider the provision within the *context of the system*. In considering previous judicial interpretations on a provision, the Court may also consider adopting the *teleological interpretation* which, although literal to a certain extent, focuses on the intention of the legislature in the light of the conditions prevailing at the time of the judgment.

Secondly, and not necessarily in the alternative, the Court has been known to adopt the following approach: (i) It asks for comparative materials on the issue, based on legislation, academic opinion and caselaw of the Member States, on the existence and scope of the disputed rule or concept. It should be remembered that in accordance with the Continental courts' practice, and the close connection between continental judges to the academic world, the ECJ has found the contribution of learned writers' opinions extremely helpful to the clarification and development of the Court's *jurisprudence*. Nevertheless, the Court goes for quality rather than quantity and is highly eclectic in its choice of doctrinal opinions, choosing only the most eminent of experts with established reputations in the field, and the actual number of judgments citing these writers' opinions are fairly few in number in relation to the abundance of writing on Community law.

(ii) It invites the parties and the advocates or interveners to submit their views as to the existence and scope of the disputed principle.

(iii) It reviews the case carefully, and then consider whether there are any 'general principles of law' which are sometimes, but not always traceable to international law principles, municipal law concepts and institutions/doctrines or are simply not traceable to any recognisable source (for example, relating to equality and discrimination: see *Re Electric Refrigerators*, Case 13/63 [1963] CMLR 289, at p.303) or on the status of international administrative tribunals: see *Bourgaux* v. *ECSC Common Assembly*, Case 1/56 (1956) 2 Rec. 451. As we have already indicated, the ECJ has also begun to adapt various concepts to suit the particular style of the Court and the needs of the parties. There is no doubt, however, that the Court makes extensive use of comparative material and is perfectly happy to utilise its own version of 'legal transplants' where it deems it appropriate or necessary to do so.

v. Distinctive Legal Institutions/Doctrines

5.7.4   Under this criterion, the term 'institutions' refers to the characteristic legal concepts and doctrines of a legal system, rather than the administrative, judicial or legislative organs of a particular entity. Hence, in the Romano-Germanic legal family, typical legal institutions include rules protecting the moral and economic integrity of a family against outsiders, the abuse of right, direct action, oblique action and their unique versions of the concept of Good Faith. (see chapter 9). In the Germanic legal family, there are concepts such as that of the general clauses, the abstract real contract, the institution of unjustified enrichment, and the doctrine based on collapse of the foundations of a transaction.

When we examine the European Community, we find that there is an inevitable mixture of concepts, and civil law and common law influences, for reasons explained above, but also that many of these concepts have begun to be clothed with a distinctive EC flavour. As we have seen above, the *doctrines* or *concepts* that have become part of Community Law are certain *general principles of law* such as 'market freedoms' which are essential prerequisites of the integration of national economies: free movement of goods, free movement of workers, freedom to exercise professional activities and so on. Another set of principles concerns setting limits to the exercise of Community powers, and yet another set may broadly be called principles of legality developed in administrative law and practice in member states, particularly with regard to economic law and the protection of legitimate expectations. Prominent among these sorts of doctrines are:(a) the principle of equality and non-discrimination; (b) the principle of freedom;(c) the principle of solidarity (against member refusing to fulfil its obligations); (d) the principle of unity (ie of the common market); (e) the principle of proportionality; (f) the rights of the defence, including the right to a hearing;

(g) confidentiality of correspondence between lawyer and client; (h) prohibition of arbitrary acts; (i) general principles of human rights. (j) general commercial principles such as good faith and fairness in dealing. (k) abuse of dominant position(Article 86: EEC Treaty).

vi. Choice of Sources of Law

5.7.5   The phrase 'sources of law' in the present context refers to the authority from which it is derived rather than the historical, social, political or economic reasons or causes of the law. Hence, the sources of Community law may be divided into *primary* and *secondary* sources of law. The primary sources of Community law are the founding *Treaties* (in particular the EEC Treaty) .As far as *Treaties* are concerned, apart from the founding treaties, other treaties such as the Accession Treaties, the Merger Treaty of 1965, the 1970 Budgetary Treaty, and the Single European Act 1986 would be included. Finally, any pre-existing Treaties such as GATT, treaties guaranteeing human rights (the UN Covenants and the ECHR) and treaties between the EEC and third states would also qualify as primary sources.

 The secondary sources of Community law are the *law-making acts of the Community organs* which result in a body of law, namely, the *administrative* and *judicial acts* emanating from the respective organs:

 (i) Administrative Acts: regulations, directives and decisions made by the Council or the Commission in order to carry out their task in accordance with the Treaty (Article 189: EEC Treaty). There is some confusion over the status of *Recommendations* and *Opinions*; the position appears to be that Opinions cannot be regarded as sources of Community law but Recommendations might be, although only under the ECSC Treaty. (ii) Judicial Legislation-decisions of the ECJ.

 As we have seen, cases are the predominant source of law in the common law tradition although the modern trend is to have greater reliance on statutes, wherever possible. Although codes and legislation are the main official sources of law in civil law countries, we have seen how they are sometimes merely a facade for the actual sources, which are court decisions.

vii. Ideology of the System

5.7.6   The objectives of the European Community are probably the best guide to its underlying ideology in the sense of its *motivating political and economic doctrines*. It is in the Preamble to the EEC Treaty that we find a general and rhetorical statement of principles, commencing with the intention '*to lay the foundations of an ever closer union among the peoples of Europe*', to which we have earlier alluded. But the basic principles of the substantive law of the EEC are contained firstly in Article 2 of the EEC Treaty which sets out the objectives of the Treaty and the means by which they are to be achieved. The *objectives* are: 'the harmonious development of economic activities throughout the Community, a continuous and balanced exanpansion, an increase in stability, an accelerated raising of the standard of living, and closer relations between the states belonging to the Community'.

146

From this Article, it appears that the goals of the Community are to be attained by the *two mechanisms* of a *'common market'* and the *'progressive approximation of economic policies'* of Member States. Article 3 then develops these means into eleven heads of activity, or statements of intent, such as '(a) the elimination, as between Member States, of customs duties, and of quantitative restricitons on the import and export of goods, and of all other measures having equivalent effect; (b) the establishment of a common customs tariff and of a common commercial policy towards third countries; (c) the abolition as between Member States, of obstacles to freedom of movement for persons, services and capital'. Further categories then specify the adoption of a common policy on agriculture and transport and the application of procedures to co-ordinate the economic policies of Member States.

The wording of these heads suggest that they are by no means exclusive or limitative which is clear from Article 3 and Article 235. each of these heads of activity is the subject of particular Articles of the Treaty containing specific provisions. Some of these provisions constitute directly effective rights (and in some cases, obligations) for nationals and enterprises of ·the Member States, directly effective obligations for the Member States and also obligations or powers to enable the Community institutions or the Member States to adopt implementing or further regulatory measures.

A great deal has already been achieved to implement these objectives such as a customs union and various measures intended to achieve the removal of retrictions on the 'four freedoms': free movement of goods, persons, services, and capital. The major step taken towards this goal was the Single European Act, a treaty agreed by the Member States in 1986, in force in the UK from 1 July 1987 (Cm 372/1988). This Act has set the further objective of the Community, of 'an area without internal frontiers in which the free movement of goods, persons, services, and capital is ensured' in accordance with the Treaty, to be achieved by 31 December, 1992. There is now a common agricultural policy, and provision is made in the Treaty for the co-ordination of economic and monetary policies (see Article 6, 102a-105). The Community has also been moving toward the goal of Economic and Monetary Union.

Among the stated objectives in Article 3 is the ninth head (i), which shows that the Community has also undertaken certain social objectives, which are fully developed in Title III of the Treaty. They include equal pay without discrimination based on sex, improvements in the health and safety of workers, a common vocational training policy, and the maintenance of a European Social Fund which provides assistance for such schemes as the retraining and resettlement of workers. The Single European Act deals expressly with the objectives of social and economic integration (including reduction of regional disparities), research and technological development and protection of the environment. It also contains provisions which formalise political cooperation between the member States in questions of foreign policy.

The objectives are supplemented and intended to be promoted and realised by certain fundamental principles in Articles 5, 6 and 7 which deal with the basic principles of Community loyalty and co-operation between Member States and Institutions of the Community in the co-ordination of the economic policies of the Member States, as well as a general prohibition of discrimination on grounds of nationality. These encapsulate the principle of

147

Community 'solidarity' which under Article 5, imposes the obligation on Member States to take all appropriate measures to endure fulfilment of the obligations arising out of the Treaty. There is also an obligation on the national judge to ensure the legal protection which subjects derive from the direct effect of provisions of Community law. It should perhaps be noted that the general non-discrimination provision in Article 7 does not prohibit all discrimination but only discrimination on the grounds of nationality.

The non-discrimination provisions only become specific when dealing with state commercial monoplies (article 37:EEC), cartel agreements (Article 85:EEC), enterprises with a dominant economic position (Article 86:EEC) and dumping (Article 91:EEC).

It will be noticed, therefore that apart from primarily economic objectives, there are also social ones and at root, there is the historical motivating objective of a certain degree of European political unity or at least integration. Perhaps at a rather prosaic level, as a generation of French political leaders has argued, uniting with one's neighbours could enable France and ultimately, all European countries, to play a much more dominant role in European economic and political affairs than they have done in modern times. It might also provide a safeguard against future domination by any major superpower in war or peace. The true objectives of the Community may well be characterised as both regional and ultimately, global.

The Maastricht Treaty, signed in December 1991, calls for European monetary union by 1999 and seeks to point the way to closer European cooperation in defence and foreign policy. In the light of the very narrow French referendum result (*le petit oui*, as one French newspaper called it) on 20 September 1992, and the Danish rejection in its referendum, it remains to be seen if the objectives of this Treaty will indeed be a reality by the year 2000, in the light of the current uncertainties and pan-European debates surrounding its implementation.

I. CONCLUSIONS

5.8 Even a brief examination of the salient features of the European Community reveals the wealth of legal tradition, legal institutions and doctrines that the Community embodies. Although a predominant legal tradition is the French legal tradition both in Community institutional structure and methods of reasoning predominantly adopted by the European Court, there have also been concepts which, at least initially, derived from German law. Having been conceived, developed and promoted by Frenchmen, it is inevitable that French ideas and French legal philosophies also dominated the early legal and administrative development of the Community legal order. However, our brief survey also reveals that like all great and enduring ideas, the Community legal order has now acquired a life of its own. Although rooted in French or German legal philosophies, it has started to adopt and adapt elements of the English common law tradition, to the extent of developing its own unique system of precedent.

Its methods of legislative and statutory interpretation are a truly international combination of techniques and styles. Since the founding Treaties are really international agreements which are governed by international law, and the European Community is an international organisation, it is equally subject to the rules that govern international organisations. Yet as a regional grouping, it has also created a unique relationship between the national law of Member States and Community law and even appears to traverse the interface between international law and domestic (national) law. For example, it echoes Article 38 of the Statute of the International Court of Justice, which refers to the general principles of law recognised by civilised nations, by also referring to general principles of law as well, and the ECJ's caselaw suggests there is no limit to these principles and that they are traceable to and reminiscent of, international law and national law concepts, as contained in Treaties, codes and cases all over the civil and common law world.

Our comparative study therefore shows that European Community law is unquestionably a unique form of European law, even at the most fundamental level, but has more practical and immediate significance than any other legal system, by virtue of the twin pillars of its legal order. In other words, by virtue of its primacy over national law and the direct applicability of some of its provisions, it has already begun to direct the flow, if not actually turn the tide, of European law.

As we approach 1993, European lawyers are coming to grips with more and more Community law, and observing the frequently disorientating and fluctuating fortunes of Eastern Europe. The need to employ the comparative method to be able to deal with different European systems of law is becoming increasingly evident-to prepare for further developments and a new legal order in an ever-changing world and to provide much-needed assistance to ravaged Eastern European countries who will one day wish to return to some semblance of law, peace and order. What our study reveals is that the process of change, adaptation and transplantation has already begun.

SELECTIVE BIBLIOGRAPHY

Keeton & Schwarzenberger ENGLISH LAW AND THE COMMON MARKET (1963)

Hartley 'Federalism, Courts and Legal Systems: The Emerging

Constitution of the European Community' (1986) 34 Am.JCL 229

Lord Mackenzie Stuart THE EUROPEAN COMMUNITIES AND THE RULE OF
        LAW (1977)

Louis EUROPEAN COMMUNITY LAW (1990)

Lasok and Bridge LAW AND INSTITUTIONS OF THE EUROPEAN
        COMMUNITIES (1991)

Hartley THE FOUNDATIONS OF EUROPEAN COMMUNITY LAW (1990)

Freestone & Davidson THE INSTITUTIONAL FRAMEWORK OF THE EUROPEAN
        COMMUNITIES (1990)

Turpin BRITISH GOVERNMENT AND THE CONSTITUTION (1990)ch.5

Mathijsen A GUIDE TO EUROPEAN COMMUNITY LAW (1990)

Spencer 1992 AND ALL THAT: Civil Liberties in the Balance

Kapteyn & VerLoren van Themaat INTRODUCTION TO THE LAW OF THE
        EUROPEAN COMMUNITIES (1990)

Green, Hartley and Usher THE LEGAL FOUNDATIONS OF THE SINGLE
        EUROPEAN MARKET (1991)

Koopmans 'The Birth of European Law At the Crossroads of Legal Traditions' (1991) 39 Am.J CL 493

CHAPTER SIX

Socialist Law and other Types of Legal Systems

A. SCOPE OF CHAPTER

6.0   This chapter first examines the socialist concept of law, before discussing differences and similiarities between civil law and socialist systems. It then conducts a brief inquest on the former Soviet Union, which was the prototype of the socialist legal systems and ideology. It concludes that section with an appraisal of the current Russian reforms and hypothesises on the future development of Russia. We then examine the Chinese and Japanese concepts of law, as examples of unique, *sui generis* systems of law.

B. THE SOCIALIST SYSTEM AND RUSSIA

6.1   The system of law that existed in the former Union of Soviet Socialist Republics (USSR), was the law that governed the world's second super-power and communist prototype. In Europe today, the Socialist legal system is no longer a dominant and equal partner with civil law and common law parent legal families but is now relegated to being an example of just another legal system. Indeed, as a result of the events of the past three years in Eastern Europe and the former Soviet Union, it is arguable that many former Socialist countries will return to their civil law roots but if they retain some of their former ideology, or are 'converted' to capitalism and adopt Western-style laws, they will certainly be 'hybrid systems' of law. The traditional conception of a hybrid legal system is one in which more than one legal system co-exists, for example, where both common law and civil law types of law can be found, and are operative.

The present section traces the typical features of the Socialist legal system and the key characteristics that distinguished it from being regarded as a civil law system. We then conduct a very brief inquest on the former USSR before looking ahead to the new decrees that have already emanated from the new regime under President Yeltsin and assess the future configuration of the new Russian law.

At the end of that outline, we shall consider some of the latest edicts that President Yeltsin has passed and consider the prerequisites for a successful transformation of the former Soviet Union into a social democracy.

i. The Socialist Concept of Law

6.1.1 The word 'socialist' when used in connection with the law, means many different things to different lawyers. At its most basic it signifies a philosophy and ideology which is based on what is commonly referred to as the 'Marxist-Leninist' school of thought. The Socialist ideology is predicated on the principles *inter alia*, that all law is an instrument of economic and social policy and the common law and civil law traditions reflect a capitalist, bourgeois, imperialistic, exploitative society, economy and government. Marxist theory, as such is founded on the doctrine of 'dialectical/historical materialism' which argues that a society goes through various stages or phases in the course of its evolution and development. It might begin with no legal system, then become a slave-owning one, followed by a stage of medieval feudalism, before moving on to capitalism, then socialism, before law finally 'withers away' in a classless society with no necessity for any legal system, because all men will treat each other as equals.

Writers have long debated the 'true' meaning of terms like 'socialist' and 'socialism' and 'Marxism', and even now, when Communism appears to be in terminal decline in Eastern Europe, with a commensurate rise in social democracy, there is still debate on issues connected with Socialist law, not least because of the continued Communist colours of the People's Republic of China.

Szabo believes that the Socialist concept of law 'may be considered as part of a homogeneous scientific theory with a particular aim.' (see Szabo in *International Encyclopedia of Comparative Law* p.49). That aim, of course, is the creation of a new legal system: Socialist law. Quigley (1989) describes (rather than defines) socialist law as 'the law of countries whose governments officially view the country as being either socialist or moving from capitalism to socialism, and which hold a communistic society as an ultimate goal.

In her recent book *The Socialist Concept of Law* (1991), Christine Sypnowich defines 'socialism' as 'a society where private property in the form of capital has been eliminated and replaced by common ownership of the means of production, thereby permitting a large measure of equality and fraternity in social relations'. (Sypnowich (1991) preface). She argues that that it incorrect to believe that an ideal socialist society would have no need of law. She concedes that Left-wing thought has long espoused the view that law will wither away under socialism, which was a view developed by Marx and Engels. It is also a view which has been supported by Western and Soviet thinkers in the Marxist tradition. But she strongly disagrees with the conventional or common view taken on the nature of socialist legality. The classical doctrine of Marxism is that law and state are determined by and subservient to, the economic structure of society and the political and economic aims of the State, as revealed in the State Plan. Marxist-Leninist theory extolls the primacy of economic relations in society, which takes precedence over politics and law. Stalinism could be described as one-party rule, central planning and state ownership of the means of production-on the domestic front. In international terms, it meant isolation from the West occasionally leavened with selective interactions with foreign communist parties.

Law, when used by Soviet leaders, has therefore been a mere tool in the planning and organising of the economic and social structure of the country. It is simply part of the ideological superstructure which controls the material reality of the means of production; it is determined and defined in terms of its political function.

The groups of countries that have received socialist law may be divided into two main categories: (i) the *older socialist jurisdictions* such as Poland, Bulgaria, Hingary, Czechoslovakia, Romania, Albania, the People's Republic of China (see, especially 6.10.7-6.10-8), the People's Republic of Vietnam, the People's Democratic Republic of Korea, Mongolia (the oldest national legal system in this group) and Cuba; and (ii) the *newer* or nascent *socialist legal systems* such as the Democratic Republic of Kampuchea (Cambodia), Laos, Mozambique, Angola, Somalia, Libya, Ethiopia, Guinea and Guyana.

The Communist Party is the only real governing and planning body within the socialist legal system. Once it decides a particular policy, it communicates its plans to all its constituent organs and this policy will be carried out by its legislative, executive and judicial agencies.

ii. Differences Between Civil Law and Socialist Systems

6.1.2   The majority of Western scholars have argued that socialist law forms a family of law separate from the civil law family and these include David, Hazard, Merryman, Ancel, Osakwe, Bogden, and Constantinesco. However, Friedmann, Lawson, Losano and Ehrenzweig belonged to the school of thought that believed that socialist law simply a member of the civil law group or sub-species of civil law. Many scholars identified the differentiating features of socialist law from civil law. As summarised by Quigley (1989), these were: (a) socialist law is programmed to wither away with the disappearance of private property and social classes and the transition to a communistic social order; (b) socialist countries are dominated by a single political party; (c) in socialist systems, law is subordinated to creation of a new economic order, wherein private law is absorbed by public law; (d) socialist law has a pseudo-religious character; (e) socialist law is prerogative instead of normative.

iii. Similarities Between Civil Law and Socialist Systems

6.1.3   There are many similarities between the civil law and the socialist system. Quigley (1989) mentions: the inquisitorial style of trial, codes and the passing of legislation/regulations as the basic style of lawmaking, division of law into its civil (private) law categories, and the method of investigation of crime (written documentation compiled by a law-trained investigator). He also points out that socialist legal systems have utilised civil law institutions, methodology, and organisation. (see Quigley (1989) p.800, 803) Further, he refers to Hazard's observations that family law and the civil code provisions on inter-personal relations do not differ from those of other civil law countries.(see Quigley (1989) p.803)

Indeed, Quigley argues that despite significant differences between civil law and socialist law, 'when one looks at Soviet, or socialist, law from a global perspective, these differences do not erase the basic identity of socialist law as part of the civil law tradition.' (Quigley (1989) p.804) He maintains that it is impossible to understand socialist law without viewing it within the tradition of which it is a part. He concludes that the points of difference between civil law and socialist law have not removed socialist law from the civil law tradition and to think otherwise, is to overlook the historical connection of socialist law to civil law and 'the continuing relevance in socialist law of civil law rules, methods, institutions, and procedures (Quigley (1989) p.808)

The *Russian tradition of codification* goes back many centuries. The *Pravda Russkaia* (Russian Law) commonly thought to be oldest surviving compilation of Russian laws, was adopted in the eleventh century. This was followed by many more in the fifteenth, sixteenth and seventeenth centuries. In 1830, Speranskii published a complete collection of the Lws of the Russian Empire, consisting of a forty-two volume reproduction, of more than thirty thousand legislative edicts and enactments, promulgated since 1649. In 1832, a sixteen volume Code of Laws was published, which represented a systematic codification of the whole Russian law, dealing with division by division. This contained sixty thousand Articles covering all branches of law. In 1845, a new Criminal Code was enacted, which preceded even more codes being promulgated, culminating in the last tsarist codes of 1903 and 1913.

After the Bolshevik Revolution in 1917, it was nearly five years before any codification took place and although the new regime were overtly seeking to destroy all pre-revolutionary law, during 1917 to 1920, a system of judge-made law was utilised. It was only in 1922 that Soviet codification revived, wherein the existing codes were modified and promulgated afresh, the great legal philosopher Pashukanis being a dominant scholar of the era of codification.

The Soviet civil code was clearly influenced by the German Civil Code, the Swiss Civil Code and the Russian Draft Civil Code of 1913. The intention appeared to be to blend the best of German codification with the high aims of the French Code.

It may be added that as with civil law systems, *legal scholars* constitute an extremely valuable intellectual source of law in all socialist countries. Since there are usually very few reported court decisions in most socialist countries, the legal expert or doctrinal writer actually comments on judicial decisions, giving not just the bare facts and ruling but also the background and explanation of the consequences of a decision. For a case in point, one may cite the poignant 1971 case of *Poltavskii*, the stevedore who saved a young child from certain death in a storm by flinging an electric cable that had entangled itself near the child, away from the child's legs, at the cost of his own life. This was not just reported by Stavisski, a doctrinal writer, but the aftermath of this case was then reported up to its remakable conclusion: that the so-called analogy of law could be used to award compensation to the stevedore's wife by virtue of the Electrical Company's lack of control over securing of electric cables; *and* that *a legal precedent had thereby been created.* (see Hazard, Butler and Maggs (1977) p.466)

In other words, legal scholars play a *major role* in analysing, developing and disseminating legal doctrine. They also play a significant role in training all the members of the legal profession and are the most highly compensated of all lawyers. They are the most conversant with the law of all the professionals through their training and teaching of the law to future lawyers, and wrought an invaluable influence on the law through their systematic commentaries, consultations of legislative drafting committees, and on consultative committees attached to the different supreme courts. Just as they have had a tremendous impact on the development of Soviet law in the early twentienth century, perhaps the legal scholars of the more modern era will play a part in the radical restructuring of the new Russian society.

iv. Was the Socialist System Part of the Civil Law System?

6.1.4   With respect, the present writer must disagree with Quigley's overall conclusion. Even though he is perfectly correct to highlight the similarities between civil law and socialist law, as many other writers do, it is surely the Marxist/Leninist ideology and its manifestations that were once all-pervading, all-encompassing and totally dominant in societies like the former Soviet Union, that unquestionably distinguished it from civil law systems and any other system. The former Soviet Union punished any individual who made 'profits' derived from 'unearned income' which had been gained from private enterprise; it had no separation of powers, its agencies were not allowed to criticise Soviet laws, doctrinal writers could only do criticise laws if they were obsolete laws, and even if they were, criticism had to be analytical rather tham political. The Courts simply carried out government policy or the Communist Party's policy. They developed the remarkable institution/office known as the Procurator who combined the roles of Prosecutor, Investigator, Appellate Agency, Advocate and Welfare Officer.

Another important point of differentiation is that whereas the French Code was seen as the epitome of French liberty and the Revolution, the Soviet Codes were seen merely as a basis for the furtherance of political aims and objectives, which would have to be modified as socialist society changed, in accordance with the building of a truly communist society.

Yet another point of significance was in the socialist *treatment of property.* Under Soviet socialism, property was limited to two categories: socialist property and personal property. Personal property was that which individuals were permitted to own for their own consumption. Socialist property included property owned outright by the State, ownership by 'public' organisations and collective farms. These nominally independent bodies functioned as if they were organs of the State. Four basic characteristics of the Stalinist-style economy are: 'collective ownership of the means of production; enterprise performance evaluated in terms of gross quantitative output targets; fixed prices bearing no relation to market forces; and a centralised hierarchical administrative apparatus'. (see Stephan (1991) p.39)

Upon assuming power, President Gorbachev indicated his determination to face the problems of deteriorating standards of living and erosion of the *nomenclatura*'s position in society. Although initially imposing authoritarian measures to deal with these problems, by the end of 1986 saw the leader altering his approach to the increasing economic problems. In December 1986, the Law on Individual Labour Activity established a procedure whereby individuals could engage in small-scale production of consumer goods, sell services such as repairs, and open family-run hotels. By 1990, there was a distinct trend towards the full restoration and reinstatement of private property. (see Stephan III (1991) p.49)

In the field of foreign investment, access of Soviet firms to foreign markets was radically expanded by 1988, together with the liberalisation of the rules governing joint ventures. In fact, the Law on Cooperatives of the USSR, which was enacted in the spring of 1988, legalised private economic activity. It permitted private firms organised as cooperatives to hire labour, sell shares, and to 'engage in any kind of activity except those prohibited under ligislation of the USSR and the Union Republics.' In October, 1990, the Soviet legislature endorsed a plan for privatisation of the state economy.

v. Inquest on the Russian Empire

6.1.5   The Empire in Russia really began in 1552, when Tsar Ivan IV ordained the building of the Cathedral of the Annunciation in Kazan to celebrate his victory over the Tartars. This was to mark the moment when Muscovy first conquered infidel territory and imposed its rule over non-Slav people. In the intervening years, the Russian Empire has been the largest in the history of the world, and outstripped the British empire for sheer longevity. The empire was unusual in that it made no clear distinction between metropolis and colonies. The colonised territories were not overseas but all adjacent to or encircling the heartlands. Russians found it natural to resettle there as if they were simply moving into another region of their home territory.

Thus, until recently, Russians readily accepted the right of all citizens to move freely and live in different parts of the country. But Russia continued to assert its control over the Eurasian expanses because of fear of subjection to some other power. The cost of defending and administering a huge and diverse territory has exacted its toll and the price paid by the Russian people has been despotism, serfdom, heavy taxation and an oversized bureaucracy.

Alexander II (1855-81) attempted to create the institutions of civil society by abolishing serfdom, and setting up elective government assemblies, the beginnings of land reform, reforms in local administration, a hierarchy of law courts and a citizen army based on adult male conscription. During his 'period of great reforms' judges were made independent of the administrative wing of the givernment for the first time.

Nicholas II then established an elected parliament. But the Russian people created institutions of their own, such as the soviets of workers', soldiers' and peasants' deputies, modelled on the village community. It was those soviets which, in 1917, seized power under the leadership of the Communist party, and then gave their name to the state which emerged from the ruins of imperial Russia.

Under the communists, the empire acquired a fresh start and renewed vigour but the the new era was short-lived. Although Lenin and Stalin managed to turn the empire into the second mightiest state in the world, this had its price. While encouraging mass literacy in the numerous vernacular languages of the Soviet Union, and created virtually sovereign state structures for even small ethnic groups, all states were tightly controlled and severely restricted by the ethos of the planned economy and the centralised power and overweening influence of the one-party rule of the Communist Party.

Thus, even small doses of *glasnost* (opening of Russian society) were enough to cause a stir and upset the odd balance of national fervour and repression of individual liberty that is typical of Russian society. Gorbachev's other innovation-*perestroika*-the restructuring of Soviet society, may have failed during his short presidential reign, but surely he has blazed a trail for others, the democratic and privatising aspects of which Yeltsin and his successors will surely endeavour to pursue.

iii. The End of the USSR and the New Commonwealth

6.1.6 Marxist/Leninist ideology inspired the classical planned economy of the former USSR and other Socialist countries, which contrasted with the market economy of the West. The Soviet Union's form of Communist rule began with the October Revolution of 1917 (or strictly, 30 December, 1922) and ended in December 1991. On 2 September, 1991, President Gorbachev and ten of the fifteen republic leaders, signed a declaration recommending that central government be suspended until a new constitution is signed. This declaration, presented at the opening session of the full Soviet parliament, effectively declared the end of the USSR.

On 21 December, 1991, eleven of the twelve remaining republics who were willing to form a new confederation met and signed a Treaty establishing a new Commonwealth of Independent States, with Russia under its President, Boris Yeltsin, its acknowledged leader. This was pursuant to an earlier agreement signed between Russia, Belorussia and the Ukraine on 8 December 1991, which announced that the headquarters of the new Commonwealth would be not Moscow but Minsk, the Byelorussian capital.

The great ideological experiment begun by Lenin's Bolshevik revolution lasted just over seventy-four years. The Soviet state which had been constituted on 30 December,1922, ceased to exist a few days before its seventieth year.

The Treaty creating the Commonwealth begins with a preamble stating the objectives of building democratic, law-governed states on the basis of mutual recognition and respect for sovereignty, and the eleven states then say: 'Co-operation between members of the commonwealth will be carried out in accordance with the principle of equality through co-ordinating institutions formed on a parity basis and operating in the way established by agreements between members of the commonwealth, which is neither a state nor a superstate structure.' Crucially, it also states: 'With the formation of the Commonwealth of Independent States the Union of the Soviet Socialist Republics ceases to exist.'

Republics which have not joined the Commonwealth are Estonia, Latvia, Lithuania, and Georgia. Of course, the new Commonwealth is not a State, it has no central government or common citizenship. It has some attributes of both the British Commonwealth and the European Community but is unlike either. It really resembles most closely a federation of states, with each state retaining independence in many matters. However, like the former Soviet Union, it faces extremely serious economic problems and once President Gorbachev resigned on 25 December, 1991, the Russian President Yeltsin has proceeded to issue decrees which will carry on the Gorbachev legacy of *glasnost* and *perestroika*, moving the new Commonwealth into an era of private enterprise, capitalism and some form of social democracy.

vii. Russian Law-Return to Civil Law or Hybrid System?

6.1.7 It should be noted that during the era of the Soviet Union, the 1922 Civil Code of the Russian Socialist Federated Soviet Republic derived from the German Civil Code. Before the Revolution, Russian was in fact a civil law country. Accordingly, the style of lawmaking in the USSR was through codes and legislation. In fact, a code or set of laws would often be enacted at federal level, and then expanded into the codes of the constituent republics. Hence, it is apparently President Yeltsin's intention at the present time to leave undisturbed any existing laws which do not conflict with civil liberties' reforms or economic and criminal law changes he is implementing (such as family law codes) or the reforms in private ownership which he has begun to introduce. Laws that were passed under the former Soviet regime were therefore all-union laws, being applicable to all republics, republic laws, and local legislation.

The courts were used to promote and carry out State and government policy. All this is supposed to change under the new laws in the new Commonwealth. If the old republic codes remain undisturbed for non-economic regulation, a hybrid system which is similar to the African legal system, may result. Certain socialist-based procedures will remain, alongside new 'democratic' and capitalist laws, within a civil law legislative and judicial framework. Here is a sample of some of the planned and ongoing legal changes based on information that is presently available:

(i) Russian Federation Reforms

6.1.8 (i) *Reform of the judiciary*: The Russian Justice Minister announced on 25 December, 1991, that judicial reform had begun in Russia and that 'reliable guarantees-juridical and constitutional-have been created for the irreversibilty of this reform.' A 'very substantial' increase in the pay of judges and the removal of the budgetary system of judicial power in Russia, will also be introduced. Efforts will be made to make it a competition to become a judge so that 'from now onwards, jurists might consider it their greatest dream to become a judge as the peak of a juridical career.' Recruitment of people of the highest calibre will be sought.

(ii) *Institution of the Jury*: 'once again the stage-by-stage introduction of this institution whereby whether a person is guilty or not will be decided by the public'; but 'only the issue of guilt or innocence, not the measure of punishment' will be their task.

(iii) *A New Draft Law on the Pledging of Security* will be introduced.

(iv) A *New Criminal Code* will be introduced: this will have its first reading in the spring of 1992. For the first time, priority will be given for the protection of the individual's rights. The interests of owners will be recognised as paramount. Articles dealing with punishment for private enterprise 'crimes' have been annulled (repealed). There will no longer be any punishment of close relatives of a criminal for the failure to report the crime. The list of crimes punishable by death has been considerably decreased. The list of articles under which capital punishment could be ordered, has been reduced from twenty-seven to three and women and minors will not be included. The maximum period of imprisonment will probably remain at fifteen years.

There will also be *new articles dealing with criminal responsibility* for example, for setting up fraudulent businesses.

On 29 January 1992, President Yeltsin approved a Decree whose intention is to accelerate privatisation. This basically encourages applications of privatisation of state and municipal enterprises, which may be submitted by work collectives of enterprises, their subdivisions, Russian and foreign legal persons and citizens on the basis of the RSFR Law, *On the Privatisation of State and Municipal Enterprises of the RSFSR.*

(ii) The New Russian Federation Draft Constitution

6.1.9   The Russian Federation has been debating its *new draft Constitution*. It is too long to reproduce here but some salient points may be noted:

(i) There is a clear statement as to 'Man and His Rights and Liberties' in Article 2, which states that 'The Russian Federation secures the rights and liberties of man and citizen according to the provisions of the constitution of the Russian Federation and the generally accepted principles and rules of international law. The recognition, observance and defence of the rights and liberties, and honour and dignity of man and citizen is the principal obligation of state power.'

(ii) The principle of 'Government by the people' is stated in Article 4. This stresses *inter alia*, that the elections of state authorities specified by the Constitution of the Russian Federation are free and are conducted on the basis of universal, equal and direct suffrage by ballot. It also states that ' Citizens of the Russian Federation have the right to resist any attempt at the forcible elimination or revision of the current constitutional system.'

(iii) Article 5 emphasises that 'Democracy in the Russian Federation us exercised on the basis of political and ideological diversity, a multi-party system and the participation of non-party persons.'

(iv) Article 6 states that 'The system of state power in the Russian Federation is based on the principles of the separation of legislative, executive and judicial power, and also delineation of the terms of reference and authority between the Russian Federation and its constitutent republics, krays, oblasts, autonomous oblasts, autonomous okrugs and local self-government.'

(v) Article 7 declares that the state and territorial arrangment of the Russian Federation is based on the principle of federalism.

(vi) In the second section of the draft constitution, there are enumerations of basic rights, liberties and obligations. Article 14 states, for example, that all are equal before the law and have the right to equal protection by the law. It also declares: 'All are equal in their rights and liberties, regardless of race, colour of skin, nationality, sex, language, social origin, social, property and official position, beliefs, attitude towards religion, participation or non-participation in voluntary associations, place of residence and other circumstances.'

(vii) Chapter III, headed Civil and Political Rights and Liberties contains Articles which declare everyone's 'right to life' the right to freedom, and freedom of movement and choice of residence, and 'inviolability' of one's person and abode, rgw right to freedom of thought and speech and the unimpeded expression of one's opinions and beliefs and the right to renounce them. Article 26 guarantees freedom of worship-'the right to freely confess any religion or not confess any religion, to choose, hold and disseminate religious, non-religious or other beliefs and to act in accordance with them, given compliance with the law.'

(viii) Chapter V is headed *Guarantees of Rights and Liberties* and includes, inter alia, the right to have one's case examined by a competent, independent and impartial court of law. The presumption of innocence is stated as well as the fact that a defendant is not required to prove his innocence. It also asserts that 'everyone has the right to a review of his case by a superior court' and that 'no one should face the prospect of double jeopardy.'

(ix) Compulsory labour is prohibited.

(x) Article 61 declares that the State guarantees free enterprise.

(xi) Article 76 guarantees the freedom of the mass media, and the massa media may be established by citizens, voluntary associations, enterprises, establishments, bodies of local sel-government and state authorities.

160

(xii) Article 105 makes it clear that 'judicial power belongs only to courts established by the constitution of the Russian Federation and federal law. It is exercised by means of constitutional, civil, criminal and administrative judicial proceedings.' It goes on to say that 'the creation of special courts and military tribunals is not permitted.'

(xiii) Article 132 declares that temporary limitations of rights and liberties may, in accordance with federal law, be imposed in a period of a state of emergency. Such limitations must be directly indicated in the state of emergency enactment.

(iii) Belorussian Reforms

6.1.10 On 23 April 1992, the Belorussian parliament recognised the need to implement a legal reform as one of the conditions of building in the republic a rule-of-law state, and confirmed the basic provisions of the plan of the reform. The main purpose of the reform is the creation of of a legal system capable of ensuring the functioning of a rule-of-law state, assertion of an independent judiciary as the main guarantor of civic (citizens') rights and liberties, the implementation in the legislation of democratic principles of the organisation and activity of law-enforcement bodies in accordance with generally-recognised norms of international law. It was stressed that the 'judicial authorities' would be separated from the 'legislative and executive authorities' as well as from political parties and public associations.

Legal reform in Belorussia will be implemented in three stages: (i) Changes will be made to the existing legislation, dealing with adoption of laws on the constitutional court, the public prosecutor's office, the bar, notary's service and national security service.

(ii) Organisational measures will be implemented to create basic elements for the new system of judiciary bodies, such as the jury, the investigating committee, and courts of appeal.

(iii) The final aims of the legal reforms will be implemented, including the creation of the new system of judicary bodies acting on the basis of the new legislation.

viii. Towards a Russian Social Democratic State?

6.1.11 It would appear, therefore, that the foundations have certainly been laid, in this most complex and contradictory of countries, for a social democracy to replace whatever form of socialism that existed. All the prerequisites of a democratic state seem to be there-civil liberties, separation of powers, independent judiciary, guaranteed freedoms, media freedom, the right to decide whether to join a trade union (Article 64: draft RSFSR Constitution), even the switch to private ownership in the capitalist mode, inter-country economic ventures and a preponderance of leaders who at least say they wish to have a more democratic society.

But new federations and newly-declared independent states apart, the future for the new republics or of the finge republics is far from assured. Old conflicts are unresolved, economic problems are rife, scarcity of basic supplies is still prevalent, productivity remains low, new problems continue to emerge. The method of privatisation currently being favoured is a system of vouchers awarded to every Russian citizen in order to break up the old state companies into a number of democratically-owned units. Yet this system has never worked in capitalist countries, and the value of the vouchers is already falling as people try to exchange them for money.

President Yeltsin is also seeking to extend the special powers he was given by the parliament last year so that he can have the right to 'hire and fire' ministers at will. He has postponed the local elections due by the end of 1992, and has an ambivalent attitude towards answering questions from MPs but agrees to talk to the press 'as a favour' to the journalists. It is still unclear what the division of responsibility between Parliament and President is, but rather than create a system of democratic institutions, Yeltsin prefers to rule by decree.

There is therefore no true accountability in the Russian Commonwealth such as an equivalent of the American system of regular presidential press conferences and no equivalent of the Prime Minister's Question Time in the British House of Commons.

The brooding omnipresence of the Russian armies maintains the dark cloud of a potential *coup* and an internal *coup* is never to be discounted. The battlegrounds in places like Moldavia and Georgia indicate that a lasting peace may not be possible without more bloodshed and suffering. Historians will doubtless continue to debate the question of whether the union could have been preserved and whether the old USSR was even truly 'socialist'.

In terms of the convergence of legal systems, there appears to be a trend towards social democracy, and this will probably develop within a civil law framework. But the current signs of its successful implementation are not encouraging.

At the end of the day, if the law of the new Russian republics is a combination of civil law (based on Roman law or more recent Continental versions) and a quasi-military government, in some ways resembling a South American *junta* or some form of benevolent dictatorship or even a completely new version of social democracy, it will not really matter. What will matter is whether the Russian people will ultiamtely be allowed to live in a stable society which is able to provide the average family minimum living standards, and the provision of their basic needs. It is anybody's guess whether this new Russian political and economic experiment will eventually succeed in transforming Russian society so that, in the words of the draft Russian constitution, its people will be able 'to affirm the liberty and rights of the individual' to have 'a worthy life, ensure civil peace and harmony, preserve the historically evolved state unity, revive Russia and make permanent its democratic statehood.'

C. HYBRID LEGAL SYSTEMS

6.2 Jurisdictions in which there is more than one system co-existing with one another, are sometimes described as *mixed jurisdictions or systems* or *hybrid systems of law*. Hooker (1975) uses the term 'legal pluralism' to describe the situation where two or more laws interact. Examples of jurisdictions where common law and civil law co-exist and interact include South Africa, Sri Lanka, the Seychelles, Scotland, Louisiana, Quebec, the Philippines, Japan, Mauritius, the Cameroons and St. Lucia.

D. OTHER TYPES OF LAW

6.3 The meaning of 'law' is a many-sided question, to which several eminent writers have responded with different conceptions and interpretations. We turn now to other non-Western conceptions of 'law', namely the Chinese and Japanese conceptions of law.

i. Eastern Legal Conceptions

6.3.1 A number of general comments may be made on Eastern laws: First, these systems traditionally perceive law as playing a minor role, in the sense that it is simply another vehicle for maintaining peace and social order. Secondly, law and the recourse to the courts is traditionally seen as a last resort, where all other methods of mediation, conciliation, persuasion and moderation have failed. Many Far Eastern countries adopted codes on Romano-Germanic lines but a number of these then opted for the Communist ideology. Countries like Indo-China, Japan, Malaysia and Burma also experienced major wars, or uprisings or colonisation in one form or another which have left their imprint on the development and composition of their laws. Japan underwent codification using German and French legal models and then experienced a radical Americanisation of laws and culture in the aftermath of the Second World War which has, in no small measure, resulted in their spectacular economic development, to become the leading industrial country in the world. These diverse influences have left Japan with a unique blend of Western and Eastern conceptions of law and legal tradition.

ii. The Chinese Conception of Law

6.3.2 A predominant principle of the traditional Chinese conception of law has been the belief in a cosmic order of the universe, involving an interactive relationship between heaven, earth and men. The universe is seen as the basis of law. China's three thousand year-old history produced numerous philosophical ideas, with three main philosophical traditions influencing the development of the legal system in China: the Confucian, Legalist and the Buddhist. Chinese sources of law thus derive from these traditions.

163

While the Confucian believes in a natural harmony between man's ritual propriety and the natural principles of the universe, the Legalists' theory, which originated in the third century B.C., argued that there should be government by law (obeying legal prescriptions) rather than government by men. These theories proved too remote and alien to the Chinese of the time and by 206 B.C., Confucianism was re-established as the favoured philosophy and the ideology of the State by the Han dynasty.

Three levels of law operate within Buddhism or the *Buddha-Dharma*: (i) *karma* (action): the law of action and reaction; the most general of all laws, which includes good and evil, physical or psychic; (ii) the Buddhist law of causation: a belief that good and evil follow are a direct consequence of the actions of the mind. Buddhism draws much sharper distinctions between the intention to commit evil, or acts committed with intent, and actions committed without premeditation or forethought.

None of these traditions have been eradicated despite the outward conversion to Communism in China.

(i) Codification

6.3.3   Chinese codes appeared at the time of the Han dynasty but dealt only with administrative and criminal law matters. It continued to dominate all aspects of life for the next two thousand years. In an attempt to unshackle themselves from Western ideas and Western domination, the Chinese adopted a series of codes ironically based on Western prototypes. They passed a Civil Code in 1929-31 (dealing with private and commercial law), a Code of Civil Procedure in 1932 and a Land Code in 1930. Since Hong Kong was annexed by the British, these codes were never in force there. Chinese law underwent a period of Europeanisation and on one level, can be included within the Romano-Germanic legal family. But if one lifted the veil of codification and legislation, one would find the old Chinese traditions and societal hierarchies, family and kinship networks still very much alive. In fact, despite the codes and the apparent Westernisation of Chinese law, Chinese judges have been quite prepared to ignore the codes and formalistic laws if they conflicted with more humane Chinese customs. Despite China embracing Communism on October 1, 1949, the Buddhist ethics of motivation have continued to be followed up to today, although the government of the new People's Republic has officially adopted a Marxist-Leninist ideology.

(ii) Different Versions of Communism in China

6.3.4   Whenever a conflict between Maoism and older traditions has occurred, Chinese Communists have been quick to follow the established tradition of advocating *li* (interpersonal law) rather than *fa* (new law based *inter alia*, on punishment for compliance). Although avowedly Marxist-Leninist in ideology, the Chinese have been at pains to emphasise moral development and civic consciousness among its citizens, much more than in the former USSR. In the first few years of Communism, law would be given primacy and urgent measures were taken to build a new society and new social order. All existing laws, decrees and courts had been abolished by the 'common programme' of 1949 so that speed was of the essence in rebuilding the social matrix. In fact, China adopted a Soviet model of Marxism until 1957 when relations between China and the former USSR began to deteriorate and and in 1960 China decided to pursue their own version of communism, emphasising a more individual-based social transformation in preference to economic growth, allowing greater participation by the managers and directors of enterprises, settlement of disputes rather than litigation, compromise by persuasion, repentance for misdemenours, and a return to ancient tradition. One noticeable consequence of these changes in philosophy, social relations and rejection of the 'principle of legality' has been the virtual disappearence of any transcendental philosophy linking man's behaviour with the cosmic order and nature.

The doctrines of Chairman Mao have replaced Soviet approaches to a Marxist-run society. Some of Chairman Mao's most potent ideas became the subject of a 'Mao cult,' motivated by the Socialist Education Movement, promoting the ideas that political leaders must share the concerns and life style of the peasant or commoner and that the masses are a progressive political force with revolutionary potential. There was a general wave of anti-elitism primarily among middle-rank officials. Law was once again seen as the last resort and a constant tension between right-wing and left-wing groups. Almost no legislation was passed after 1949 right up to the death of Mao in 1976. The traditional Chinese antagonism toward rigid forms of legislative prescription re-surfaced. Consequently, there is only a small body of judicial decisions, and a mere handful of reported Supreme Court decisions. No doctrine of judicial precedent is known. Neither has there been any substantial amounts of doctrinal writing.

(iii) Chinese Law in the Post-Mao Era

6.3.5   In the aftermath of the arrest of the 'gang of four', China has developed two systems of justice:(i) 'popular' justice; and (ii) bureaucratic justice.   The popular model is based on the radical ideals of continuing revolution and self-reliance, rejecting codification, and opposing any sort of formalising legislation which would stultify current social structures while social inequities still persist in China, which is still in a state of transition. The workers, farmers, women and neighbourhood residents play a large part in policing this sort of system. The bureaucratic model is based on the premise that law is necessary to consolidate past gains, to control and govern future changes, to maintain state control and ensure the continued progress and means of production. Police, courts and the Procurate (modelled on the Soviet quasi-military office) play an essential part in this sort of system. Co-operation and confrontation between the two models continued throughout the 1970s.

In 1978, a new Constitution was enacted, and legislation once again began to appear. Since 1979, laws have been passed on elections, court organisation, joint ventures, Chinese and foreign capital investment, marriage, local government, the environment and there is now a code of criminal procedure

165

and a criminal code. With the passing of several more laws which *ex facie*, appear to eradicate uncertainty and injustice, the new legal system has also sought to control dissent and centralise state power, as well as extend and unify Peking's modernisation programme. Maoist traditions have been breached by favouring expert management rather than worker participation and relying on material incentives, encouraging a more capitalist ideology, buttressed by making profitability a central goal, and borrowing from capitalist countries and encouraging foreign investment. There has been a growing emphasis on legalism, since law is seen more and more as a controlling mechanism as well as an educative one.

The gulf between the elitist 'privileged' class of 'haves' and the 'have-nots' has, unfortunately been widened so that any dissent or dissatisfaction has been dealt with severely. Although Chinese law has a positive input of revisionist and progressive laws, the shortage of lawyers, judges and courts as well as the lack of legal education and anti-legalist thought, all operate to repress rather than encourage the growth of jurisprudence or more pragmatically, individual freedom of expression.

Current Chinese law is in a state of transition, and the events of Tiananmen square are only one manifestation of a country rich with tradition and culture, caught between the need to modernise under pressure from a body of youthful opinion wanting some form of democracy, coupled with the desire for China to take a more exalted place in the international community and the perceived need to preserve its incomparable heritage with dignity. The success or failure of China in coming to terms with this ongoing conflict will determine the shape of its laws in the twenty-first century.

iii. The Japanese Conception of Law

(i) Background to Japanese Law

6.3.6   It is well-established that Chinese ideas exerted an extremely strong influence on Japanese culture and ultimately influenced the overall Japanese conception of law. The fifth century saw the infiltration of Chinese writing and in the sixth, the 'importation' of Buddhism. The major forces that have shaped Japanese conceptions of law are multifarious: historical, physical, and cultural. Japan is an island nation which enjoyed relative isolation which enabled it to achieve a national ethnic unity. This was maintained for thousands of years. It was also a rural agricultural nation up until the last century, with settled populations in localised farming communities. Japan also possessed a stable hierarchical social structure but this was disrupted by civil wars, which came to an end around the end of the sixteenth century, with the ascendency of the Tokugawa Shogunate. In the succeeding generations dominated by Tokugawa officials, Japan appeared to be permanently settled into a stable and regular routine of administering 'one big rice estate' (Henderson: 1965) where Shintoism, Buddhism and Confucianism continued to have an impact on Japanese traditional ideas.

It was Chinese Confucianism that had the single greatest impact on early Japanese thought, and, in the way in which the Japanese have achieved acclaim with their globally renowned technological advancements and innovations in modern times, they earlier adapted Confucian ideas to the Japanese psyche and way of life. None the less, there are several typically Japanese characteristics in their conception of law. First, there is the 'aversion to law' which refers to their general antipathy toward the law as the means of resolving disputes through the courts, resulting from their 'norm-conscious sense of values, combined with their emotional anarchism' (Noda: 1971) as well as their propensity towards intuition and emotion, and their belief that law is simply a corpus of legal rules without any connotations of legal or personal rights. It is only respected as a teacher of morals and an expedient for maintaining social order but not a great deal beyond that. Other reasons for the Japanese aversion to litigation and preference for conciliation may be the fact that the earliest Japanese codes were never seen by anyone other than the magistrates, for whose use they were specifically designed. Further, the early Japanese Codes were descended from the Chinese codes which were almost exclusively penal, so that law came to be associated with pain, punishment, constraint and the idea of prison, which connotes severity.

Secondly, there is no room for Western ideas of logic in Japanese law since logic is anathema to their subjectivity, emotion and honour. Life is seen as 'indeterminate, immensely varied and subtle' (Kawashima: 1967) and should therefore be accepted and lived as it is, not placed into neat segments by logic. This is partially explicable by their 'racial and cultural homogeneity of thought' (Noda: 1976) which has nurtured the environment of a common understanding and consensus about life experiences and life in general.

Thirdly, there is the belief that life should be governed by non-legal rules of conduct (*giri*) and the obligations incurred towards benefactors (*on*) such as parents, the emperor, the nations and the law. The guiding principle is that it is one's duty to repay this life-long debt which cannot, in fact, ever be fully repaid. These obligations must be fulfilled by a special friendliness towards the other party so that the spirit in which a duty is performed should be one of affection and benevolence. The main duty is to avoid discord and achieve harmony.

(ii) European Influences on Japanese Law

6.3.7   In the nineteenth century Western nations became extremely interested in trade with Japan which threatened the isolation sought by the Shoguns-the military overlords of the day. Initially, only the Dutch received special permission to enter specified harbours for the specific purpose of trading. However, with increasing interest from other Western countries, the so-called 'unequal treaties' were entered into by the Shogun with the United States, which had sent a fleet of warships to cruise off the Japanese coast in 1853, and Japan eventually entered into treaties with England, Russia and the Netherlands. The essence of these treaties was to give foreigners the right to settle in specified cities, have the right to trade and have consular representation. These moves were met with considerable opposition from the people and were widely seen as a national humiliation so that even the Emperor emerged from his semi-retirement which had been forced upon him by the Shoguns and led the opposition to these treaties. By 1867, the Shogun had no option but to withdraw and the Meiji emperor was reinstated with full governmental powers. This heralded a remarkable Westernisation of Japanese legal thought and in the next few decades, the army and administration were also modernised on European lines, Western technology was adopted and a new Constitution was introduced in 1889. This followed a Prussian model which turned Japan into a constitutional monarchy although the emperor retained all powers of decision. Further Europeanising influences followed as a result of a number of factors:

(a) The Japanese were anxious to remove the discrimination of the unequal treaties which gave consular courts jurisdiction over Japanese courts in matters affecting foreign nationals. The French professor, Boissonade was therefore commissioned to draft a new criminal code and code of criminal procedure. This came into force in 1880 and was inevitably strongly reminiscent of French law. At the same time, the German professor, Roesler had also been asked to draft a commercial code, which he based on the French civil code but left the family and succession law to be drafted by a Japanese committee. Both these drafts provoked criticism from the conservative and liberal wings of the Japanese parliament when they were presented to them. As you might have expected, they were seen as too French, and insufficiently Japanese, or that codification was inappropriate at that time.

(b) The preparation of the Japanese civil code was therefore handed to a commission of three Japanese professors who ultimately followed two drafts of the German BGB (Civil Code) in key points of structure and content, although there were French and English law traces as well. No one can be sure as to why the German model eventually won favour, but it is certainly possible that the BGB was rated as the most mature and sophisticated example of the continental art of legislation; that the French Code was already seen as having technical defects; that Japanese scholars found German conceptualism and systematic exposition attractive and in accord with their own systematic modes of theorising. It is also likely that as the BGB was the product of the German empire, this would have impressed the more conservative members of Japan. Perhaps the answer lies in a combination of these reasons.

The Japanese Civil Code and Commercial Code accordingly came into force in 1898 and 1899, respectively, both being based predominantly on the German equivalents. Indeed, the Japanese code of Civil Procedure and their organisation of courts was also modelled on the German scheme. Inevitably, towards the end of the First World War, it was German legal philosophy that provided the main inspiration to Japanese private law scholarship.

(iii) The Influence of Anglo-American Law

6.3.8 In 1945, after the Second World War, there is little doubt that Anglo-American law exerted a very strong influence on Japanese law. Whether it succeeeded in transforming the essence of Japanese legal thinking or centuries of tradition remains a point of contention. In terms of actual changes to existing written laws, however, the following may be noted:

(a) The new Japanese Constitution has been based predominantly on American legal ideas, which included strengthening the position of judges, the status of public officials, reforming administrative organisation, and including a list of basic rights which the courts are required to enforce.

(b) Both the codes of criminal procedure and civil procedure have been amended so as to curtail the judge's power to restrict the parties and their counsel in presenting evidence during the trial. The old Japanese family system has been abolished in favour of the principle of equality of husband and wife which is embodied in the civil code.

(c) Democratising laws were implemented, at the insistence of the American occupying force, in relation to company law, bringing in anti-monopoly laws as well as more supervisory laws to regulate the stock market and share issue.

(d) Judicial review and conciliation are envisaged by law. A special pre-trial procedure (*wakai*) is available which usually suffices to settle the dispute but if it fails to do so, the parties have the right to go to court.

(iv) Continuing Influence of Japanese Traditions

6.3.9 However, very much in line with indigenous Japanese philosophy, the Code of Civil Procedure requires the judge to attempt to bring the parties to reach a settlement; indeed, the judge plays the role of mediator as often as possible. In addition, there is a procedure that allows a panel of conciliators, composed of a judge and two conciliators, to adjudicate on a dispute (*chotei*) and the judge tries not to take an active part in the proceedings which must be seen to have been resolved without judicial intervention. There is an obligation in the case of family law or labour law, for *chotei* to be referred to. As a result of a Supreme Court decision, it is now established that the *chotei* procedure is only possible if the suggested solution is voluntarily accepted by the parties. The procedure has been in decline since 1958, and the parties now tend to go before the court and request that it resolve the issue 'in strict law.'

Furthermore, in the case of Japanese contracts, should a dispute arise, there are clauses which require the parties to confer in good faith, or to settle the matter harmoniously by consultation. This is in sharp contrast to the typical Anglo-American contract, which may refer the dispute to independent arbitration but also utilise a whole range of other legal devices to deal with the situation.

Finally, there is the principle of 'both parties are to blame' which Japanese law used to apply to disputes; in a quarrel, each party was seen as attacking the other so that there was no room for the concept of self-defence to be applied to acts committed in the course of a quarrel (see *Osada* v. *Japan* (1932) Great Court of Judicature Judgment, Jan.25;). This case was subsequently overruled in 1957, and self-defence was accepted as a defence.

(v) Future Trends in Japanese Law

6.3.10   At one level, Japanese thought and Japanese law continue to move inexorably towards the West. Newer types of legal actions are being brought to the courts fairly frequently and the Japanese popular press now devotes much more attention to law, litigation and international economic and political relations with the West. As we have seen, the post-war democratisation of government, Westernisation and modernisation of Japan has continued apace. This has occurred alongside dramatic reform of the traditional rural order through land reform, and demographic changes such as the movement towards and concentration within big cities, changing family values and relationships accompanying other changes in social conditions. But, despite their remarkable industrial and economic progress, Varley suggests that: 'the Japanese remain strongly enthralled by their own unique heritage and uncertain...of their moorings in the cultural gulf that still separates East and West in the modern world.'

On the other hand, Kawashima (1979) has maintained that although Japanese legal thinking is predominantly influenced by German legal thought, this does not mean that the legal thinking of Japanese lawyers is completely westernised. There are 'significant elements' which indicate non-Western ways of thinking. The reference to German thought has already been discussed and again, in many respects, Kawashima is correct. Nevetheless, it is probably true to say that Japan is in a state of flux and a society in transition. Despite all these radical legal transplants and massive injections of Western culture, the heart of the Japanese legal mind remains an Eastern one, operating on a different plane, in tune with different rules and still very much steeped in tradition. As with other Far Eastern legal conceptions, at many levels below the facade of written laws and codes, Japanese law remains, as Noda first expressed it, "the law of the subtle mind" (see Noda: 1971) and an exotic example of a fusion of Western and Eastern legal traditions seeking to come to terms with the demands of modernity.

SELECTIVE BIBLIOGRAPHY

Knapp (ed.) International Encyclopaedia of Comparative Law:

vol I: National Reports; vol.II: Legal Systems of the World

Hazard, Butler and Maggs THE SOVIET LEGAL SYSTEM (1977)

International Encyclopaedia of Comparative Law: vol II

Lee and Lai 'The Chinese Conceptions of Law: Confucian, Legalist, and Buddhist' (1978) 29 The Hastings Law Journal 1307

Kim & Lawson'The Law of the Subtle Mind: The Traditional Japanese Conception of Law'(1979)ICLQ 491

Kawashima 'Japanese Way of Legal Thinking' (1979) International Journal of Law Libraries 127

Ioffe and Maggs SOVIET LAW IN PRACTICE (1983)

Butler SOVIET LAW (1987)

Zweigert and Kotz AN INTRODUCTION TO COMPARATIVE LAW (1987): vol. I

Quigley 'Socialist Law and the Civil Law Tradition' (1989)

    AmJCL 781

Sypnowich THE CONCEPT OF SOCIALIST LAW (1990)

Stephan III 'Perestroika and Property: The Law of Ownership in the Post-Socialist Soviet Union' (1991) AmJCL 35

PART THREE: SUBSTANTIVE STUDIES

CHAPTER SEVEN

The Law of Obligations: A Comparative Study of Contract and Tort

A. INTRODUCTION

7.0 In 1953, Prosser declared that 'When the ghosts of case and assumpsit walk hand in hand at midnight, it is sometimes a convenient and comforting thing to have a borderland in which they may lose themselves.' (see Prosser *The Borderland of Tort and Contract* (1953) p.452) In modern English law, the areas of tort and contract are usually placed in separate legal compartments for analytical, pedagogical and conceptual purposes. On the other hand, civil law legal systems group both tort and contract as belonging to one category-the general Law of Obligations. The common law has adopted the dichotomy since the mid-nineteenth century, and contrastingly, the civil law's treatment of both areas as being part of the same generic law of obligations appears to date from early Roman law.

Yet, in terms of legal theory and legal history, tort and contract are by no means invariably independent or mutually exclusive concepts. In many respects, they are closely related and as Winfield put it in 1931, 'The segregation of the law of tort from other parts of the law is quite modern.' (Winfield (1931)p.8). Winfield himself emphasised the fact that liability in tort arose from the breach of an obligation primarily fixed by law, but in contract it is fixed by the parties themselves. This generalisation was certainly true when liability in contract arose from the mere exchange of promises but not in more modern times when contractual liability is seen as arising as soon as the plaintiff has conferred a benefit on the defendant or has incurred loss by relying on the defendant's behaviour (see Dias and Markesinis (1989) p.7).

Indeed, despite their conventional separation, there are situations even *within* English law, where, for example, a party's conduct may be tortious in character, but may also have contractual overtones. Similarly, the behaviour of a party may be the consequence of a contractual relationship which he has entered into with another, but which may also give rise to tortious liability.

Common examples in English law of overlap between tort and contract arise, for example, in 'economic torts' and certain cases of misrepresentation where a remedy may lie in the tort of deceit (for fraudulent misrepresentation which induced a party to enter into a contract) or for conduct which induces someone to commit a breach of contract, which may also be regarded as tortious behaviour.

There are a number of striking differences between common law and civil law systems in their approach to delictual obligations (or the law of tort, in common law parlance) and contractual obligations. These differences are seen in their method of division into separate areas of law, their different remedies and their divergence in bases of liability. While the civil law groups both tortious and contractual obligations under the general area of law which they call The Law of Obligations, the common law retains its nineteenth century division of the law of obligations into the categories of contract, tort and restitution. There are, of course, other types of obligations which, for example, French law is prepared to admit but which it will not enforce by legal process. These are called 'natural obligations' using the Roman law terminology, from which the concept derives. A typical example is a civil obligation which is unenforceable for technical reasons such as a statutory limitation period within which to bring the suit. Certain obligations have to be converted into a 'civil act' in order to be actionable and this usually requires a solemn notarial act.

For the purposes of this chapter, we shall compare the historical development of the notion of tortious (or delictual) liability and contractual liability in English law and the two main civil law countries. We shall also analyse certain common elements such as 'fault' and illustrative situations in tort and contract as developed in these jurisdictions.

B. HISTORICAL DEVELOPMENT: A COMPARATIVE ANALYSIS

i. The Early Roman Law of Obligations

7.1   It appears to be well established that Roman law's greatest contribution to modern Civil law has been in the law of obligations and especially in the law of contract. It is also in the law of contract that Common lawyers have most frequently looked to Roman or civil law. But in Gaius' *Institutes*, followed by Justinian, having dealt with property and succession, writes about a subject called *Obligationes*, which he classifies under two headings, those arising from contract (*ex contractu*) or from delict (*ex delicto*). To these categories Justinian added *quasi-contract* and *quasi-delict*.

ii. Contracts

(i) Early Roman Law

7.1.2 The word *obligatio* does not appear to have been used as a legal term until the time of the Empire. Yet as early as the Twelve Tables, there is mention of a formal act which embodied the bare essentials of an agreement. This was the *stipulatio*, which consisted of an exchange of a question and answer in formal words. In its earliest forms, the prospective creditor/promisee would say: 'Do you solemnly promise [to pay me X...or to convey to me your horse]? and the prospective debtor/promisor replied 'I solemnly promise.'

But the validity of the *stipulatio* derived from its *form*, not from the agreement which the form embodied. Agreement played no part in early Roman law, being neither necessary nor sufficient. The *stipulatio* thus came to be generally enforceable as *a formal promise in which an obligation is imposed on only one party, the promisor or debtor*. But the *form of words* had to be correct.

Legal historians such as Nicholas (1962) stress that the idea of contract was one which, as in English law, emerged gradually and probably began with a notion of *debt*-that someone owed someone else a certain sum or thing. The presence or absence of agreement was not a significant consideration. The origins of contract probably lie in the existence of two types of debt, one deriving from a formal act, and the other from an informal transfer or payment. The crucial difference between the two is that whereas the first is a *promissory debt*, the other is a 'real' debt in that it is limited to the return of something already received from the creditor (Nicholas (1962) p.160).

The implications of the 'promissory debt' for the development of commerce were extremely significant because the needs of a more sophisticated commercial society could be better served by the utilisation of a concept that could be adapted to more complex transactions. Performance of services or of undertakings incidental to a sale, required a more flexible means of interaction.

Hence, an even more significant development which occurred in certain other transactions (such as sale or hire), was the evolution of the principle of a party being bound by a formless agreement. This meant that a contracting party could be bound when neither had performed their part of the agreement, (under an *executory* contract) a notion which English law recognised only as late as in the seventeenth century. Consensual contracts appear to have been established in Roman law sometime in the first century B.C.

The four consensual contracts were: (i) *emptio venditio* (sale); (ii) *locatio conductio* (hire); (iii) *societas* (partnership); and (iv) *mandatum* (mandate). All four of these shared a common denominator: they arose by *mere agreement*, without the need for any form or any physical act, such as delivery which was a prerequisite for 'real' contracts. The important concept of *bona fides* was also developed through the application of these consensual contracts and especially in contracts of sale and hire.

(ii) Early English Law

7.1.3   Yet, in English law, the notion of an enforceable agreement had appeared at an early stage, but then lost currency until around the late fifteenth or early sixteenth centuries. In England,the ecclesiastical courts began to impose spiritual penalties in certain cases of breach of agreement where no remedy existed at common law. This practice was, however, checked very early by writs of prohibition and does not seem to have made any impact on later law. Much later on, in the fifteenth and sixteenth centuries, before the common law courts had created a viable notion of contracts, the English Court of Chancery was apparently establishing a consistent practice of enforcing agreements of several different kinds without actually deciding the principle upon which it was acting.

(iii) Principal Feature of Contracts in Roman Law

7.1.4   The main characteristic of the Roman law relating to contracts is that it consisted of a law of *contracts*, rather than a doctrinally unified law of contract. There were therefore no generalised rules but really many *different rules governing a recognised list of contracts*, and the legal requirements of each contract varied according to its particular species. An informal agreement in Roman law did not constitute a contract unless it satisfied the legal requirements of this particular contract.

Contracts in Roman private law, thus became extremely important and various commentators have argued over the nature of contractual obligation. The traditional explanation, however, is that it was the promisor's declaration of his will which made a contract binding, by obliging him to keep his word (*De iure belli*, II.II; *De iure naturae*, III.5).

Nicholas (1962) highlights three practical consequences that flowed from the lack of generalised theory: (i) Lawyers were therefore able to determine in detail the 'incidents' of each type of contract in advance, so that these could be adapted to the commercial needs of the particular parties; (ii) Since each type of contract had an appropriate form of action according to the *formulary system* of the time (see chapter 3), the plaintiff had to prove that he had entered into the type of contract specified in the *formula* of his action or would have his case dismissed at this preliminary stage; (iii) Any agreement could be cast in the form of a *stipulatio*, which would then render it legally effective, since the *stipulatio* was a *method of contracting* rather than a type of contract. It was the *stipulatio* which gave the Roman system a much-needed degree of flexibility as well as generality.

The classical Roman view that only certain types of contracts should be enforced hence eventually came to be rejected under the influence of canon law, the law merchant (*lex mercatoria*) and natural law. Under these three influences, it came to be accepted that in principle *any agreement of two parties, which had been voluntarily entered into and intended to create legal obligations, should* prima facie *be enforced as a contract*, irrespective of the presence or absence of what a Common lawyer would call 'consideration'. This general principle came to be known as *freedom of contract*.

Of course, there were many exceptions to the rule, such as the need to comply with certain form requirements; or exceptions based on duress, fraud, illegality or mistake. This was the position on the eve of the age of codification, and the same general principle enunciated above-freedom of contract-was consequently integrated into all the Codes. It is also often stated, and with some justification, that there was no doctrine of consideration in Roman law. However, civil law appears to have developed a doctrine of 'cause' (*causa*) which has been vigorously debated and analysed by legal historians, and which has even been incorporated into the French Civil Code.

(iv) Cause and Consideration in Roman and English Contracts

7.1.5   On the question of consideration in contracts, there certainly did not appear to be any rule in Roman law which required that every promise must be supported by 'consideration' as a condition of its validity, in the sense of *quid pro quo*, and equivalent to the English notion of consideration. Under modern English law, consideration has been described as the price of the promise, or 'the price for which the promise is bought' (Pollock). This is, of course, exceedingly vague. It has, however, traditionally been defined as *involving either some detriment to the plaintiff or some benefit to the defendant* (see *Currie* v. *Misa* (1875) LR 10 Exch 153,162; *Thomas* v. *Thomas* (1842) 2QB   851) but almost invariably involves both, and must be of some economic value in order to be legally significant. In fact, the English 'doctrine of consideration' refers to a number of complex rules (see below:7.1.8). As many legal historians such as Buckland and McNair (1952) observe, the Romans did not think in terms of consideration in any common law sense, but other writers such as Lawson (see *Excursus* to Buckland and McNair (1952)pp.228ff.) also pointed out that there are apparently four sets of ancient Roman texts which support the similar notion of *causa* or 'cause' in the Roman law relating to contracts. First there is a text in the *Corpus Juris* which suggests that contracts needed *causa* as well as consent, in order to be enforceable: see D.2.14.7.4; and D.14.1.49.2. (*cum nulla subest causa praeter conventionem*). Secondly, another set of texts also suggests that an agreement is void or voidable if it is based on an illicit or non-existent *causa*. The central difficulty with the first set of texts is that there were four consensual contracts in Roman law which existed at the time these statements appear to have been made which were binding solely on the basis of consent (see above). 'Cause' therefore applies, if at all, to the innominate contracts and the upshot of it is that 'executed consideration is required where no regimes have been set up for particular contracts' (Lawson: Excursus).

With regard to the second set, Buckland and McNair's analysis (see Buckland and McNair (1952) pp. 224ff.) suggests that the usage of *causa* varies with the context and certainly does not refer to meanings similar to the English model, but to the failure to perform something which was at the root of the contract or to an ulterior motive for the transaction which vitiates its legality. Hence, the various Roman contracts which appear to support the notion of *causa* really deal with situations where some fraudulent intention was the real basis of the contract, or recovery of money was ordered because a *causa* (a particular service or undertaking) which was the basis of the whole transaction, was not carried out.

A third Roman origin of cause, unearthed by Lawson, is sometimes called the 'interdependence of promises' which arose from the obligations in a contract of sale. The obligations of the buyer and seller were 'mutually independent', so that neither could refuse to perform his part on the ground that the other had defaulted or was not ready or willing to perform. Nevertheless, classical Roman law mitigated this rule so that either party could refuse to perform unless the other party was ready and willing to perform his side of the agreement. In cases of failure to pay the price at the agreed time, the insertion of a *lex commissoria* clause into the contract was the solution, since this gave the seller the option of declaring the contract at an end if the buyer did not pay within an agreed time. Once it was inserted, the two promises became interdependent.

A fourth source of the doctrine is the practice that grew up in Roman times of requiring acknowledgement of debts to specify their basis, because of the fear (mainly by the canonists) that vague or abstract promises would pose difficulties of proof and therefore enforceability. The rule therefore emerged that an acknowledgement of debt *nudum a causa*, could not be enforced. This had nothing to do with consideration.

Nevertheless, the medieval lawyers utilised *causa* as the basis of their system of contract in order to distinguish between promissory transactions which would be legally enforceable and those which would not. The concept has accordingly passed into the French Civil Code, in Italy and other European systems though not in Germany. But it has been criticised as unmanageable, undecipherable and in the words of Bonfante, 'the battle ground for metaphysical elucubrations and juridical psychology' (Bonfante, Scr. Giur.iii.p. 125).

(v) The Notion of Contract in Early English Law

7.1.6   In the Middle Ages, the word 'contract' was engulfed within the larger idea of property. The medieval usage of the term denoted a transaction involving the transfer of a material thing (*res*) so that the earliest contracts were all 'real' contracts, where the legal duty was based on the delivery of a chattel. Thus, as with early Roman law, the element of agreement or consent did not seem to be relevant and the majority opinion of legal historians appears to be that *agreement was not recognised as a basis of liability* (see, for example, Street (1908)pp.1,5; Holmes(1881),p.264;Pollock and Maitland (1968) p.212; Holdsworth: vol.III,p.349; Potter(1958)p.452; Fifoot (1949) pp.225-226). A judicial statement from a 1428 case which is typical of the cases which support the majority view is: 'The ground of the action is a duty' YB.7 Hen. 6,f.5,pl.9.

Professor Simpson (1975) appears to agree with this to some extent but points out that the 'duty' was *a duty of indebtedness*, and although he thinks that medieval law did sometimes enforce parol or verbal agreements, this was not necessarily enforceable in the common law courts. Commentators such as McGovern and Arnold also disagree with the majority view, arguing that their research suggests that a wide range and fairly large number of arrangements in the fourteenth century were analysed in terms of a *promise*, and the writ of covenant was used for this purpose (see McGovern (1969) and Arnold (1976)). It is submitted that the ambiguous nature of the Year Book accounts, and different use of terminology therein coupled with the absence of authoritative treatises on the subject make it impossible to know what the actual legal position was at the time. It is noteworthy, however, that in the early contracts, any notion of duty seemed to originate from the defendant's receipt of property that was perceived as rightly belonging to the plaintiff. Indeed, as with early Roman law, all the early transactions also seemed to create some 'debt' in the mind of the medieval lawyer.

On the point of terminology, *'covenant'* appears to be the medieval equivalent of our legal usage of 'contract', so that to medieval lawyers, 'covenant' and not contract was the term that signified a legally binding agreement. Thus, although the word 'contract' appears in the Year Books, it does so infrequently and its usage certainly does not seem to correspond to any theory of contract based on agreement. Year Book evidence also suggests that counsel and judges are careful to distinguish between 'contract' from a sealed writing. Both Hale and Blackstone treat contract as 'only a means of acquiring ownership or possession'.

The earliest from of a 'real' contract appears to be *bailment*, wherein the main duty seemed to be the return of the chattel, or its value, to the original owner. English law required the actual delivery of the chattel before it could impose any legal duty. It appears, therefore, that Anglo-Saxon law did not possess any theory of contract and only recognised written agreements under seal, 'real' contracts and the simple contract of suretyship.

'Contract' was later broadened to include all transactions (consensual or otherwise) which gave rise to the action of Debt. Further, another notion associated with the early forms of informal contracts was that of *quid pro quo* (something for something), which was often said to be an essential element of a valid contract. Thus, even in early times, 'contract' was perceived as a *bargain* involving some element or notion of *reciprocal exchange*.

It is important to note, however, that although the notion of *quid pro quo* made its appearance in contracts like the sale of goods, the doctrine of Consideration in the modern or nineteenth-century sense, was unknown to lawyers of the fourteenth and fifteenth centuries. In any event, all it meant was that in informal transactions, a duty to pay a debt arose when either performance had been tendered or services had been rendered. Hence, some sort of part performance yielding a benefit to one of the parties must have taken place for some sort of duty to arise. But this was only relevant to the question of actionability, *not* the question of when an agreement became binding.

a. Actions on the Case

7.1.7   The modern law of contract appears to have originated from a form of *actions on the case* known as *assumpsit* (undertaking). As we have seen in chapter 4, the early history of the common law saw the establishment of central courts and the procedure which enabled these courts to summon defendants to answer complaints against them was the form of summons known as the *writ*. It should be remembered that parol or oral agreements of an informal nature were few and far between in medieval times, since the King's courts were only prepared to recognise agreements which were 'under seal'. Consequently, for a long time, no writ existed for breach of parol agreements.

Thus, there were gaps in the common law of obligations, before the mid-fourteenth century, since there were no writs to deal with informal, unsealed agreements which could be proved by wager of law (production of a certain number of witnesses to prove one's case). Eventually, a new writ of trespass developed, which contained the *vi et armis* (with force and arms) clause which gave the courts jurisdiction to hear the case. The trepass writ eventually spawned the 'Actions on the Case', which were actions which local custom classified as wrongs and which were admitted to the courts even *without* the *vi et armis* clause, because they were actions based on previous or established cases.

It was against this procedural backdrop that the writ known as *assumpsit* was developed from the actions on the Case, derived from the original writ of trespass. Assumpsit appeared in the mid-fourteenth century, from which the common law developed an action for breach of informal promises. The essence of assumpsit was that the defendant had vountarily assumed an obligation, as illustrated by the case of *Skyrne* v. *Butolf* (1367) YB 3, Ric 2,223, in which the plaintiff, who sought a cure for ringworm from the defendant doctor, alleged that the doctor undertook (assumpsit) to cure him for a sum of money which had already been paid. The gist of the plaintiff's claim was that the defendant performed this undertaking or promise so negligently that the defendant suffered unjury.

This action was then extended to persons such as blacksmiths, innkeepers and surgeons in the famous *Humber Ferry Case* (1348) YB 22 Ass, p.141, where the ferryman was held liable for his breach of his undertaking (assumpsit) in overloading his ferry such that the plaintiff's mare, which the defendant had promised to carry across the river, perished. The plaintiff sued in trespass but pleaded a breach of the *promise* made by the defendant.

These were clearly cases of misfeasance or intentional harm, but the action was later broadened to include cases of non-misfeasance, or unintentional harm, which was established in *Pickering* v. *Thoroughgood* (1533) 93 Selden Society 4. The landmark decision was *Slade's Case* (1602) 4 Co Rep 92, in which it was definitively established that any undertaking or promise could be actionable. In its form, assumpsit constituted an action for a detriment suffered by the person to whom the promise had been made, in reliance on that promise. Assumpsit therefor shifted the focus of liability arising from parol transactions from the delivery of a chattel to whether a promise had been unfulfilled either by defective performance or nonperformance.

b. The Doctrine of Consideration

7.1.8 As we have seen from the previous discussion, the doctrine of consideration began to be developed by the English courts in the mid-sixteenth century, as a touchstone of the seriousness of contractual intention. But this is was obviously not the modern-day (or nineteenth century) version of the doctrine. It gradually acquired a technical meaning and became the pivotal prerequisite for the enforceability of promises. By the nineteenth century, it had become entrenched in the doctrine of English law and, to a certain extent, is the basis of other contractual rules such as privity of contract. The doctrine itself comprises a number of rules such as: (i) *Past consideration is no consideration*-a promise to pay for services already rendered is not usually enforceable; (ii) *Consideration need not be 'adequate'* -it may be a 'tomtit or a canary' but need only be of some value in the eye of the law; (iii) *Consideration must move from the promisee*-a party wishing to enforce a contract must show that he has furnished consideration for the promise of the other party; this is sometimes cited as another of the reasons for the inability of a third party to a contract to sue on such a contract-since he has not provided any consideration for the promise. (iv) *Performance of an existing duty is not valid consideration*-for example, where a duty is already owed under a contract or by law, as with an existing public duty.
It is well-known that the English doctrine has come under severe criticism from various commentators and the courts themselves, as well as by the Law Revision Committee in 1937 who suggested that an agreement should be enforceable if either the promise was made in writing by the promisor or his agent, or if it was supported by valuable consideration, past or present. English legislators and latterly, the Law Commission have not responded to these suggestions until recently, and a comprehensive study of contracts is currently being undertaken.

iii. Tortious or Delictual Liability

(i) Origins and Development

a. Common Law

7.1.9 In the early common law, there was no differentiation between crimes and torts. Wrongs were first classified into (i) felonies and (ii) those that were not felonies. If an offence was punishable by death, dismemberment, escheat, or outlawry, it was a felony. The same classification applied if it could be prosecuted by means of the private criminal prosecution known as an appeal of felony, wherein the accused's guilt was decided by battle. If it did not fall within that grouping, it was one of a vast group of offences referred to as trespasses or transgressions. In the famous words of Bracton, 'Every felony is a trespass, though every trespass is not a felony.' Within the group of trespasses, misdemeanours and torts were all mixed in a hotchpot so that it was impossible to distinguish them.

The word 'trespass' itself was used to mean 'wrong' and applied to many types of actions that involved tortious civil wrongs. Trespass was one of the earliest writs in the royal courts, appearing around 1250, but it possessed criminal overtones and had criminal sanctions. It was directed at serious, direct and forcible breaches of the peace and was the remedy for all such injuries or damage, whether caused to persons, land or chattels. As in France, it was concerned with the punishment of the crime and gave compensation to the injured plaintiff only as supplementary to the sentence.

It developed rapidly during the thirteenth century, and towards the end of the thirteenth century, was supplemented by an action of trespass *'on the case'* to accommodate wrongful conduct which was neither direct nor forcible, which did not fit within the confines of the original writ of trespass. These sorts of claims were therefore granted writs 'on the case', in the light of and on the basis of the particular circumstances.

Thus, there were *nominate and specific torts* which were directly covered by the original trespass writ, and *innominate torts* which varied according to their individual circumstances.

A scholarly debate developed which focussed on the true interpretation of chapter 24 of the Statute of Westminister II of 1285. For many years, this was thought to have created the authority in the Courts of Chancery to issue writs of trespass on the case (also known simply as Case). A subsequent theory was that trespass on the case grew out of trespass as a natural progression. Professor Milsom has argued, in what has become known as a more modern theory, that trespass was used in obvious cases involving forcible trespass such as asault and battery and trespass on land, but Case was used where the cases were not so obvious. Professor Milsom therefore argues that the term 'case' did not appear until 1370.

After various developments had taken place, wherein the royal courts started to hear the actions on the case by plaintiffs' insertion of the 'with force and arms' formula, it eventually reached the stage where fault was the basic element in actions of trespass on the case, but did not feature in the case of taking someone's personal property or invading someone's land. Here the nominate torts were used.

Up to the development of industrialisation during the nineteenth century, the emergence of fault as a criterion of liability had certainly dominated the English civil liability scenario. However, the notion of fault was found to be inappropriate to the new industrialised nineteenth century society, and new principles were needed to take care of the new phenomenon of 'accidents' which came to include not just fortuitous mishaps but also harms caused by human errors, predominantly because 'more machines are used and more accidents happen'. (see International Encyclopedia of Comparative Law, vol.xii, chapter 1,p.41).

It was probably in England that the industrial revolution had its first impact on the law of tort. Railways trains appear to have been the first source of injuries and actions upon the case for negligence. The process began with an action on the case, supported by an allegation of negligence. This focussed the issue on negligence and after a slow and gradual evolution, the tort of negligence emerged and was unequivocally recognised in the landmark case of *Donoghue* v. *Stevenson* [1932] AC 562, a Scottish appeal which went to the English House of Lords. In a famous passage by Lord Atkin, which has come to be known as the 'neighbour test' he said a man is required to take 'reasonable care to avoid acts or omissions which he could reasonably foresee would be likely to injure his neighbour' and in answer to the question 'Who is a neighbour?' he replied, 'persons who are so closely and directly affected by my act that I ought reasonably to have them in contemplation as being so affected when I am directing my mind to the acts or omissions which are called into question.'

This was not the first statement (indeed, it was strictly only *obiter dicta*) acknowledging a general theory of duty in negligence but was the first which gained general acceptance and influenced the whole course of development of the English law relating to negligence. Judges initially only found negligence in cases where an established duty was said to exist (eg in *Otto* v. *Bolton and Norris* [1936] 2 KB 46,pp.54-55) but during the period of the 1970s and 1980s was accepted as a statement of general principle.

b. French Law

7.1.10   In French Law, only particular torts were actionable as in Roman law and Roman jurists devised a formula (*neminem laedere*:injure no one) which became the basis of Article 1382 of the Civil Code. The French law on torts is essentially a 'praetorian law founded on judicial decisions.' (*International Encyclopedia of Comparative Law*, vol II. chapter IV, p.F-70). The law of early France had three main sources, namely Germanic customs, Roman law and canon law. Germanic customs were predominant in the field of tort, mostly in the North but also in the South, at any rate, up to the second life or revival of Roman law at the beginning of the thirteenth century. The *Germanic law of the Salic Franks*, dating from the fifth century, defined in great detail various offences and the appropriate fines and even prescribed different types of compensation commensurate with the social status of the victim. For example, slaves cost less than an important officer in the army, and a thief had to give compensation not just for the value of the thing stolen but for the loss of its use. Part of the compensation went to the king and part to the victim or his family.

This was a remarkably sophisticated system for its time. Canon law was later responsible for the intention element in the law, adding to the degree of morality of the offender. From about the twelfth century, Gratian made a clear distinction between damage caused unwittingly and intentionally which led to a distinction between criminal justice and civil justice. Where criminal law proceeded by a list of specific offences, civil law could develop using more general principles of compensation.

The delict provisions in the French Civil Code are almost completely attributable in their formulation, to the French scholar Jean Domat, who, in the seventeenth century, distinguished between intentional breaches of the law, breaches of contract and mere negligence. Fault was made the criterion of liability. Even when coupled with harm, proof of fault was necessary in order to create liability. As far as the question of what conduct should be considered 'wrongful' the French adopted the Roman approach as expressed by their jurists, and used the criterion of conduct which fell short of the standards of a *bonus paterfamilias*. (see International Encyclopeadia of Comparative Law, vol.xii, ch.1, p.36)

Very little progress was made in the period between Domat and the enactment of the French Civil Code. Domat's work inspired Pothier who divided conduct which involved liability in damages into *delits* and *quasi-delits*.

c. German Law

7.1.11 Before the enactment of the BGB, the law of tort in Germany was a mixture, with the *Gemeines Recht* being based partly on traditional types of liability inherited from Roman law and other parts of the country being governed by a general clause of liability in tort. The Prussian Land Law stated in paragraph 1 ff. I 6 that 'a person who injures another intentionally or by gross negligence must pay full compensation to that other' while 'the person who injures...another by only moderate carelessness' need only pay for 'the palpable harm cause thereby'. (see Zweigert and Kotz (1987) p.293). After seriously considering whether to follow the French Civil Code, the draftsmen of the BGB decided not to adopt a general clause, not least because they wanted greater precision in the German version but also because they feared that excessive generality would empower judges to resolve the ambiguities and fill the gaps too frequently, which would be inconsistent with their perception of the judicial function. (Zweigert and Kotz, *ibid.*)

Three heads of tortious liability were therefore laid down in *two paragraphs*, supplemented by other specific provisions. Under the *first head*, paragraph 823 I BGB, liability for causing injury in an unlawful and culpable manner will arise if the injury affects the victim in one of the legal interests enumerated in the text, namely life, body, health, freedom, ownership and any other right.

The second head of general tort liability arises under paragraph 823 II when 'a statute designed to protect another' is culpably contravened. The kinds of statutes referred to will include all the rules of private and public law, particularly criminal law, 'which are substantially designed to protect an individual or a group of individuals rather than the public as a whole.' (Zweigert and Kotz 91987) p.296).

The third head of general tort liability arises under paragraph 826 BGB. A person is liable under this provision if he 'intentionally causes harm to another in a manner which offends *contra bonos mores*'.

iii. Law of Obligations: Contract in Civil Law

(i) Legal Obligations and Freedom of Contract

a. French Law

7.1.12   In pre-codification times, in Roman law, the contracting parties' consensus was the central and decisive element of the law of contracts. This was also called the principle of 'freedom of contract'. The Civil Code treats obligations in accordance with a classification of their sources, that is, the facts which give rise to the obligation. The draftsmen *distinguished* between those obligations which arose from the *agreement of the parties* and those which *did not*. In the section on Obligations, the first title or chapter deals with contracts and the second title with other obligations. Non-contractual obligations are subdivided further into those obligations which arise solely from the authority of the law and those which result from a personal act on the part of the debtor. This last group is finally subdivided into obligations which arise from quasi-contracts, from delicts and from quasi-delicts respectively.

 Obligations therefore derive from four sources: contract and quasi-contract, which are broadly similar to the areas covered in English law; and delict and quasi-delict, which are roughly equivalent to the law of tort (excluding areas covered by the law of property). Contract and tort are therefore seen as forming one category much more in French law than in English law. The lack of distinction is also facilitated by the view that liability under both heads rests on fault. (see below,C. *Fault in the Law of Contract and Tort*).

 Under the Code, legal obligations arise because the debtor wishes them to arise; in other words, they are created by his will and with his consent. Under Article 1108 of the Civil Code, one element necessary for an agreement is the consent of the party who obligates or 'binds' himself. This indicates that a promise is necessary for an obligation to arise but not an acceptance. Under the ideology of the Civil Code, an agreement is binding because and in so far as the parties have consented to it. Thus the obligations created by the parties could be modified, altered or rejected by them.

 Hence the *norm* in the law of obligations was the contractual obligation and extra-contractual obligations were limited in scope. The Code seeks to ensure that effect is given to the will of the parties.

b. English Law

7.1.13   Of course, the notion of freedom of contract is a dominant principle in English common law as well. The phrase itself has many meanings: (i) freedom to choose to enter into any sort of contracts; (ii) freedom to decide whether or not to contract; (iii) freedom of each contracting party to fix the terms of his own promise, subject to the agreement of the other party. True or absolute freedom of contract cannot really exist, since parties are rarely completely equal in economic or social terms, and one's freedom to contract is clearly limited by social, commercial and legally acceptable norms, some of which is contained in criminal law and others in the law of contract itself (the contracts that would be void for illegality-contracts to promote illegality or immorality; contracts in restraint of trade).

Much academic ink or, these days, word-processor printer ribbons have been used to debate and discuss this concept which appears to have fallen in and out of fashion from time to time. Professor Atiyah's monumental book *The Rise and Fall of Freedom of Contract* (1979) surveyed the genesis of the notion and traced political, economic, social and legal influences which have shaped this phenomenon. He concluded that freedom of contract was in decline towards the end of the 1970s, but in the last decade, there has been a strong resurgence of the free market ideology, a revival of interest in the right of the individual to make his own free choices and that individuals should be left to make their own mistakes, if that is what they wish to do. Concomitant with this has been the growing distrust of bureaucratic and State-controlled decision-making. The tremendous rise in the use of administrative and employment tribunals in Britain (see Chapter 4) is not so much an affirmation of belief in the power of quasi-judicial powers but of the individual's right to an impartial hearing and the right to be heard. Thus freedom of contract's star has been rising in the 1980s and the inevitable tension between legal paternalism and an individual's right to make his or her own contract have come into play yet again.

The use of *standard form contracts* represents an attempt to introduce generalised terms and conditions of business, primarily for economies of scale. However, these have meant that the average consumer has had to cope with the full might and power of a large commercial enterprise, thus reducing any semblance of equality of bargaining power. The English Courts have devised concepts such as Fundamental Breach of contract and adopted a strict interpretation policy towards widely-worded exemption clauses in order to equalise the consumer's bargaining power with that of the large corporation. Parliament has also intervened to pass the Unfair Contract Terms Act 1977 (UCTA), requiring, *inter alia*, that any exemption clause which is sought to be relied upon, must be 'reasonable in all the circumstances'. Schedule 2 of the UCTA lists factors which the court is directed to consider to promote equality of bargaining power in applying the 'reasonableness test'.

However, in 1980, the House of Lords in *Photo Production* v. *Securicor Ltd* [1980] AC 827, appears to have advocated a non-interventionist approach, leaving it to the parties to decide which sort of breaches would entitle the innocent party to repudiate the contract. In other words, the parties' agreement should be the controlling factor. This has been followed in cases such as the *TLF Prosperity case* [1984] 1 WLR 48, but goes against another earlier House of Lords case, the *George Mitchell Case* [1983] 2 AC 803. Hence, the caselaw on the English judges' approach to the interpretation of the UCTA indicates: (i) There are two different approaches to the interpretation of the 'reasonableness' requirement in the UCTA. The *Photo Production* approach suggests a party-centred, non-interventionist approach and the *George Mitchell* approach advocates leaving the matter to the discretion of the trial judge. (ii) Trial judges seem more likely to operate within the *George Mitchell* approach rather than the Photo production one. (iii) Judges seem willing to apply the Schedule 2 guidelines which include the strength of the bargaining positions of the parties relative to each other, the presence or absence of an

inducement to agree to a term, and whether the customer knew or ought reasonably to have known of the existence and extent of the particular contractual term.
(see UCTA and Adams and Brownsword 'The Unfair Contract Terms Act: A Decade of Discretion' (1988) 104 LQR 94).

c. German Law

7.1.14 Freedom of contract, an essential concept to German private law, is protected under the Basic Law in Germany as part of the general freedom of action (article 2, par. 1: Basic Law). As a crucial element of a free economy, contract facilitates private enterprise and promotes the development of economic relationships and commercial enterprise. German law distinguished between the freedom to form contracts and the freedom to decide their content. The freedom to enter a contract or not is limited whenever there is a monopoly of some description. Although there is a general freedom to contract on virtually anything, there are both constitutional and legal limits to this freedom, as with every other legal system.

The limits to contractual freedom are discussed by Horn, Kotz and Leser (1982): (i) Statutory prohibitions under paragraph 134: BGB, which include criminal conspiracies and dealings in prohibited drugs. (ii) An assortment of cases where the court decides on their legality or otherwise depending on the gravity, the danger or turpitude of the transaction, including medicaments without presription, and transactions to evade tax which will only be illegal if their principal aim was to evade tax;

(iii) prohibition of usurious contracts(paragraph 2: BGB); (iv) a legal transaction will be void if it is 'contrary to good morals' (paragraph 1: BGB). Apparently the legislator applies general principles of ethical conduct in order to demarcate the limits within which contractual freedom is permitted. The judges have to give content to this principle, and very much like the English law relating to the tort of defamation, the standard of good moral behaviour has often been described as as the 'feeling of propriety entertained by all right-thinking people' (see BGHZ 10,228, 232,; BGHZ 69, 295, 297 (Supreme Court decisions)

In a codified system, it is particularly noteworthy that it is to caselaw that one has to turn to discover the types of contracts that have been held contrary to this statutory provision. They include contracts which oppresively restrict personal and economic freedom of movement (BGHZ 22, 347, 355), contracts that pay people for changing their religion (RG *Seuff Arch* 69,no. 48: Imperial Supreme Court decisions), and contracts that benefit one creditor to the detriment of others (BGHZ 55,34, 35 (1970); BGHZ 30, 149,153; RGZ 143, 48, 51).

Another restriction on freedom of contract is in the context of immoral transactions and this is covered by the good faith and fair dealing requirement under the German Civil Code (paragraph 242:), which applies to all obligations and contracts. Paragraph 242 has made it possible to invalidate any part of a legal transaction that is inconsistent with good faith and fair dealing, according to the interpretation of the courts. This resembles the 'blue pencil test' that is sometimes used in English law (see, eg, *Mason* v.

Provident Clothing & Supply Co. Ltd [1913] AC 724) where the offending or illegal part of the contract will be severed from the rest of the contract provided it is possible to do so without having to redraft the rest of the contract. (see further Chapter 13)

Certain rules of the BGB cannot be excluded by contract: (i) paragraph 276 (II): BGB, dealing with invalidity of exclusion of liability for intentional fault and paragraph 248 (I) dealing with invalidity of prior agreement to pay compound interest; and (ii) other restrictions dealing with property law, family law, and the law of succession.

Another restriction to contractual freedom relates to formalities, regulated by the requirements of paragraphs 126-9 BGB and paragraph 313 BGB, which are particularly important to sales of land. Failure to comply with these provisions will usually invalidate the transaction (see paragraph 125:BGB).

There have also been Acts of Parliament outside the BGB dealing with mandatory rules, which first appeared after the First World War. These protect tenants against eviction by landlords and employees from dismissal by employers. Although labour law remained separate from the BGB, the mandatory rules for landlords and tenants were integrated into the BGB in the 1960s and 1970s.

The Standard Contract Terms Act (or General Condititons of Business Act) consists of substantive law and provisions which came into force on 1 April 1977. It is designed to protect the weaker party in a transaction, as well as seeking to regulate other aspects of general conditions of business. The two most important provisions are (i) the General Clause; (ii) the 'black list'; and (iii) the grey list. If one wishes to ascertain if a clause is void, this may be done by consulting the black list which is a section in the Act which enumerates clauses which are void in every case. Those clauses which are enumerated in the grey list are *prima facie* void but may not be so interpreted in every case.

If one is unable to find a number in the black or grey list that is similar to the clause being used in any given agreement, the general clause should be consulted, which states that: (a) provisions in standard contract terms are void if they place the other party at an unreasonable disadvantage to such an extent as to be incompatible with the requirements of good faith; (b) In case of doubt, an unreasonable disadvantage shall be presumed if a term (i) is incompatible with the fundamental principles of the provision from which it deviates, or (ii) restricts fundamental rights or duties inherent in the nature of the contract to such a degree as to jeopardise its object. (Tonner *Characteristics of German Contract Law* Lecture at Keele University (March 1990)).

The second part of the Standard Contract Terms Act deals with the right of associations like consumers' associations a right to complain against unlawful individual standard terms (section 13).

C. TORT AND CONTRACT: CONTEMPORARY COMPARATIVE ASPECTS

i. Formation of Contracts

(i) French Law and Common Law

7.2   The absence of any doctrine of consideration in French law means that agreements of all kinds are legally binding in France, so long as a true consensus has been reached between the parties and provided that, where legally required, there has been compliance with the necessary requirements of form. Hence French law will recognise the existence of gratuitous contracts, so that any seriously intended agreement is binding and no difficulty arises when a contractual obligation is gratuitously reduced or even discharged.

In addition, there is no conceptual obstacle to the recognition of the binding effect of an offer in the French system. Nevertheless, under the French system offers may not be freely revoked. In the analysis of offer and acceptance, French law tends to see a display of priced goods in a shop window or supermarket shelves or in catalogues as an offer rather than as an invitation to treat. The basis of this is that a display indicates a continuing intention to sell, thus the buyer's actions indicating the intention to purchase means that the contract is formed from that moment. On the other hand, English law bases its rule on convenience for delaying the moment of completion.

The French law on the question of acceptance appears to have clarified in a 1981 case decided by the *Cour de Cassation*. The point to remember is that there are conflicting academic and judicial opinions as to whether the manifestation of acceptance is necessary in French law. Thus, the *emission theory* argues that the contract is complete as soon as the offeree has emitted a declaration of his acceptance of the offer. A variation of this is the *expedition theory* which argues that the contract is formed when a letter or telegram has been despatched accepting the offer. In contrast, the *information theory* holds that the communication of the acceptance must be received by the offeror before a contract may be said to have been formed. Most decisions have favoured the expedition theory but the matter has not been definitively settled until this Cour de Cassation 1981 decision.

In the case referred to, an offer to A was to be accepted by C within a set period of thirty days. C actually disptached his acceptance seven days early but could not prove that it had been received in time. On the basis of the emission theory, the contract was formed as soon as the offeree 'emitted a declaration of his acceptance of the offer'. Some academic opinion seems to believe this now resolves the question, but as Nicholas points out, there is less agreement on whether it applies only to the particular situation of lapse or to all cases of revocation of the offer, or whether it is a universally applicable test. (see Nicholas (1992)p.74).

On a point of terminology, as Nicholas (1989) points out, the French 'unilateral contract' denotes 'an agreement which creates only rights in one party and duties in the other, as in the case of a gratuitous promise to pay money'. On the other hand, a bilateral contract creates rights and duties in both parties. In English law, a unilateral contract means a promise in return for an act and this will not be enforceable in French law unless it can be said that it conforms to the definition of a contract as an agreement, that is, when the offer has been accepted. At that point it will be a bilateral contract. (see Nicholas *in* Harris and Tallon *Contract Law Today* (1989) p.19)

(ii) German Law

a. Declaration of Will

7.2.1   The BGB uses the concept of the *declaration of will or intention* in regulating the formation of a contract. This comes from the Pandectists, and encompasses not only offers and acceptances by persons negotiating a contract but also unilateral declarations such as giving notice or effecting a cancellation. (see Horn, Kotz and Leser (1982) p.75). Offer and acceptance have to correspond in order to produce a contract although there is no express provision regulating this in the BGB, which assumes the formation of the contract has already taken place. The offer and acceptance are declarations of intention which occur at different times, the former simply preceding the latter. If, as is common, the contract is the last stage of a series of negotiations, any distinction between offer and acceptance simply fades into insignificance. (see Horn, Kotz and Leser (1982) p.76)

b. Juristic Acts

7.2.2   Thus offer and acceptance are reciprocal *juristic acts* (*acte juridique, Rechtsgeschaft*) and the contract to which they give rise is the normal source of obligation. The notion of juristic act embraces all those declarations of intention which are capable of creating, transforming or determining legal relations. Examples are making a will, rescinding a contract, granting power of attorney, transferring property, exercising an option. Unilateral juristic acts are recognised as capable of generating obligations and apart from the example given above, include the establishment of a foundation, promise of a reward and the acceptance of a negotiable instrument. The *Rechtsgeschaft* is a concept that gives rise to general rules which govern all juristic acts.

c. Legal Position of Offers

7.2.3   There is no specific 'indicia of seriousness' in German law. But every offer is irrevocable unless the offeror has excluded the binding effect of his proposal. As with Swiss law, the only gifts which require a special form are promises to transfer property. All other gratuitous promises, such as a promise to give an interest-free loan, or a contract in favour of third parties, or to do or refrain from doing something are all valid, even if made informally. (see Zweigert and Kotz (1977) p.69).
 In the case of postal offers, the arrival within the offeree's sphere of influence will be sufficient, even if he is unaware of its existence at the moment of arrival. The offeree need not have read it but it is sufficient if he had the capacity to do so.(see RGZ 50, 191: the lottery ticket case).

The offeror is bound by his offer for a reasonable length of time (paragraph 145 BGB). However, it is common for the offeror to exclude the binding effect of the offer by inserting express words such as '*freibleibend*' (subject to change) or '*widerruflich*' (revocable). If this is done, then there is only an invitation to make offers or an 'invitation to treat' as English law calls it. This will apply to declarations to the public as in the case of a catalogue, price list, newspaper advertisement or display in a shop window. Unless an offer and acceptance are given orally or by telephone, they must usually arrive at the recipient's address. There is no equivalent of the 'posting rule' as in English law, where mere posting of a letter of acceptance constitutes an acceptance where negotiations are conducted by post.

Rather than any doctrine resembling consideration or *causa*, German law has opted for 'the construction of the transaction' approach (see Zweigert and Kotz (1977) p.68) in most areas of the law. It is only in the sphere of the law of property that *causa* plays any sort of role, where the *causa* is the right to hold on to something which one has received-'a thing is received with *causa* and its retention justified by it if the thing was transferred pursuant to a valid contract, or pursuant to a liability or to a gift...and if at the time of the transfer the transferor knew that he was not obliged to make it.' (Zweigert and Kotz (1977) p.69).

d. Silence in Negotiations

7.2.4   On the question of silence in negotiations, German law rules that it is not always necessary for the declaration of acceptance to reach the offeror. But it depends on the individual circumstances of the case. For mail-order cases, once a mail-order organisation *dispatches* the goods which have been ordered, this constitutes an *acceptance of the offer*. In the case of unsolicited goods being sent to a person, unlike English law, he will be treated as having accepted them when he starts to use them.

Apart from these cases, if there is no response to an initial declaration of intention, in any written form or by conduct, no legal consequences would normally follow. An exception to this is contained in the German Commercial Code (paragraph 362) which requires a merchant to make it clear, in certain circumstances, that he is not going to fill an order he has received. If he keeps silent, the legal rule is that the contract will be deemed to have come into force and *silence will constitute acceptance* of the contract.

German courts have applied this rule to commercial letters of confirmation, which are different from the English approach to counter-offers (or responses to the original offer which includes different terms). In English law, it will depend on whether the response constitutes a *counter-offer*, which may be accepted or rejected or whether it is merely a *request for information*, which does not affect the original offer. It turns on a matter of interpretation of the exact terms. In German law, subsequent to oral negotiations between merchants, if a letter of confirmation is sent on terms which accord with the oral agreement, this will serve as evidence of it, but if it contains different terms from the oral agreement, but is accepted without comment, the agreement will be treated as modified in accordance with the written terms. Here the letter of confirmation has been held by German courts as having a 'constitutive effect' (see BGHZ 54, 236,240), which means that the contract will be deemed valid on the terms of the confirmation. The point to note is that once the letter of confirmation proceeds on the basis that a contract has been formed, a binding contract may now be *deemed by the courts to be in existence* despite the fact that no contract was actually crystallised in the original negotiations. (Horn, Kotz and Leser, *ibid*)

If a recipient of a letter of confirmation wishes to reject its contents in any material particular, he should reject it immediately in very clear terms. It does not seem too much to ask of commercial parties to respond in this manner, although it is, of course, quite possible and no doubt not uncommon, that an oversight might result in a contract being formed despite silence on the part of the recipient of such a letter.

e. Culpa in Contrahendo

7.2.5   The formation stage of contract may also be afftected by the doctrine of *culpa in contrahendo*.   This comes from Roman law, in a passage by Modestinus in the *Digest*, as developed by the German jurist Jhering. As it has come to be known and embodied in the German Civil Code, it recognises that contractual negotiations engender a relationship of trust which obliges the parties to observe a certain standard of care. Thus, whenever a supposed contract fails to materialise through the negligent misrepresentation and non-disclosures of one of the parties, this would be actionable if the other party suffered damage as a result of being induced to rely upon the representation, even though no contract comes into being.

This is very similar to English law relating to negligent misrepresentation, which also imposes liability in similar circumstances, where the representor had the means to ascertain the true state of facts and where there is a 'special relationship' giving rise to a duty of care between the parties (see *Howard Marine* v. *Ogden* [1978] QB 574). This has been further strengthened in English law by the Misrepresentation Act 1967, which makes it unnecessary to establish a special relationship between the parties, and reverses the burden of proof, so that the representor (rather than the representee, as at common law) must prove, under section 2(1), that he had reasonable grounds for believing and did believe up to the time the contract was made that the facts were true. Thus statutory liability complements and amplifies the liability which also exists 'at common law' (under caselaw).

The French Civil Code does not refer to this doctrine as such, but it is generally accepted by French jurists and has been cited in various decided cases.

ii. Frustration of Contract, Impossibility and Supervening Events

7.2.6   Throughout history, contracting parties have grappled with the problem of non-performance of the contract after its formation (or 'conclusion' in civil law terminology) but before its completion, caused by political, social or economic upheavals beyond their control. Various systems have coped with these situations in different ways, using a variety of approaches. Continental law has utilised notions such as mistake, abuse of rights, impossibility (which includes financial impossibility within physical impossibility), a want of good faith (in the sense of a want of reasonableness), the collapse of the foundation of the contract and the 'gap-filling' doctrine. There is no unity between the different civil law systems or even within systems, with one system of French courts adopting a different approach from another.

a. French Law

7.2.7 French law proceeds on the basis that a promise to do the impossible is null and void (*impossibilium nulla obligatio*). The principle is widely accepted although not expressly stated in the Civil Code. It appears to be implicit in a number of Articles such as Articles 1108, 1126-30, 1172, 1302, and 1601 (see Nicholas (1992) p.200). If performance is impossible from the outset, the *objet* is impossible and therefore no contract can exist. if there is supervening impossibility, a contract has already come into existence but the debtor is no longer under an obligation to perform. Where the non-performance is due to the fault of the debtor, or rather, where he cannot show that the non-performance is due to *force majeure* or *cas fortuit*, a claim for damages will be available. In these circumstances, of course, a claim for performance would not be available.

The scope of *force majeure* in French law is much narrower than the English legal doctrine of frustration. Article 1148 of the Civil Code refers to *cas fortuit* as well as *force majeure* but attempts to distinguish these terms have not been successful. According to Cour de Cassation cases, 'force majeure refers to events which make performance impossible, not to those which make it more onerous.' (see, eg. Civ. 4.8.1915, S. 1916.1.17). This is invoked if a change of circumstances renders the implementation of a contract not just commercially impracticable to perform but legally or physically impossible to perform.

The impediment to performance must be absolute, unforseeable and irresistible, as well as unavoidable and insurmountable (see Nicholas (1992) p.203). According to *force majeure*, a contract may be rescinded when the court is satisfied that it has become impossible to perform the contract as the result of a supervening event which could not have been reasonably foreseen by the parties.

The French civil courts have never accepted any doctrine of *imprevision* (unforeseeability) which has been applied by the *Conseil d'Etat*, as established in a 'leading case' of 1916 (see CE 30.3.1916, S. 1916.3.17, D. 1916.3.25), and which resembles the English doctrine of frustration. It would seem to be derived from Article 1134 of the Civil Code which stipulates good faith in the performance of contracts, and the principle of *rebus sic stantibus*. The doctrine is therefore only found in administrative contracts not civil contracts.

b. German Law

7.2.8   In German law, there is a doctrine known as *Geschaftsgrundlage* or basis of the transaction. This is usually applied under paragraph 242 of the BGB. It recognises that performance of a contract can no longer be insisted upon when, as a result of a complete change in conditions, the performance has become completely different from that originally contemplated by the parties. However, since German courts still insist on compliance with paragraphs 157 and 242 of the BGB, the doctrine often results in a modification of existing duties under the contract. The doctrine is usually applied strictly and there is no lapse of the foundation of the contract unless there has been an economic upheaval of a really fundamental character. A total failure of the contractual basis entitles each party to rescind the contract and German law allows this to have a retrospective effect. Consequently, rescission will restore the parties to the *status quo*, as if the contract had never been concluded.

If there is only a partial failure of the basis of the contract, the courts have the power to vary the terms of the contract so as to adjust it to the changed circumstances.

As far as other types of impossibility are concerned, the rules have been summarised by Horn, Kotz and Leser as follows: (i) A debtor will be liable for all irregularities of performance for which he is to blame or is responsible; even if he is not to blame personally, he may be liable if the persons who assisted him in his performance (a sort of vicarious liability), or (ii) because of the strict guarantee in contracts requiring the procuring and delivery of generic goods; or (iii) because he has assumed the risk by contract or (iv) because his obligation was 'subjectively' impossible when the contract was formed. (see Horn, Kotz and Leser (1982) p.101)

German law distinguishes between *objective impossibility*, meaning the case where all debtors would be prevented or impeded in the same way; and *subjective impossibility*, meaning a case where the particular debtor is unable to perform but someone else is in a position to do so. The final result is not really different from English law but the different forms of irregularity employed in German law present a more complex scenario than the common law.

c. English Law

7.2.9   In English common law, contractual liability is in principle absolute-a party is generally bound to perform what he has promised and is not excused from his performance merely because it turns out to be more difficult, inconvenient, and more burdensome than expected. However, the doctrine of Frustration was devised to deal with situations involving impossibility of performance. It can be viewed as an exception to the general principle of *pacta sunt servanda* (agreements should be kept) which is basic to both civil law and common law jurisdictions. English law utilised the notion of the implied term to excuse parties from performance (see *Taylor* v. *Caldwell* (1863) 3 B.& S. 826). It was postulated that certain contracts, by their nature, were subject to an implied condition that the parties should be excused. For example, if it became 'physically impossible' to perform a contract, then parties were discharged from the obligations. This rule was then extended to include legal impossibility, caused by a subsequent change in the law. In the course of this development, the broader question of the extent of the court's jurisdiction in litigation concerning contracts was raised. This led to a marked difference of opinion between the Court of Appeal and the House of Lords in 1951 (see *Br. Movietown News* v. *London and District Cinemas Ltd* [1952] AC 166). It was unanimously suggested by the Court of Appeal that any uncontemplated change in circumstances was sufficient to justify the court's intervention and the exercise of its discretionary power. The House of Lords, however, equally unanimously disagreed, denying the Court of Appeal's 'inherent jurisdiction' to interfere in such matters and declared that a fundamentally different situation, rather than any unforeseen change, was the prime prerequisite for a contract to be frustrated.

Five years later, Lord Radcliffe defined the doctrine in terms which have been approved by subsequent courts (and writers), declaring in *Davis Construction Ltd* v. *Farnham UDC* [1956] AC 696 that:

> '[F]rustration occurs whenever the law recognises that without default of either party, a contractual obligation has become incapable of being performed because the circumstances in which performance is called for would render it a thing radically different from that which was undertaken by the contract. *Non haec in foedera veni*. It was not this that I promised to do.'

The English courts have indicated that the doctrine which operates to terminate the contract is to be applied within very narrow limits and that mere commercial inconvenience and material loss are not sufficient to invoke it (see eg, *Tsakiroglou* v. *Nobles and Thorl GmbH* [1962] AC 93).

There is a rather small area covered by the Law Reform (Frustrated Contracts) Act 1943. This Act does not state when a contract is frustrated and its chief feature is that it gives the court the power, subject to certain conditions, and excepting instances covered by section 7 of the Sales of Goods Act 1979 or trade practice, to make such adjustment between the parties as the court might consider just.

All other cases of non-performance caused by events beyond the control of the parties which might occur after conclusion of a contract for the sale of specific or unascertained goods, have to be resolved on the basis of common law rules. Since the adoption of the 'radically different' rule, which Lord Radcliffe called the test of the changed significance of the obligation (see the *Davis Case* (above), at p.729), an objective interpretation of the common intention of the parties seems to be called for. Hence the doctrinal differences between the two theories appear to have disappeared and the scope of the judicial discretion has been widened. Today, the court decides in every case whether a 'fundamentally different situation' has been created which qualifies as a legally frustrating event. Hence each case will have to be decided on its particular set of circumstances and it will be a matter of degree whether the stringent requirements of the doctrine will be met.

iii. Scope of Tortious Liability

(i) Common Law

a. General

7.2.10   The common law of tort is dominated by the duty of care notion, and English courts in previous times had based liability on other torts such as trespass, conversion, and nuisance. Four subsequent House of Lords cases have added their own glosses to the law of negligence. The first was *Hedley Byrne* v. *Heller* [1964] AC 465, which broadened the scope of liability from physical to economic loss, if caused by a negligent misstatement by someone who would owe a duty of care to the plaintiff, if he voluntarily assumed responsibility to him. The second is *Home Office* v. *Dorset Yacht Co. Ltd* [1970] AC 1004, where Lord Reid emphasised that the neighbour principle ought to be applied to all cases of negligence unless there were good reasons for its exclusion. Further, the House of Lords held that if there is between the defendant and plaintiff 'a sufficient relationship of proximity or neighbourhood such that, in the reasonable contemplation of the former, carelessness on his part may be likely to cause damage to the latter', then a duty of care will be found so long as there are no policy factors which 'ought to negative, or to reduce or limit the scope of the duty or the class of the person to whom it is owed or the damages to which a breach of it may give rise.'

The third case is *Anns* v. *Merton* [1978] AC 728 which saw another expansion of liability in tort when Lord Wilberforce also strongly supported the notion of a duty of care should be assumed if the parties are proximate, and the duty dislodged or limited only if there are sound reasons of policy for doing so. In the fourth case, *Junior Books* v. *Veitchi* [1983] 1 AC 520, where the Wiberforce approach was used to allow recovery in tort for economic loss (the cost of repair) where the parties, the owner of a building and a sub-contractor) were extremely 'proximate' without being in a contractual relationship. Recent indications are that the courts are reverting to more narrow constructions of a 'proximate' relationship.

The elements of an action for negligence are: (a) a duty of care owed by the defendant to the plaintiff; (b) a breach of that duty by the defendant; (iii) consequential damage suffered by the plaintiff, which is (iv) caused proximately by the breach. In fact, these requirements are similar to the civil law requirements that there be negligence, harm, and causation.

b. Liability for Nervous Shock

7.2.11   In English law, actions for nervous shock were first allowed if they were accompanied by or flowed from actual physical injury, so that the courts were less inclined to doubt the seriousness or genuiness of the shock symptoms. Compensation was also allowed where the plaintiff was put in fear of physical injury through the defendant's negligence and suffered nervous shock but not physical injury as a consequence. A further development which the courts sanctioned was the instance where the defendant had intentionally

194

done an act calculated to cause nervous shock to the plaintiff-in this case through a 'practical joke' which resulted in the plaintiff's nervous shock (*Wilkinson* v. *Downton* (1897).

More recently, in *McLoughlin* v. *O'Brian* (1983) AC 410, the House of Lords extended the range of claimants, to a close relative or spouse who suffered nervous shock although he had not actually witnessed the incident wherein the injury had been caused, but had witnessed the extent of the injuries very soon afterwards and had been informed of a fatality in the family, in the immediate aftermath of the accident. After this case, although there was difference in opinion as to the exact policy that should be adopted in these cases among the Law Lords, it was clear that the plaintiff must show that he has suffered some form of psychiatric illness through apprehension of injury to himself or shock as a result of injury or the threat of injury to others caused by the defendant. The plaintiff must prove that the defendant was negligent, that is that he owed him, and breached, a duty not to cause him harm by way of nervous shock. Only those who are sufficiently proximate to the victim are owed this duty. Proximity must exist in relation to the relationship to the actual victim of the physical harm and to the manner in which they perceive that harm being inflicted. As Lord Wilberforce explained, as regards the means by which the shock was suffered, it must come through sight or hearing of the event or of its immediate aftermath. Further, foreseeability did not of itself, automatically give rise to a duty of care owed to a person or class of persons.

In the Hillsborough football stadium tragedy of 1989 where ninety-five people died, and four hundred were injured, the question of the scope of liability for nervous shock again went all to the way to the House of Lords (see *Alcock et al* v. *Chief Constable of South Yorkshire Police* (1991) Times, 29 November. Several psychiatric claims by plaintiffs in close family relationships with the victims of the disaster were brought against the Chief Constable of South Yorkshire, who had accepted responsibilty for the overcrowding and ultimately the tragedy. In *dismissing* the appeals, and holding that the Chief Constable did not owe a duty of care to to the plaintiffs, the House of Lords made the following important points:

(i) Injury by psychiatric illness was more subtle than the ordinary case of direct physical injury suffered in an accident at work or elsewhere where reasonable foreseeability of the risk was the only test that was needed to determine liability.

(ii) Liability for injury in the form of psychiatric illness must depend on a relationship of proximity between the claimant and the party said to owe the duty, as well as foreseeability.

(iii) The kinds of relationships which would qualify as sufficiently proximate were not confined to husband and wife or parent and child.

(iv) Other plaintiffs not present at the football ground all watched scenes from Hillborough on television but none of these depicted suffering of recognisable individuals. 'The viewing of these scenes could not be equiparated with the viewer being within sight or hearing of the event or of its immediate aftermath, to use the words of Lord Wilberforce (see above), not could the scenes reasonably be regarded as giving rise to shock, in the sense of a sudden assault on the nervous system.' (per Lord Keith, The Times). he stressed that 'the viewing of the television scenes did not create the necessary degree of proximity.'

A subsequent case heard in 1992 by the English Court of Appeal confirms this approach. In *Ravenscroft* v. *Rederiaktiebologet* (1992) Times, 6 April, the respondent's son had been crushed to death by a runaway forklift truck belonging to the appellants, his employers, who had admitted negligence. But the respondent had not seen the accident, nor was present at her son's death in hospital and did not see his body immediately afterwards. In allowing the appeal, and denying the mother's claim, the appeal court relied on *Alcock's case* (above), stating that the House of Lords had held that relatives or friends of victims of the Hillsborough stadium disaster who had suffered nervous shock, were not persons to whom the chief constable responsible for policing the stadium owed a duty of care. Sir Christopher Slade, LJ, conceded that 'the rules of the law of tort which giverned recoverability for psychiatric illness resulting from nervous shock might not appear to present a logical and consistent whole' but the *Alcock case* was clear authority for the proposition that 'a claim for damages for psychiatric illness arising from nervous shock was not sustainable in law unless the shock had arisen from sight or hearing of the relevant event or its immediate aftermath'.

c. American Law

7.2.12   It is perhaps a little surprising that American jurisdictions have not really developed radically in the area of recovery in tort for nervous shock. Having abandoned the original rule which required contemporaneous persoanl injury before nervous shock could be compensatable, the majority of jurisdictions, in conformity with section 313 of the Restatement (Second) of Torts, require the plaintiff to be in the danger zone (or zone of foreseeable danger) before he can recover. The controversial case of *Dillon* v. *Legg*, (1968) 68 Cal. 2d 728, 441 P. 2d 912, extended recovery to persons outside the immediate danger zone or zone of foreseeable danger provided (i) the 'plaintiff was located near the scene of the accident...(ii) the shock resulted from a direct emotional impact upon plaintiff from the sensory and contemporaneous observance of the accident, as contrasted with learning of the accident from others after its occurrence, (and) (iii) ...plaintiff and the victim were closely related...' (441 P.2d 912 at 920). Other Californian courts have not pursued a strict or sometimes easily discernible line in this area but it seems reasonably clear that different interpretations notwithstanding, 'spatial and temporal proximity' remain 'crucial factors even though they are likely to be understood differently by different courts' (Markesinis (1990) p.108).

A notable feature of the American development is the apparent extension of recovery to cases of mere 'emotional distress' even where this is not accompanied by physical injury (see, eg *Molien* v. *Kaiser Foundation Hospitals* (1980) 27 Cal. 3d 916, 616 P. 2d 813). All the court required in this case was that the emotional distress should be 'serious'. Two Hawaiian cases provide an insight into some judicial attitudes. In the first, *Rodrigues* v. *State* (1970) 52 Haw. 156,472 P.2d 509, 'serious emotional harm' was defined as 'serious mental distress...found where a reasonable man, normally constituted, would be unable to adequately cope with the mental stress engendered by the circumstances of the case'. In the second, *Campbell* v. *Animal Quarantine Station* (1981) 63 Haw. 587,632 P.2d 1066, five plaintiffs were awarded a total of US $ 1000 for the anguish that they suffered when they were told over the telephone that their ageing dog had died the previous day after it had been forgotten in an unventilated van for over an hour and had been left exposed to the Hawaiian sun.

(ii) Civil Law

a. French Law

7.2.13 Tortious or delictual liability in French law is known as the law of delict or civil wrongs (*responsabilite civile*) which derives from Roman law and the further refinement of the early concepts, such as the delict *damnum injuria datum*, which was effected by the Continental jurists in the centuries before codification, resulted in the formulation of principles of liability for civil wrongs in the Civil Code. The delict provisions in the Civil Code are expressed in a remarkably concise and compact form, with the entire subject covered in five short articles, of which Article 1382 is the key provision:

> 'Any act by which a person causes damage to another makes the person by whose fault the damage occurred liable to make reparation for such damage.'

The text does not mean that any damage caused by fault gives rise to liability.
Article 1383 states that 'A person is responsible for the damage which he has caused whether by positive act, or by his negligence or imprudence.'
Article 1384 states that 'One is responsible for the damage that one causes by one's own act, but also for that which is caused by the act of the persons for whom one ought to answer, or the things that one has under one's control...'
Article 1385 states that 'The owner of an animal, or the person making use of it, while it is in his service, is responsible for the damage which the animal has caused, whether it was under his care or had strayed or escaped from it.'
Various French doctrinal writers have offered interpretations on these provisions, and in the nineteenth century, Toullier suggested that Article 1382 applies to actions that cause damage unless the actor is exercising a right. This explanation fell out of favour towards the end of the nineteenth century and it came to be accepted that the defendant may be liable when it is difficult to identify an injury which infringed the right of the plaintiff, as in cases of unfair competition, seduction, or entering into a void contract. After undergoing further scholarly scrutiny, the earlier views have had to give way to induction, so that an examination of the case law in each case needs to be undertaken to ascertain some general rules. The current interpretation is that liability may be excluded if a justification can be found for the activity of the person causing the harm.

The landmark decision of the *Cour de Cassation* (19.1.14) appeared to establish that liability will exist for the 'custodian' of a 'thing'. The word 'custodian' would cover someone who had use, management, and control and disposition of a 'thing'. A 'thing' would include vehicles and vessels like cars, trains, elevators and ships-any corporeal object. However, such a custodian might avoid liability if he could prove that the damaging occurrence was due to (a) *force majeure*: that is, an unforeseen event which either occurred with unforeseeable suddenness or irresistible violence so that the custodian could not possibly have prevented the harm; or (b) the fault of the victim; or (c) the fault of a third party. The *Jand'heur* decision (13.2.30; S. 1930,I 121) ruled that the 'thing' need not be something that was inherently dangerous, but it must not have played a purely passive role.

In order to recover damages in delict or tort under French law, the plaintiff must show that he suffered damage and that the damage was caused by an act or omission for which the defendant was responsible. The responsibility may exist because the defendant was personally at fault, or because he was vicariously laible for another's fault, or because the damage was caused by a 'thing' in his care. Damage, causality and responsibility have all to be proven.

It is not just physical injury that is recoverable in damages if the delictual requirements are satisfied. Damage to a person's honour is covered, such as damage occasioned by insults, defamation and seduction, deprivations of liberty and invasions of privacy. It also includes mental suffering caused by the death by the death of one's loved ones and the pain and suffering occasioned by physical injuries to oneself. This is called 'moral damage' in French law and it is not always possible to quantify it in terms of money and in any demonstrably direct way. (see Amos and Walton (1967) p.209).

In relation to injuries to the feelings caused by another person's death, there is no textual limitation which restricts the scope of persons who might be potential claimants (Req. 10.4.1922,D. 1923.1.52; Civ. sect. com.15.12.1923,D.1924.1.69). However, the only limit is the need for proof of real and sufficiently profound sorrow (Amos and Walton (1967) p.210) The courts seem to approach these cases on the basis that it is presumed to exist in the case of certain close relatives, especially the deceased's parents, spouse, and children. In other situations, the 'facts and circumstances must point unequivocally to the presence of a continuing and deep injury to the sentiments.' (Amos and Walton, *ibid*.) There is therefore no requirement of sight or hearing of the actual event, or being present in its immediate aftermath as in English law.

An illuminating illustration of how French law treats cases involving landowners exercising their rights in an 'abusive' manner, which French law addresses through the notion of 'abuse of rights' or *abus d'un droit* which means an abusive exercise of rights. (see also chapter 3). English law would approach these sorts of cases falling within 'nuisance' under the law of tort. Three illustrative cases are: (i) The Chimney case (Colmar 2.5.1855, D. 1856.2.9); (ii) The Water Pump Case (Lyons 18.4.1856, D. 1856.2.199); (iii) The Airplane Hangar Case (Affaire Clement-Bayard) (Req. 3.8.1915, S.1920.1.300, D.P. 1917.1.79). In each case, the defendant purported to act in accordance with his rights over his property, in case (i): to erect a chimney which effectively deprived a neighbour of his access of light to his some of his rooms; in case (ii) to install a pump, the effect of which was to diminish the water supply of a neighbour's adjoining spring by two-thirds; and in case (iii) to erect an immense wooden structure topped with metal spikes which made the launching of zeppelins from the neighbouring hangar difficult, if not impossible.

In each case, the Court found no difficulty in finding that the proprietor had abused his right of ownership because the action was carried out with spiteful intent, with the deliberate intention of inflicting harm. The basis of such actions is actually quasi-delictual rather than delictual.

Under English law, all three cases would be treated as instances for which an action might lie in tort (specifically-the tort of nuisance) but in which the results might not have been the same as in the French cases.

Case (ii) is very similar to the English case of *Bradford Corporation* v. *Pickles* [1895] AC 587, wherein the defendant stopped an underground stream which flowed under his land from flowing to the plaintiff's land, in order to compel them to buy his land at an inflated price. The House of Lords found that the defendant was not liable and was merely acting to protect his interests and even said that they would have reached the same conclusion if the defendant had acted maliciously. Motice was said to be irrelevant to liability.

An earlier English case, *Christie* v. *Davey* [1893] 1 Ch.316, had taken a different approach. There the defendant had blown whistles, banged trays and hammered on the plaintiff's wall solely to annoy the plaintiff in retribution for the annoyance the defendant felt he had been caused by the plaintiff's piano lessons. He was held liable in nuisance for acting so maliciously.

Subsequent English cases such as the 1936 case of *Hollywood Silver Fox Farm* v. *Emmett* [1936] 2 KB 468, have not followed the *Bradford Case*. In the *Hollywood Case*, the defendant was found liable in nuisance when he discharged guns on his own land, but close to the boundary of the plaintiff's fox farm, when he knew that the foxes were sensitive to noise and acted maliciously. It would appear that *Bradford's Case* should be treated as a case involving absolute rights over land and therefore a case of servitudes, where the plaintiff, a corporation, had no legal right to receive water.

b. German Law

7.2.14   The German BGB devotes thirty paragraphs to the law of torts, in contrast to the five articles of the French Civil Code. However, in essence, the Code proceeds on the basis of *three general provisions*, paragraphs 823 I, 823 II and 826 BGB and some *specific provisions* which deal with a number of particularised tortious situations.

In addition, therefore, paragraph 824 BGB deals with cases of untrue statements which damage one's credit, paragraph 824 requires any person who induces a female person to have sexual intercourse with him, to pay compensation and paragraph 834 deals with the liability of animal supervision.

As Markesinis stresses, 'the Code system of liability is a system of fault-based liability' (Markesinis (1990) p.21) and he would analyse it according to three main sets of provisions. First, there are provisions which impose liability for fault (paragraph 823 I and II, 824-6, 830, and 839); secondly, there are provisions which make liability depend on a rebuttable presumption of fault (paragraphs 831, 832, 833 (second sentence), 834, 836-8 BGB);

thirdly, there is also liability for 'created risks', independent of fault. There are several statutes which deal with these situations, primarily the Strict Liability Act and the Road Traffic Act. There are also cases where one person is liable strictly but for some other person's fault. (see Markesinis (1990) pp. 21-2).

Three further points are stressed by Markesinis (1990) pp.22-3): (i) the BGB is a typical product of the Pandectist school, 'abstract, conceptual and meticulous in the extreme.' (ii) paragraphs 823 ff. are not independent and self-sufficient provisions of the Code but must frequently be read in conjunction with other parts of it, especially the general part of the law of obligations (see above) and he gives four illustrations: (a) *contributory negligence of the victim* is regulated by paragraph 254 I of the BGB 'which makes the obligation to compensate the negligent plaintiff depend on how far the injury has been *caused* predominantly by the one or the other party (plaintiff/ defendant).' (b) the concept of *unlawfulness* is satisfied 'whenever one of the interests listed in paragraph 823 I BGB has been infringed in the absence of a legally recognised defence.' But it is necessary to consult paragraphs 227-31 BGB and their interpretation by caselaw in order to determine whether the concept has been satisfied. (c) paragraph 847 BGB allows monetary compensation for injuries to body or health or for the deprivation of liberty. This forms an exception to the general rule in paragraph 253 BGB which prohibits monetary compensation for harm which is not damage to property unless otherwise provided by the Code. One of the questions which arises in connection with these provisions is whether paragraph 847 can be extended by analogy to cover instances other than the ones which it expressly provides for in the light of the phrasing of paragraph 253. (iv) the final caveat is directed to common lawyers-not to expect to find in German tort law all the material included in common law tort courses. (see Markesinis (1990) *ibid*)

Returning to the concept of unlawfulness, according to Zweigert and Kotz (1987) this is satisfied by 'any invasion of one of the legal interests specified in paragraph 823 I BGB, provided it is not justified by one of the special privileges, for example self-defence or necessity. They further suggest that *culpability* or *fault* is satisfied 'if the harmful conduct is either intentional, that is, accompanied by the intention of invading the protected legal interest, or negligent.' (Zweigert and Kotz (1987) p.293). According to paragraph 276 BGB, negligence means 'a want of that degree of care which is generally regarded as necessary in society.'

According to Zweigert and Kotz, the courts have applied paragraph 826, the third general head of liability to 'a whole range of cases where one party has caused harm to another by behaviour so offensive and improper as to incur strong disapprobation from the average person in the relevant section of society.' (Zweigert and Kotz (1987) p. 297).

The experience gained from the caselaw in this area is that there are considerable areas left uncovered by these three heads of liability, such as gaps in the protection given to rights of personality and for pure economic harm which is negligently caused. The German courts have therefore been filling in the gaps, and again we see how the courts have, in practice, taken a much more active 'lawmaking' role though they have proceeded on the basis of merely 'interpreting' the BGB provisions.

As far as injury to feelings are concerned, mere fright, anguish, 'normal' distress or grief which is occasioned by the accident, will not be sufficient grounds for recovery of damages. In German law, nervous shock is 'clearly, injury to health in the sense of paragraph 823 I BGB, so long as it entails medically recognisable physical or pschological consequences which would not have been suffered by the ordinary, not over-sensitive, citizen.' (Markesinis (1990) p.35). As Markesinis points out, the problem of where to draw the line is being treated as a question of legal cause and is being approached increasingly as a matter of policy. The caselaw indicates that German courts are prepared to allow rights of recovery not just to eye-witnessing relatives but beyond this to persons who suffered trauma from hearing of an accident to a loved one or close relative, that is, cases of 'distant nervous shock'. However, recovery must be limited to cases of recognisable medical illness or nervous shock. (see the Federal Supreme Court case reported in BGHZ 56: translated in English and fully discussed by Markesinis (1990) pp.95-103). This approach has been followed in a number of subsequent cases.

In another earlier case the question was whether the defendants were liable for the plaintiff wife's nervous breakdown which she suffered upon receiving news of her son's death in the accident (see RGZ 133,270: Markesinis (1990) pp.103-9). The *Reichsgericht* held in 1931 that an action could lie since the plaintiff's wife has suffered injury to her health as a result of the tort. Adequate causality was held to exist. German law has shown it is prepared to adopt a liberal view than either English or American law. French law is also fairly liberal in its approach to such cases. Occasionally, of course, an American case demands a suspension of disbelief as in the case of *Campbell* v. *Animal Quarantine Station* (see above, 7.2.12, under *American law*).

D. TORT LAW AND TRAFFIC ACCIDENTS

i. French Law

7.3   Some brief observations may be made in connection with traffic accidents of one kind or another, as treated in different jurisdictions. In French law, if a collision occurs between a moving vehicle and a properly parked one, the presumption enacted by Article 1384(1) of the Civil Code will not attach to the 'custodian of the car'. However, if the collision occurs at night and the car was not adequately lit or happened to be parked in a place where visibility was poor, the stationary car could well be seen as a 'productive cause of the harm'. If a cyclist is injured by a collision with a van, it cannot sue the custodian of the van if at the time of the accident, it was travelling at the proper speed on the correct side of the road (see Civ.26 Oct.1949.Gaz. Pal. 1950.1.79 and Civ. 22 Jan.1940,S.1940.1.19) In the latter case (called the Poyet case) a car owned by the Societe Montbarbon and driven by one Redt at an excessive speed, suddenly blocked the road at a crossing, causing M. Poyet, who was approaching the crossing on his bicycle, to swerve sharply. There was no contact between Poyet and the car but he fell from the bicycle and was killed. Having lost her action based on Article 1384 of the Code civil, on the basis that Article 1384 does not apply unless there had been contact between the object and the victim, Mrs. Poyet brought a *pourvoir en cassation* (application for review on legal grounds) to the *Cour de Cassation*. The Court held that as the absence of contact between the object in question and the damage does not necessarily exclude the causal connection, the decision should be quashed.

In cases where an automobile accident has been caused by something internal which the custodian could not have foreseen such as a sudden failure of brakes or steering or a tyre exploding, the driver will still be liable for any harm or damage caused, because the rules of force majeure demand that the event causing the accident must be external to the thing which causes the harm. It must be both unforeseeable and unavoidable in its consequences (see Zweigert and Kotz (1987) p.358).

Drivers falling unconscious at the wheel of the car have also been found liable for the consequences of their actions while still driving (see Civ. 18 Dec. 1964,D. 1965,191). This is similar to the English law approach (see below). Many cases dealt with custodians of motor vehicles arguing that the unexpected occurrence of a patch of oil on a highway constituted *force majeure*. These claims were rarely accepted and were completely abolished by the Law on Traffic Accidents of 5 July 1985.

As a result of the *Desmares case* (Civ.21 July 1982,D.1982,449), wherein the *Cour de Cassation* appeared to say that contributory negligence was irrelevant in reducing the amount of compensation payable, the Law of 85-677 of 5 July 1985 (cited above) was passed. Its main objective was to limit the extent to which the negligence of a traffic accident victim may reduce the amount of compensation payable under his claim for bodily injury or death. This sort of reduction is not permissible if the victim is under sixteen or over seventy years old, or if he is at least eighty-per cent disabled. Claims may also be reduced if the accident was the inexcusable fault of the victim or the exclusive fault of the victim. But if the victim is a driver, the Law does not protect him. This gap in the law has been addressed by the introduction of a type of insurance marketed by the insurance industry covering drivers and their families.

It has been estimated by Tunc that the result of this legislation and insurance scheme has been that compensation in eighty-five to ninety per cent of all accident cases have been awarded independent of the negligence of tortfeasor and victim(see Tunc *Essays in Memory of Professor Lawson* (1986) p.71). Tort liability for traffic accidents is now largely replaced by a system of insurance protection (see Zweigert and Kotz (1987) p.360).

ii. English Law

7.3.1   English law utilises the same general law of tort in dealing with civil or private law claims for compensation for injury, damage or loss caused by traffic accidents. Hence a duty of care must be held to exist and the usual requirements concomitant with this duty must be proved, on a balance of probabilities. The standard of care required of even a learner driver is that of a an average, competently qualified driver (see *Nettleship* v. *Weston* [1971] 2 QB 691). In the case of a driver who lost control of his car through suffering a cerebral haemorrhage which caused him to be unaware of what he was doing and incapable of driving properly, a *strict liability* approach was adopted and the Court held the driver liable in negligence for colliding with another car (see *Roberts* v. *Ramsbottom* [1980] 1 WLR 823). A truck driver had also been held liable for a defect in the brakes which no layman could possibly have discovered (see *Henderson* v. *Jenkins & Sons* [1970] AC 282).

English law allows the defence of contributory negligence to reduce the amount of damages payable to the plaintiff where the plaintiff was also negligent to a certain extent. Under the Law Reform (Contributory Negligence) Act 1945, damages may be reduced to the extent that the court thinks 'just and equitable having regard to the claimant's share in the responsibilty for the damage.' Another possible defence to actions for negligence is the plea of *volenti non fit injuria* which means that a plaintiff is barred from bringing an action that arises from a situation to which he consented.

iii. German Law

7.3.2 German law relating to the custodian of a motor vehicle is contained in the Road Traffic Act 1952 and section 7(1) thereof states: 'If in the course of the operation of a motor vehicle a person is killed...or injured, or an object is damaged, the keeper of the motor vehicle is obliged to compensate the injured party for the damage resulting therefrom.' Section 7(2) goes on to declare that: 'The duty to compensate is excluded, if the accident was caused by an unavoidable event which is not due to a defect in the construction of the vehicle or to the failure of its mechanism.' The provision explains further that an event is deemed to unavoidable in particular if it is 'due to the conduct of the injured party or an animal; and if both the keeper and driver have applied that care which is required in the light of the circumstances.'

Hence, unforeseen and unavoidable failure of the parts of a vehicle, such as axle fracture, brake failure, a tyre defect or the seizing up of the steering will not excuse the custodian or keeper of the vehicle. Liability will only be excluded 'if the accident is due to an 'external' event such as the occurrence of black ice or an animal running in front of the vehicle or faulty driving on the part of other motorists' (Zweigert and Kotz (1987) p.349) and the defendant observed all the care necessary in the circumstances.

Liability will also be excluded or the amount of compensation reduced if an accident is attributable to (i) the behaviour of the victim; or (ii) of a third party not involved in the operation of the vehicle; or (ii) of an animal and both the custodian and the driver of the driver have taken all the care called for in the particular circumstances (see section 9: Road Traffic Act 1952 and paragraph 254 BGB). The standard of 'all the care called for in the circumstances' has been described by a German court as 'care going beyond what is usually required...extreme and thoughtful concentration and circumspection' seems to be required: BGH VersR 1962,164). This standard has been affirmed by several subsequent court decisions and needless to say, is usually very difficult to prove to the satisfaction of the court. If the victim was partially at fault, damages will be reduced accordingly.

It is worth noting that injured passengers in a vehicle can only sue the custodian under the Road Traffic Act 1952 if they were being carried by way of business and for reward, for example, in a taxi or bus. In all other cases, injured passengers would have to use the the general provisions of the law of tort or delict (paragraphs 823 ff. BGB) (see Zweigert and Kotz (1987) p. 349).

The custodian of a motor vehicle must take out liability insurance in Germany and his victim is given a direct claim against the insurer, and will have this right even if he has not insured the vehicle at all, or if the insurer is unidentifiable (in hit-and-run cases) or insolvent. It has long been demanded that the scope of the custodian's liability be extended (see Zweigert and Kotz (1987)p.377).

E. FAULT IN THE LAW OF CONTRACT AND TORT

7.4   The word 'fault' is derived from the French *faute* which is itself derived from the Latin verb *fallere*. The original meaning of that word was 'to deceive' but it later came to express the notion of failing in some way (see Lawson (1977) vol.II. p.348). Hence, 'fault' here appears to resemble 'default', which is rather vague and general in meaning. As Lawson neatly described it, '[the word] 'fault' is not a term of art in the common law.' (Lawson (1977) *ibid*,p.347)

In the English Law Reform (Contributory Negligence) Act 1945, 'fault' is defined as meaning 'negligence, breach of statutory duty or other act or omission which gives rise to a liability in tort or would, apart from this Act, give rise to the defence of contributory negligence'.

'Fault' occurs rarely in the English common law of contract, and features mainly in the sale of goods and where the frustration of a contract is said to be self-induced. (see above, under Frustration) On the other hand, apart from special cases, the general ground of liability in the civil law system is the fault (*dolus aut culpa*) of the defendant.

The 'duty of care' component which is an integral part of the common law tort of negligence is not explicitly stated in the civil law codes. However, the Continental courts have also had to face the problem of demarcating the boundaries of liability in delict. In dealing with omissions which cause physical damage to person or property, German law has treated this as governed by paragraph 823 of the BGB. Pecuniary loss is recoverable only where it is a case of malice, and not merely negligence (Paragraph 826: BGB).

In French law, *faute* is interpreted as not just *culpa* in the sense of negligence, but in the sense of *wrongful*. This approach approximates the English 'duty of care' characterisation. In French law, therefore, faut is a question of law, as duty of care is in English law, so that the judges in both systems have the discretion to delimit the scope of liability for damage resulting from a failure to act with reasonable care. Crucially, *any* fault which causes damage is actionable irrespective of whether it is a delictual or contractual obligation that has been breached. There is therefore a *single concept of fault under French law*, and Mazeaud and Tunc define *faut* as an error of conduct and stress that he who conducts himself in an antisocial manner will be at fault. Various writers have seen *faute* in French law as meaning a failure to observe a behavioural norm which the defendant should have respected or as culpable behaviour on the part of the defendant (see Zweigert and Kotz (1977) p.286).

The *justification of the concept of fault* in the context of tort has been debated at great length by various commentators. Its advantages appear to be considerably outweighed by its disadvantages. Briefly, the case for retaining some notion of fault is derived from its logical strength, since it is generally accepted that a person should be answerable for the damage he has caused. There is also a strong moral content to such a principle, and indeed fault derives from the canon law notion of sin and the need for atonement for one's sins. Fault also seems necessary to social expectations and socially accepted standards of behaviour. If tort law is seen as a means of ensuring the balance between freedom of the individual and the duties and responsibilities which arise in modern society, then fault is the yardstick which can distinguish the boundaries of liability.

On the other hand, if we accept that the main function of tort is to compensate losses, there is no reason for retention of fault. Fault appears to be a condition of penal liability and should thus be removed from labelling less serious conduct. In more realistic terms, the tortfeasor's capability to bear the loss or to pay the compensation for the loss or damage caused has come to the fore. The idea has grown that, particularly in the field of industrial accidents, the organisation or person best able to afford to pay compensation to the injured party, should be the one who should bear the costs of the loss suffered. Fault fails when confronted with modern technology because it is often the machinery that is really to blame, because it causes harm which is unforeseeable and which no one could possibly have prevented. The position of the victim has also changed since the value of the objects which he exposes to being damaged or destroyed has a much higher economic value. There are also much greater sums which are needed in modern times to compensate the victim for his loss of earnings, in the long and short term.

F. INTERACTION OF TORT AND CONTRACT

7.5   We conclude the substantive part of this brief survey of tort and contract by noting that there are clearly criticisms which can be levelled at the continuing separation of tort from contract law. While one writer has said that 'Contract is productive, tort law is protective' and that 'tortfeasors are typically liable for making things worse, contractors for not making them better', the following are some of the problems which Tunc (1974) has highlighted:

(i) In every country where the distinction has practical consequences, many cases appear not to follow the conventional dichotomy. One writer even called attention to what he labels 'hermaphrodites' (Stevens (1964) 27 Mod.LR 121,161) where the cause of action fits either category. Application of the distinction in the common law is compounded by the undertainty of the criterion.

(ii) The complexity of the relationships between tortious and contractual liabilities has led to 'answers which vary from country to country and is itself a complex one in many countries'.

(iii) Among the many criticisms that have been levelled at the distinction, French doctrinal writers have argued that if you base liability upon fault, and define fault as a violation of a pre-existing legal obligation, there is no justification for distinguishing between tort and contract.
(iv) It is often very difficult to say whether damage has been caused within or outside the scope of a contract.
(see Tunc *International Encyclopedia of Comparative Law* (1974), vol.XI, chapter 1, pp.19-20)

In contrast, Tunc (1974) argues that the scope of the 'obligations' owed by persons in contractual and non-contractual relationships has to be considered carefully. Surely, contractual obligations are owed to persons who have entered into the contract, are involved in its negotiation stages and who might be beneficiaries under it. On the other hand, the 'obligation' of a driver is a general obligation owed to all persons who could be injured by his conduct. It is as different as the rights of ownership in different situations-rights *in rem* and rights *in personam*-and different durations of limited rights exist, for instance, under bailment, as opposed to full legal ownership in English law.

Tunc (1974) therefore advocates not fusion but unification of the rules of tort and contract, leaving them in separate fields but making the consequences of liability identical whether liability existed from a breach of a contract or from a tort. The only qualification which he would advocate is that the law should respect any agreement which may have been made between the parties, provided it is not contrary to public policy. He recognises that such agreements would be usual in contractual liability, and exceptional in tortious liability. However, it is possible that the potential perpetrator of a possible private nuisance (or abuse of right) may agree to pay a periodical and reasonable indemnity to the person inconvenienced by his operations and on the basis of 'assumption of risks', this might be a way of ensuring that all parties reach a satisfactory compromise. (see Tunc (1974) *ibid*, pp. 28).

In fact, some modern systems have already moved toward effecting a desirable fusion in, for example, the English legal system, by allowing plaintiffs a choice of contractual of tortious remedies; the English courts are also beginning to assimilate the rules on remoteness of damage. The Warsaw Convention 1929 and the Brussels International Convention for the Unification of Certain Rules Relating to Carriage of Passengers by Sea (article 10-1) specifically submit all suits to the same rules. The duality of divisions and regimes has also been rejected by the Czechoslovakian 1950 and 1964 Civil Codes and the Senegal Code of Civil and Commercial Obligations 1963, has also abandoned the strictness of the old rules, by stating that fault refers to the failure to satisfy a pre-existing obligation, whatever be its nature.

As far as English law is concerned, the differences between 'obligations assumed and imposed' (Weir) are being constantly whittled away. Five factors have been identified by Fridman (1977) as responsible for this process: (i) the rise of the concept of restitution or unjust enrichment, including the idea or practice of 'waiver of tort'; (ii) the emergence of a common law remedy for innocent misrepresentation; (iii) the possibility of using *volenti non fit injuria* in a contractual situation to provide a way of avoiding the privity of contract and consideration strait-jackets in relation to exemption clauses upon persons not parties to the contract, but who wish to claim its benefit; (iv) the

'advent and extension' of the collateral warranty doctrine which has both contractual and tortious overtones; (v) the doctrine of promissory estoppel,
which, despite contractual roots, has links with principles originating from
tort. (see Fridman (1977) pp.436-7). In contrast, Professor Markesinis argues
that, particularly in the light of American developments in this area, the common law tort solutions to problems involving an overlap between tort and
contract should not be abandoned, but that contract law should be expanded
with tort correspondingly restricted. (see Markesinis (1987) p.397). No doubt
the debates will continue to occur between various comparatists. In many
respects, of course, it is symptomatic of a rapidly changing society which is
seeking more progressive solutions and modern policies to cope with
everyday problems, while attempting to free itself from the philosophical and
historical shackles of a byegone age.

G. COMPARATIVE OVERVIEW

7.6　　As our comparative survey indicates, there is clearly some basis for
saying that just as civil law places the divisions of contract and tort within a
single law of obligations, the common law has also succeeded in blurring the
edges of the distinction between tort and contract in a variety of contexts, not
least in the area of 'economic torts'.

As far as the formation of contractual obligations is concerned, the analysis
of contract in terms of offer and acceptance is basically similar in common
law and civil law systems. However, individual problems are not solved in the
same way. Theoretical differences and the different approaches to commercial and non-contractual contracts in the civil law systems have produced different rules and different results. An offer in France is seen as continuing in-
definitely if it is not withdrawn, but in commercial contracts, the offer lapses
after a reasonable time. In Germany, every offer is irrevocable unless the offeror has excluded the binding effect of his proposal.

On the so-called indicia of seriousness in the civil law, French law and other
Romanistic systems have flirted with *causa* or cause, as the criterion for distinguishing legally binding transactions from non-legally binding transactions
and German law has used the *construction of the transaction* approach. An
important observation is that in the civil law countries, despite the general
statements of rules and purported definitions, the application of the law in
practice is very much the province of the courts, so that recourse to cases has
become ever more significant. English law continues to utilise its much-
criticised consideration doctrine but the nature of its detailed rules generally
allows some scope for judicial discretion.

In the field of tort, we find a number of similarities in approach between
civil law and common law jurisdictions, particularly in the requirement of a
certain standard of care which must be exercised in order to found liability
for unintentional harm and the ubiquitous influence of the industrial revolution. On the question of intentional harm, the common law has proceeded by
having specific torts and continental legal systems categorise particular
groups of cases utilising a general clause.

If extensive harmonisation of legal systems ever takes place, the legal categories of tort and contract will arguably be one of the most easily adaptable. If the law's clear policy is to provide a remedy in those cases where a breach of a legal rule or norm has occurred, this could be done far more simply by adopting this principle as an explicit policy, and using the contract/tort dichotomy purely as a means of identifying the source of the legal obligation. In this way, particularly in the common law, the ghosts of the past will be exorcised forever and enable claimants to obtain legal redress or compensation more expeditiously and more frequently.

SELECTIVE BIBLIOGRAPHY

A. TORTIOUS OBLIGATIONS/DELICTUAL LIABILITY

Holmes THE COMMON LAW (1881) Lecture III

Winfield 'The History of Negligence in the Law of Torts'
    (1926) LQR 184

Williams 'The Foundation of Tortious Liability'(1939-1941)
    Camb.LJ 111

Lawson NEGLIGENCE IN THE CIVIL LAW (1950)

Lawson A COMMON LAWYER LOOKS AT THE CIVIL LAW (1953)

Catala & Weir 'Delict and Torts: A Study in Parallel' (1963)
    Tul. LR 573; (1964) Tul. LR 701

Amos & Walton INTRODUCTION TO FRENCH LAW (1967)

Lawson MANY LAWS (1977) vol.I and II

Horn, Kotz & Leser GERMAN PRIVATE AND COMMERCIAL LAW (1982)

Lawson & Markesinis TORTIOUS LIABILITY FOR UNINTENTIONAL HARM IN THE COMMON LAW AND THE CIVIL LAW (1982) vol.I and II.

Holyoak 'Tort and Contract after *Junior Books*' (1983) 99 LQR 591

Zweigert & Kotz AN INTRODUCTION TO COMPARATIVE LAW (1987),
    VOL.II

Markesinis 'An Expanding Tort Law-The Price of a Rigid Contract Law' (1987) 103 LQR 354

Winfield & Jolowicz (ed. Rogers) LAW OF TORT (13th ed.)

Dias & Markesinis TORT LAW (1989)

Markesinis THE GERMAN LAW OF TORTS (1990)

Kahn-Freund, Levy & Rudden A SOURCE-BOOK OF FRENCH LAW (1991)

International Encyclopedia of Comparative Law,vol. X1, ch.1(Tunc)(1974); ch. 12 (Weir)(1976)

B. CONTRACTUAL OBLIGATIONS

Buckland & McNair ROMAN LAW AND COMMON LAW (1952)

Parry THE CHANGING CONCEPTION OF CONTRACTS IN ENGLISH LAW (1958)

Pound 'Promise or Bargain?' (1959) 33 Tul.LR 455

Nicholas INTRODUCTION TO ROMAN LAW (1962)

Amos & Walton AN INTRODUCTION TO FRENCH LAW (1967)

Cohn MANUAL OF GERMAN LAW (1968) vol.I: Chapter 3

Fridman 'The Interaction of Tort and Contract' (1977) 93 LQR 422

Zweigert & Kotz AN INTRODUCTION TO COMPARATIVE LAW (1977) vol.II

de Cruz 'A Comparative Survey of the Doctrine of Frustration'
    [1983] Legal Issues European Integration 51

Trietel THE LAW OF CONTRACT (1987)

Cheshire & Fifoot (Furmston) THE LAW OF CONTRACT (1990)

Atiyah   AN INTRODUCTION TO THE LAW OF CONTRACT (1979)

Atiyah   THE RISE AND FALL OF FREEDOM OF CONTRACT (1979)

Treitel   REMEDIES IN CONTRACT (1988)

Cook & Oughton   THE COMMON LAW OF OBLIGATIONS (1989)

Tallon & Harris   CONTRACT LAW TODAY

Atiyah & Summers FORM AND SUBSTANCE IN ANGLO-AMERICAN LAW

O'Connor GOOD FAITH IN ENGLISH LAW (1990)

Whincup   CONTRACT LAW AND PRACTICE (1990)

Nicholas FRENCH LAW OF CONTRACT (1992)

Owsia 'The Notion and Function of Offer and Acceptance under French and English Law' (1992) 66 Tul.LR 871

CHAPTER EIGHT

Corporate and Commercial Law

A. SCOPE OF ANALYSIS

8.0   Of the major legal families in the world today, it is the Romano-Germanic jurisdictions and Common Law jurisdictions that have played dominant roles in the development of a company law ethos. Company law has sometimes been subsumed within the broader category of Commercial Law, as in the German system. In the Soviet system, for most of its legal history right up until 1992, the category of commercial law has not featured in the Soviet classification of divisions of law, primarily because of its basic ideology. However, in the light of the dramatic changes which have been taking place between 1990 and 1991, and which are continuing to take place, leading to the disintegration of Communist rule in the former Soviet Union, it is likely that a distinct branch of law known as 'commercial law' may soon develop, if their moves toward a capitalist economy are eventually successful. It is proposed to concentrate on European company law for a number of reasons. First, it is within Europe that a greater concentration of dominant legal systems can be found. Secondly, the institutions of the European Community (EC) has brought a new dimension to the field of company law. The programme of harmonisation promoted by the EC has the long-term goal of creating a new environment for companies at international level as envisaged by art. 54(3) of the Treaty of Rome. Other EC initiatives will also result in more European companies and firms being involved in closer inter-country contact than ever before. We also undertake a brief comparative survey of Agency or Representation in civil and common law countries before examining the shape of EC Corporate Law.

B. PROBLEMS IN COMPARISON OF COMPANY LAWS

8.1   Several *caveats* need to be made about the study of different European company laws as with other comparative analyses of substantive topics as developed by different legal families. These may be summarised as : (i) terminological; (ii) conceptual; (iii) underlying similarities despite differing

211

terminology; and (iv) systemic;

The *terminological caveat* refers to the fact that even if the same term is used to describe a feature or institution of a branch of law, the term can refer to different things, despite the similarity in terminology.

The *conceptual caveat* refers to the fact that legal concepts may exist in every country, these may be understood differently; an example is the concept of share capital.

The third caveat refers to underlying similarities which may exist in spite of *ex facie* differences; for example although certain countries do not recognise the distinction between authorised and issued share capital, most European countries have the power to issue new shares although this power may be regulated by time limits or by different parties.

The final *caveat* deals with *systemic* problems arising from the nature of the legal system of the country where the company is formed or operates. Obviously, where, for example, there is a fused profession, only one legal practitioner may be dealing on behalf of a company. In England, therefore, it may be necessary to be aware of the different functions of a particular legal representative so that a company is aware of the legal ramifications of his actions in relation to the company.

C. KEY CONCEPTUAL QUESTIONS

8.2   Drury and Xuereb (1991) suggest that an analytical framework which goes beyond mere descriptive analysis is required if one is to discover how different systems solve particular problems and why certain solutions are appropriate for one system but not for another. They argue that the underlying concepts, policy considerations and assumptions of each system need to be addressed before the real nature and relative importance of key matters within each system can be properly understood. Among the key conceptual questions that have dominated the study of company law are: What is a company? Is there a contractual relationship betweeen persons intending to form a company, pre-registration/incorporation? What are the theories that have underpinned the study of the company?

8.2.1   The significance of these questions will be familiar to company lawyers but it should be noted that during the last 30 years we have witnessed a dramatic change in the concept of the company, originating in France. The latest approach is to view the company as *the entity that provides a legal structure for the enterprise*. Under this new approach, it is no longer critical to determine whether the company is a contract or an institution but rather to ask: *what are the social and economic characteristics of that enterprise which has been set up by law*? (see Paillusseau in Drury & Xuereb (1991)). Nevertheless, in order to place the new developments in historical and comparative perspective it is instructive to examine the 'contract theory' and 'institution theory.'

8.2.2 The *contract theory* is predicated on the basis that 'the company is a contract whereby two or more individuals agree to put something in common, with a view to sharing the possible profits.' This was the definition derived from Roman law, as contained in Article 1832 of the French Civil Code and various other definitions subsequently enshrined in the Italian Civil Code (Article 2247), the Swiss Code of Obligations (Article 530) and the Civil Code of Belgium (Article 1832). This definition endured in France until it was first amended in 1978 and then decisively in 1985 when the Act of 11 July 1985 introduced the one-man company in France. The new form of words now reads: 'The *societe* is instituted by two or more persons who agree by way of a contract to combine their assets or their labour in a common enterprise with a view to sharing the profits or benefitting from the savings which result'.

A *societe* can be created in the situations provided for by statute, by the voluntary act of a single individual.

This appears to signify a move towards regarding the company as an *institution*. It is pertinent to note that the word *societe* in French law covers both companies and partnerships. Nevertheless, the words *contrat de societe* have been translated as 'the company contract'. In any event, as soon as the company is registered in France, it becomes a legal entity (see Article 1842: Code Civil) and only 'silent partnerships' (see below) are not legal entities. It is the judicial conception of the company as a legal entity that has shaped the development of the corporate contract. For example, in 1945 and 1956, the *Cour de cassation* acknowledged the legal personality of enterprise committees and of a bankrupt's estate. Hence, the two main consequences of this contract theory are:

(i) The corporate contract creates the company whereby the group of individuals who wish to combine their assets is formed. The group becomes the legal entity when it is registered as a company.

(ii) The company is therefore a contract; this organisation is to be effected by the parties themselves and their organisation can only be contractual.

8.2.3 The *institution theory* stresses the predominance of the legal person over the contract. The company as Hauriou puts it, is:

> 'a concept of work or enterprise which takes shape and has a legal existence in a social environment. To implement this idea, an authority is established which provides the enterprise with organs. In other respects, between the members of the social group concerned with the realisation of the idea, some manifestatons of their common will are produced which are directed by the duly empowered organs and regulated by their procedures.'

8.2.4 The *new conceptual approach* has been described by Paillusseau as 'a technique for the organisation of the enterprise.' However, it seems more illuminating to describe it as the legal and institutional framework for the organisation of the commercial enterprise. The notion of the 'enterprise' is apparent not just in French company law but also in its labour law, tax law, accountancy law and competition law. At the pragmatic level, it is clear that the advent of the one-man company in French law has rendered the traditional concept of company law obsolete. What exactly is the 'enterprise'?

Paillusseau's Enterprise Notion

8.2.5   The concept of *enterprise*, as developed by Paillusseau, has two main features:
(i) The enterprise as a *business*; and
(ii) The enterprise as a *focus of interests*;

The enterprise as a *business* would therefore include the production, transformation and distribution of goods, or the supply of services, or some of these features. As with most businesses, it would also include a range of resources, skills, finance, contracts, planning strategies, and decision-making procedures.

 The enterprise as a *focus of interests* would assume a particular size, range and   complexity depending on the nature of the enterprise, and would inevitably include not just those of the founder or creator of the enterprise. Creditors, partners, shareholders, moneylenders and managers would inevitably come into the picture and the unique nature of the enterprise would dictate the role of entrepreneur.

8.2.6   The law provides the statutory framework for the enterprise's structure, functioning, financing, decision-making procedures, sale, reorganisation and winding-up. Paillusseau suggests *five main lines of intervention* by the law in determining respective rights and levels of protection to be accorded to parties having an interest in the enterprise. These are:
(i) The protection of different interest groups by means of the
    dissemination of information;
(ii) Increasing the rights and protection accorded to certain
    categories of individuals;
(iii) Protection of different interest groups through the concept
    and structure of the company;
(iv) Using company law to establish an 'institutional
    equilibrium' between the different interest groups; and
(v) External protection of different interest groups.

In each legal system, the amount of State intervention and State regulation will vary according to the nature, complexity and extent of the interests involved and it is still accurate to say that the role of contract remains relevant to those situations where parties are capable of a greater degree of self-regulation.

D. FORMS OF BUSINESS ORGANISATION: A COMPARATIVE OVERVIEW

i. Corporate Terminology in France and Germany

(i) 'Company' and 'Partnership'

8.3   In the Continental systems, one term may cover *both* companies and partnerships in the European Continental systems, namely the French term *societe* or the German term *Gesellschaft*.

The two main forms of business organisation in Western Europe are:

(i) The *partnership*, where some or all of the members are responsible for the liabilities of the business; and

(ii) The *limited company*, where none of the members has personal liability for the company's debts.

(ii) Public and Private Companies

8.3.1   There are two basic types of limited company in Latin and Germanic countries, namely the 'share' company (*societe anonyme* (SA): French; *Aktiengesellschaft*(AG): German) and the limited liability company (*societe a responsibilite limitee*(SARL): French; and *Gesellschaft mit beschrankter Haftung*(GmBH)): German.

The Continental 'share' company finds its strict English equivalent in the registered company limited by shares which may be public or private. However, despite the term 'public' they shares are not publicly held or necessarily listed on the Stock Exchange; they need not be held by the public although they might well be so held.

The difference between share companies and limited liability companies on the Continent is distinguishable by the name of each type of company utilising a different designation for each type of company. Similarly, in England, by s.25(2) Companies Act 1985, the last word of a private company's name must be 'limited' or 'Ltd'. This gives notice to persons dealing with the company that they will not have access to the private funds of the members to satisfy the company's debts. A partnership must not end with the term 'limited'. Under s.25(1)of the same Act, a public company's name must end with the words 'Public Limited Company' or 'plc'. There is a facility for certain companies in England to dispense with the term 'limited' for example a private company limited by guarantee. (see s.30: Companies Act 1985(UK))

ii. The English Approach to Company Law

(i) Meaning of 'company' in English Company law

8.3.2   A company is an association or organisation with a legal personality distinct from that of the human members who control and administer the organisation. The inclusion of the name 'company' in an association's title does not necessarily mean it is a registered company; the mere adoption of the word carries no legal consequences. When a company is registered, it becomes in law a separate legal entity from its members and this is a fundamental principle of English company law which was established by the English House of Lords in the case of *Salomon* v. *Salomon & Co.* [1897] AC 27. The significance of this case is discussed in detail below (see 11.4.2) For the moment, it should be noted that the *corporate personality* is referred to as the '*veil of incorporation*' and its members are generally shielded from the legal consequences of the company's actions. However, there are several situations in which the law is prepared to 'lift the veil' of incorporation which are also discussed below.

(ii) Sources of Law

8.3.3   English company law is to be found in several companies Acts (Companies Acts of 1948, 1967, 1976, 1980, 1981, 1985, 1989) as well as in the European Communities Act 1972, delegated legislation and Stock Exchange regulations with regard to listed companies. As is the classic common law style, fundamental governing rules and principles were to be found in caselaw, which were gleaned from judicial pronouncements but these have been increasingly supplemented by a mass of legislation and regulation, which have, in turn, been subjected to judicial interpretation which have modified some of the more antiquated principles of law.

(iii) Types of Business Units in the United Kingdom

8.3.4   There are three main types of business units in the United Kingdom, ie (i) Registered Companies; (ii) Partnerships; and (iii) Sole traders.

a. Types of Companies

8.3.5   There are three types of companies in Britain at the present time:(a) Public corporations; (b) Chartered companies; and (c) Registered Companies.
 The *Public Corporations* are the nationalised industries such as British Rail and British Gas, which were created and are regulated by their own Act of Parliament so that they do not register under the Companies Act 1985 like registered companies. They are not subject to the control of the shareholders since there no shareholders or board of directors.
With the current British Government's privatisation policies, these types are becoming increasingly extinct and there is a question as to whether there will be any such companies left in Britain by the end of the twentieth century.
 Chartered Companies used to be created by Royal Charter, ie by the power of the Crown, but Royal Charters are no longer used to create trading companies, but are confined to universities and professional organisations such as Chartered Accountants and Surveyors.
 Registered Companies, which form the majority of trading associations in the UK, are created by registration under the Companies Act 1985 and are usually classified by either (i) the method by which their liability is limited; or (ii) depending on whether they are public or private.
b. Methods by which Liability may be limited

8.3.6 The two main methods by which liability may be limited are:(a) by shares; (b) by guarantee. There are *Public* and *Private* Companies.

A *public company* is defined by the Companies Act 1985 as a company limited by shares and guarantee and where:
(i)   the Memorandum states that the company is a public limited company;
(ii) the company has at least two members;
(iii) the name of the company ends in 'plc';
(iv) the company has an authorised (nominal) share capital of not less than 50,000 pounds.

A *private company* is not defined in the Companies Act 1985 but under s.1 of the Act, a private company is any company which is not a public company. Thus any company which does not fall within the defintion of a public company is a private company.

(iv) Consequences of Incorporation

8.3.7   The most significant effect of incorporation is that the company becomes in law *a separate legal entity* and becomes a legal personality distinct and therefore separate from the members of the company: *Salomon* v. *Salomon* (above). Other consequences are:

(i) The case established the 'one-man company' as a legally recognised entity and that incorporation was available to small and large businesses.

(ii) As a result of the separate legal personality theory, the company can make contracts on its own behalf and neither the benefits nor the burdens of such contracts can be claimed by its members. (this is the result of the privity of contract doctrine)

(iii)The company has contractual capacity and can sue and be sued in its own name.

(iv) Perpetual succession of the company is possible; the death or incapacity of its members will have no effect on the company or its property. Even if all its sharegolders are dead, the company must be put through a 'winding-up' procedure if it is sought to dissolve it legally.

(v)   The company may own property in its own right so that the members only have a right to shares in the company but own no direct interest; members are precluded from having any insurable assets in the assets of the company (eg in the *Macaura* case (1925) the one-man owner of the company had no right to claim under an policy when the company-owned estate suffered damage by fire since he had the policy not in the company's name but his own.)

(vi) Under the limited liability principle, the members are not liable for the company's debts if it was a limited company; members would be personally liable for the company's debts if it was an unlimited company.

(v) Companies and Contracts

a. Pre-Incorporation Contracts

8.3.7   The basic English law rule is that a contract (so-called *pre-incorporation contracts*) made on behalf of a company in the course of its formation but before its formation (or incorporation) does not bind the company. It cannot therefore be ratified by the company after ratification. In *Kelner* v. *Baxter* (1866) a company was about to be formed for the purpose of purchasing a hotel. Before the company was formed, the promoters signed a contract 'on behalf of' the proposed company for the purchase of a quantity of wine. The company was formed, and the hotel was purchased. The wine was also delivered and consumed but the company then went into liquidation before payment for the wine had been made. The court held that the promoters should be held personally liable for payment of the wine. Any purported ratification by the company therefore had no legal effect.

b. Persons Purporting to Contract on Behalf of the Company

8.3.8   Under section 36C of the Companies Act 1985, where a contract purports to be made by a company, or by a person as agent for a company, at a time when the company has not been formed, then subject to any agreement to the contrary the contract will take effect as if it had ben entered into by the person purporting to act for the company or as agent for it, and he is personally liable on the contract. This section effectively abolishes any distinction that might have existed at common law between signing *as an agent* of the company and signing to *autheticate* the signature of the company.
  However, a promoter may protect himself from the statutory personal liablity imposed by s.36C, by (i) agreeing that the promoters' liability shall cease when the company enters into a similar agreement, after incorporation; or (ii) by agreeing that if the company does not enter into such an agreement within a fixed period either part may rescind the contract.

c. Public Company Trading before Issue of Certificate

8.3.9   A public company may not commence trading before it has obtained a certificate of compliance with the capital requirements of public companies under s.117 of the Companies Act 1985. This, rather than the certificate of incorporation, is the 'birth certificate' of the English public company.
  However, if a public company does commence business in contravention of s.117 (above), the transaction will *prima facie* be valid unless the company fails to comply with its obligations within 21 days of being called upon to do so. Its directors will then be liable to indemnify the other party if he suffers loss as a result of the company's failure to comply. The company and its officers may also be fined. Clearly, in these circumstances, the law is prepared to 'lift the veil' of incorporation and go behind the company facade.

(vii) Company Auditors

8.3.10   The Companies Act 1989 introduces new rules regarding the auditing of a company. They seek to ensure that only persons who are properly supervised and appropriately qualified are appointed company auditors and that audits are carried out in a proper manner and with integrity and independence. The two types of supervisory bodies established under the Act are: (a) Recognised Supervisory Bodies (RSBs) of which all company auditors must be members; and (b) Recognised Qualifying Bodies (RQBs) which will offer the professional qualifications required to become a member of an RSB. The same body can be both a RSB and a RQB. However, the existing professional bodies, such as the Chartered Association of Certified Accountants and the Institute of Chartered Accountants will probably fulfil both functions.

8.3.11   Under the RSBs' rules, auditing must be carried out properly and with integrity. Two areas have been highlighted by a Department of Trade and Industry consultative document, namely: (i) the standards of performance of the audit, and compliance with approved auditing guidelines; and (ii) General ethical standards, including rules dealing with independence, objectivity and client confidentiality. Eligible persons who carry out audits must also continue to maintain an appropriate level of competence.

Under English common law, auditors may be liable to the company for loss of dividends if, despite their suspicions, they accept an explanation from an officer of the company (such as a managing director) without undertaking any further investigation: see *Re Thomas Gerrard* [1967] 2 All ER 525, where the auditors were found guilty of negligence and breach of duty under s.333(1): Companies Act 1948. If auditors believe that entries in or omissions from the books give rise to suspicions, they must make a full investigation into the circumstances: see *Fomento* v. *Selsdon* [1958] 1 All ER 11, where the House of Lords held that auditors were entitled to information relating to certain types of refills of writing instruments even though they did not appear to be items which were strictly covered by the particular deed of terms.

(viii) Lifting the Veil of Incorporation

8.3.12   Despite the principle that the separate corporate personality of a company prevents outsiders from taking action against the members of a company, so that the members are shielded behind this '*veil of incorporation*', there are several examples of cases where the law is prepared to 'lift the veil' or to 'pierce the veil' so as to go behind the corporate personality. This means they will either discover who were the individual members responsible for the particular act or be able to ignore the separate corporate personality of several companies and proceed against the economic entity constituted by the group as a whole. Examples of such instances include:
(i) cases of fraudulent or wrongful trading:
    s.213 1A; s.214 1A : Companies Act 1985;
(ii) cases of individuals using the company to evade their legal obligations:
see *Goodwin* v. *Birmingham City F.C.* (1980);

(iii) cases involving holding and subsidiary companies.

In a number of instances, such as the presentation of financial statements, the companies in a group have been treated as one legal entity. Other examples are where the courts have held that the holding company and its subsidiaries really constitute a single commercial entity:see *DHN Food Distributors* v. *Tower Hamlets LBC* [1976] 3 All ER 462; and where, on the particular facts of the case, the company and its manager have been treated *de jure* as one person where this was the *de facto* position:see *Goodwin* v. *Birmingham City FC* [1980]. The modern tendency appears to be that courts are more willing to 'lift the veil of incorporation' than hitherto.

(ix) Partnership Law

a. Partnership Companies

8.3.13   Under s.8A of the Companies Act 1985, it has become easier to set up *partnership companies*, since such a company is defined therein as 'a company limited by shares whose shares are intended to be held to a substantial extent by or or behalf of its employees'.

b. Differences between Partnerships and Companies

8.3.14   Under section 1 of the Partnership Act 1890, a partnership is defined as a 'relation which subsists between persons carrying on a business in common with a view to profit'. 'Business' includes any trade, occupation or profession. There are several differences between partnerships and companies in English law:

(i) A partnership may be created by the express or implied agreement of the partners, and no special formalities are required. Hence they may be created by conduct, orally or, as is usual, by writing. A company is created by registration under the Companies Act 1985.

(ii) A partnership incurs far less expenses than a company from the stage of formation, throughout its life and upon dissolution.

(iii) A partnership is not a separate legal person but as with a company, it may sue and be sued in the firm's name. The partners are personally liable on the firm's contracts but there is no limitation placed on their contractual capacity; such limitations are sometimes written into a company's memorandum and articles of association.A company is a separate legal person which may make contracts and of course, sue and be sued in the company's name.

(iv)   The liability of a general partner is unlimited, although it is possible for one or more partners to limit their liability. There must, however, be one general partner remaining. A company's liability may be limited by shares or by guarantee. The limited liability may not, however, be of any practical value for small companies whose directors or majority shareholders will have to give a personal guarantee for any loans that are advanced.

(v) Partners have the power to sell goods or personal chattels of the firm since they own the property of the firm jointly and severally. Companies may, of course, hold property in their own name.

(vi) A partnership has confidential accounts whereas a company is obliged to file accounts at the Company Registry where they are available for public inspection and accounts for most companies must be submitted to an annual audit.

(vii) There is no free transferability of shares for a partnership, and the agreement of all the partners is required before shares may be transferred. A partner may assign the right to his share of the profits but the assignee does not thereby become a partner.

(viii) A partnership should generally not have more than 20 persons in a firm, apart from exceptions such as solicitors, accountants, auctioneers and estate agents. A company must have a minimum of 2 members but there is no maximum limit.

(ix) All partners are entitled to share in management, unless there is provision to the contrary in the partnership agreement. Members of a partnership who are not managers are still liable as though they were. Only those members of a company who become directors may take part in its management.

(x) A partner is an agent of for his co-partners, therefore he may bind the firm in contract provided the contract falls within the scope of the partnership business. A member of a company is not prima facie an agent of the company and thus cannot bind the company in contract.

(xi) Partners may agree on their own arrangments for drawings of profit and capital whereas company law requires that dividends may only be declared out of profits, so that there is maintenance of issued capital.

(xii) Partnerships have the right to make their own arrangments for the management and organisation of the firm, and may carry on any business they wish. Companies, however, are fairly tightly regulated in their powers and duties by the Companies Acts, its constitution is clearly laid down in its Memorandum of Association and its internal rules are contained in its Articles of Association.

(xiii) A partnership may publicise as little or as mch as it wishes of its management details, whereas a company has to give far greater publicity to its directorate, charges on its assets and its financial position generally.

(xiv) A partnership often finds borrowing difficult since no floating charges are possible, whereas companies generally find borrowing easier.

(xv) A partnership ends on the death of a partner unless there is a specific agreement to the contrary and provision for new members. A is an artificial and discret legal entity which is capable of perpetual succession, which may continue irrespective of a change in its members or management.

In English law, therefore, there are many significant differences between partnerships and companies and each term has its own legal, economic, philosophical and political significance. Of course, both the company and the partnership are a means of carrying on business and the benefits of incorporation (such as a separate legal personality and limited liability) must be weighed against the more intimate relationship of mutual trust and confidence that is more typical of partnerships.

c. Relevance of Partnership to Agency

8.3.15 The central feature of a partnership is agency. The English courts have confirmed that the liability of a partner for the acts of his co-partner is similar to the liability of a principal for the acts of his agent. Agency is the relationship which arises whenever one person (the agent) acts (or purports to have the authority to act) on behalf of another person (the principal) and has the power to alter or affect the principal's legal position in relation to the third party. The most important feature of agency is therefore the agent's *power to alter the legal relationship between the principal and a third party*. This can be done by making contracts on behalf of the principal's behalf or by disposing of the principal's property.

A crucial distinction that is made in English law is between the agent's *actual authority* and his *apparent authority*.

Actual authority is the authority which the agent actually holds, based on *consent between agent and principal*, where the principal authorises the agent to act on his behalf, expressly or impliedly; or by operation of law.

Apparent (or 'ostensible') authority is the authority which an agent appears to hold. This may mean either *any* authority which an agent appears to have (based on the maxim: apparent authority is the real authority) or authority which appears to exist but did not in fact exist. In this second sense, apparent authority is a form of *estoppel*, which is pleaded by showing: (i) a representation was made; (ii) reliance was made on that representation; (iii) alteration of the plaintiff's position took place as a result of that reliance.

Under section 5 of the Partnership Act 1890 (PA), every partner is an agent of the firm and his other partners, for the purposes of the business of the partnership. It indicates that a partner's apparent authority is confined to acts which are connected with the business of the kind carried on by the firm and performed in the usual way. Whether or not a partnership will be bound by a particular act is a question of fact in every case. The test adopted by the courts is an *'objective test'* meaning that the courts would ask whether a *reasonable man* dealing with the firm would be put on enquiry as to the authority of the active partner who was dealing with the matter in hand: see *Mercantile Credit Co. Ltd.* v. *Garrod* [1962] 3 All ER 1103.

iii. Company Law in France

(i) Types of Business Organisations

8.3.16 Anyone wishing to carry on a business in France may do so either as a sole trader (*entreprise individuelle*) or through a corporate body (*societe*) or as a GIE (*Groupement d'Interet Economique*), commercial associations which are business entities peculiar to French law. While the sole trader is the simplest form of business organisation wherein no distinction is made between the capital of the business and that of the trader, the *societe* has a *separate legal personality* so there is a distinction between the private capital of its participants and the business capital of the corporate body or company. The liability of the participants for the debts of the *societe* may or may not be limited, depending on its type. Corporate bodies may therefore be divided into two groups depending on the different liability of the participants in each group: (i) *Limited Liability Companies* (*societes de capitaux*); and (ii) *Partnerships of various kinds* where members have unlimited liability for the debts of the *societe* (*societes de personnes*) (see below). However, although the first type of company corresponds to the English-style limited liability company, and the second is similar to partnerships in English law, there is far less precision in the criteria for the division of these different types of business enterprises. Unlike English law, French law makes a distinction between *commercial partnerships* and *companies* (*societes commerciales*) and civil partnerships and companies (*societes civile*). Different rules will apply depending on whether the *societe* is classified as *commerciale* or *civile*. Under Article 1 of the Law of 24 July 1966:'the following forms of *societe* are *societes commerciales*(SA), regardless of their objects: *societe anonyme, societe a responsabilite limitee*(SARL), *societe en nom collectif, societe en commandite simple* and *societe en commandite par actions*.'

Other *societes* will be classified as commercial or civil in accordance with their stated objects.

8.3.17 The following are considered *societes de capitaux*, where the key distinguishing feature is the pooling of capital:

> (a) *societe anonyme* (SA), which is the closest in characteristics to an English company;
> (b) *societe en commandite par actions* (SCA), which is a partnership limited by shares.

In contrast, those commercial enterprises which are primarily characterised as associations of persons (*societes de personnes*) are:

> (a) *societe en nom collectif* (general commercial
>   partnership);
> (b) *societe en commandite simple* (limited partnership);
> (c) *societe en participation* (undisclosed/sleeping
>   partnership);
> (d) *societe civile* (civil partnership).

A French *societe* is based on a contractual agreement, irrespective of whether it is a civil or commercial *societe*.

The SARL (*societe a responsabilite limitee*) is modelled on the German GmbH (see below) and resembles a *societe a capitaux*, although not classified as such. The problem in classification derives from the fact that the capital of an SARL is divided into *parts sociales*(non-negotable shares), as it is in a general partnership, and yet the liability of its members is limited to their contributions, which is the same as shareholders in an SA. It is therefore something of a hybrid *societe*.

8.3.18 The *societe commerciale* is now largely subject to mandatory rules and since 1985, all registration applications for *societe commerciales* have to be made directly to a Business Formalities Centre (*centre de formalites des entreprises*) which now exists in most *departements*. The purpose of such a centre is to convey information about the *societe* to the appropriate government authorities including the *greffier* of the *societe*'s local *tribunal de commerce* (commercial court). The *greffier*, which is technically translated as *registrar*, is an *officer of the court* who assists judges at court hearings and performs various administrative duties but undertakes no judicial functions. *Greffiers* are therefore not 'registrars' in the English courts' sense but civil servants. Their functions are closer to 'clerks of the court' in English courts, and among their duties will be to publish the relevant announcement informing the public of the formation of the *societe commerciale* in the *Bulletin official des Annonces Civiles et Commerciales* (the equivalent of the Official Gazette).

8.3.19   No French company may be incorporated for more than 99 years although on the first expiry of this period, its term may be extended by special resolution but for no longer than one other period of 99 years. The French doctrine of *ultra vires* is more restricted in its scope than the English equivalent although the UK Companies Act 1989 has greatly reduced the extent of the divergence.

(ii) Legislative Sources of Law

8.3.20   In typical civil law style, the sources of law for the French *droits des societes* are to be found in Codes and legislative enactments. The three main statutes relating to French *societes* are: (i) Commercial Companies Law (*Loi sur les Societes Commerciales*) 66.537 of 24 July 1966; (ii) Commercial Companies Decree (*Decret sur les Societes Commerciales*) 67.236 of 23 March 1967; and (iii) The General Companies Rules (*Dispositions Generales sur les Societes*) of the Civil Code: Book III, title IX, Articles 1832-1844. The first two pieces of legislation apply only to *societes commerciales* and the third applies to *societes civiles* generally and to *societes commerciales* to the extent that they are not in conflict with provisions of the Commercial Companies Law. Other statutory provisions relevant to this area of law are:
(i) Commercial Register and Companies Decree (*Decret relatif au registre du commerce et des societes*) 67.327 of 23 March 1967;
(ii) Economic Co-operation Group Decree (*Decret relatif au Groupement d'interet Economique*) 67.821 of 23 September 1967; and
(iii) Law of 30 April 1983: see French accounting principles in relation to individual companies' financial statements; Law of 3 January 1985 (consolidated financial statements) and the Stock exchange Commission Rules (*Commission des Operations de Bourse*-COB) Ordonnance 67833 of 28 September 1967.

(iii) Incorporation of a Societe

8.3.21   It is usually a fairly lengthy process to form a French *societe*, taking an average period of three months, unlike the much speedier processes available in England. The following are the steps which should normally be taken in order to form a *societe*: (i) Preparation of the Articles of Association (hereafter 'Articles') (*statuts;*) (ii) Signature of the Articles (iii) Payment of Registration Tax (*droits d'enregistrement*) and Stamping of the document; (iv) Opening a *Societe* Bank Account, in return for a certificate from the bank (*certificat de depot*) which will acknowledge the share capital deposited; (v) Publication of a Notice in a legal gazette, informing the public of the formation of the *societe*; (vi) Deposit with the Clerk of the Commercial Court copies of the following :

(i) Two originals of the Articles (*statuts*);

(ii) Two copies of the documents listing the officers of the company (eg the manager or the directors) if they have not been appointed by express provision of the Articles.

(iii) Two originals of a subscription certificate listing the shareholders;

(iv) Two copies of the report of the special auditor if contributions have been made in kind;

(v) Two copies of a declaration (the declaration of conformity or *declaration de conformite*) certifying that the proper steps have been taken in conformity with the legal requirements.

(iv) Status of a Societe Pending Incorporation

8.3.22 Pending the full incorporation of a company, before its registration at the appropriate Register of Commerce, a *societe* is still able to enter into contracts *en formation*, that is, during the period between the signature of the Articles and registration, subject to subsequent ratification of the contract once the company is registered. A clause may be inserted in the Articles whereby stated obligations to be assumed by the *societe* on its registration will receive automatic ratification by the *societe* on its registration. (see modification of this position for SAs and SARLs: below 12.5.6 ff.). The liability of a person acting on behalf of a *societe en formation* will generally be a personal one but this has been modified for SAs and SARLs. A sole trader only requires registration at the appropriate Register of Commerce.

(v) SAs and SARLs

a. *Societe anonyme* (SA)

8.3.23 The SA closely approximates the English plc in structure and purpose, and, apart from the SCA, is the only other form of company which may offer its shares to the public. It requires a minimum of seven shareholders, who may be individuals or legal entities, and may be French or foreign but no maximum number is imposed. Shares cannot be issued before registration of the company in the Commercial Register for which the penalty is a fine. Since 1 October 1982, only those corporations listed on a stock exchange may issue or maintain bearer shares and these must be held by authorised institutions like banks.

An SA may, as with an English plc, obtain finance by different means such as share issues, debentures, or through public advertisements other than those required by law. Shares must have a nominal value which is fixed by the Articles but since 1988, there has been no minimum nominal value requirement except in the case of a publicly-quoted company whose shares must have a nominal value of at least FF 10 expressed in francs excluding centimes.

8.3.24   *Directors* are appointed either by the Articles or by the SA in general meeting and he may also be removed by the SA in general meeting. The *Board of directors* of an SA exercises the *management powers* of the SA as do their English counterparts.

8.3.25   French law requires at least one *independent statutory auditor* (*commissaire aux comptes*) to be appointed for a six-year period, but unlike the English company law counterpart, such an auditor has the duty to not just verify that the *societe*'s accounts have been drawn up in accordance with the law, but also to report to the public prosecutor if any irregularity or mis-managment of the company of a criminal nature, is detected. Further, every time a statutory auditor is appointed, a potential *substitute* must be named, to allow for the possibility that the appointee retires during the period or is dismissed. Grounds of dismissal include serious misconduct. As we have seen, the UK Companies Act 1989 has introduced new rules to govern auditors of English companies. In cases where British auditors have been held liable for not carrying out their duties properly, an action may be brought against them by the company through its liquidator under s.212 1A of the UK Insolvency Act 1986.

b. *Societe a Responsabilite Limitee* (SARL)

8.3.26   A SARL, the most popular form of *societe*, which is used extensively in France, possesses characteristics which are similar to a SA and an English private limited company in that its members are liable only to the extent of their contributions to the company's capital. However, it also resembles a partnership in that its participants are treated more like partners than shareholders. Its shares will be made up of non-negotiable shares (*parts sociales*) which are freely transferable among members but transfers to third parties (non-members) require the consent of the majority of its members representing at least three quarters of the corporate capital.

8.3.27   A *minimum of only two members is required*, with a *maximum of fifty members* of either individuals or legal entities, which may be French or foreign. Under the Law 85.69 of 7 July 1985 a SARL may be subscribed to and may continue to exist with only one shareholder, who may be an individual or a legal entity. He is known as a sole member. This type of SARL is still subject to the same provisions as those governing other SARLs but will be known as an *Entreprise Unipersonnelle a Responsabilite Limitee* or EURL. If the sole shareholder is a *legal entity*, it may not also be a EURL and the sole member who happens to be an *individual* is not permitted to be the sole member of another EURL.

8.3.28   The management of a SARL may be run by one or more managers (*gerants*) who may be non-members but will have full authority and unlimited powers to represent the company and bind the SARL both in respect of third parties and, subject to its Articles (*statuts*), its members.

(vi) The GIE and the GEIE

a. The GIE

8.3.29   The French GIE (*Groupement d'Interet Economique*) is an entity which was created by Ordonnance No.67-821 of 23 September 1967, to enable any group of businesses to pool their resources to carry on some joint activity whilst maintaining their independence, and individuality in other fields of commercial enterprise. It is noteworthy since it is not strictly a corporate body or partnership. The GIE is formed by executing a written agreement between the members and is incorporated by being entered in the commercial register. It may be classified as civil or commercial depending on its stated objects.

Setting up a GIE can enable a group of businesses to co-operate in respect of a number of commercial activities such as exports or sales, and to co-ordinate their activities in one specialised area such as distribution, while maintaining their separate identity for other activities.

A GIE may be set up *for a specified term* in order to employ means to facilitate or develop the economic activities of its members, or to increase the profits or benefits of such activites': Article 1: Ordinance of 23 September 1967. A GIE must be an extension of the economic activities of its members, and it must have an economic purpose. Two points flow from these requirements. First, each member must retain its economic and magerial independence in non-GIE activities. Secondly, the GIE must actually engage in economic activites.

However, an economic activity is not necessarily commercial. For example, if farmers and commercial partnerships form a GIE to provide its members with special services, the GIE will be regarded as *civil* in character. It will therefore not fall within the jurisdiction of the commercial courts but only within that of the civil courts (ie, the *tribunaux d'instance* exercising their civil jurisdiction).

A GIE has *legal personality* and full legal capacity as soon as it is entered in the Commercial Register. It is a *separate legal entity from that of its members*. It can also be set up without having any share capital. A GIE contracts directly and its members are jointly and severally liable for its debts provided certain procedures have been carried out, such as service of a formal demand for payment on the GIE by registered letter or service of a written notice delivered by a baliff (Article 2: 1967 Ordinance).

b. GEIE

8.3.30   The *Groupement Europeen d'Interet Economique* (GEIE) or European Economic Interest Group is a legal entity which was inspired by the GIE and is designed to facilitate co-operation between businesses in different Member States of the EEC, who wish to combine their resources for certain joint activities, such as research or manufacture. It was created by Regulation 2137/85 on 25 July 1985 by the Council of Ministers. The Regulation defines its basic charactcristics and lists the rules regulating the formation and operation of a GEIE. Individuals, partnerships and companies are all entitled to form a GEIE and as with the GIE, various joint activites may be undertaken. The basic rules applicable to GEIEs are similar to those of the GIE, but a GEIE is not allowed to issue debentures. GEIEs which are established in France are now governed by the Law 89/377 of 13 June 1989, whereby the GEIEs acquire legal personality as soon as they have been registered in France on the commercial register.

c. Partnerships

8.3.31   It will be recalled that in France, the term *societe* may include *both* companies and partnerships. Although a partnership is formed by a contract between the parties, there are still *de facto* partnerships if: (i) there a a form of contribution by the partners; (ii) a sharing of profits and losses and (iii) a common intention amongst the partners to achieve a common goal (*affectio societatis*).

French law recognises general partnerships (SNC) (*societe en nom collectif*) and limited partnerships (*societe en commandite simple*). If the latter have a share capital (*societe en commandite par actions*: SCA), they are also reconised by French law but the SCA has become increasingly obscure. Civil partnerships (*societes civiles*) will be governed by the Civil Code (Articles 1841 *et seq.*), and are restricted to non-commercial activities. All forms of partnership other than the silent partnership (see below) and the GIE (see above) must have a corporate capital.

8.3.32   The *silent partnership* (*societes en participation*) was, for many years, by definition, undisclosed to third parties and is therefore not a legal entity. Accordingly, it need not be registered. Since 1978, a silent partnership has the option to decide whether to be disclosed to third parties or to remain secret. Such a partnership may be classified as civil or commercial depending on the nature of its activites. It cannot have a corporate name and its shares cannot be represented by certificates. Its members remain personally liable for their acts.

8.3.33   Each of the five main types of partnerships (and companies), namely (i) the general commercial partnership; (ii) the limited partnership; (iii) the share company; (iv) the limited liability company and (v) the partnership limited by shares, is referred to as a *societe commerciale*. These five types will be regarded as commercial partnerships irrespective of their objects. Thus, so long as a *societe* has adopted the form of a general commercial partnership or limited partnership, it will still be classified as a *societe commerciale*, even though some of its activities may not be regarded as commercial under French law. On the other hand, if a *societe* has not adopted a commercial form, its classification as a *societe civile* or *societe commerciale* will depend on its objects.

8.3.34   *Societes civiles* or civil companies are unusual in that they are completely governed by the Civil Code (Articles 1841 *et seq.*). Examples of business activities which such partnerships carry out involve real estate and agriculture, and relate to the exercise of a profession by, for example, doctors, architects, lawyers and accountants. If such partnerships have commercial objects or activities, they will be treated as companies for the purposes of tax. No statutory minimum registered capital is prescribed, and their capital is divided into non-negotiable shares (*parts*) for which there is no statutory minimum par value. The unanimous prior consent of all partners is required for the transfer of shares and such transfers must be executed by a written contract of sale and duly registered with the tax authorities.

Any decisions, including a resolution to amend the articles of a *societe civile*, may be taken at a meeting of the members usually by a majority vote as laid down in the articles. However, should the articles be silent on the type of majority needed to carry an amendment thereof, a unanimous vote will then be required.

8.3.35   The general partnership (SNC) or *societe en nom collectif* is a partnership wherein all partners are deemed to be merchants. This means they will have to abide by the rules applicable to merchants. Liability for the debts of the partnership will be unlimited, joint and several. This form of partnership resembles the English general partnership but a key difference from the English version is that the French general partnership does possess a separate legal personality.

8.3.36   The limited partnership (SCS) and partnership limited by shares (SCA) are rarely used forms of *societe* but famous examples of SCAs, which may offer their shares to the public, are Yves Saint Laurent and Michelin. SCAs have: (i) general partners, who have *unlimited personal liability*. They manage the partnership in much the same way as their English counterparts; (ii) limited partners, who are shareholders with limited personal liability and do not have the right to manage the partnership but have the right to supervise its affairs on the lines of the supervisory board of an SA. They are represented by a supervisory board which exercises powers similar to statutory auditors. The rationale behind this fundamental distinction between managers and investors is apparently to forestall hostile takeover bids.

iv. Company Law in Germany

8.3.37   The political reunification of Germany has given rise to a number of significant developments. Upon the accession of the former GDR to the Federal Republic of Germany on 3 October 1990, the West German legal system became the law in force in the territory of the former GDR. Special transitional legal provisions are to apply to the former GDR area, in some cases, for several years to enable a proper transition from planned to market economy to take place. The reader is referred to the annexes to the Treaty of Unification for these transitional provisions. For present purposes, we shall proceed on the basis that the law is that which applied to West Germany.

Accordingly, most commercial matters would fall within the jurisdiction of the *civil courts*, which are traditionally divided into four regional units. The lowest civil court is the *Amtsgericht* or county court, but claims in excess of

DM 6,000 have to be brought in the regional or district court, the *Landgericht*, where each party has to be represented by a German lawyer who has the right to appear at that particular court. A special chamber deals with commercial cases in the *Landgericht*, which, on request, deals with proceedings between merchants as well as with other urgent commercial matters.

Commercial parties are also permitted to enter into agreements conferring jurisdiction for disputes concerning property on whichever regional court they choose, so that particularly between commercial companies, the most convenient forum may be chosen. (see Bocker *et al* (1992) p.3)

Appeals to the Court of Appeal (*Oberlandesgericht*) are available against decisions of both the *Amtsgericht* and the *Landgericht*, but the amount at issue has to be at least DM 1,200 in order for leave to appeal to be granted. An appeal to the Federal Supreme Court of Justice(*Bundesgerichtshof*) on points of law can also be made in cases involving an amount greater than DM 60,000 or in disputes concerning matters of fundamental importance. There is no further appeal against the decisions of the small claims court.

The German Civil Code (BGB) also contains the provisions dealing with civil partnerships, and the Commercial Code (*Handelsgesetzbuch*)(HGB) which contains provisions governing commercial partnerships. Special statutes regulate the public company (*Aktiengesetz*) (AG) and the private company (*GmbH-Gesetz*) (GmbH), reorganisations and mergers (*Umwandlungsgesetz*) (UmwG), compositions with creditors (*Vergleichsordnung*), and bankruptcy (*Konkursordnung*). There are also special statutes dealing with insurance, banking, mutual funds, and the Stock Exchange but the the abovementioned list contain the important codes and statutes dealing with German company law.

(i) Types of Business Organisation

8.3.38   Two basic types of legal structures for the formation of a business exist: (i) the partnership; and (ii) the legal corporation or legal entity, of which the most widespread are the limited company and the public limited company. Partnerships include the following categories: (a) General Partnership (oHG); (b) Limited partnership (KG); (c) Silent Partnership; (d) Ship-owning partnership (*Reederei*).

Legal corporations or entities include: (a) the Limited Liability Company(GmbH); (b) the Public Limited company(AG); (c) the Mutual Insurance company (VVaG); (e) the Cooperative Company (eG). There is usually a statutory requirement for most of these companies to be registered in a commercial register (*Handelsregister*) which is kept at the local county court (*Amtsgericht*). Companies which are legal entities come into existence upon registration, whereas partnerships and sole trading companies begin their legal existence as soon as they commence their business. In certain cases, fines may be imposed for non-registration of partnerships and sole traders.

Implementation of recent EEC publicity directives has occasioned another difference between partnerships and legal entities. Legal entities are obliged to publish detailed accounts whereas partnerships are exempt from this requirement.

230

(ii) Partnerships and Sole Traders

8.3.39   The question of whether a single businessman and a partnership fall under the rules of the BGB or the HGB depends on their qualification as a 'merchant' (*Kaufmann*). This is partly dependent on the nature and size of the business. German commercial law is a special law for merchants. The definition of the merchant is therefore the basis of commercial law. The first paragraph of the HGB states: 'For the purpose of the present Code any person exercising a commercial business activity is a merchant' and paragraph 2 then lists business activities regarded as commercial. These are mainly activities concerning dealing (purchase for resale) and transformation (manufacture) of goods and related activities-brokers, bankers, insurers and transporters. A rule of practice appears to be the value of yearly sales, which, if exceeding a certain amount, must be registered (say, DM. 200,000) if they are regarded as qualifying as merchants who must register their business.

Partnerships and sole trading companies are the most utilised forms of organisation for a business in the case of small or medium-sized family companies. Partnerships trade under the names of their partners and it would seem that incorporation is comparatively rarer in Germany than in other countries such as Britain. Partnerships between non-merchants are called BGB *Gesellschaften-civil partnerships*, which is a form that is also available to enterprises who want to form a partnership for a special purpose of short duration. This is often the case with construction businesses or underwriters.

a. Sole Traders

8.3.40   One-man businesses can be run as a one-man limited company (GmbH) or as a sole trader. Minimum capital investment for a GmbH is DM 50,000. Hence, sole trading companies are the norm. Anuone carrying out a business under his or her name can be a sole trader. There is a distinction between 'major' and 'minor' traders (see Bocker *et al* (1992) p.53). The Commercial Code (HGB) only applies to major traders. Minor traders are not allowed to register their company and do not have to comply with the strict requirements of the HGB.

Article 1 of the HGB contains a traditional list of who can be a major trader and among the most important businesses listed are those involved with: (i) buying and selling goods; (ii) trading with securities (excluding land); (iii) manufacturing of goods); (iv) trade representatives.

If other types of trade wish to be registered as major trades, the registrar must be 'satisfied' that the size of the business justifies registration (proceeding on the basis of necessary bookeeping, the employment of several employees and a certain amount of bank credit). Estate agents and building businesses do not traditionally form part of the group of major traders.

Although no restrictions exist for the formation of a sole trading company, two notifications must be made: (a) to the local trade authority; and (b) to the local tax authority. Specialised trades such as auctioneers, brokers, real estate developers, casinos and gambling establishments have to obtain permission from the local trade authority before commencing trading. Fines may be imposed for non-compliance but the legal existence of the particular company is unaffected.

A sole trader must use his own name as his trading name. He may add a supplementary phrase describing the nature of his business such as 'Kurt Wilhelm, Dealer in Quality Watches'. A sole trading company is represented by the proprietor who may confer full commercial powers of attorney to other persons. A sole trading company incurs unlimited personal liability for all debts and obligations which arise in the course of business. Creditors may therefore seize both company assets as well as the sole trader's private assets.

A sale of a trading company may be performed through the transfer of its assets to the purchaser. It is only possible to sell the 'goodwill' and the 'trading name' together with the company. It is therefore possible for the purchaser of the company to continue to use the name of the original proprietor once he has bought the business.

b. Partnerships

8.3.41   There are two main types of commercial partnerships in German law: *limited partnerships*(KG) and *general partnerships* (OHG), both of which are based on the same basic principles. Their main objective is to pursue a business purpose together, pursuant to which each usually makes a financial contribution or a service. It is also possible and reasonable common for a wealthy financial 'backer' to enhance the company's creditworthiness by adding his name to the list of partners.

The liability of the partners will vary according to whether it is a limited or general partnership. All partners will have equal rights, equal standing and full liability in a general partnership but in a limited partnership, some partners may be fully liable while others may limit their liability to a fixed sum.

i. General Partnerships (OHG)

8.3.42   According to the HGB or Commercial Code, a partnership of two or more persons formed for the purpose of running a commercial business under a firm name is a general commercial partnership(OHG), if the personal liability of none of the partners is limited. There must be a partnership agreement which does not restrict the liability of any partner, have a Firm name and the OHG must be registered in the commercial register. An OHG is governed by the terms of its partnership agreement, the relevant provisions of the HGB and the provisions of the BGB if it is a civil partnership above) insofar as they are not modified or excluded by the HGB (see Horn *et al* (1982) p.244).

An OHG, under its firm name, can, in accordance with Article 124 I HGB, acquire rights (including rights over real property), incur liabilities, sue and be sued, although it is not a legal entity and does not have a separate legal personality. Hence an OHG may be a plaintiff or defendant in a court action. Its assets are held by the partners in joint co-ownership and may be seized by the creditors of the OHG pursuant to a judgment against it. Since all partners have equal standing, each of them may represent and conclude contracts on behalf of the company. Contractual provisions for joint representation may be made but such provisions will have to be registered in the commercial register in order to be legally valid in any third party dealings. Any unregistered restrictions will not affect third parties which act in good faith.

Creditors of the general commercial partnership may take legal action against both the partnership as such and against each individual partner. Since, apart from in England, a judgment against the partnership cannot be enforced against a partner and vice versa, it is usually preferable to sue both the company and its most creditworthy partners as joint defendants in order to secure a claim.

A partner is not usually permitted to sell has share ina partnership without the prior permission of all the partners. But it has now become common practice to insert a clause in the articles of associations which allows the sale of partnerships.

ii. Limited Partnerships (KG)

8.3.43   The general partnership may be converted into a limited partnership if some of the partners begin to limit their liability in accordance with Article 170-75 of the HGB. The Firma will then be a commercial business with two types of partner: a general partner and a limited partner. The latter will be personally liable to the creditors of the KG only up to the amount of his unpaid partnership contribution. If he has paid his contribution and not had it paid back to him, he is not liable to them at all (Articles 171-2 HGB). In order to limit the liability of a partner, the partnership contract must name a fixed amount of money which the limited partner is willing to put into the company. This amount has then to be registered and publicised and the liability of that partner will then be limited to the registered amount. The partner concerned need only guarantee future payment with no obligation to pay the set sum immediately. If this is done, the creditors may then sue him directly for payment of the fixed sum.

The general partner will have to remain fully liable and his liability cannot be excluded. Of course, the general partner can also be a limited company (GmbH) in which case the limited partnership is called a GmbH & Co. KG, and will enjoy full limitation of liability. As one group of commentators put it, this entity is 'a German peculiarity because it combines the advantages of limitation of liability with the freedom to organise the company structure in a partnership contract.' (see Bocker *et al* (1992) p.57). The managing director of the GmbH & Co. KG represents this form pf partnership and he will usually hold a share as a limited partner in the KG.

There is also the *'massed partnership'* which is gaining in popularity wherein a large number of limited partners have a holding, which are often styled investment companies or 'writing-off companies'. This final form of company produce yearly losses for their partners which can be written off for purposes of tax.(see Bocker *et al*, p.58).

Limited partners must not consent to the partnership starting business before registration or they will be personally liable without limit to any partnership creditors who had no prior notice of their status as limited partners (Article 171 HGB). They have a limited role in the management of the company's affairs unless the article of association provide differently and they cannot represent the KG unless they have obtained express authority from the general partner to do so, as the general partner is the only official representative of the partnership. They have the right to inspect and check the annual financial statement, have the right to participate in any increase in the internal value of the assets and, subject to the terms of the partnership agreement, may even compete with the partnership.

However, all matters of outstanding importance for the company need to be decided by an assembly of all partners and any clauses which attempt to abolish voting rights of limited partners are void and unenforceable.

iii. The Silent Partnership

8.3.44   Unlike the French version of a silent partnership (see 8.3.32, above) the German version of a silent partnership has remained true to its name, remaining anonymous and secret. The silent partner is not known to the outside world, so that all third party dealings are handled by the owner of the business. It is a *contract* between a financier who acts as silent partner and the proprietor of a mercantile business (individual, partnership or company) whereby the silent partner receives a share in the profits of another persons's business in exchange for his investment in that business. One purpose of such an arrangement might be to provide a member of a family with a source of income without having to involve that person in the management of the business. Creation of a silent partnership can also be a useful to avoid inheritance tax in Germany (which is up to seventy per cent) so that children can accrue considerable assets over many years and not be subject to inheritance tax, if they are made silent partners at an early age (see Bocker *et al* (1992) p.61).

The contract setting up a silent partnership should usually be in writing and the parties may decide the terms on which the arrangement may be made. The silent partner may be made the internal manager of the company by requiring his approval for all external transactions(see Bocker *et al* (1992) p. 60). No registration is required and the company will continue to be run under the name of the proprietor. Third parties will obviously only deal with the proprietor whom they have the right to sue, but the silent investment will be treated as part of the proprietor's assets for these purposes. The silent partner cannot be made personally liable for company debts since there is no privity of contract between silent partner and third parties. (see Bocker *et al, ibid*).

Of course, the partnership may well provide for the silent partner to have rights in the management of the business or participation in the capital appreciation of the business property.

(iv) Limited Companies and Public Limited Companies

a. The Limited Company (GmbH)

8.3.45   The GmbH is probably the most popular form of company in Germany for small to medium sized businesses. Public limited companies(AG) are more suited to the needs of large businesses. They are both corporations which have separate legal personality. There are several advantages enjoyed by the GmbH. First, its shareholders and managers will normally avoid personal liability. Secondly, its articles of association will usually provide it with greater flexibility than the AG in relation to the organisation of the company. Thirdly, it can be owned by a single person and the minimum capital needed to effectg registration is only DM 50,000, up to fifty per cent of which may be inserted by non-cash contributions. Fourthly, it fulfils many functions of an AG but within a much simpler legal structure.

As a result of these advantages, the GmbH is often called 'the joint stock company of the little man' (see Bocker et al (1992)p.61).

As with other corporations and legal entities, the GmbH comes into existence once all the formalities of incorporation have been complied with and upon registration. Before the prescribed procedures have been completed, and full registration has not been effected, something like a quasi-company exists which may commence business but for which there will be no limitation of liability. All founders and other persons dealing on behalf of the company will be strictly liable for all debts incurred before registration (Bocker et al, p.61). Of course, as soon as a GmbH has been registered, its liability is restricted to its assets.

The GmbH operates through the management and the general meeting of the company. Many GmbHs also have an advisory board or some version of a supervisory board. Every GmbH must have one or more business managers who represent it when dealing with third parties. An important point to note is that even if the company contract or resolution limits the company's management powers, this will only be effective in relation to the company and its members. It will have no legal effect on the company's powers of representation in relation to third parties (see Article 37 GmbHG 1892: Law on Limited Liability Companies). As Horn puts it 'This is [a] good example of the distinction so strongly made by the German law of agency between the external relationship-the power of representation-and the internal relationship-the power to manage the business.' (Horn et al (1982) pp.252-3). Again, although internal restrictions may be imposed, it is not possible to limit the power of attorney of the managing director of a GmbH. Hence, any such restrictions would not be enforceable against a third party.

A GmbH comes to an end on the expiry of the period of time provided in the contract of incorporation, on a resolution carried by the majority of the members, on a court decision, on the commencement of bankruptcy proceedings, or on a final determination by the register court that the contract of incoporation is defective (see Article 60 GmbHG; Horn et al,p.257). Of course, the contract of incorporation may also provide its own grounds for dissolution.

b. The Public Limited Company (AG)

8.3.46   There are four hundred and one articles in the Companies Act 1965 (AktG) dealing with the AG which are also more detailed in coverage compared to only eighty-four in the GmbHG. These are more mandatory and offer far less flexibility. This is perhaps understandable when it is realised that their purpose is clearly to protect the general public, especially investors.

The AG has a legal personality and is the only company which has a capital that is divided into shares which can be quoted on the market. The AG's closest equivalent is therefore the British public limited company. At the end of 1987, there were two thousand five hundred such companies registered in Germany while only four hundred and seventy-one of them had their shares quoted on the stock exchange. It is also possible, though very rare, for a one-man AG to be formed. The constitution of an AG is contained in a single company contract and is not split into memorandum and articles of association.

An extremely complicated formation procedure is required, requiring a number of stages, commencing with a minimum of five founders being required to take up the shares and being obliged to draw up the company contract in notarial form. Articles of association must contain shares and capital stock (minimum DM 100,000), the face value and number of the shares, the issue price of the shares (minimum face value), and the shares must be held by the founders. A company contract or constitution must contain: the name and location of the company, the object of the company, and the names of the board of directors. There must then follow another series of stages including the appointment of the supervisory board, auditors, board of directors, a written formation report, submission of a copy of it to the local Chambers of Commerce which will issue a certificate. The application for registration must include: the articles of association; any special privileges which may have been granted, a report on non-cash investments, documentation on the appointment of all board members, a formation report, a copy of the certificate issued by the local Chambers of Commerce, and evidence to show that the sum paid in for the shares is at the free disposal of the board of directors.

The AG will exist as a legal person when it is registered and anyone who acts in the name of the AG before it is properly registered will incur personal liability. (see Article 41 I AktG). As a legal entity, an AG will be liable to all its creditors as such. Any member of the Board of Directors or supervisory board could face personal liability if they violate their obligations.

The Board of management is responsible for conducting the business of the company (article 76 I AktG) and it may act free from any directions from the supervisory board or the shareholders' meeting on how to run the business. Decisions should be taken by mebers of the Board acting jointly or, if the rules permit, by majority decision. (see Horn *et al*,p.259). Under Article 77 of the AktG, decisions by a minority or the chairman of the board are not permissible.

The Board of management also represents the company in court and wherever necessary and its members must usually act jointly in order to represent the company. The scope of the managing board's power of representation cannot be limited, since German law does not have any doctrine of *ultra vires*.

It certainly seems plain that any notion of flexibility or freedom to contract on more *ad hoc* terms has been greatly restricted in pursuance of safeguarding investors and creditors.

(v) The European Economic Industry Grouping(EEIG)

8.3.47 We have already discussed the EEIG in relation to French Company Law . Since 1 July 1989, a new European form of company, the EEIG has existed in all EEC member countries. Germany implemented the EEC Directive No. 2137-85 by means of an EEIG Law which regulates the formation and management of an EEIG in accordance with the Directive. EEIGs are intended to provide a suitable organisational form for joint ventures between small and medium-sized companies from different EEC member states. (see Bocker *et al*(1992),p.69).

In Germany, the EEIG is treated in the same way as a general commercial partnership so that it is not a legal entity but may be the bearer of rights. It acts though its managing directors, who may represent the company either jointly or severally. Each member is usually taxed according to his national tax law but German turnover tax may be applicable. No minimum capital is required to form an EEIG. Since it may therefore lack any assets of its own, all members of an EEIG are fully liable to the company's creditors. (Bocker *et al,ibid*).

(vi) Disclosure Provisions

8.3.48   As a result of recent EEC Directives on disclosure, all large AGs and some very large partnerships are obliged to publish their accounts. Disclosure obligations for smaller partnerships and sole traders have also been amplified. In the case of large partnerships: proceeds from turnover; proceeds from holdings; wages, pension, maintenance costs; valuation methods; and the number of employees have to be published. Profit and loss calculations do not have to be published. On the other hand, all AGs, regardless of their size, must publish the following: their balance sheet; a list of all shareholders; profit and loss calculation; situation report; auditing note; report of the supervisory board; annual profits and proposals and decisions on how to use those profits.

The extent of these obligations might well persuade businesses to opt for a GmbH & Co KG in preference to an AG when planning which company structure to adopt.

E. A COMPARATIVE OVERVIEW OF AGENCY

i. Historical Origins

8.4   The basic concept of agency exists in civil law and common law jurisprudence, and indeed has existed in those jurisdictions since earliest times. Civil law systems of the French pattern find in the contract of agency (*mandat*) the consensual basis for representing another in the process of pre-contractual and contractual negotiations. The contract of *mandat* dates from the Roman law agreement for management of a patrimony: see Ripert and Boulanger *Traite Elementaire de Droit Civil*, vol.II, no.3020 (see further: French law, below). The English common law general principle, recognised from as early as Edward I, is '*Qui facit per alium facit per se*' (any person can act through an agent) was established for obvious reasons of practical convenience. This basic rule was later modified by caselaw and statute. The genesis of agency in early English law is traceable to the relationship of *master and servant*, at least with regard to the history of agency in *tort*.

In the course of the thirteenth century, mercantile necessity and canon law cohered to encourage the fairly rapid rise of agents. Thus the Salman, and later the *feoffee to uses*, was an agent for the transference of property. Similarly the attorney was an agent for purposes of litigation. The records of the medieval courts of the fairs show that a species of commercial agency existed from an early date, and that during the fourteenth and fifteenth centuries the devlopment of trading companies provided further impetus to the need for agents.

Throughout the Middle Ages, *canon law* also encouraged the development of agency since monks, as corporate bodies, needed agents in order to function, communicate, and interact with the outside world. Merchants subsequently borrowed some of the ecclesiastical rules which they then applied to their own agents.

With the rise of negotiable instruments, and forms of banking practice, the commercial doctrine of negotiability was one of the earliest instances of deviation from the primitive concept of each party acting for himself. There was also the influence of the law merchant (*lex mercatoria*) (see next chapter for an account of the historical development of the law merchant), the body of law that developed from the law and practice of the international fairs.

Other early examples of agency in operation were innkeepers and shipowners/carriers. Such persons, either because of their special status (the innkeeper) or their particular circumstances, such as the remoteness of the ship from the control of others, were charged with a special responsibility for the acts of those under their care, or for the goods in their care. They may well have been more in the nature of insurers, but these individuals were held responsible for the loss of goods, or for damage caused thereto by their servants or agents.

The law in Europe therefore recognised from early times that a contract could be made through an agent and that it was the principal and not the agent who would be liable on these contracts, provided they were ratified by the principal.

Further,as mentioned above, since agency derived from the master-servant relationship, agents were seen as a particular class of servant and the sole distinction between 'servant' and 'agent' was to be found in the business in which they were respectively employed. In the last century, however, a split occurred between the law relating to master and servant and that of principal and agent. This was the result of two developments: (i) Commercial growth led to enormous importance being attributed to the principal-agent relationship as a branch of contract law; and (ii) The law of master and servant became inextricably associated with the law of domestic relations.

The key distinction between master and servant, and principal and agent, is that in the latter case, a person becomes the representative of another for the purpose of bringing the principal into a legal contractual relationship with a *third party*. On the other hand, servants were properly those who were employed to perform services subject to the control and direction of their employer/superior. From the sixteenth century onwards, certain classes of agents-brokers and factors-were becoming more closely associated with commercial law. Agency had become essential to the necessities of commerce. There clearly came a time when, in the commercial context, the status of servant was eventually transformed into the higher status of an agent.

Thus agency which began as a *status*, emerged in modern times as founded on *contract* and *consent*.

ii. Modern Agency Law: Common Law v. Civil Law

(i) English Law

8.4.1   We have already noted the relevance of agency to partnerships, given the special significance of partnerships to English law and we have seen that English law places significance on whether an agent has actual authority or only apparent or ostensible authority. Another noteworthy principle is the question of contracts made by the agent on the principal's behalf. In essence, the legal position of the parties will depend on whether the principal was named, disclosed or undisclosed.

If the agent made the contract on behalf of a named principal, the *de jure* contracting parties will be the principal and the third party, the agent being merely a conduit who will drop out of the picture once his work is completed. The principal will be liable provided the agent had express, implied, usual or apparent authority or if he ratifies the agent's acts. The principal may also sue the third party if the agent had actual authority.

Where the agent informs the third party that he is acting on behalf of a principal but does not disclose the identity of the principal, the legal rights and liabilities of the principal and third party are generally the same as with a named principal, but the agent might nevertheless be liable on a contract if:

(i) he signs the contract in such a way as to assume personal responsibility; this will usually be the case if the agent is sued on a written contract wherein he appears as a contracting party; or

(ii) on the facts of the case, the court decides that this is the correct inference to be drawn.

The agent's personal liability may ultimately depend on the particular interpretation or construction that is placed on the contract in question.

(ii) German Law

8.4.2   In German law (ie West German law which is applicable to the newly unified Germany, since 3 October 1990), the basic concept of agency (*Stellvertretung*) is very similar to that of English law. However, although several *de facto* varieties of agency exist in Germany, which include disclosed and undisclosed agency, strictly speaking, German law does not recognise undisclosed agency in the sense that the agent must act in the name of the principal before any legal significance will be attached to the acts of the agent: paragraph 164 (II) BGB. This is because under paragraph 164 (I) of the BGB, an agent (*Stellvertreter*) is a person whose conduct in transactions, wherein making and receiving declarations of will occur, has a direct legal effect on the position of the principal (*Vertretener*).

i. The Disclosed Agency

8.4.3 The reference to 'disclosure' is to the name or even existence of the principal in dealings between agent and third party. Where the agent reveals he is acting for someone else, this becomes a disclosed or proper agency, and the principal has usually to be named. *Two contracts* are therefore involved in a disclosed agency, one between the agent and the third party, the other between agent and principal which transfers the rights obtained from the third party to the principal.

If the agent does not reveal he is acting on behalf of someone else, this is an undisclosed agency since the principal remains unknown and German law does not recognise any privity of contract between principal and third party.

ii. The Commission Agent

8.4.4 Of course, there are clearly situations in which an agent does act for an *undisclosed principal*, such as the *agency for commission*. This involves a person who is an independent merchant under paragraph 1 (II) no.6: Commercial Code (HGB) whose business consists of buying and selling goods or securities in his own name on the account of another, called the *Kommittent*, whereby he earns his commission: paragrpah 383 HGB. This type of *commission agent* is called a *Kommissionar* and since he acts in his own name, the agency (and principal) is undisclosed so that this is not recognised as agency in German law.

There seems to be three contracts involved in the *Kommissionar*'s business: (i) the contract of commission between *Kommittent* (the principal) and *Kommissionar* (commission agent) whereby the *Kommittent* engages the *Kommissionar* to buy or sell specific goods for a commission. This comes under paragraph 675 BGB, for which the HGB has special rules under paragraphs 383-405; (ii) the contract of sale entered into between *Kommissionar* and third party, performed by the transfer of the object of the sale. Since there is no direct contact and no privity of contract between *Kommittent* and customer, the *Kommissionar* will usually acquire ownership of all goods purchased on behalf of the *Kommittent*; (iii) there is the transfer of ownership of the goods from agent to principal, or an assignment of his right to claim delivery of the goods from the third party.

In general terms, the commission agent must carry out the business with care and safeguard the interests of his principal, submit accounts or transfer any proceeds of sale to the principal: paragraph 384 HGB. Where the commission agent makes a personal intervention which is not strictly within the terms of the commission contract, his duty to account and safeguard the principal's interests will be satisfied by showing that he kept to the market or exchange price. If the commission agent does go beyond the *Kommittent*'s instructions, this will be permissible only if he can prove that the final outcome is more favourable to the *Kommittent* than it would otherwise have been.

(iii) French Law

8.4.5   Today, *mandat* in French law is the agreement pursuant to which a person is authorised to enter into certain acts of legal significance *actes juridiques* ('acts in the law') on behalf and in the name of another. *Actes juridiques* are actions or expressions of will which are intended to alter the legal position of its author. There is no general treatment of agency (also referred to as 'representation') in the Civil Code but, as in Germany, there are commercial agents, independent agents and commission agents. A *commercial agent* is an individual who carries on 'ordinarily' and 'independently' and 'professionally' (and otherwise than as an employee) the negotiation or conclusion of contracts for the sale, purchase or letting on lease or hire of goods or other property or the provision of services, for and on behalf of manufacturers, producers or merchants: see Article 1 of the Decree of 23 December 1958. The Decree makes a clear distinction between the commercial agent (*commissionaire*) and the commission agent, to the effect that the former is a representative whereas the latter acts in his own name on behalf of a principal (*commettant*).

As a general proposition, the principal is bound only within the limits of the power or authority granted to the agent: see Article 1989: Civil Code, which is similar to the English common law position. However, an agent may be liable to third parties in cases where he has not revealed the full extent or scope of his authority: see Article 1997: Civil Code.

a. Commercial Agents and Commission Agents

8.4.6   As far as *commercial agents* are concerned, the principal will only be liable to third parties for the acts of these agents if these were made within the scope of the commercial agent's authority. However, a *commission agent* is *a party to the contract* which he transacts on his principal's behalf so that he becomes *personally liable to third parties with whom he contracts*. Since a principal is not a party to the contract made by a commission agent, third parties cannot bring an action against the principal if they wish to have the contract performed. Of course, the corollary to this is that the principal has no direct action against third parties. Nevertheless, an indirect action may be allowed (*action oblique*) subrogating the plaintiff to the claims of the agent against his principal or against the other party to the contract: see Article 1166: Civil Code.

b. Agents and Apparent Authority

8.4.7   As in German and English law, an important issue in French law relating to agency is the scope of an agent's apparent or ostensible authority. Since there has been no express Code provision on this matter, court decisions have had to determine this matter. Earlier cases relied upon the Article 1382 concept of fault (*faute*) as the basis of the principal's liability to an innocent third party. More modern cases suggest that, as in English law, initially an objective test must be applied, namely: would a reasonable person come to the conclusion, on an objective view of the particular circumstances, that the agent had the requisite authority to act as he proposed to do? If the answer was yes, it was then to be ascertained whether the plaintiff's mistaken reliance or belief in the agent's authority justifiable or 'legitimate'? It would appear that if these two questions could be answered in the affirmative, the burden would then be placed on the principal to disprove the justification for assuming the existence of apparent authority, even if there was an absence of fault on his part.

The courts appear to be adopting a policy of protecting a third party who acts in good faith, provided there was nothing in the nature of the transaction to arouse the suspicion of that third party. (see *Societe Civ. Immob. Les Genevriers* v. *Bonnin*, Cass. Civ. 29 April, 1969, 1970 D.S. Jur. 23; and *Societe Minsallier et cie.* v. *Societe Lambert et Freres*, Cass. Comm., 29 April, 1970, JCP. 1971. II.16694)

iii. Comparative Analysis of Agency

8.4.8   The institution of Agency or Representation has certainly became an indispensable part of modern commercial life. Modern technological developments have changed the context in which agency relationships exist, especially where intricate relationships are involved. With the advent of instantaneous transmission of documents through the use of facsimile machines, agents are receiving far more closer scrutiny than before, but there is also the possibility of a speedy response to changes in commercial conditions, and perhaps less possibility of misunderstanding of contractual intent. The German system of making the agent's power independent of the contractual relationship between principal and agent and of emphasising this independence in the system of the Code has had a considerable influence on all civil law countries. It has, for instance been adapted into the Swiss Civil Code and the Italian Civil Code.

F. EUROPEAN COMMUNITY CORPORATE LAW

i. The Notion of European Community (EC) Law

8.5   EC corporate law is but one component of the many institutions created by the internal market (see Chapter 5 for an overview of EC law). It is 'that part of Community law which enables companies to do business across frontiers in the internal market and which enables third parties to deal with them secure in the knowledge that they may do so within a framework of common standards.' (Richards: (1991)) Thus, it consists of the creation of a business environment favourable for corporate enterprise and a set of standards of protection for those engaged in corporate dealings. The EEC Treaty provisions embody the spirit of these abovementioned objectives. Article 52 enables nationals of one member State to establish themselves in another State, without any of the traditional barriers. This includes the right to set up agencies, branches or subsidiaries. The right to set up and manage undertakings is also included in the definition of freedom of establishment.

Article 58 specifies the legal persons that benefit from rights of establishment. The relevant criteria, as set out in Article 58(1) require companies or firms to be formed in accordance with the law of the Member State and to have *either* (a) their registered office, or (b) their central administration or (c) principal place of business to be within the Community.

Article 58(2) then specifies the types of companies and firms that would qualify under the legislation, namely those 'constituted under civil or commercial law, including co-operative societies, and other legal persons governed by private or public law' *except for those which are non-profit making.* (author's emphasis)

(ii) The Daily Mail Case

8.5.1   The *Daily Mail Case* (Case 81/87 *R v. H.M. Treasury and Commissioners of Inland Revenue, ex p. Daily Mail and General Trust plc* [1988] ECR 5483) which was decided by the European Commission ruled, *inter alia*, that despite the defintion of Article 58, Member States stll have the right to impose fiscal and other requirements on the transfer of the company from one Member State to another without these necessarily constituting a breach of the rights of establishment. Further clarifying legislation may therefore be required.

(iii) Non-Profit-making Undertakings

8.5.2   In relation to non-profit making undertakings, the EC Commission has never adopted a restrictive view of this aspect. What should be the approach to those undertakings dealing with health, pensions and insurance which often operate as co-operatives or mutualised companies? If their primary purpose is to reduce costs to their members rather than to make profits for distribution, it would appear to be unduly harsh to classify or regard them as profit-making enterprises simply because they may incidentally make profits. If no clarification is made of the legal position of such enterprises, it will be left to the courts to demarcate the boundaries of acceptable commercial activity. The interim uncertainty is not conducive to true freedom of establishment.

(iv) Removal of Restrictions on Freedom of Movement

8.5.3   A General Programme to remove restrictions on the freedom of establishment was adopted on 15 January 1962, pursuant to Article 54 which provides for such a programme to be adopted. Article 54 thus supplements Article 58 so that companies which rely only on the 'registered office' requirement for qualifying under Article 58, must also show that they have a tangible link with the economy of a Member State.

(v) Statutory Foundations of Harmonisation of Laws

8.5.4   Various objectives in the pursuit of abolition of barriers to freedom of establishment are defined in Article 54 but the key Article is *Article 54(3) (g)* which enunciates the task of "co-ordinating to the necessary extent the safeguards which, for the protection of the interests of members and others, are required by Member States of companies and firms...with a view to making such safeguards equivalent throughout the Community." This Article has been used as *the legal foundation of the entire harmonisation programme* and the tenor of it suggests that minority shareholders, creditors, employees (ie,company participants and third parties) will continue to be protected by each country's legislation on company law.

Harmonisation of the companies of the financial sector is dealt with by Article 57 which encourages the coordination of the provisions laid down by the Member States with regard to taking up and pursuing activities as self-employed persons.

(vi) Nature of EC Company Law

8.5.5   The Treaty framework provides for two main legal instruments which are available to the legislator, excepting Conventions and Recommendations. These are: the *Directive* and the *Regulation* whereby the Community can create legal entities and means of Incorporation. The Community may adopt directives to implement changes in national or domestic company laws. These directives have a binding effect as to the result but leaves the national authorities the choice of form and methods: Article 189(3): EEC Treaty. A Member State may be brought before the European Court of Justice if a directive is not incorporated into national law within the stipulated period: Article 169: EEC Treaty.

A regulation is binding in every material particular and is directly applicable in all Member States: Article 189(2): EEC Treaty. In the context of Company law, the principle of immediate application of directives is somewhat less significant. Company law proposals require the two reading process before the European Parliament, and the experience so far of the EEIG Regulation indicates that complementary domestic legislation will usually be a prerequisite to the smooth integration and transition of a particular Regulation into national law. Richards (1991) highlights the variety of provisions that are contained in the directives:

(i) Certain provisions set a minimum (eg the minimum capital requirement for plcs:25,000), beyond which the Member States are free to go, but they must respect the overall objectives of each provision;

(ii) Member States may sometimes be given alternative means of achieving the same result(eg the accounting directives);

(iii) Member States may have an option as to whether to do something or not; they will, of course, then have to observe the rules which regulate the particular option.

(iv) Company law is also unusual in having a wholly optional directive;

(v) The directives sometimes prescribe a minimal margin for manoeuvre.

244

The question arises as to whether these directives are too complicated to be readily usable for Member States. It is as well to bear in mind that a clearly structured framework is better than no framework and that Article 54(3)(g) requires the Community to co-ordinate safeguards 'to the necessary extent'.

(vii) Directives already in force in UK

8.5.6   Directives which have already been implemented in the United Kingdom are now contained in the 1985 and 1989 Companies Acts as follows:
(a) Directives in the Companies Act 1985, are:
  (i) The First Directive (1968) on co-ordination of safeguards
     required by companies; this includes amendments to the
     ultra vires rule;
  (ii) The Second Directive (1976) dealing with the maintenance
     and alteration of public company capital; and
  (iii) The Fourth Directive (1978) dealing with company
     accounts.

(b) Directives in the Companies Act 1989, are:
  (i) The Seventh Directive (1983) dealing with consolidated
     accounts; and
  (ii) The Eighth Directive (1984) which lays down audit
     regulations and minimum qualifications for auditors.
Other directives on prospectuses, mergers and divisions, admission of securities to listing and disclosure of information have also been implemented through the utilisation of delegated legislation such as the Companies (Mergers and Divisions) Regulations 1987 and the Stock Exchange (Listing) Regulations 1984.

G. COMPARATIVE CORPORATE LAW: CONCLUSIONS

8.6   As we have seen, the term 'company' refers to different legal entities in French, German and English law, and thus between civil law and common law jurisdictions. The difference between partnership and company in English law is not merely terminological but is substantively different. Both civil law and common law jurisdictions have some form of sleeping/silent partner on the premise of a someone who provides capital in return for a share of the profits but plays either a minimal part or no part in the management of the partnership/company.
The sheer flexibility, inventiveness and adaptability of the various forms of the company/partnerships appear to strike a balance between serving the needs of its managers, its members and the demands of commercial fairness. It is the variety of forms which demonstrates the similarity of response on both sides of the English Channel and the perceived need for such variety to continue to exist to cope with the rapidly changing commercial world.
However, the EC directives do not always seem to recognise this fact and only the accounting directives appear to deal directly with this divergence by using a size criterion rather than a terminological one. Some EC corporate law directives apply indiscriminately to all forms of limited company while

others refer specifically to plcs. Whereas the SA would be the most conventional type of corporate legal entity in France, the vast majority of companies in Germany and the UK are private limited companies. The EC is also looking into the best way of allowing other associations such as co-operatives to participate in the internal market.

There is clearly the hope that Europe is heading towards a 'greater mutual recognition of national laws on the one hand combined with more sharply targeted instruments on the other...and the European Company Statute falls squarely within this type of approach' (Richards (1991)). However, in the light of the ongoing Maastricht Treaty negotiations, there would seem to be some distance to go yet before we can be realistically sanguine about true harmonisation and widespread cooperation in corporate and commercial law.

SELECTIVE BIBLIOGRAPHY

Le Gall (ed. Pennington) FRENCH COMPANY LAW (1974)

Wurdinger (ed. Pennington) GERMAN COMPANY LAW (1975)

Horn, Kotz & Leser GERMAN PRIVATE AND COMMERCIAL LAW (1982)

Tunc 'A French Lawyer Looks at British Company Law' (1982)
    45 Mod.L.R. 1

Raiser,T 'The Theory of Enterprise Law in the Federal Republic of Germany' (1988) Am. JCL 111

Teubner, G. 'Enterprise Corporatism: New Industrial Policy and the Essence of the Legal Person' (1988) Am. JCL 130

Farrar et al FARRER'S COMPANY LAW (1990)

Drury & Xuereb (eds.) EUROPEAN COMPANY LAWS (1991)

Bentley et al CORPORATE LAW: THE EUROPEAN DIMENSION (1991)

Maitland-Hudson   FRANCE: PRACTICAL COMMERCIAL LAW (1992)

Bocker et al GERMANY: PRACTICAL COMMERCIAL LAW (1992)

Richards, H: 'What is EC Corporate Law?' in CORPORATE LAW (1991)
    (above),p.1

Murray 'New Concepts in Corporate Law' in CORPORATE LAW (1992)
    (above) p.17

Werlauff 'The Development of Community Company Law' (1992)
    Eur.LR 207

CHAPTER NINE

Sale of Goods

A. INTRODUCTION

9.0   A sale of goods is possibly the most common type of commercial transaction in practically every country in the world. This area of law is predominantly regulated by statutes or codes, supplemented by caselaw, in both the civil law and common law world. It derives from the *lex mercatoria* (law merchant) or ancient mercantile law (the body of law that developed from international fairs and mercantile practice: see, below, at 9.1.1). and is today generally classified as a body of law within 'Commercial Law.' However, there are significant differences between English law, German law and French law on the basic approach towards the sales of goods. There are, of course, many reasons for this, despite common features of mercantile law having been absorbed into both common law and civil law systems. The current European statutes are all based on creations of the nineteenth century and there is little doubt that they were products of their time. The French Civil Code of 1804, the English Sale of Goods Act 1893 and the German Civil Code of 1896 all reflect the notion of freedom of contract or the 'autonomy of the parties.' However, in French law, for instance, there is no distinction drawn between the sale of goods and sales of any other type of property, whereas the English common law approach does draw such a distinction. French law treats all sales under the single head of *vente*, which is governed by the general rules stated in Title 6 of Book III of the French Civil Code. However, there are special rules for sales of particular kinds of property, the rules of which are contained in separate legislation. As one might have expected, German law deals with sales of goods in its Civil Code (paragraphs 433-515) but this should be read together with the entire first part of the Code and the General part of the Law of Obligations and the General part of the BGB. If the sale is a commercial one, provisions of the German Commercial Code will also apply. The Law on General Conditions of Business (AGBG 1976) and the Law on Instalment Contracts (AbzG: 1894) are both also relevant to sales as well as the all-embracing general principle of good faith (paragraph 242: BGB).

German law contains elements of Roman law, Germanic law and the *lex mercatoria*. Most of the principles of German contract law come from the German law of sale, an extrapolation which had already begun by the nineteenth century and the time of the Pandectists (see Chapter 3). Their agreement of sale concept is also based on the fundamental principle of freedom of contract.

For a variety of historical reasons, the English law of sales of goods is today a combination of statute and caselaw, predominantly based on the law of contract but also imbued with distinctive features inherited from its rich and colourful history.

B. THE HISTORICAL BACKGROUND

i. Sale of Goods in Roman Law

9.1   In Roman law, the rule was *'periculum rei venditae nindum traditae est emptoris'* which meant that the risk of a thing sold but not yet delivered is on the buyer. Sale - *emptio venditio* - was a contract but never effected transfer of property. When the *emptio* was *perfecta* (ie when identity, quality and quantity of the thing had been ascertained and the price had been settled, and when all all suspensive conditions (if any) had been fulfilled: Lawson (1949)) the risk fell upon the buyer. Subsequently if the subject-matter of the sale was destroyed, the buyer was nevertheless bound to pay the price and, if he paid in advance he could not recover his payment. The Romans regarded the transfer of property (or ownership) in a sale of goods as an exception to the general principle of *res perit domino* (the risk of destruction falls upon the owner of a thing). Hence, as regards a specific thing of which future delivery has been promised, Roman law took the view that the agreement only produced an obligation that the seller shall convey the thing to the buyer. Indeed, the process of transference of the property (in the sense of *ownership*) in the goods by sale was seen as consisting of two distinct parts: (i) the contract or agreement to transfer regulated by the law of obligations; and (ii) tradition by which the transference is completed, which constituted the right of property. Germany and the Netherlands follow the Roman law but France, Italy and English common law see 'property' in the sense of ownership or title, passing by the fact of agreement, that is, when the contract has been formed (or 'concluded', in the civil law parlance). Since there was no 'reception' of Roman law in England, in the manner in which it occurred in civil law countries and Scotland, there is no strong Roman law presence in the English law relating to sales of goods, although any features it has in common with French law are attributable in part to its *lex mercatoria* inheritance.

ii. The Law Merchant

9.1.1   The intermingling of concepts and experience in commercial law is not a new phenomenon. The historical development of the law merchant or ancient mercantile law may be divided into two distinct phases:

(i) The Law Merchant of the Middle Ages; and
(ii) The period of National Codifications.

There was also the impact of nationalism and the influence of the leading doctrinal writers of the nineteenth century.

(i) The Middle Ages

9.1.2   In the Middle Ages, international commercial law evolved in the form of 'a body of international customary rules governing the cosmopolitan community of international merchants who travelled through the civilised world from port to port and fair to fair' (Schmitthoff: 1968). The prevailing legal situation of the time has been described by one historian as one that developed from the 'law of the fairs born of the peace of commerce' that was 'acting strongly on institutions under the ordinary law still imbued with its ancient rigours' (Huvelin: 1895).

It is now reasonably well established that this body of law was virtually universal and that the jurisdiction of the fairs extended to all parts of the known trading world. The international character of mercantile law was and remains its distinguishing feature. In the Middle Ages, this 'internationalism' was brought about mainly by the unifying effect of the law of the fairs, the universality of the customs of the sea, the special courts dealing with commercial disputes and the activities of the notary public, who handled a great deal of commercial legal work (see Schmitthoff :1968).

A unique feature of this first phase of development is that international merchants themselves sat in the courts of 'pie powder'(or 'dusty feet') and administered courts at various ports which had 'half-tongue juries' (so named becaused these juries consisted of one-half of native and the other half of foreign merchants). The piepowder courts were so known because the word started as a nickname but came to be known as the official style of the court. Its origins have been variously explained. Coke (Coke, *Fourth Institute*,p.272) believed the name originated because justice was administered as speedily as the dust could fall from the feet of litigants but Cross (Cross *Select Cases of the Law Merchant* (S.S.) i, xiii,xiv) was of the opinion that 'piepowder' referred to the dust on the clothes and boots of the itinerant merchants who used the court. Derivation apart, it seems clear that these courts administered a form of speedy justice, a fact which highlighted the tardiness of the common law courts. Merchants whose livelihood depended on speedy resolution of matters did not relish the stately and contemplative progress of the common law courts and preferred to sort out their affairs as soon as possible.

Thus, the mercantile law of this period was developed by the international business community itself and not by lawyers. By 1622, in England, Chief Justice Herbert could say: 'The custom of merchants is part of the common law of this Kingdom of which judges ought to take notice; and if any doubt arise as to them about their custom they may send for the merchants to know their customs'. Out of this early period came commercial institutions like the bill of exchange, the bill of lading, the charterparty and even the commercial corporation. As Schlesinger (1900) put it, 'the law merchant by the end of the medieval period had become the very foundation of an expanding commerce throughout the Western world.'

(ii) National Codifications

9.1.3   The second phase of development of the law merchant lasted from the 17th to the 19th century, during which this cosmopolitan and universal law merchant was incorporated into the national laws of various jurisdictions. In *England*, this transformation and incorporation of the mass of commercial usages into the common law was undertaken by Lord Mansfield (1756-1788), when sitting at Guildhall in the City of London with his special jurymen, whom he also met out of court. By clearly stating in his judgments the general principles on which he based his decisions, he gradually managed to give definite form and substance to what became a distinctive and recognisable system of mercantile law. In 1893, the English Sale of Goods Act was passed, which has served as a model or protoype to many countries, European and non-European. In France and Germany, national codifications of commercial law were also undertaken. In France, Colbert, the minister of Louis XIV carried out his codification on a national scale. His two ordinances, the *'ordinance sur le commerce'* (1673) and *'ordinance de la marine'* (1681) paved the way for Napoleon's *Code de Commerce* of 1807. German codification occurred only in the nineteenth century. In 1834, the *Zollverein* sponsored a Uniform German Bills of Exchange Act (promulgated in 1848) and in 1861, the German Confederation adopted a Uniform Commercial Code which was the precursor of the German Commercial Code of 1897.
  Despite these early codifications, however, commercial law retained its international flavour and the antecedents of the law merchant and Roman law, have survived through the ages. As a result of these developments, commercial institutions which benefited directly were negotiable instruments, insurance and carriage by sea and forms of sales contract were created such as f.o.b. and c.i.f. (see below English law: 9.4.9) as well as bankers' commercial credits which have become the most frequently used method of payment in the export trade.

(iii) Influence of Nationalism and Contemporary Writers

9.1.4   In the eighteenth century, legal thinkers in Europe had already expressed the need to codify the law to make it more homogeneous and accessible. Adam Smith's book, *The Wealth of Nations* (1776) which included a number of liberalist ideas also included freedom of contract as a concept. Many of his ideas were accepted in France even before the French Revolution and undoubtedly had an impact on the lawyers who drafted the *Code Napoleon*. Before this, of course, the School of Natural Law had dominated

250

legalistic thinking in the seventeenth and eighteenth centuries, and this particular philosophy also argued that the contract alone should decide the legal effects of agreements and transactions. Furthermore, the Roman law heritage never completely left the scene as far as French law was concerned, and the nineteenth century Pandectists also left their mark on German legal philosophy. But it was not until the nineteenth century that codification actually took place in the wake of the emergence of a wave of nationalism and independence, and the new Nation States of Europe, such as Italy, Austria, Switzerland and Germany. By the end of the eighteenth and beginning of the nineteenth century, largely through the efforts of Lord Mansfield, the modern English law of sale came into its own as a distinct body of law. Many principles of law which were established in the preceding century were embodied in the English Sale of Goods Act of 1893. Even the United States originally adopted a Uniform Sales Act based on the 1893 Act which was only superseded in 1951 by their Uniform Commercial Code, which has retained many of the English ideas and juridical components.

C. KEY ISSUES IN SALES OF GOODS

9.2   As far as civil law and common law countries are concerned, the main issues that arise in relation to sales of goods are related to: (i) The Legal Effects of the Contract of Sale on the Transfer of Ownership and Risk; (ii) Rights and Obligations of the Seller and Buyer under the Contract of Sale (iii) Warranties as to Fitness of the goods (v) Remedies of the parties. It should be remembered that up to now, or at least in 1992, Socialist systems of law have had a totally different view of contracts of sale. Since the adoption of a Marxist/Leninist ideology in several European countries, China and the former USSR, the contract of sale has been seen there as merely a further device which assists in promoting and implementing the purposes of the State economic plan. However, in view of the collapse of the former USSR and the increasing decline of communism in several Eastern European countries, it is certainly likely that the Westernisation and democratisation of the contract of sale is about to happen. The newly formed Russian Commonwealth of Independent States has already begun to implement economic changes which are intended to introduce a more 'capitalist-oriented' society which signals the beginning of a new era of private ownership.

D. COMPARATIVE STUDY OF EUROPEAN CIVIL LAW COUNTRIES

i. French Law

(i) Transfer of Ownership

9.3   In French law, a commercial contract of sale will be subject to certain special rules found in the Civil Code, Commercial Code and in separate legislation (cf. L. 13.6.1866). Proof in commercial contracts is governed by article 109 of the Commercial Code which which states the general rule that oral evidence is admissible in any commercial matter in which the court thinks fit to admit it. With regard to the legal effects of a transfer of goods, once the goods have been ascertained and the price agreed upon, *the effect of the conclusion (formation) of a contract of sale is that of immediately transferring the property in the goods to the purchaser*. This rule will operate unless the parties have expressly or impliedly agreed to postpone the transfer of title: art. 1583: Civil Code. If there is a proposed sale of goods which have yet to be ascertained, then the property does not pass until specific goods have been appropriated to the contract. In French terminology, there is a need for 'individualisation' of the goods. If there is a contract for the sale of goods 'on approval' then again the property or right of ownership in the goods does not pass by reason of the 'conclusion' of the contract, until the buyer has signified his approval of the goods.

(ii) Responsibility for Risk of Loss

9.3.1   The question of who bears the 'risk' (of loss, damage or deterioration of the goods) in relation to the goods depends on the particular circumstances involved and the particular arrangement that the parties have entered into. If the contract has been concluded (formed) the buyer would normally bear these risks, even though they have not yet been delivered since conclusion of the contract itself transfers the property in the goods to the buyer: art. 1138: Civil Code. Of course, if the goods have not yet been appropriated to the contract or where the parties have expressly or impliedly agreed to depart from the principle of the Code, or it is the seller's fault that they have been damaged, the risk of loss or damage remains with the seller. Similarly, the risk is borne by the seller if he delays in making delivery: art. 1138: Commercial Code. On the question of future or generic goods, ownership and risk will pass when the goods are ready (*achevee*) for delivery to the buyer in accordance with the contract. Thus a quantity of rice ordered by the buyer, once put into sacks and labelled with the buyer's name signifies that ownership and risk of loss have then passed to the buyer. If goods are bought *en bloc*, with reference to the place where they are stored, they are then at the buyer's risk until delivery provided the seller is not negligent in his care of them. Once goods that have been specifically ordered have been delivered to a carrier, they are then at the buyer's risk, but the buyer retains a right to damages if the goods are then lost or damaged. Goods that require weighing and measuring before delivery will remain at the seller's risk until they have been weighed and measured: art. 1585: Civil Code. It is important to bear in mind that all these rules may be overriden by the parties themselves, as already indicated. The parties have a free rein in deciding when the passing of ownership or risk should take place and may agree that the seller shall remain owner until he has been paid. These agreements are regulated by the Law of 12 May 1980 which deals with cases of the buyer's bankruptcy. An appeal court has ruled that a seller can rely on a retention of title clause even though the buyer did not give his written consent to such a clause and that the risk of loss or damage remains with the seller until the price is paid: *Cour* *d'Appel de Metz*, 29 October 1980. It should also be noted that French law differs from the Hague Convention on International Sales of Goods 1964, which supports the German approach (see below).

(iii) Rights and Obligations of Buyers and Sellers

9.3.2   The seller has a duty to deliver the goods sold as soon as the contract is concluded: para. 1138: Civil Code. Of course, the seller's duty to deliver ceases if the buyer fails to pay for the goods on the agreed day (in the case of non-credit transactions) or if he becomes bankrupt: arts. 1612-3: Civil Code. *Delivery* takes place when the goods are transferred into the control and possession of the buyer: art. 1604: Civil Code. The seller also has a duty to guarantee that the buyer is protected against any undisclosed rights of third parties over the goods.: art. 1138: Civil Code. The buyer is obliged to pay the price and expenses and to take delivery of the goods. Payment should be made at the time and place of delivery, unless the parties have agreed to the contrary. If the contract does not specify where delivery is to be made, it must be at the place where the goods are when the contract is made: art. 1609: Civil Code. When goods are not delivered at the agreed time, the buyer has a right to seek *cancellation of the contract*: art.1184: Civil Code or apply for delivery to be enforced under article 1610. The seller may have to pay damages and interest in any event (art. 1610-1) but if there is no agreed stipulation by the parties on this point, the court may decide the time for delivery: Cas.Civ. 4.4. 1973.

9.3.3   Under article 1641 of the Civil Code, the seller warrants that the buyer is protected against *hidden defects* which make the goods unfit for their purpose or reduce their usefulness to such an extent that the buyer would not have bought them or would have paid a lower price had he known of their existence. Thus *four conditions* are required to activate this provision:
(i) the defects must have been hidden (*vives caches*) and not apparent on reasonable inspection; second-hand goods might not necessarily be covered on the basis that their defects are attributable to their used condition: Civ. 10.7.1956, D. 1956.719; Civ. sect. com. 11.6.1954, D.1954.697.
(ii) the buyer was unaware of them; this will not apply if the defect is so common that the buyer ought to have been aware of it (such as certain types of antique furniture whose antiquity and susceptibility to disintegration have been and are often wrongly assessed even by experts) in which case the buyer must prove his ignorance of the defect. A usual practice to forestall this occurrence is for the buyer to require the insertion into the contract of the clause 'seller undertakes to supply goods free from defects.' for classes of things especially prone to defects.
(iii) the defects lessen the fitness or usefulness of the goods;
the criterion used is not an aesthetic one, only economic.
(iv) the defects antedated the sale; unless, of course, some evidence of such defects was already present at the time of the sale.

All sellers, whether or not they act in the course of a business, are 'caught' by article 1641. However, French law distinguishes between the professional and non-professional seller in the extent of their liability for defective goods. The professional seller is deemed to have been aware of the faults and will be liable in damages for physical injury and economic loss, whereas the non-professional seller will be obliged only to take back the goods and repay the price (*action redhibitoire*: action for rescission) or repay a part of it if the buyer keeps the goods (*action estimatoire*) unless he was aware of their defects. Either action must be brought promptly since the Code mentions allowance for a 'a brief delay' which may be tolerated depending on the nature of the defects and the custom of the place where the sale was made. The court has a discretion to simply disallow a claim that has been delayed unreasonably. The buyer may still have a remedy if the merchandise delivered does not correspond with the seller's express or implied description of its quality. If the seller was aware of the defects, the buyer may rescind the contract and claim damages on the ground of fraud (*dol*).

Irrespective of the good or bad faith of the seller and regardless of any undertaking the seller might have given, the buyer may rescind on the ground of an *erreur sur la substance* under article 1110 of the Civil Code. Claims under this Article must be made within 5 years of the discovery of the mistake. This type of error exists where the buyer can prove that he was mistaken as to the substantial quality of the merchandise sold; substantial quality would mean that quality which goes to the essence of the thing the buyer wished to acquire in making the purchase. It refers to the identity of the thing which is the basis of the decision to enter into the contract. A relatively recent case in French law involved the seller who wrongly believed that he was selling a painting in the style of Poussin but not by him. On realising the painting was actually by Poisson, he was allowed to avoid the contract: *Cour d'Appel de Versailles*, 7 January, 1987.

The test applied under art. 1110 is entirely subjective in contrast to art. 1641 which applies an objective test. A final point is that irrespective of whether the contract is nullified, a party may be ordered to pay damages if he was to blame for the other's mistake, or acted fraudulently or in bad faith.

9.3.4   On the question of *exclusion clauses*, the *Loi Scrivener*-Law of 10 January 1978 has been passed to give the government very wide powers to issue decrees to control unfair clauses. Under the decree of 24 March 1978 clauses excluding or limiting consumers' rights against sellers who are in breach of contract may no longer be inserted into contracts. Additionally, clauses entitling sellers unilaterally to change the characteristics of the goods or services contracted for, are also forbidden. A second decree has established a model standard form for contracts of guarantee and after-sales service relating to domestic electrical equipment: see Decree of 22 December 1987. Another law, the Law of 5 January 1988, enables approved consumer organisations to prohibit the use of particular forms of words in traders' standard form contracts with consumers.

9.3.5   The contractual action known as *action directe*, which is unique to French law, may be used where there has been a series of sales of the same thing. At any stage in the chain of sales, a buyer may sue any previous seller, up to and including the manufacturer, for breach of warranty, despite the absence of any contract between them. This has developed from the basic warranty rule embodied in art. 1641, and the basis of *action directe* is that each successive sale implies a transfer of all rights of action relating to the thing sold. Hence, the warranty is attached to or is part of the thing sold, so that each successive buyer has the rights of each seller against the previous seller: Cass. Civ., 12 November 1884. If the person sued is not the first seller in the chain, that person will have an *action recursoire* against any previous seller; and this will continue, back to the first seller. Claims for breach of warranty should usually be made within a 'short time': art. 1648. Six to twelve months is the usual acceptable time after discovery of the fault.

9.3.6   Articles 1382-4 enunciate general remedies for any injured party who is unable to establish any contractual or quasi-contractual right. Under Article 1384 every act or omission which damages another person must be paid for by the person at fault. But French case law has ruled that mere delivery of goods which are not reasonably safe is sufficient to prove fault, unless the supplier can prove that the defect was caused by a stranger or Act of God. Suppliers are vicariously liable for their employees' defective workmanship and also as 'guardians' of things under their control. Physical control is usually the basis of this rule but there may arguably be liability for defective design or production.

(iv) Remedies of Buyer and Seller

9.3.7   If the seller has not been paid, he may, of course, sue for the payment and cancellation of the contract but in addition, has four special remedies :
(i)   a lien on the goods (*droit de retention*);
(ii) a right to take possession (*droit de revendication*);
(iii) a prior charge on the goods (*privilege*); and
(iv) a right of rescission (*resolution*);

9.3.8   The *lien of the unpaid seller* entitles the seller to refuse to deliver the goods so long as he has not been paid the price: Article 1612: Civil Code. He is, however, deemed to waive this right where it was provided in the contract that the buyer should be allowed credit. Nevertheless, if the buyer becomes insolvent or bankrupt or if the term of credit expires, the right will automatically revive. The insolvent buyer may still claim delivery of the goods provided he can find security for payment at the appointed time.

9.3.9   The *seller's right to retake the goods* exists only if:(i) no credit has been given, the goods have remained in the buyer's possession, are unchanged in their condition, and the claim has been made within eight days of delivery: art. 2102-4: Civil Code; or (ii) where the goods, having been delivered to a carrier, have not yet come into the possession of the buyer or his agent, but the buyer has, in the meantime, become bankrupt or insolvent. The third special remedy is seldom exercised, since the unpaid seller will usually rescind the sale rather than claim his privilege. Nevertheless, if the eight days have expired, or credit facilities have been given, and both ownership and possession of the goods sold have passed to the buyer, the seller can compel a judicial sale of the goods and claim *payment of the price out of the proceeds in priority to other creditors*. This privilege is no longer available if the goods are no longer in the buyer's possession (excepting the unpaid seller of a motor-vehicle under the terms of D.-I.30.9.1953 which applies to credit sales), or have perished, or where the bankruptcy or 'judicial administration' of the buyer has supervened. *Judicial administration (le reglement judiciare)* refers to a judicially-controlled process whereby the court seeks to preserve the bankrupt's business and to restore it to him when the bankruptcy proceeedings have been completed. This is to be contrasted with *la faillite* or bankruptcy proceedings of another sort, wherein the object of the court is to wind up the business and terminate the debtor's commercial trading.

9.3.10   The *seller's right to rescind* is provided for under the Civil Code which states that: 'If the buyer does not pay the price, the seller may claim rescission of the sale.': article 1654: Civil Code. Where the goods have already been delivered, the court may give the buyer more time to pay, unless there is a contrary provision in the contract: article 1183-4: Civil Code. The right to rescind is part of the general right to rescind for non-performance in any synallagmatic (two-sided) contract: article 1184: Civil Code. It applies regardless of whether the seller has parted with ownership or possession or both. If the buyer fails to collect the goods within the contractually stipulated time, the seller has the automatic right to rescind without first obtaining a court judgment or even without issuing a formal summons to the buyer. In any other situation, the court must pronounce upon the seller's claim to rescind: art. 1184 (2): Civil Code.

9.3.11   French law distinguishes between a merchant or commercial company and a non-merchant (*societe civile*). Broadly, the law leaves the individual creditors to obtain payment as best they can from a non-merchant. However, since there is a public interest in the prompt payment of debts where a commercial company is concerned, there is an elaborate judicial administration involved in settling the debts of the company, designed to preserve equality between the creditors and, if possible, to restore the creditor to commercial viability. Hence, once a merchant debtor has become bankrupt or gone into judicial administration, the right to rescind is lost as soon as the goods have come into his shop or warehouse.

9.3.12 In the case of *supervening events* which make it difficult or impossible to carry out the performance of the contract, French law also has rules equivalent to the English contractual doctrine of *Frustration* (see Chapter 7). These are dealt with under the headings of *force majeure* and *imprevision* (unforeseeability) or unforeseen events. French law is far more rigid than the German or English parallels and is applied more strictly. The doctrine of *imprevision* is only found in administrative contracts and there is no similar doctrine in civil contracts. Contracts between private parties cannot therefore utilise the doctrine of *imprevision*. Article 1134 of the Civil Code declares that contracts have the force of law, hence the judges cannot change their terms simply in the interests of fairness. *Imprevision* is admitted in contracts to which the French State or another French public body is a party. The *Conseil d'Etat* has held that administrative contracts may be revised in 'radically altered circumstances' (imprevision). A change in circumstances may render a contract commercially impracticable or more expensive to fulfil but the contract will nevertheless be enforced according to its terms. However, if a change of circumstances renders the contract legally or physically *impossible* to perform, the doctrine of *force majeure* may be invoked.

If the impossibility is merely temporary this will not terminate the contract but simply suspend its execution and only relieve the party from liability for the damage caused by the delay. In the contract of sale, if there is an obligation to deliver a specific thing, the ownership of that item will pass, together with the risk by virtue of the consent of the parties. if the item perishes before delivery, the obligation to deliver it will disappear but the obligation of the buyer to pay for the price will remain unless he can prove fault on the part of the person in whose hands the itme perished.

In the famous 1916 case of *Compagnie du Gaz de Bordeau*, the *Conseil d'Etat* held that as a matter of principle, a contract could only be modified with the consent of both parties but where the whole economic basis of a contract had been altered by executive action the private individual was entitled to an indemnity from the State agency because of the unforeseen loss it had caused him. A French judge does not have the same discretionary powers afforded an English judge to terminate a contract completely in these circumstances. A strike or a war will not necessarily be regarded as an event of *force majeure* but subsequent illegality will usually suffice terminate a contract by judicial resolution. Article 1148 of the Civil Code permits *force majeure* to be used as a defence to a claim for damages for breach of contract but only where unforeseeable and irresistible events make it impossible for the contract to be performed. Judicial modification of the terms of the contract may, in exceptional circumstances be permitted, for example, under Article 1124 of the Civil Code which allows extension of time for the repayment of debts or the Law of 9 July 1975 which allows penalty clauses to be nullified.

It should be remembered, however, that under Article 1147, a debtor may be ordered to pay damages either because of his failure to carry out an obligation or because of his delay in executing it, in every case where he is unable to prove that the delay has proceeded from some external circumstances for which he cannot be made responsible.

ii. German Law

(i) General

9.3.13   There are no rules equivalent to common law concepts of consideration or estoppel in German law. Hence, contracts which have been concluded without consideration are enforceable. However, this is of little practical significance since sales contracts are invariably entered into so that possession and title may be transferred for a consideration. Moreover, most modern-day sales contracts are reduced to writing and standard form contracts are also common in Germany with German law favouring the 'last shot' rule (ie the form that was received last will prevail) unless there was a specific contractual stipulation to the contrary, or one specifying which form would govern the contract. A creditor's written agreement to accept part payment is binding in full settlement will also be binding on him and manufacturers' guarantees are directly enforceable, since they are seen as separate from the contract of sale. There is also no general requirement of written form for sales contracts although contracts for the sale of real property, including mortgages, and concerning the statutes of a company, must be embodied in writing authenticated by a notary or judge: para. 313: BGB. Similarly, writing is required in contracts between landlords and tenants and contracts of financial guarantee (para:766:BGB) and hire purchase contracts. Another general principle is that the BGB imposes strict liability in contract upon retailers if their goods and services are not reasonably fit. This rule only applies to the goods or services themselves, and does not cover any injury or damage caused to the buyer or his property by usage of the goods. Such claims would require proof of *negligence* which may be established either though a *breach of contract action* against the dealer or in a *tort* action against someone like the manufacturer.

The difference between contractual and tortious liability is clearly highlighted by this approach. Tortious liability is enunciated in paragraphs 823 and 831 of the BGB but there is a special rule of strict liability for injuries caused by drugs.

(ii) Transfer of Ownership

9.3.14   The German code provisions which specifically deal with sale only relate to the contract between the parties and its legal consequences. It is the third book of the Code that deals with the law relating to the ownership of the object which has been sold. The German term *Kaufvertrag* although translated as 'sale' does not does not connote the transfer of ownership but merely that there has been an agreement to sell. The contract of sale creates rights and duties but it does not, *per se* transfer property. The *property* in the goods will pass depending on the rules of para.929 *et seq* of the BGB. German law follows the Roman law principle whereby *the transfer of ownership requires transfer of possession*. This differs therefore from both French and English law, under which the mere sale will normally transfer ownership of the goods. Thus, *a concluded contract will not operate as a conveyance*. There is therefore a split between duty and performance which leads to a potential problem if the property is sold twice. In theory, the seller can undertake several conflicting duties to deliver the same piece of merchandise. If the seller then transfers the goods to the second purchaser, the first purchaser is only entitled to sue the seller for damages. It is only in cases where the first purchaser can prove that the second purchaser 'induced a breach of contract' by the seller that the first purchaser may claim the goods from the second purchaser in tort (see BGHZ 12, 308,318 and RGZ 108, 58).

If the seller goes bankrupt before he can perform the contract and transfer the goods to the purchaser, the purchaser has no right to the merchandise but is left with a claim in bankruptcy which is generally unsatisfactory.

(iii) Responsibility for Risk of Loss

9.3.15   As far as risk of loss or damage to the goods is concerned, German law states that the risk passes to the buyer only with the delivery of possession (para. 446: BGB; *'periculum est vendoris'*). This usually, but not always, means that risk passes when ownership is transferred. This differs from Roman law, wherein risk of accidental damage and destruction passed with the completion of the contract of sale (*'periculum est emptoris'*) and from English law, under which *prima facie* risk passes to the buyer with the 'property in the goods' that is, with the transfer of ownership, which usually occurs at the point of conclusion of a contract of sale, irrespective of the transfer of possession (s.20(1): Sale of Goods Act 1979) under the *'res perit domino'* rule (the loss falls on the owner). In other words, the goods remain at the seller's risk until ownership passes, which is when the contract is concluded (see below for English law exceptions).

In German law, despite the rule that risk passes on delivery, there are exceptions to this rule:

(i) In sales of land, risk passes with either transfer of possession or registration, whichever is the earlier: para. 446(2): BGB).

(ii) If the place of performance and place of transfer are not identical, then risk passes upon the delivery of the goods to the person or organisation designated to carry out the transfer from the place of performance to the place of delivery: para. 447(1):BGB)

(iii) The parties may agree that the risk may pass earlier. This is similar to English law where, in the case of c.i.f. and f.o.b. contracts, the risk passes at the moment the goods are delivered to the ship. German law accords with English law on this point. The German law approach here is that of *'cujus periculum, ejus est commodum'* so that the burdens and advantages of the thing which has been sold will pass to the purchaser at the same time as the risk passes: para. 446: BGB.

(iv) There may be a *retention of title clause* in the contract.

Under para.454 of the BGB, such clauses are declared valid. Any problems that arise must be settled by case law. The *Romalpa* clauses (*The Romalpa Case* [1976] 2 All ER 552; and see English law, below, at 9.4.19) used in common law jurisdictions are very common but are rarely contested.

(v) If unascertained goods are destroyed by flood or fire, the seller will only be liable for the buyer's loss in cases of negligence. If the seller has not been negligent, he has no obligation to perform the contract and the buyer has no obligation to pay for the goods.

(vi) Ownership passes to the buyer only if he obtains actual possession. If the seller has entrusted goods to an independent carrier, risk but not ownership will pass, in the absence of a contrary contractual provision.

(iv) Duties of Buyer and Seller

9.3.15   Under German law, the seller is obliged to deliver the goods and transfer ownership in them, while the buyer is obliged to pay the price and take delivery of the goods: para. 433: BGB. After delivery, the *buyer's main right is to cancel the contract* if the goods are defective but he also has the option to pay a *lower price*. Unlike Roman and English law, the seller warrants that he has title to the goods he is offering to sell :para. 433(1) BGB. This applies not just to things sold but also to rights. A seller who sells a non-existent right cannot therefore argue that the sale if void because of the non-existence of the right. In the case of a defect of title, a purchaser has all the rights that he has in the case of a breach of contract: para. 440: BGB. The purchaser will have these rights even if the seller may not have acted negligently or intentionally. However, the seller will not be responsible for defects of title which are known to the purchaser: para. 439: BGB. There are two exceptions to these rules:

(i) In sales of movable property, the purchaser can demand compensation for non-transfer of title, after delivery, provided the defect in title has resulted in the merchandise having been delivered to a third party who is entitled to it; or the object has been returned to the seller; or the merchandise has been destroyed: para. 440: BGB. This is similar to the Roman principle of eviction, which has also had an impact on English law:see s.12: Sale of Goods Act 1979 (UK).

(ii) In sales of immovable property, the seller is obliged to procure the cancellation of all charges on the land, even though they are known to the purchaser: para. 439(2): BGB.

9.3.16   The contract of sale gives rise to a number of *collateral duties* (*Nebenpflicten*). These are derived partly from the Civil Code, partly from the contract and partly from the general principle of good faith (see discussion on Good Faith, below at 9.3.28) One example is the duty of the seller to refrain from competing with the purchaser of his business; another is the duty of the seller to point out to the buyer the existence of any special dangers that are not immediately apparent in the property sold.

(v) Remedies of Buyer and Seller

a. Buyer's Remedies

9.3.17 Irregularities in the performance of the contract of sale must first be categorised before it is possible to know where the various statutory remedies may lie. Various *remedies for non-performance by the seller* are available to the buyer under the General Part of the Law of Obligations and there are additional rules in the law of sales, particularly for defects in the goods. Two points should be noted:

(i) In the case of a sale of a thing, there is the right of the buyer to demand that the contract be performed, ie the equivalent of the English action of specific performance except that in Germany this *'claim to performance'* (*Erfullungsansspruch*), which entails asking for the transfer of title and delivery of the merchandise, is the standard remedy rather than the exceptional one unlike the English practice. In Anglo-American law, it is viewed as exceptional and at the court's discretion whether specific performance of the contract should be ordered. Thus German law frequently adopts the exact opposite of the English common law law approach where there is non-performance of the contract by the seller.

(ii) If the seller fails to perform, and the risk has not yet passed, rules relating to *impossibility of performance* (which is part of the doctrine of Frustration in *English* law: see Chapter 7), and *delay* will apply (see paras. 323-6: BGB). There is some doctrinal dispute as to whether certain cases wherein the seller was unable to perform his part of the contract should accurately have been called cases of impossibility or whether they should have been treated within the notion of good faith (*Treu und Glauben*: para. 242: BGB). However, the key determinant of the seller's liability would appear to be whether he was 'at fault' in some way and therefore responsible for the impossibility of performance. English law regards cases where one party was partly or wholly responsible for the impossibility as 'self-induced frustration' which does not qualify as legally valid frustration. There is no identical conceptual doctrine of Frustration in German law but there is a concept known as a 'fundamental change in circumstances underlying the in contract' (*Wegfall der Geschaftsgrundlage*) which is similar to certain aspects of English law. In German law, where the seller has been responsible in some way for his inability to perform the contract, the buyer has the right to claim damages for non-performance of the sales contract: paragraph 325 BGB. He also has the right to claim damages for lost profits. Should neither party be responsible for the impossibility, obligations for both parties are terminated. Thus the buyer need not pay anything for goods which were not, in any event, delivered but neither will he have any right to claim damages.

9.3.18 The rules for *delay* are similar to those which operate for impossibility: para. 325: BGB. Delay has proved to be a more important practical and popular basis for legal actions than impossibility because as long as non-performance can be proved, the fate of the actual goods is only indirectly relevant to the question of responsibility for the delay. In respect of a unilateral obligation on the part of the seller to deliver on time, this obligation continues in spite of the delay, hence a right to claim damages will arise for the loss attributable to the delay in supplying the goods. On the other hand, for reciprocal contracts, the buyer has the unique option of fixing an additional time for delay in delivery after it has first occurred, a period of grace (*Nachfrist*), after which *no further obligations* will remain under the contract. This is not derived from Roman law, but came into the BGB from the Allgemeines Deutsches Handelsgesetzbuch of 1867. Thus, the buyer may, for example, fix a final date for performance of the contract, so that the seller may either comply by this date, or let the date pass, so that the contract may then be resolved by a claim for damages *or* rescission. The contract is then void, and no further claim for performance can be made. If this option of giving a period of grace is not exercised by the buyer, he has the usual right to claim compensation for any loss attributable to the delay. Note that this right to set a subsequent date for delivery exists *in addition to any claim for performance*, provided, of course, the goods may still be delivered.

9.3.19 Before delay in the legal sense arises, there must, of course, have been an obligation to deliver. *Notice* is required to put the seller on enquiry, unless the contract has identified the delivery date with sufficient precision, that is, so it is easily identified by reference to the calendar. Words such as 'as soon as possible' or 'with all speed' will not suffice. A seller may be responsible for a delay in delivery if he deliberately delays performance to satisfy another customer, or does anything or fails to do something which he knows would result in delivery being delayed. This will include failure to employ sufficent workmen to ensure delivery on time, or to get necessary permit permission, or raw materials, or having a shortage of funds, as with any general obligations:para. 279: BGB. In other words, the seller must have been negligent in some way before the buyer would be entitled to claim damages. The seller will also be responsible for any fault on the part of those he employs to assist him in performance: para. 278: BGB. This last principle resembles the 'vicarious liability' principle utilised in English law. Of course, the seller will not be liable for delays caused by *force majeure* such as fire, theft, other natural disasters, blockades, wars, and similar occurrences over which he has no control, which might have resulted in the unavailability of transport. Such clauses are frequently included in written contracts, particularly in standard form contracts.

9.3.20 The purpose of the award of damages for delay is to compensate for all disadvantages caused by the delay. However, as we have seen, damages constitute only one of the remedies available for breach of contract. Cancellation of the contract or payment of a lower price, or a claim for performance (subsequent delivery: para. 480:BGB) are other possible options for the buyer, depending on the circumstances. The purpose of an award of damages in the context of delay is the same as in English law, as laid down in *Robinson* v. *Harman* (1848) 1 Exch. 850, namely that 'where a party sustains a loss by reason of a breach of contract he is, so far as money can do it, to be placed in the same situation...as if the contract had been performed.' Thus if the market for the goods has fallen sharply and the buyer has to resell them at a lower price, he would be entitled to the difference between the market price now and its rate when delivery was promised. If the delay results in extra cost being incurred by the buyer, necessitated by giving notice, or having to defend a legal action, this will be taken into account in computation of the compensatory figure.

b. Contributory Fault in Damages

9.3.21 There is also acceptance of a rule of 'contributory fault' (*Mitverschulden*) in the law of damages: para. 254:BGB and there is no distinction between direct and indirect (or consequential) losses, although the contract may specify different limitation periods.

9.3.22 Delay also affects the operation of the rules of impossibility. If goods have been accidentally destroyed while the seller was in delay, then he will be liable to compensate the buyer for losses incurred as a result of that destruction, contrary to the general rule regarding impossibility of performance.

9.3.23 Under para. 459 BGB, the seller of a thing also warrants that at the time when the risk passed to the buyer, it possesses the following qualities:
(i) it is free from defects diminishing or destroying its value or fitness for either ordinary use or the use as impliedly or expressly stated in the contract. If there is only a trivial defect in value or fitness, this will not be sufficient (this follows the English *de minimis* principle).
(ii) it possesses all the qualities which have been promised.
If this warranty is breached, the two normal remedies provided by para. 462 of the Code are the right to *cancel the contract* (*Wandelung*), which is the conventional right of *rescission*, which includes the right to return the goods and the *right to demand a reduction in price* (*Minderung*). Rescission is dealt with under para. 467 of the BGB, and para. 472 deals with the *Minderung*. The reduction of the price is computed by subtracting an amount equal to the deficiency in value from the orginal agreed price: para. 472: BGB. Paragraph 462 also entitles the buyer of defective goods to demand a replacement. Defect is construed in a similar manner to English law (see eg. 9.4.11). There is no statutory right to have the defect removed and the goods put right, but such a right is frequently incorporated in contracts by the parties or through application of the General Conditions of Business. Instead of bringing a claim for *Wandlung* (rescission), the buyer may bring a claim for *Minderung* (abatement of price) or even switch from one remedy to another unless the seller is relying on the remedy first selected. Apart from the reduction, which is made proportionally, the rest of the sales contract remains intact with all its rights and duties untouched by a claim for a lower price. *Actions for breach of warranty* must be commenced within six months of purchase. Under the Commercial Code, business buyers must make their complaint immediately after delivery.

9.3.24   The Civil Code also provides a number of other remedies aimed at dealing with a number of special circumstances:

(i) The purchaser has the right to refuse to accept performance and demand damages for non-performance if:

(a) A quality whose presence has been asserted is lacking (para. 463: BGB) but it must be established that the assertion was part of the contract and not merely 'sales talk' preliminary to actual negotiations which was therefore not part of the contract.

(b) The purchaser has kept silent with malicious intent, despite being aware of a defect, and knowing that it would prevent the conclusion of the contract, and being aware of his duty to report such a defect under the rule of good faith (para. 242:BGB) Mere silence under these conditions is sufficient, without the need for any positive act of concealment.

(c) The seller has maliciously misrepresented the existence of some qualities or the absence of defects. There is no necessity for any actual promise to have been given. Although not included in the Code, this is a rule derived from customary law, which was introduced by the courts and has commanded universal acceptance by legal writers: see *RGZ* 132,78.

(ii) In the case of things sold which have been specifically designated in the contract of sale by their particular characteristics (*Genuskauf*). Here the purchaser also has the right to demand delivery of an object without defects: para. 480: BGB.

9.3.25   These remedies are not available to the buyer in the following cases:

(i) If the purchaser was aware of the defect at the time when the contract was concluded: para. 460:BGB.

(ii) If the purchaser was ignorant of the defect as a result of his gross negligence and the seller had neither guaranteed that the object was free from that defect nor had maliciously kept silent about it: para. 460. The same rule would apply if the seller had not maliciously asserted that the thing sold was free from defect.

(iii) In the case of sales by public auction, where the object has been sold by way of an auction of objects given as a pledge or taken by way of enforcement of a court judgment: para. 461; section 806: *ZPO* (Code of Civil Procedure).

c. Seller's Remedies

(i) Buyer's Failure to Pay the Price

9.3.26   Paragraph 433(II) BGB, requires the buyer to pay the purchase price and take delivery of the goods. The debt so created is normally to be paid at the domicile of the seller or by sending the money to him there: para. 270 BGB. In modern-day practice, mere crediting of the seller's account will suffice to constitute performance of the buyer's promise. The buyer is required to keep himself solvent. The seller may set down a period within which payment should be made, however once this stipulated period has elapsed, the seller can no longer claim performance of the promise to pay the price of the goods that have been delivered, but *only damages* will then be available. This claim for damages will usually amount to at least as much as the purchase price. Of course, the seller can still insist on delivering the goods, even if the buyer does not want them. The seller can then claim full damages, including the purchase price.

(ii) Impossibility of Performance

9.3.27 If the buyer is responsible for impossibility of performance, for example, if he damaged the goods while inspecting them prior to delivery, the seller may still claim for the price and need not perform: para. 324:BGB.

(iii) Buyer's Delay in Acceptance of Goods

9.3.28 Although there is a general principle under para. 288 of the BGB which specifies the rate of interest for delay in the payment of money (four per cent), which applies even if the creditor/seller is not paying any interest himself, the most beneficial right which a seller may claim nowadays is the compensation for any interest he has actually paid to his bank during the period of delay (see BGH MDR 1978, 818). If the buyer does not accept the property as agreed, the seller may claim compensation for any harm or loss he has suffered as a result and may even resell the goods if it is a commercial sale: para.373:BGB. Where acceptance of the property has been made a principal duty under the contract because the seller has a special reason in disposing of it (eg., perishable goods, or if there is a need to clear the particular warehouse) the seller may then stipulate a precise period within which performance by delivery should take place, and is if this is not complied with, he may *either* rescind the contract *or* claim damages for non-performance.

(iv) The Principle of Good Faith in German Law

9.3.29 Good faith is a *general principle* in German commercial law enshrined in para. 242 of the BGB (German Civil Code) which simply states that 'The debtor is obliged to perform in such a manner as good faith requires, regard being paid to general practice.' As the commentary explains, the aim of the legislator was 'to make people conscious of the true content of the contractual obligation' and the scope of the provision was to be restricted to 'regulating the manner and method of the duty to perform: I *Protokolle zum BGB 303*.

Paragraph 242 has been used to elaborate on routine commercial matters such as what performance entails and to cover matters such as the proper packing of goods, and the necessary provision of adequate instructions for use with the goods. In this sense, the concept may alrcady be distinguished from the English use of the term 'good faith' which in the commercial context, applies to buyers of goods who have purchased them from third parties who, unknown to the buyers, were not the owners of the goods. Under section 23 of the Sale of Goods Act(SGA), purchasers may only defeat the original owner's competing claim to the goods by proving they are *bona fide* purchasers of the goods without notice, ie they purchased them while unaware of the seller's defect in title. In these circumstances, he may therefore give a good title to a (second) purchaser provided he is unaware of the defect in title. The specific good faith rules in the SGA really only deal with 'honesty in fact' and the closely linked concepts of good faith and notice in the SGA (and the sale of a motor vehicle under the Hire Purchase Act 1964) are really based on commercial convenience and expediency, as exceptions to the general *nemo dat* rule stated in section 21(1) of the SGA. They do not really deal with the broader notions of justice, fairness and reasonableness which are redolent of good faith itself. The requirement of good faith in English contract and commercial law is really a requirement of a standard of honesty and fair dealing, and in contracts of insurance, for example, is really an application of well-established common law and equitable rules on fraud.

In short, English law has no general requirement as such that parties should perform their contractual obligations in good faith nor is there any general principle of common law which implies any sort of duty along these lines. Rather, it deals with the need for goods to be fit for their purpose and of merchantable quality, and all the other prerequisites through concepts such as 'implied terms' or conditions or warranties and though certain sections of the Sale of Goods Act 1979.

In contrast, paragraph 242 of the BGB has outgrown its original function by being used as a statutory enactment of a general requirement of good faith, a principle of legal ethics (Larenz: *Methodenlehre*: 1979) and in fact 'dominates the entire legal system' (Leser: 1982). Its content today is seen as primarily 'reliance' whereby it acts as an integrating element in the legal culture, and particularly through reciprocal reliance which caters to the needs and interests of others (Fikentsher, I *Methoden des Rechts* 109f., 179f, (1975).

In the context of the present chapter, suffice to say that the principle of Good Faith continues to play an important supplementary role in German sales law, performing an *ethical function* by giving a legal foundation for ethical values, a *contractual function* by developing contractual rights and duties and a *regulatory function* by controlling and demarcating the exercise and scope of rights in conjunction with other business statutes, codes and principles.

D. THE ENGLISH COMMON LAW APPROACH

i. General

9.4   The English law of sale of goods originated from the *lex mercatoria* or ancient mercantile law and is predominantly based on principles developed by the law of contract. Until the end of the nineteenth century, the principles governing sales of goods lay buried in the larger mass of contract law. The ninteenth century eventually produced the Sale of Goods Act 1893 which remained unchanged on the statute books for eighty years. The sources of the law of sales may now be found in the Factors Act 1889, the Sale of Goods Act 1979 ('the 1979 Act') which consolidates the original Act of 1893 with later amendments, the Unfair Contract Terms Act 1977 and the rules of common law (ie case law) which have been left intact despite these pieces of legislation. In keeping with the English common law tradition, statutes are not intended *ipso facto* to create new rules or procedures but to consolidate and sometimes clarify the existing law. Indeed, section 62(2) of the 1979 Act declares:

'The rules of the common law, including the law merchant, except in so far as they are inconsistent with the express provisions of this Act, and in particular the rules relating to the law of principal and agent and the effect of fraud, misrepresentation, duress or coercion, mistake or other invalidating cause, apply to contracts for the sale of goods.'

The 1979 Act therefore makes no attempt to codify existing legislation. Hence, as *Bank of England* v. *Vagliano Bros.* [1891] AC 107 emphasised, if the Act's provisions were ambiguous in any way, earlier cases may help to resolve the ambiguity; and if a term had acquired a technical meaning, previous cases may be cited to illustrate this meaning. A necessary corollary of this is that if a point arose which was not covered by the Act, earlier decisions would have to be referred to and followed. Since it is primarily derived from the law of contract, it is inevitable that a great deal of its key concepts and main remedies have a strong contractual underpinning, supplemented by modified 'commercial law' principles. The 1979 Act defines a contract of sale from other transactions. Section 2(1) states that: 'A contract of sale of goods is a contract whereby the seller transfers or agrees to transfer the property in goods to the buyer for a money consideration called the price.' Further, by s.61(1) of the same Act, the term 'contract of sale' in the Act includes both actual *sales* and *agreements to sell*.

As with the previous civil law analysis, it is proposed to concentrate on the key issues that dominate this area of law under English common law.

ii. Transfer of Property and Transfer of Ownership

9.4.1   Under English law, the basic principle is that whoever is *the owner of the goods at any given time must bear the risk of loss, damage or deterioration of the goods.* Sections 16 to 20 of the 1979 Act enunciate the rules relating to transfer of ownership. The statute refers to 'transfer of property as between buyer and seller.' Under the 1979 Act, 'property' refers to the *title to the goods*, or *rights of ownership*, as in 'the property in the goods.' Further, the rights expressly dealt with are those which arise between seller and buyer, which are not necessarily identical against the third parties and the world at large. *'Property' or ownership must be distinguished from possession* since the property in goods sold may pass to the buyer but the seller may nevertheless retain possession of the goods. Possession of the goods may also be transferred without transferring the ownership of them, as in hire purchase contracts and contracts whereby the seller has reserved his title: see *The*

Romalpa Case [1976] 2 All ER 552. Rights of third parties over the goods are covered by sections 21-26 of the 1979 Act. English law does not follow Roman law and so, 'property' may pass by agreement.

9.4.2   As far as English law was concerned, the doctrine of the 'passing of property' by consent was combined with the principle of *nemo dat quod habet* (no one can give a better title than he holds himself) which was subsequently modified by the Factors Act 1889 and the 1893 Act. It also sees problems of risk and ownership as quite separate from those arising from breach of contract. Hence, if the buyer has become owner of the goods, this does not *ipso facto* affect his right to repudiate the contract or claim damages for goods which are not in conformity with the contract. If he retains the right to repudiate, ownership will then revert to the seller, although the contract may stipulate that the buyer will be responsible for returning the goods at his own risk. In the United States, article 2-510 of the Uniform Commercial Code seeks to protect a buyer in these circumstances so that he will not be at risk even temporarily. It stipulates that risk of loss remains on the seller until the defect is cured or the goods have been accepted.

iii. Transfer of Ownership and Risk of Loss

(i) Sales and Agreements to sell

9.4.3   A clear distinction is drawn between sales and agreements to sell in the 1979 Act:
(a) Where under a contract of sale, the property in goods is passed from the seller to the buyer, the contract is called a sale: s.2(4).
(b) Where the transfer of the property in the goods is to take place at a future time or subject to some condition to be subsequently fulfilled, the contract is called an 'agreement to sell':s.2(5).
(c) An agreement to sell becomes a sale when the time elapses or the conditions are fulfilled subject to which the property in the goods is to be transferred: s.2(6).

(ii) Ownership and Responsibility for Risk of Loss

9.4.4   These distinctions should be noted because the actual moment 'property' or the right to ownership passes is important for the following reasons. First, the *risk of loss or damage will pass with the property*, that is, *with the transfer of ownership*: section 20 (1): 1979 Act, unless otherwise agreed. The risk of accidental damage or loss will therefore follow the transfer of ownership under the *res perit domino* principle (see 9.1). It is important to note that the risk of accidental loss or damage will fall on the owner of the goods, *irrespective of whether he is in possession of the goods*: see *Tarling* v. *Baxter* (1827) 6 B&C 360. Nevertheless, the Act's provisions on, *inter alia*, passing of risk, may be varied by agreement of the parties or by trade custom:

'*Risk*' within the meaning of section 20, would seem to include only loss or damage caused by accident and without negligence on the part of either buyer or seller.

Secondly, *if ownership has passed to the buyer the seller has the right to sue for the price*. Thirdly, if the seller re-sells the goods after ownership has passed to the buyer, the second buyer acquires no title unless he is protected by one of the exceptions to the *nemo dat* rule (see below 9.5.42). The same sort of principle applies if the buyer re-sells the goods before the property in them, ie, the *title* to them, has passed to him.

(iii) Ownership and Unascertained Goods

9.4.5   Under section 16 of the 1979 Act, where there is a contract for the sale of *unascertained goods* (namely, goods identified by description only and not identified until after the contract is made), *no property passes to the buyer unless and until they are ascertained*. Hence, a particular article or collection of articles must be identified as the unique subject matter of the contract before ownership can pass to the buyer who will then bear the risk of loss, damage or deterioration of the goods.

9.4.6   In *Healy* v. *Howlett* [1917] 1 KB 337, a buyer ordered 20 boxes of fish from the seller. These were separated from a large consignment at a time when the whole consignment had already gone bad. Although the seller had given instructions for the boxes to be appropriated for the buyer the fish had gone bad before this appropriation had been carried out. It was held that since property did not pass until appropriation for the buyer had been carried out, when the fish went bad, they still belonged to the seller and so the fish remained at the seller's risk.

Similarly, in *Re London Wine Co.* [1986] PCC 121, buyers bought certain quantities of wine, which they also identified by specific descriptions, which they then left in the seller's warehouse. The seller went into liquidation and his creditors claimed all the wine in the warehouse. The court held that even though the quantities and descriptions ordered by the buyers accorded with the wines stored in the warehouse, it was still not necessarily the only wine which could have been used to fulfil the buyer's orders and so property had not passed, and the sellers remained the owners. Hence the buyers were left with claims for damages from sellers who were insolvent. It is worth noting that under Article 2-105 of the American Uniform Commercial Code, the buyer of part of an undivided whole becomes owner in common with the owners of the remaining parts.

9.4.7   However, the provisions of the Act can be *varied by agreement or trade custom*. Thus, if it appears that the parties have agreed that the risk will pass *before* the property or ownership does, the courts may find such an agreement crucial to their determination of whether the property in the goods has in fact, passed to the buyer. In *Sterns Ltd.* v. *Vickers* [1923] 1 KB 78, the seller agreed to sell 120,000 gallons of spirit, out of a total quantity of

200,000 in a storage tank on the premises of a third party. A delivery order was issued to the buyer, which the third party accepted, but the buyers decided to leave the spirit in the tank for some months for their convenience, during which time the spirit deteriorated. The Court of Appeal held that although the property in the goods had not passed (because no appropriation had taken place) the parties must have intended the risk to pass when the delivery order was delivered and accepted by the third party. Consequently, the buyer remained liable for the price.

(iv) Ownership and Ascertained Goods

9.4.8 Under s.17 of the 1979 Act, if the contract is for the sale of specific or ascertained goods the property passes *when the parties intend it to pass*. In other words, *the parties may decide when ownership shall pass if they are dealing with ascertained goods*. This may be expressly stated in the terms of the contract. An extremely common practice (see Whincup (1990)) is for a clause to be inserted which says either that ownership shall pass on delivery or when payment is made after delivery. A typical *reservation of title clause* might read: 'The property in the goods shall remain in the seller until the price and any other payment due to the seller has been discharged in full.' Such clauses are also called *retention of title clauses*. The seller may, nevertheless disclaim responsibility for risk and impose liability on the buyer as soon as the latter takes delivery, despite retaining ownership by having a clause in the contract stating the precise legal position and terms of the agreement, to this effect. As with unascertained goods, risk may even pass before delivery by the same device of a clause expressly stating this to be the case, but the buyer will, of course, have to agree to this being so stated. The seller may therefore wish to '*reserve title*' to the goods until the buyer's outstanding debts are paid and s.19 expressly deals with such clauses and is discussed below (see 9.4.18-19), but under the 1979 Act, s.17 is also wide enough to enable such reservation of title clauses to be made. If there is no clear statement of the parties' intentions, it may be inferred from the conduct of the parties, and the circumstances of the case: section 17(2) : 1979 Act.

9.4.9 The courts will generally endeavour to give effect to the contracting parties' intentions, as far as they may be discoverable. Nevertheless, a number of business practices have grown up surrounding various types of contracts, despite a lack of written evidence of intention in any given case. For instance, ownership of goods shipped under c.i.f. contracts (where the price includes cost, insurance and freight) is usually deemed to pass upon delivery of the documents of title (ie, the bills of lading). In f.o.b. contracts (free on board), ownership passes when the goods cross the ship's rail (cf. the rules on passing of risk are different for each of these contracts. If a seller retains the documents of title after delivery, the implication appears to be that he still owns the goods: *Cheetham* v. *Thornham* [1964] 2 Lloyds Rep. 17. On the other hand, there are cases like *The Albazero* [1977] AC 774 which suggest that ownership might be deemed to pass upon shipment of the goods or upon posting the bill of lading. It will clearly turn on the individual circumstances of the case and the court's perception of the parties' intentions. However, if any intentions were expressed *after* the contract was made, these will be disregarded: *Dennant* v. *Skinner and Collom* [1948] 2 KB 164.

9.4.10   If the parties have not indicated their intention (at the time of contracting) as to when property in ascertained goods should pass to the buyer and it cannot be discovered, even by using all the above means, the matter must be decided by applying the *five rules contained in s.18 of the 1979 Act*. s18 begins by stating:'Unless a contrary intention appears, the following are rules for ascertaining the intention of the parties as to the time at which the property in the goods is to pass to the buyer.'

We now consider the five rules, bearing in mind the words 'unless a contrary intention appears' as an all-embracing proviso.

9.4.11   *Rule 1* of s.18 provides that in unconditional contracts for the sale of specific goods in a deliverable state ownership passes when the contract is made. The term 'unconditional contract' appears to refer to a contract that is not subject to either a condition precedent or condition subsequent, so that it takes effect immediately. 'Specific goods' under s.61 of the 1979 Act are goods 'identified and agreed upon at the time of sale.' Two contrasting cases are *Kursell* v. *Timber Operators & Contractors Ltd* [1927] 1 KB 298 and *Reid* v. *Schultz* (1949),SR (NSW) 231 (an Australian decision). In *Kursell*, a sale of all the trees in a Latvian forest which conformed to certain measurements which by a given date had reached a certain size was held by the Court of Appeal not to be sufficiently specific, as the goods were not sufficiently identified. This was because it was impossible to say then which trees would qualify; not all the trees were to pass but only those conforming to the stipulated measurements. However, in *Reid*, a sale of all the millable or marketable hardwood timber on a certain site was held to be a sale of specific goods.
'Deliverable state' for the purposes of this Rule refers to the goods being in such a state in which the buyer would under the contract be bound to take delivery of them: section 61(5): 1979 Act; in other words, if nothing more needs to be done to the goods under the contract; this does not include anything that needs to be done to them to remedy any defects or deficiencies. Hence if they need to be repaired or dismantled, they are not immediately deliverable, and reamin the seller's responsibility and he must bear the loss of accidental damage or deterioration. As under all these rules, the parties may agree that the goods concerned are deliverable before anything that needs to be done to them has been completed.

9.4.12   It appears somewhat unsatisfactory to make ownership pass at the time the contract is made even when the goods remain with the seller, albeit temporarily. Coupled with the rule that the owner then bears the risk of accidental loss or damage, if a buyer orders a specific item in a shop, he therefore becomes the owner of that item. Should it be accidentally damaged before it has been delivered to the buyer, the buyer would still be bound to pay for it. To avoid this, most commercial firms usually insert a clear contrary provision to the effect that risk shall not pass until delivery. Courts have, in any event, shown themselves unwilling to apply Rule 1 and have been quick to seize any ambiguity or uncertainty in the contract to find it is unconditional and therefore not covered by this Rule. As Diplock, LJ put it: 'In modern times very little is needed to give rise to the inference that the property in specific goods is to pass only on delivery or payment.': *Ward* v. *Bignall* [1967] 1 QB 534,545.

9.4.13   Rules 2 and 3 deal with acts that are required to be fulfilled by the seller. If these necessary acts must be done by the buyer, ownership will pass upon the making of the contract. *Rule 2* of s.18 states that where the contract is for specific goods and the seller is bound to do something to the goods to put them into a deliverable state, ownership does not pass until this has been done and the buyer has been notified accordingly. Hence, if a seller agrees to fix a handle to a piece of furniture which he has sold, ownership will not pass until the buyer has been notified that the work has been carried out.(see *Underwood* v. *Burgh Castle Brick and Cement Syndicate* [1922] 1 KB 343.

9.4.14   *Rule 3* states that where the specific goods are in a deliverable state but the seller is bound to weigh, measure, and test the goods to establish their price, ownership does not pass until these things have been done and the buyer is notified accordingly. Clearly, this Rule is not applicable to a situation where nothing further needs to be done to the goods to render them deliverable.

9.4.15   *Rule 4* deals with goods sent on approval or on sale or return. In this case, ownership of the goods will pass to the buyer only when he informs the seller that he wants them or confirms to the seller that he wants them or in some other way indicates that he wants them. Three examples of the kinds of action that could signify the buyer's intentions were given by Lopes, LJ in *Kirkham* v. *Attenborough* [1897] 1 QB 201,204:(i) The buyer may pay the price; or (ii) He may retain the goods beyond a reasonable time for return; or (iii) He may do an act inconsistent with his being other than a purchaser.
 In accordance with the third of these possibilities, the buyer may therefore sell the goods to someone else and would, it appears, pass a good title, unless the terms of the original contract prohibited him from this. If the contract says 'The goods remain the seller's property until paid for or charged' pursuant to the all-embracing proviso ('unless a different intention appears'), then ownership will not pass. If the seller holds his buyer as authorised to sell the goods, then the seller may lose them to an innocent third party: s.21: the 1979 Act.

(v) Unascertained Goods and Rule 5

9.4.16   *Rule 5(1)* of s.18 deals with future or unascertained goods. In other words, it covers goods which are not specific at the time of sale. These were the sort of goods in *Healy* and *London Wine* (above) and are generic or simply unidentified parts of a whole. This Rule determines the precise moment after the contract has been made at which the goods become the buyer's property. It states:'Where there is a contract for the sale of unascertained or future goods by description the property passes when the goods of that description and in a deliverable state are unconditionally appropriated to the contract by one party with the express or impled assent of the other.'
Hence the goods must be *'unconditionally appropriated'* to the contract by the seller or buyer with the express or implied approval of the other.
The case of *Pignataro* v. *Gilroy* [1919] 1 KB 459 is instructive. The seller sold 140 bags of rice to the buyer, 15 bags of which were appropriated by the seller for the contract. The buyer was told where he could collect them. The bags were then stolen through no fault of the seller before the buyer was able to collect them. The buyer failed in his action to recover the price paid for the 15 bags. It was held that the buyer had by his conduct assented to the seller's appropriation; the seller's appropriation of the bags for the contract, without any objection by the buyer, constituted transfer of title to those bags. The property in the goods (and therefore the risk) had passed to the buyer. The bags thus belonged to the buyer when they were stolen.
No appropriation occurs in an f.o.b. contract until the goods are shipped: *Carlos Federspiel & Co.* v. *Twigg Ltd.* [1957] 1 Lloyd's Rep. 240. The words of Pearson,J in the *Federspiel case* are illuminating:

> 'A mere setting apart or selection by the seller of the goods which he expects to use in performance of the contract is not enough. If that is all, he can change his mind and use those goods in performance of some other contract and use some other goods in performance of this contract. To constitute an appropriation of the goods to the contract, the parties must have had or be reasonably supposed to have had an intention to attach the contract irrevocably to those goods and no others are the subject of the sale and becomes the property of the buyer...if there is a further act, an important and decisive act, to be done by the seller, then there is *prima facie* evidence that probably the property does not pass until the final act is done.'

The appropriation must therefore be 'irrevocable' and conclusive to be legally effective. It is perhaps also worth noting that if the goods are in the hands of a third party bailee such as a warehouseman, the goods may still be deemed to have appropriated if, for example, the third party ackowledges that he holds the goods on the buyer's behalf: see *Sterns* v. *Vickers* (1923) (discussed above at 15.4.7). The rationale for this decision appears to be that by giving a delivery order to the buyer, the seller has done all that he can to enable the buyer to collect the goods. In commercial sales, the American Commercial Code (see UCC: 2-509) adopts the same approach.

9.4.17 *Rule 5(2)* of section 18 must be read in conjunction with s.16. Rule 5(2) provides that a seller who delivers goods to the buyer or to a carrier for transmission, without reserving a right of disposal, is deemed to have unconditionally appropriated the goods to the contract. Under s.16, no right of ownership passes until the goods are ascertained.

(vi) Reservation/Retention of Title Clauses: s.19

9.4.18 Under s.19, the seller may reserve the right of disposal of the goods until certain conditions are fulfilled and ownership will not then pass to the buyer until the conditions imposed by the seller have been fulfilled. In brief, this suggests that if the contract has been appropriately worded, a seller may remain owner of his goods until he is paid for them. The form of words that is frequently used for this *retention of title* or *reservation of title clause* has already been suggested (see 9.4.8, above) and the main purpose of the seller in inserting such a clause is to attempt to give himself the best available security in the event that the buyer becomes insolvent. The opening words of s.18 again come to mind, namely 'unless a different intention appears' which means that provided this different intention is suitably worded, a so-called *Romalpa* clause (named after the case containing that type of clause: see 9.4.19, below) has been utilised as a useful device for hard-pressed sellers.

a. The Romalpa Case

9.4.19 In the *Romalpa Case* (1976), the plaintiffs (AIV), who were a Dutch supplier of aluminium foil, provided in their conditions of sale that 'The ownership of the material to be delivered by AIV will only be transferred to the purchaser when he has met all that is owing to AIV no matter on what grounds.' After taking delivery of a consignment of aluminium the purchaser went into liquidation. The plaintiffs, who had not received the purchase price sought to enforce the above provision so as to secure payment prior to the distribution of the insolvent buyer's assets to the general creditors. The Court of Appeal held:
 (i) that the clause enabled the plaintiffs to recover from the insolvent buyer all the unsold foil still on his premises; and
 (ii) that since the object of the clause would be defeated unless it impliedly obliged the buyer to hold the proceeds of sale of unmixed foil on trust for the plaintiffs, the plaintiffs had a right to follow such monies into the buyer's bank account and require payment from it.
 On the special facts of *Romalpa*, the seller succeeded in recovering the unsold foil and the identifiable proceeds of sold foil from the buyer's liquidator. The remedy of possession appears to be wider than than the remedy of lien which is for the price only. Further, the *Romalpa* remedy may be exercised until 'all that is owing' has been paid. In addition, it is wider than the right of stoppage *in transitu* since the right to stop in transit ends when transit ends. The *Romalpa* remedy is only available after delivery of the goods.

274

b. Effect of Romalpa Case

9.4.20 The *Romalpa Case* was widely regarded as a controversial decision which has resulted in the floodgates of many such 'Romalpa clauses' being inserted in contracts. The effect of the decision seemed to be to give comfort to sellers who used such clauses but not to unsecured creditors of companies in the *Romalpa* circumstances. Neither the proceeds of sale nor the buyer's stock in trade would be available to these creditors and even the bank might not be first in priority. Since English law does not require reservation of title clauses to be publicly registered, nor any form of mandatory notice to be given, it appears extremely difficult to discover a company's real creditworthiness. Such a clause, if prudently drafted, however, could still give an unsecured creditor a measure of protection from a buyer's insolvency.

9.4.21 Caselaw has established that the inference from s.19 is that payment of the buyer's debts must be made in full before property in the goods would pass: see *Mitsui* v. *Flota* [1988] 1 WLR 1145; and that a Romalpa clause will not apply once the goods or material in question have been incorporated into other goods or subjected to the manufacturing process. In *Re Peachdart* [1983] 3 All ER 204, leather which was intended to be used in the manufacture of handbags, was sold on reservation of title terms, with the seller being entitled to ownership of *both* leather *and* handbags. It was nevertheless held that once goods were incorporated into other goods they ceased to exist, hence the supplier's title ceased to exist when the leather had been made into handbags. The seller's claim to the proceeds of sale of the bags was also dismissed, inter alia, on the basis that there was no way of relating the proceeds of sale of the bags to the value of the leather in them.
In *Clough Mill* v. *Martin* [1984] 3 All ER 982, the material concerned here was yarn which the buyer would spin into fabric. The reservation of title clause stated that the ownership of the yarn remained with the seller until the seller had received payment in full, or the yarn was sold by the buyer in a *bona fide* sale at full market value. When a receiver was appointed the seller claimed a quantity of the yarn. The receiver refused to return it. The case was heard on the claim for wrongful use (conversion) of the yarn and is not therefore a direct authority on the *Romalpa* clause. However, the Court of Appeal upheld the seller's claim and the receiver was held personally liable for wrongful use of goods. Significantly, Oliver,LJ suggested that they saw 'no reason in principle why the original legal title in a newly manufactured article composed of materials belonging to A and B should not lie where A and B have agreed it shall lie.'

c. Principle of the Romalpa Case

9.4.22 The broad principle discernible from the *Romalpa* case appears to be that if goods have been delivered to the buyer under a contract which contains a stipulation that ownership of the goods is only to pass on payment, the seller may be able to recover the goods and possibly the identifiable proceeds of sale from the buyer's liquidator, in the event of the buyer's bankruptcy. As a final observation, it would appear that everything turns on the precise wording of the individual clause in each case and the claim to mixed goods and, arguably, their proceeds of sale, will succed or fail depending on the specificity of the wording of a *Romalpa* clause.

(vii) Delivery at Seller's Own Risk

9.4.23   If the seller agrees to deliver specific goods at his own risk, then s.33 of the 1979 Act becomes relevant. Section 33 reads: 'Where the seller of goods agrees to deliver them at his own risk at a place other than that where they are when sold, the buyer must, nevertheless, unless otherwise agreed, take any risk of deterioration in the goods necessarily incident to the course of transit.'
The implication of this provision is that the seller would take the risk of unusual or extraordinary deterioration or loss.

viii. Duties of Buyer and Seller

(i) Conditions and Warranties

9.4.24   Under English law, rights and duties granted or imposed under a contract of sale are divided into conditions and warranties. There has also been considerable academic and judicial discussion prompted by certain leading cases over the proper legal effect of terms of the contract which could not be definitively categorised as either condition or warranty and were sometimes called 'innominate terms.' There are also statutory rules which supplement the common law rules which govern the duties of buyers and sellers. A *condition* is an essential term, which goes to the root of a contract, the breach of which normally entitles the innocent party to *repudiate* the contract and *claim damages*. A *warranty* is a stipulation of secondary importance, ancillary to the contract, the breach of which only entitles the innocent party to damages but not the right of repudiation. Conditions and warranties have been integrated into the Sale of Goods Act 1979 which elaborates and adapts the terminology and concepts to the sale of goods. It is not possible in a book of this nature to explore the many terminological and legal difficulties that have been raised by the terms 'condition' and 'warranty' which have been the subject of many decided cases and fairly extensive academic opinion. Suffice to say that the legal meanings of the words differ from their meaning in common English usage; even more confusingly, they have also been used interchangeably in law. To give an example of each:
(a) The word 'condition' may be used as a *condition precedent*, or as an essential prerequisite of contractual liability, eg, as in 'If I manage to sell my shares, I will sign the contract.' There will not be any liability for breach of the proposed contract if the shares are not sold.

(b) The word 'warranty'(in old English usage) used to mean a promise of any kind, whether of crucial importance or merely subsidiary. Today it often refers to a manufacturer's guarantee, which may carry no legal consequences whatever, or to an insured party's obligations, the breach of which may nullify the contract even though the breach was not the cause of the insured ' loss!

(ii) Innominate Terms

9.4.25   Given that it may be very difficult in certain cases to decide whether a particular term should be regarded as a condition or warranty, the English courts have decided that the final classification of a term may depend on either (i) the intention of the parties; or (ii) the nature and consequences of the breach of the contract rather than on the prior classification of the terms. In the absence of evidence of intention, the court will consider the consequences of the breach. The leading case, from which (ii) is derived, is the Court of Appeal decision, *Hong Kong Fir Shipping* v. *Kawasaki Kisen Kaisha* (*The Hong Kong Fir Case*) [1962] 1 All ER 474. This did not involve a sale of goods but a contract of hire of a ship -a charterparty- in which one of the terms was that the ship should be seaworthy. *Prima facie*, it might have been thought that a ship which was in no fit state to go to sea at all with no prospect of being repaired sufficiently so as to make it fit to sail again, would surely entitle the charterer to repudiate the contract altogether. Seaworthiness might therefore have been regarded as a vital term and therefore a condition. However, on the case authorities, seaworthiness was a comprehensive standard and a ship might therefore be pronounced unseaworthy for a trifling defect which could be rectified quite easily but might fail the legal standard. Accordingly, the Court of Appeal held that the shipowner's duty could not be classified beforehand as a condition or warranty but remained an'innominate term' until the nature and consequences of its breach could be assessed. Subsequent cases have merely confirmed the existence of such a category which cannot be classified and will be adjudicated upon only when the consequences of its breach are known.

For example, the *Mihalis Angelos* [1971] 1 QB 164 held that some contract terms should still be properly regarded as conditions, so that any breach of them should entitle the innocent party to repudiate the contract; the House of Lords in the *Reardon Case* [1976] 1 WLR 989 appeared to say that express contractual conditions in a contract of sale of goods should be subject to the general rules of contract and not the peculiar and specialised rules laid down in the Sale of Goods Act. The position is clearly unsettled and the most that can be said is that judges have a wide discretion as to how to rule in any case of ambiguity.

The uncertainty caused is certainly unsatisfactory from the strictly commercial point of view since business certainty, at least within a measure of reasonableness, is generally essential to commercial dealings. However, it is still up to contracting parties (or their legal advisers) to devise contracts which will leave no doubt as to the importance that they wish to attach to individual terms of a contract so that if the matter comes to court, the judges will have very little room within which to manoeuvre and have no option but to implement the clearly-stated wishes of the contracting parties.

(iii) Breach of Entire and Severable contracts

9.4.26   Another possible scenario which the courts have faced is the question of construing when a breach has taken place is in the context of *entire* and *severable* contracts. The 'entire' contract is a contract in which no payment is due to the seller or supplier of services until he has fulfilled *all* his commitments precisely in accordance with the terms of the contract. A 'severable' contract is one in which part payment is due as soon as *each stage of the contract* has been completed. Thus, in the case of an entire contract, the most trivial defect or deficiency in the seller's performance of the contract would, in strict law, amount to a breach of contract which would entitle the buyer to repudiate the contract. However, this might not always be an equitable solution since the buyer might not be able to return any benefits he might have already received under the contract, thus making an unjustifiable profit. Three points tend to mitigate against interpreting contracts as entire ones. First, judges apply the 'substantial performance' approach which reduces the situation to a breach of warranty which will not justify repudiation. Secondly, judges are generally reluctant to contrue contracts as entire contracts. Thirdly, there is a common law principle that does not allow a whole sum of money to be recovered unless there has been a total failure of consideration. Thus, if a buyer paid some money in advance to the seller in pursuance of a contract, and the seller had already performed part of the contract, the buyer could not usually recover the money unless he received nothing at all in return for it.

(iv) Conditions as Warranties under the Sale of Goods Act

9.4.27   Under s.11 of the Sale of Goods Act 1979, it is possible for a breach of condition to be treated as a warranty in certain circumstances. Under s.11(2) a buyer may waive a breach of condition by the seller or elect to treat it as a breach of warranty. If a contract is non-severable, and the buyer has accepted all or some of the goods, by s.11(4) a buyer must treat a breach of condition as a breach of warranty. However, s.11(4) does *not* apply to a breach of s.12 which enacts that there is an implied condition that the seller has the right to pass title to the goods. A breach of s.12 will amount to a total failure of consideration since the transfer of the property on the goods is the essence of a contract of sale. Such a breach cannot therefore be treated as a breach of warranty.

(v) Seller's Duties

9.4.28   In the nineteenth century, in the heyday of the *laissez-faire* philosophy, the basic rule was that 'the seller was not liable for a bad title unless there was an express warranty or an equivalent to it by declaration or conduct': Baron Parke in *Morley* v. *Attenborough* (1849) 3 Exch.500, 512. Thus the rule was *caveat emptor* (let the buyer beware). However, this was often countermanded by caselaw and section 12 of the 1979 Act (the Act) now enacts that *there is an implied condition that the seller has the right to pass good title to the goods*.

(vi) Sale by description

9.4.29 Where goods are *sold by description*, there is also an *implied condition* under s.13 of the Act that:
(i) The goods will correspond with the description: s.13(1)
(ii)If the sale is by sample, as well as by description, the
     bulk of the goods will also correspond with the sample:
     s.13(2).
This has proved to be a source of dispute in a number of cases because of the very open-endedness of language and its many possible meanings. Among the issues encountered is the question: Has this section abolished the distinction between mere representations and contractual terms? Cases such as *Beale* v. *Taylor* [1967] 1 WLR 1193 appear to suggest that in practice this section makes it easier for a buyer to argue that a descriptive statement by the seller is a contractual term and not a mere representation. However, the House of Lords has also suggested that a statement about the goods is only part of the 'description' if it has been used to identify the goods: see *Ashington Piggeries* v. *Christopher Hill* [1972] AC 441. The approach must therefore be to analyse the descriptive words to see if they amount to mere representations or form part of the contract. If they are contractual, the normal contractual remedies will be available. If they are *misrepresentations* then the usual rules will apply under common law and the Misrepresentation Act 1967. The case of *Grant* v. *Australian Knitting Mills* [1936] AC 35 is also instructive. Here, a buyer of underpants contracted dermatitis because of an excess of sulphite in the garment he purchased. The House of Lords emphasised that a sale may be 'by description' even if the buyer has seen the goods before buying them provided he relied essentially on the description, and any discrepancy between the description and the goods is not apparent. There was therefore a breach of s.13 in that case. There is therefore a sale by description 'even though the buyer is buying something displayed before him on the counter. A thing is sold by description, though it is specific, so long as it is sold not merely as the specific thing but as a thing corresponding to a description.': Lord Wright in the *Grant* case. His Lordship gave the examples of woolen undergarments, a hot-water bottle, and a second-hand reaping machine. Thus, s.13(3) makes it clear that a sale of goods is not prevented from being a sale by description solely because goods being exposed for sale are selected by the buyer: s.13(3).
 Hence many goods may 'describe themselves' by the way they are packed or displayed, and the word 'description' in the section does not assume that anything was in fact said or written. Hence whether the goods are new, used, their measurements and packing may all be relevant what are essential or merely secondary attributes.
 As with other aspects of this area of law, a great deal will depend on the *the consequences of the breach* and the *cost of the repairs or replacement of the goods*. If buyers receive the goods according to their description but they

then turn out to be defective, then their remedy will be under s.14 of the Act which deals with the rules on merchantable quality and fitness of the goods for the purpose for which they have been bought. In view of the uncertainty involved in establishing a case under s.14 buyers may be better advised to attempty to bring their goods within s.13. One method of doing this might be to use extremely precise language so that the goods are described and identified as clearly and unambiguously as possible rather than in general terms such as 'in good condition'.

(vii) Implied Conditions Relating to Quality or Fitness

9.4.30   Section 14 preserves the basic *caveat emptor* rule (let the buyer beware) *under certain circumstances*. It declares that there will be an implied condition that the goods will be of merchantable quality *only as provided by its subsections or by s.15*. The exceptions to the general principle are: (i) under s.14(2): implied condition of merchantable quality; (ii) under s.14(3) implied condition of fitness; (iii) under s.14(4): conditions and warranties implied by usage; and (iv) under s.15(2)(c): implied condition that goods will be free from any latent defects on a sale by sample.

9.4.31   Under s.14(2) of the Act, where goods are sold *in the course of business* there is an *implied condition* that those goods are of merchantable quality unless (i) the defects have been pointed out to the buyer before the sale, or (ii) if the buyer has examined those goods before the sale was made, and should have discovered those defects at that time.
The words *'in the course of a business'* include a profession, and the activities of a government department, local or public authority: s.61(1): the Act. It is not necessary to be the manufacturer of the goods and there is no requirement that the business must consist of the buying and selling of the type of goods which are actually sold. Hence if a milkman sold one of his milk-floats, this would still be 'in the course of a business'. Where a person sells the goods *as agent for another,* for example a trader selling something on behalf of a non-trader, then the purchaser has the benefit of the statutory protection unless he knows that the goods are being sold on behalf of a non-trader or the trader took reasonable steps to inform the purchaser of this fact: s.14(5): the Act. s.14(2) will cover goods 'supplied' as well as goods 'sold'.

9.4.32   *'Merchantable quality'* is dealt with by s.14(6), which was inserted by the Supply of Goods (Implied Terms) Act 1973, says that goods are merchantable 'if they are fit for the purpose or purposes for which goods of that kind are commonly bought as it is reasonable to expect, having regard to any description applied to them, the price (if relevant) and all the other relevant circumstances'. This appears to be somewhat unhelpful since merchantability is defined in terms of reasonable fitness which is the second of the two requirements, but which is not itself defined. The key requirement, both under the common law established prior to the s.14(6) definition (ie pre-1973), is that the goods will not be deemed merchantable if they have defects

280

which make them unfit for their proper use *within the terms of the contract description and the particular circumstances of the case.* 'Merchantable quality' appears to be a relative concept. So everything will turn on what the actual terms of the contract are. Hence, as *Bartlett* v. *Sydney Marcus* [1965] 1 WLR 1013 appears to illustrates, if a car, for example, is being sold as 'second-hand with a defective clutch' the car could not be said to be unmerchantable if the defect, once accepted by the buyer, then proved more expensive to rectify than expected. The position would certainly be different if a new car were being offered for sale which proved defective upon examination. *Wilson* v. *Rickett Cockerell* [1954] 1QB 198 suggests that the implied condition as to merchantable quality does not only apply to goods sold but also to goods supplied under the contract.

9.4.33 The question of the *extent of the defects* required to entitle a buyer to reject the goods has proved a fruitful source of litigation, where occasionaly, cases have held that even trivial defects rendered the goods unmerchantable: see. eg *Jackson* v. *Rotax Motor Cycle Co.* [1910] 2 KB 937; *Parsons (Livestock) Ltd* v. *Uttley Ingham & Co* [1978] QB 791. However. against this sort of approach is the more common one which is to apply the well-known *de minimis* principle, so that defects or deficiencies of a trivial, superficial or cosmetic nature which do not really affect the basic quality of the merchandise will not be afforded relief by the courts and will not therefore entitle the right of rejection of the goods to be exercised. It should also be noted that the right to reject the goods can be lost quite quickly when the goods have been used by the buyer for any prolonged period, or been so used substantially or repeatedly.

9.4.34 Section 14(2)(b) of the Act clarifies the position regarding a buyer who examines the goods before the sale is completed. Such a buyer will not be protected if he actually examined the goods and the defects ought then to have been discovered. If, however, the defect is not discoverable by examination, the seller will then be liable: see *Wren* v. *Holt* [1903] 1 KB 610 where the plaintiff recovered damages for breach of the condition of merchantability where beer had been contaminated by arsenic, a defect which could not have been discoverable on reasonable examination.

9.4.35 Under s.14(3) where goods are sold in the course of a business and the *buyer (expressly or impliedly) makes known to the seller the purpose for which the goods are being bought*, there is an implied *condition* that they will be *reasonably fit for that purpose*, whether or not that is their usual purpose, unless in the circumstances the buyer does not rely, or it is unreasonable for him to rely on the seller's skill or judgment.
It is usually self-evident what the purpose of most goods is, at least as far as everyday consumer goods are concerned. Hence a buyer need only state his requirements in express terms when his needs are more specialised than usual or if they happen to be for unusual purposes. But the section also requires the buyer to have *prima facie* relied on the seller's skill and judgment

in selecting his goods and reliance is normally presumed. This presumption will be rebutted if, for instance, the buyer has carried out his own expert and detailed examination of the goods; or if the buyer has specified his own design for the goods in which case the quality and workmanship of the goods are still the seller's responsibility but not the success of the design: *Cammell Laird* v. *Manganese Bronze* [1934] AC 402. As *Wormell* v. *RHM* [1987] 3 All ER 85 suggests, the standard of fitness will depend on the complexity, price and age of the goods, the way they are described and packaged and their instructions as to use. Perfection (however one might define it) is not required of this standard of fitness. Courts frequently allude to the normal expectation and usage of a given product in order to assess the standard of reasonable fitness of merchandise.

9.4.36   It would appear the buyer has no statutory duty to take defective goods back to the seller to give him the opportunity to remedy the flaw before exercising a right of repudiation but if there are potential immediate and serious dangers, the buyer may have no choice but to do so. An example would be cars expressly sold 'subject to service' which means they should be repaired or adjusted after the sale. Unless the buyer does return to the seller to ascertain the extent of the defects, the seller will have had no opportunity to have rectified any problems with the vehicles. For cases which do not have the element of imminent danger but have frequent breakdowns or many minor defects, the case of *Rogers* v. *Parish* [1987] 2 All ER 232 is instructive. This involved a new Range Rover, costing sixteen thousand pounds which, six months after purchase, still had an engine that misfired at all speeds and an excessively noisy gearbox and transfer box. Attempts were made to rectify the faults but during this time, it was clear that the plaintiff was subjected to driving the vehicle with considerable discomfort and irritation. The appeal court, overturning the lower court, held that the purpose for which this car was required was not merely that of driving from one place to another but of doing so 'with ...comfort, ease of handling and...pride in the vehicle's outward and interior appearance'. The defects present in this car were simply well outside the range of expectation given the price of the car, its newness and the expected value for money. The buyer therefore succeeded in claiming his money back.

9.4.37   There are therefore four matters common to s.14(2) and s.14(3) of the Act:
  (i) The seller must sell in the course of a business;
  (ii) This condition applies to all goods 'supplied';
  (iii) Factors taken into account in deciding whether goods are 'merchantable' and 'reasonably fit' are the age of the goods, the price (if relevant) and all other relevant circumstances (such as the purpose(s) of the goods; or their packing;)
  (iv) The condition is one of *strict liability*; the absence of negligence on the part of the seller is no defence. It all depends on the particular situation: if goods have one purpose and they are unfit for that purpose a buyer would probably succeed under both subsections; if the goods are not fit for the

buyer's purpose but suitable for other purposes, the buyer will usually only have a remedy under s.14(3). The goods are statutorily required to be *'reasonably fit'* so it is important to bear in mind that *the seller is deemed to be guaranteeing the suitability and safety of the goods* and will still be liable whether or not he tries or is able to rectify the defect. Hence the primary liability, under English law, rests on the seller, which means that if it is claimed to be a manufacturing defect, the seller must then sue the manufacturer under the same section of the Act.

Strict liability is not, however, absolute liability. If the goods are reasonably fit for their purpose but they nevertheless cause loss or injury, the seller is not liable. Hence if buyers do not exercise sufficient care in using goods, for example by incorrect electrical installation, exposure to extreme heat, continued usage while aware of dangers of such usage, the sellers will not be liable for the consequences. There is no set minimum above which the courts will find goods or products unsafe; if certain type of food has killed someone only on rare occasions, it will still be considered unfit and unsafe, unless it proved dangerous as a result of the buyer's own fault, for instance, by not cooking it properly.

9.4.38   Under s.15(2)(c) of the Act, the implied condition that goods are of merchantable quality is excluded where there is a *sale by sample* and the defect could have been discoverable by *reasonable examination of the sample*, irrespective of whether the goods have in fact been examined. s.15 (2) also stipulates that where there is a sale by sample, there is an implied *condition* that:

(i) the bulk will correspond with the sample; and
(ii) the buyer will have a reasonable opportunity of comparing the bulk with the sample : s.15(2)(a) and (b).

(viii) Exclusion Clauses and Defective Goods

9.4.39   On the question of exclusion clauses in English law, this is partly dealt with by the Unfair Contract Terms Act 1977 (UCTA) and partly by caselaw. But we focus on the question of defective goods rather than on any more detailed consideration of this substantial area of law.

Section 6 of UCTA is a very important section which deals with contract clauses or notices excluding the operation of sections 12-15 of the Sale of Goods Act 1979 or equivalent sections of the Supply of Goods (Implied Terms) Act 1973 relating to hire-purchase transactions. The section first declares that no seller or owner can escape liability for failing to give a good title to the goods sold or hire-purchased. It then draws an important distinction between *consumer sales* and *non-consumer (business) sales* or transactions. As far as consumer sales are concerned, s.12, and sections 13-15 of the 1979 Act cannot be excluded by any clause or notice.

Hence *the statutory requirements as to description, sample, merchantable quality and reasonable fitness cannot be excluded for consumer sales by any such clause..* It is also a criminal offence to use such a clause: see Consumer Transactions (Restrictions on Statements) Order 1978. For *non-consumer*

283

contracts (ie contracts between businesses), s.13-15 may be excluded by a clause or notice but only if the *'test of reasonableness'* is satisfied (see 9.4.41 below). There is an exception made with regard to exclusion of liability for sales by description, merchantability and fitness in the case of 'international sales' under the Uniform Laws on International Sales.

9.4.40   A person *'deals as consumer'* when he buys for private use or consumption, and not in the course of his own business, from a business seller, and sold to a person who does not hold himself out as buying them in the course of a business: s.12 :UCTA. The meaning of sales made 'in the course of a business' has been discussed above. The status of the seller should be made plain since the Business Advertisements (Disclosure) Order 1977 requires the business status to be declared in advertisements. If a private person uses a business agent to sell his goods, the agent will be liable for the quality of the goods unless he informs the buyer that the sale is in the course of business: s.14(5): the 1979 Act. If a business engages in an activity (such as buying a car) which is incidental to their normal business, this will not be 'in the course of the business' unless it is an integral part of it if, for example, it is carried on with a degree of regularity: see *R & B Customers Brokers* v. *United Dominions Trust* [1987] 1 All ER 847. In that case, the purchase of a car by the company for the use of their directors was construed as a consumer contract because they were occasional purchases and car buying was not an integral part of the company's business.

9.4.41   The *'test of reasonableness'* is stated as a general principle in s.11 of the UCTA, which requires contractual and non-contractual clauses to be *'fair and reasonable'* clauses *at the time the contract was made*; and various statutory guidelines as to 'reasonableness' are listed in Schedule 2, which is contained in an Appendix to the Act. The crucial time is the time the contract was being made, when the clause should have been known or at least in the contemplation of the parties: s.11: UCTA. The burden of proving that the clause is reasonable is upon the seller or supplier who relies on it. The courts have a wide discretion under the UCTA to interpret exclusion or exemption clauses in accordance with their perception of what is 'reasonable' in the circumstances.

 Under Schedule 2 of the Unfair Contract Terms act 1977, the court is required to consider in particular the parties' relative bargaining power, availability of other sources of supply, any inducements offered to the buyer, whether other suppliers used such clauses, whether the buyer had adequate notice of the clause, whether it was reasonable at the time of the contract to comply with the clause, and whether the goods were manufactured, processed or adapted according to the buyer's special needs.

9.4.42   In some cases, the buyer can acquire a good title to the goods even though the seller had neither the property nor the right to dispose of the goods, either as owner or as pledgee. This is dealt with in the 1979 Act in sections 21-26 under the general heading 'Transfer of Title'. The classic common law position is neatly summarised in the words of Denning, LJ (as he then was) in *Bishopsgate Motor Finance Corpn.* v. *Transport Brakes Ltd* [1949] 1 All ER 37, 46, when he said: 'In the development of our law, two principles have striven for mastery. The first is for the protection of property: no one can give a better title than he himself possesses. The second is for the protection of commercial transactions: the person who takes in good faith and for value without notice should get a good title.'

This passage deals with the present topic, which may also be described by the maxim *nemo dat quod habet* (no man gives that which is not his own) and its exceptions. There are nine exceptions to the *nemo dat* rule:

  (i)   Sale under order of court;
 (ii)   Sale under a common law or statutory power;
(iii)   Estoppel;
 (iv)   Agency;
  (v)   Sale in market overt;
 (vi)   Sale under a voidable title;
(vii)   Disposition by seller in possession;
(viii) Disposition by buyer in possession after agreement to
        sell;
 (ix)   Disposition under Part III of Hire Purchase Act 1964.

It is emphasised that the present work is not intended to provide a full discourse and analysis of the many permutations of the sale of goods but to merely highlight key features and draw comparisons. In that vein, the following may be noted:

9.4.43   On the question of *estoppel*,Section 21 provides that where goods are sold by a person who is not the owner, the buyer acquires no better than the seller had unless:

  (i)   the seller had the authority or consent of the owner; or
 (ii)   the owner is precluded by his conduct from denying the seller's authority to sell.

9.4.44   At common law, a sale by an *agent* will bind his principal if the agent had actual, apparent or usual authority (see further Chapter 8). Under s.1 of the Factors Act 1889,a *mercantile agent* is defined as an agent having in the customary course of his business authority to sell goods, or raise money on the security of goods. This definition includes an auctioneer or broker, but not a clerk or warehouseman. Under s.2 of the same Act, any sale, pledge or other disposition by a mercantile agent in possession of goods or documents of title with the consent of the owner, and in the mercantile agent's agent's ordinary course of business to a *bona fide* purchaser for value without notice of any defect in his authority is as valid as if expressly authorised by the owner.

9.4.45   Sale in *market overt* is the most ancient of all the exceptions, originating from the sixteenth century when trading consisted of very simple transactions. The expression 'market overt' has been incorporated into the Sale of Goods Act (s.22) and it covers a sale that takes place in an *open, public and legally constituted market*; or in a shop in the City of London, provided it is held in the public part of that shop and it is by and not to the shopkeeper: *Ardah Tobacco* v. *Ocker* (1931) 4& TLR 177. It cannot take place in a private room and all of the goods must be exposed for sale not merely a sample. The sale must also take place between sunrise and sunset: *Reid* v. *Commissioner of Police* [1973] 1 QB 551 and the goods must be of a kind usually sold in the market. It may be held by charter, by prescription or under statutory powers.

9.4.46   Under section 23, when a seller of goods has a 'voidable title' (for fraud but not for mistake) but this title has not been avoided (set aside) at the time of sale, the buyer acquires a good title provided he buys in good faith without notice of the seller's defect in title. If a seller agrees to sell goods, whereby ownership is transferred, then retains those goods and subsequently disposes of them again to a third party, the delivery or transfer by him of those goods is as valid as if authorised by the owner, provided the second buyer takes in good faith without notice of the previous sale: see s.24 of the 1979 Act and s.8: Factors Act 1889. All the first buyer is left with is a personal action against the seller. Note that the seller only needs to retain *possession* for this exception to operate, although not necessarily as seller. He may also pass valid title as hirer or trespasser, provided the good faith and lack of notice requirements are satisfied on the part of the second buyer. The converse to this last situation is where A agrees to sell goods to B and it is agreed that ownership will pass on payment. B then obtains possession or documents of title with A's consent and delivers them to C, who takes in good faith and unaware of A's ownership. C (subject to the mercantile agency exception) will take good title: s.25(1): the 1979 Act.

9.4.47   The ninth and final exception (s.27) deals with a case where a motor vehicle is held under a hire-purchase or conditional sale agreement and the debtor disposes of the vehicle before ownership has passed to him. If the disposition has been made to a private purchaser who (i) takes in good faith; and (i) without notice of the agreement, the disposition will be valid to pass good title as if the title of the creditor has been vested in the hirer or buyer immediately before the disposition. Notice in this context means actual notice: *Barker* v. *Bell* [1971] 1 WLR 983. The term 'disposition' covers any sale, contract of sale, letting under a hire-purchase agreement and transfer of property under a provision in such agreement.

ix. Remedies of the Buyer and Seller

(i) Buyer's Remedies

9.4.48   We have already discussed at some length the remedies that are available to a buyer in the context of goods that do not conform to their description, are not of merchantable quality or are not fit for the purpose for which they have been sold. The right of the buyer to reject the goods or 'repudiate' the contract and the right to claim damages (monetary compensation) in certain circumstances have, by now, become quite familiar to the preceding discussion. Nevertheless, we now list six remedies that are available to the buyer when different breaches of contract have occurred:

   (i) Rejection of the goods;
   (ii) Recovery of the price;
   (iii) Action for damages for breach of warranty;
   (iv) Action for damages for non-delivery of the goods;
   (v) Specific Performance
   (vi) Tortious action

Rejection of the goods is available for *breach of condition* (see 9.4.24 above) unless the buyer has waived the breach and elected to treat it as a breach of warranty; or the contract is non-severable and the buyer has accepted the goods or part of them: s.11(4): The 1979 Act. The buyer may recover the price of the goods where he has paid for them if the consideration has failed, for example if the seller has no title or delivers goods which the buyer validly rejects: s.54: the 1979 Act. With regard to a *breach of warranty*, the buyer may set up the loss in diminution of the price or sue for damages. If the seller has *delayed delivery*, damages for delayed delivery are assessed on the basis of the difference between the value of the goods when they should have been delivered and their value at the time of delivery. An '*anticipatory breach*' of contract occurs where, *before the time of performance*, one party informs the other that he does not intend to perform the contract. The innocent party may ignore this proposed repudiation and wait for the date of performance in the hope that it will be performed or accept the repudiation and sue for damages. *Specific performance* (s.52) is the exceptional remedy in most cases in English law, since it will usually only be ordered if damages are an inadequate remedy. The buyer may also sue the seller and third parties in tort if he is entitled to possession of the goods and possession has been withheld. The buyer may sue the third party under the *Torts (Interference with Goods) Act 1977* if third parties wrongfully interfere with the goods but the buyer must have either possession or an immediate right to possess. A buyer who has resold the goods cannot recover the loss of profit in tort if he cannot recover it in contract, since damages would be computed on the same basis as a contractual claim for non-delivery.

(ii) Remedies of the Unpaid Seller

9.4.49 It will be recalled that under s.27, the buyer's duty is to accept and pay for the goods. If a seller is unpaid, however, he has the following six remedies under the 1979 Act:

  (i) A lien:s.41-43)
  (ii) A right of stoppage in transitu: ss.44-46
 (iii) Right of resale: s.48
  (iv) Right of retention where ownership has not passed to
       buyer: s.47(2)
  (v) Action for the price: s.49
  (vi) Action for damages for non-acceptance: s.50

9.4.50 A *lien* is the right to retain possession of goods (but not to resell them) until the contract price has been paid. Section 41 (1) provides that a lien exists in three cases:(a) where the goods have been sold without any stipulation as to credit; (b) where the goods have been sold on credit, but the term of credit has expired; and (c) where the buyer becomes insolvent. s.41(2) clarifies that the seller may exercise his right of lien even though he is in possession of the goods as agent or bailee or custodier for the buyer. The rights given under this section are very useful especially when combined with a power of sale under s.48. Note that the word 'insolvent' in s.41(1)(c) is wider than 'bankrupt' because s.61(4) states that 'A person is deemed to be insolvent within the meaning of the Act who either has ceased to pay his debts in the ordinary course of business, or cannot pay his debts as they become due, whether he has committed an act of bankruptcy or not'.

9.4.51 After the seller has parted with the possession of the goods to a carrier for transmission to the buyer he has the right to stop the goods and repossess them if the buyer becomes insolvent (ie is unable to pay his debts as they become due). The right of *stoppage in transit* is covered in sections 44 to 46. Three conditions are required before the right may be exercised: (a) the seller must be an unpaid seller within the meaning of the 1979 Act; (b) the buyer must be insolvent; and (c) the goods must be in course of transit. This remedy is no longer as important as it used to be since most export sales are nowadays financed by means of banker's commercial credits, which means that a bank in the seller's country pays the seller or accepts bills of exchange drawn by him in return for the shipping documents. Once this occurs, the seller is no longer an 'unpaid seller'. Thus the right is only important when the sale is on credit. The other method of finance, whereby a bill of exchange is sent together with a bill of lading, while still used, means that since a bank normally processes the shipping documents, the buyer must honour the bill of exchange before he may obtain the bill of lading and thereby the goods. The period of transit commences from the time when the goods are handed to the carrier until the time when the buyer takes delivery of them. There are two methods of exercising the right of stoppage, enunciated by section 46:

(i) By taking actual possession of the goods; and

(ii) By giving notice of his claim to the carrier or other bailee or custodier who has possession of the goods.

Transit may be also be terminated if the buyer obtains delivery of the goods before the arrival of the goods at the agreed destination, for instance, because the carrier hands them to the buyer's agent during transit. If the carrier acknowledges to the buyer that he is holding the goods to the buyer's order or if the carrier wrongfully refuses to deliver the goods to the buyer, transit is also terminated. It should also be noted that the right of stoppage does not *ipso facto* rescind the contract.

9.4.52   As a general principle, lien and stoppage in transit do not give the unpaid seller *the right to re-sell the goods* but s.48 lists *three exceptions*: (a) where the goods are of a perishable nature; (b) where the unpaid seller gives notice to the buyer of his intention to resell, and the buyer does not pay for them within a reasonable time; or (c) where the seller expressly reserves the right of resale in case the buyer defaults in payment.

9.4.53   The unpaid seller who is still the owner of the goods will have a right of retention coterminous with the right of lien or stoppage. Under s.47, the unpaid seller's right of lien or retention or stoppage in transit is not affected by any sale or other disposition of the goods which the buyer may have made, unless the seller has 'assented' to it. In practical terms, in order for the unpaid seller to have assented, he must have effectively renounced his rights against the goods, as, for example, by selling goods and agreeing to be paid out of the proceeds of a resale by the buyer: see *Mount Ltd*. v. *Jay and Jay Ltd* [1960] 1 QB 159. However, under s.47(2), where a document of title to goods has been lawfully transferred to any person as buyer or owner of goods and that person transfers the document to a person who takes it in good faith and for valuable consideration, then, provided that last transfer was by way of sale, the unpaid seller's right of lien or retention or stoppage in transit is defeated. If the last transfer was a form of pledge or other disposition for value, the unpaid seller's right of lien, retention or stoppage can only be exercised subject to the transferee's rights.

9.4.54   As we have seen, a seller may expressly contract that property in the goods (ie ownership) will remain his even after they are delivered, until the contract price or any other debt owing to him by the buyer has been paid: *Aluminium Industrie BV* v. *Romalpa* (1976) (above). If this has been done and the seller has not been paid, the seller may re-possess the goods if the buyer, being a company, goes into liquidation or receivership. There is no right to re-possess goods from a buyer who is a private individual unless he were adjudged bankrupt or if the seller were given some indication that the goods would not be paid for.

9.4.55   There are *two personal remedies available to the unpaid seller against the buyer*: (a) an *action for the contract price under s.49*, where the buyer wrongfully neglects or refuses to pay for the goods contrary to the terms of the contract or where they were due on a specific day irrespective of delivery; and (b) an *action for damages for non-acceptance under s.50*, where there is an available market. In these circumstances, the measure of damages will *prima facie*, be the difference between the contract price and the market price on the date fixed for acceptance, or in the absence of a fixed date, at the time of refusal to accept. If the buyer has become owner, the right to sue for the price is available whereas if the buyer is not yet owner, when he rejetcs the goods the seller's claim is for damages for breach of contract which will be 'unliquidated damages'. There may also be the right to *claim for special damages under s.54* and for any *loss occasioned by the buyer's neglect to take delivery. Under s.37*, where the seller is ready and willing to deliver the goods, and requests the buyer to take delivery but the buyer does not take delivery within a reasonable time after such request, the seller may sue for any loss occasioned by this non-delivery and also claim a reasonable charge for the care and custody of the goods.

x. The Supply of Goods and Services Act 1982

9.4.56   Certain hire and service contracts are dealt with under the Supply of Goods and Services Act 1982 (the 1982 Act), which came into force in the United Kingdom on January 4, 1983. The 1982 Act has two main parts. Part I amends the law regarding terms implied in certain contracts for the supply of goods and Part II codifies the common law rules applicable when a person agrees to carry out a service. The Act applies to contracts for services which do not necessarily involve transfer of goods, hence it applies to contracts 'under which a person agrees to carry out a service.' But it does not apply to apprenticeships, contracts of employment or services rendered to a company by a director and the services of an advocate before a court or tribunal. Under Part I, problems that arose with uncertain common law rules, and inadequate protection by the Sale of Goods Act either in terms of definition or scope were noted by the Law Commission and their recommendations eventually led to the 1982 Act. Contracts for work and materials, part exchange contracts defined as barter transactions, and contracts for the hire of goods which were not orginally covered by legislation, are now covered. Hence *the 1982 Act applies to 'contracts for the transfer of property in goods' and 'contracts for the hire of goods' and sections 2-5 enact statutory implied terms on the part of the seller which are similar to those in sections 12-15 of the 1979 Act.* Sections 1 to 5 of the 1982 Act deal with goods supplied under contracts for services and sections 6 to 10 cover those supplied on hire or loan.
 The 1982 Act effectively re-enacts the obligations imposed by sections 8-11 of the Supply of Goods (Implied Terms) Act 1973 so that they apply to the contracts covered by the 1982 Act. In the case of contracts for work and materials, such as contracts for installation of central heating, double glazing, burglar alarms, repairs, construction and so on, the supplier undertakes two obligations: (a) an obligation pertaining to the goods (as now governed by s.2-5 of the 1982 Act); and (b) an obligation pertaining to the work (now

governed by ss.13-15 of the 1982 Act. Hence, in such contracts, there, for example, be an 'implied *term*' that where the supplier is acting in the course of a business he will perform the service with 'reasonable care and skill' (s.13: 1982 Act); if the time for the service to be carried out is not specified by the contract or determined by the parties' course of dealing, there is an implied term that the service will be carried out within a reasonable time (s.14: 1982 Act). Finally, if the parties have not specified the consideration for the contract the party contracting with the supplier will pay a 'reasonable price'. It will be noticed that the 1982 Act implies terms, without using the language of conditions and warranties.

This seems sensible since the very nature of services will make it impossible to repudiate in the sense of being returned to their supplier and so the right of repudiation (contingent upon breaches of *condition*) is inappropriate. Damages would therefore be the proper remedy for breach of these implied *terms*.

9.4.57   On the question of *exclusion clauses*, the Unfair Contract Terms Act 1977 (UCTA) has been amended by the 1982 Act in realtion to contracts for the supply of goods other than contracts of sale of hire purchase so that: (a) if the exclusion clause relates to title it will be void: s.7(3A): UCTA; (b) if the exclusion clause relates to description, quality , fitness or sample it will then depend on whether the buyer deals as a consumer or not. If he does, the clause is void: s.7(2) UCTA; if he docs not, the exclusion clause must satisfy the test of reasonableness as laid down in s. 11 and Schedule 2 of UCTA; (c) if the exclusion clause relates to poor quality work, which might amount to a breach of s.13, the clause must also satisfy the reasonableness requirement (as above) unless the negligent work causes personal injury or death in which case it will be void: s.2: UCTA.

If there is a complaint concerning defective materials in a consumer contract, the exclusion clause will be void. However if the materials are of acceptable quality but the workmanship is negligent the exclusion clause will again have to satisfy the reasonableness requirement (as above). Note that while a supplier of *goods* is under an obligation to ensure such goods are *reasonably fit* for the purpose for which they are supplied, a supplier of *services* is only able to undertake that he will comply with the normal standards of his trade or profession. Hence a supplier of services who carries out the contract according to the normal standard expected of him in his trade or profession, cannot generally be sued for breach unless the contract lays down some higher standard or some other special and specific requirement. As a general standard of professional work, English law expects a standard of reasonable care which will be judged in accordance with the view of a responsible body of opinion within that profession. (on the question of negligence in English law see Chapter 7).

E. THE UNIFORM LAWS ON INTERNATIONAL SALES

9.5   In 1964, two international Conventions were adopted at the Hague after nearly thirty years of preparation, involving thirty countries redrafting and negotiation: the Uniform Law on the International Sale of Goods (ULIS) and the Uniform Law on the Formation of Contracts for the International Sale of Goods (ULOF). These are commonly referred to as the Hague Uniform Laws.

This particular version was ratified with reservation by the United Kingdom (that it would only apply if the parties chose it as the law to govern their contract). The Uniform Laws on International Sales Act 1967 came into force in Britain in 1972.

Apart from France, which played a large part in the drafting of the Laws, all the other five original members of the EEC ratified the Convention. By 1989, there were some 180 reported decisions on the Hague Uniform Laws in the courts of the Member States, except for the English and Scottish courts. (see Nicholas (1989) 105 LQR 201,202). It seems fair to say that these Uniform Laws simply failed to attract sufficient support, despite them obtaining a currency in Western Europe, predominantly because it was seen as representing a narrowly West European orgin, despite the thirty-five countries that represented at the Hague-nineteen of these were from Western Europe.

In any event, further revisions were made and on 11 April, 1980, the UN Convention on Contracts for the International Sale of Goods was adopted at a Diplomatic Conference of 62 States convened in Vienna by the Secretary-General of the United Nations. The Convention became effective on 1 January 1988.

The UN Convention is a radically revised version of the original Hague Uniform Laws. For instance, there are no longer two Conventions but there is now one Convention which is divided into four parts: Part I defines the Convention's sphere of application and contains provisions dealing with interpretation, usages and requirements of contractual form. Part II deals with the Formation of Contract, Part III contains the main body of rules on Sale of Goods and Part IV deals with the public international law framework. Article 92 allows a contracting state to declare that it will not be bound by Part II or Part III.

Article 6 provides that, subject to Article 12 (see below), the *parties are free to exclude or vary the provisions of the Convention in whole or in part*. There is no mention of whether there may be implied exclusion but this is probably covered. Nevertheless, this has left the situation uncertain since it is never safe to predict when the courts will be prepared to make such an implication.

The Convention was the result of a successful project under the auspices of the the United Nations Committee on International Trade Law (UNCITRAL), set up in 1966 to promote 'the progressive harmonisation and unification of the law of international trade.'

It is proposed here only to compare and contrast the main points of the approach taken to sale of goods by the ULIS so that one may compare them with the civil law and common law approaches.

i. Meaning of 'International Sale'

9.5.1 An 'international sale' is defined in Article 1 of the Convention but, like everything else in the Convention (except as provided by Article 12) this is subject to the power to contract out. In other words, parties to whose contract the Convention otherwise applies are bound by it unless they have excluded its provisions in whole or in part: Article 6.

According to Article 1(1), the Convention 'applies to contracts of sale of goods between parties whose *place of business are in different States*: (a) when the States are contracting States; or (b) when the *rules of private international law* lead to the application of the law of a Contracting State.

Nicholas (1989) sees the rule in Article 1(1)(a) as being either too wide or too narrow depending on the circumstances but it is at least straightforward and clear. Article 10 also provides that if a party has more than one place of business, the relevant place is that which has 'the closest relationship to the contract and its performance'. However, there is clearly some uncertainty of the rule in Article 1(1)(b) since the rules of private international law, which would be the rules of the forum state, would never be realistically predictable.

ii. Sale of Goods

9.5.2 The Convention only applies to contracts of sale of goods (Article 1(1)). There is no definition of sale, although the words of Articles 30 and 53 (relating to the obligations of buyer and seller) suggest that a conventional defintion will be applied. Sales of goods bought for personal, family or household use (consumer sales) are excluded where there might be a conflict between the Convention and mandatory rules of domestic law for the protection of consumers (Article 2 (a)). Auction sales and sales on execution or otherwise by authority of law are also excluded (Article 2(b) and (c)).

It should be noted that just as the parties may contract out of the Convention, they may also agree that it shall apply to a transaction in cases where that transaction is, or may otherwise be, inapplicable.

Various other substantive matters connected with the sale of goods are covered and we may usefully highlight the following:

(a) *Fundamental Breach*: this is widely defined in Article 25 and is not without some ambiguity. A fundamental breach is committed by one of the parties 'if it results in such detriment to the other party as substantially to deprive him of what he is entilted to expect under the contract, unless the party in breach did not foresee and a reasonable person of the same kind in the same circumstances would not have foreseen such a result.' This is not quite the same scope as the English version (as propounded by Diplock,LJ in *Hong Kong Fir Shipping Co.* v. *Kawasaki Kishen Kaisha Ltd* (1962) 2 QB, at p.66), namely whether the breach deprived the innocent party of 'substantially the whole benefit which it was the intention of the parties as expressed in the contract that he should obtain.'

(b) *Specific Performance*: the Convention adopts the Continental approach which is that it is the norm rather than the exception, being the right of the promisee so that damages are generally merely a substitute for actually carrying out the contract. Nevertheless, the common law position is preserved under Article 28 which allows the court to option not to order specific performance 'unless the court would do so under its own law in respect of similar contracts of sale not governed by this Convention.' Thus the priority of specific performance remains in jurisdictions to which the provision does apply.

(c) *Modification and Termination of the Contract*: This can be done purely by the mere agreement of the parties; consideration is not required. Thus, although the Convention does not expressly deal with the validity of a contract of sale, it impliedly allows the parties to decide on matters conncected with its validity.

(d) *The Seller's Obligations*: These are in accordance with most national laws, with the seller being bound to deliver goods which are 'of the quantity, quality and description required by the contract and which are contained or packaged in the manner required by the contract.' (Article 35(1)) and Article 35(2) is similar to the merchantable quality definition in s.14(6) of the English Sale of Goods Act 1979 (SGA) (goods needing to be 'fit for the purpose or purposes for which goods of that kind are commonly bought') but without the further elaboration of those requirements which follows on in that subsection (ie 'having regard to the description.. price (if relevant) and all the other circumstances') of the English statute. Article 35(1) (b) is very similar to s.14(3):SGA (fitness for purpose known to the seller), sub-paragraph (c) is equivalent to s.15(2)(a):SGA (sale by sample) and sub-paragraph deals with adequacy of packaging.

On the question when the buyer will lose (wholly or partially) the right to rely on a lack of conformity of the goods, there was no concordance between common law and civil law solutions. Accordingly, another compromise was reached. The buyer must examine the goods as soon as practicable and he will lose his right to rely on the lack of conformity if he does not give notice of it to the seller (i) within a reasonable time after he discovered it or ought ot have done so, (ii) in any case, within two years of the actual handing over of the goods (Article 39). The meaning of 'within a reasonable time' will depend on the buyer's circumstances but he may also resort to other remedies such as reduction of the price, or damages (except for loss of profit) if he has a reasonable excuse for failing to give notice. But all this must be within the two year limit.

(e) *Remedies of Buyer and Seller*: Two remedies for the buyer are stated which will be unfamiliar to the common law : (i) in cases of lack of conformity, the buyer may request the seller to repair the goods, unless this is in all the circumstances unreasonable. (ii) if the lack of conformity constitutes a fundamental breach, the buyer may request the seller to deliver substitute goods.

The Seller, however, has the right to cure any failure to perform his obligation, including a failure to deliver goods that conform, before the time fixed for performance (as in English law) and unlike English law, after the time fixed for performance. But this right is subject to it not causing the buyer unreasonable inconvenience or unreasonable expense and the buyer may still claim damages.

(f) *The 'Period of Grace' Procedure*: There is a procedure in the Convention which will familiar to German lawyers but not to English common lawyers: the *Nachfrist*(period of grace) remedy. This allows either party to fix an additional period of time to allow the other party to perform: Articles 47(1), 49(1)(b), 63(1), 64(1)(b). During the period specified, the party fixing the period cannot resort to any remedy for breach of contract. The only real benefit of this remedy is to give a party time to consider, or a period of grace, within which he may decide what course of action to adopt in relation to the breach and to encourage the other party to perform. The legal effect of this procedure is confined to three main cases: where the seller has failed to deliver or the buyer has failed to take delivery or to pay the price. If the failure is not remedied after the *Nachfrist* has expired, the other party will be entitled to avoid the contract regardless of whether the breach is fundamental or not.

(g) *Reduction of Price Remedy*: Again, this is a civil law remedy whereby the buyer, in the case of non-conformity of goods, is allowed to reduce the price 'in the same proportion as the value that the goods actually delivered had at the time of delivery bears to the value that conforming goods would have had at that time.' This rather convoluted wording basically allows the buyer to set-off his losses caused by falls in the value of the goods, but is only really advantageous if the breach is not fundamental.

If the buyer cannot claim damages because the non-conformity is due to an impediment beyond the seller's control, the remedy of reduction of price will protect the buyer. In any event, this remedy will not preclude a claim for damages, which means the buyer will have two remedies in the event of any losses suffered.

(h) *Avoidance of the Contract*: A right to 'avoid' (ie repudiate in English law parlance) the contract exists under the Convention, provided it is done within a reasonable time, for (a) a failure by the other party to perform any of his obligations which amounts to a fundamental breach or (b) if the seller fails to deliver or the buyer fails to pay the price or take delivery of the goods within a *Nachfrist* fixed by the other party. The effect of avoidance is to release both parties from their obligations under it, subject to any damages which may be due.

There is no equivalent of s.11(4) SGA where in the case of a 'non-severable' contract, a buyer cannot reject goods or repudiate a contract if he has accepted them in their entirety or in part. The Convention more closely resembles s.2-601 of the American Uniform Commercial Code .

(i) *The Rule for Damages*: Article 74 encompasses the rules in *Hadley* v. *Baxendale* (1854) 9 Exch. 341 but is slightly wider in stating that on the point of foreseeability, all that is required is that 'a possible consequence' of the breach was the loss suffered.

(j) *Impossibility of Performance*: This is covered in the Convention under 'Exemptions' under Article 79 and the first paragraph states: 'A party is not liable for a failure to perform any of his obligations if he proves that the failure was due to an impediment beyond his control and he could not reasonably be expected to have taken the impediment into account at the time of the contract or have avoided or overcome it or its consequences.'

ticle 79(5) goes on to elaborate on the meaning of 'is not liable':'Nothing in this Article prevents either party from exercising any right other than to claim damages under this Convention.'

Attention has been drawn (see Nicholas (1989)p.235) to several points: (i) This is different from the English contract law dealing with Impossibility of Performance, in certain ways-the non-performing party has a defence against an action for damages, and the impediment does not terminate the contract. (ii) The exemption from liability is in relation to the performance of 'any of his obligations' not just to the performance of the contract as a whole; (iii) The non-performance must be due to an impediment byond that party's control, which is similar to the French force majeure requirements, namely that the events must be unforeseeable, irresistible, unavoidable and insurmountable (Nicholas *French Law of Contract* (1992) p.203) but this will be quite familiar to the English lawyer as well. Concepts which are as broad as this, as with notions of fundamental breach, cannot really be pre-empted in their judicial interpretation. Everything will surely depend on the individual circumstances. (iv) This Article's formulation will not include cases amounting to Frustration in English law, since there is a focus on 'impediment' but will include English law cases of impossibility.

(k) *The Passing of Risk*: Subject to Articles 6 and 9, that the parties are free to exclude or vary the Convention's terms , apart from Article 12, and will be bound by any trade customs or usages to which they have agreed or any practices they have established among themselves, the Convention deals with two main categories of cases and a residual set of cases. The two categories are (1) typical international sales cases involving carriage of the goods (Article 67) and (2) goods sold in transit (Article 68); the residual categories are covered by Article 69.

In (1), for the Convention to apply, this must be a situation where the contract requires or authorises the seller to arrange for the goods to be carried and that the carriage will be by a third party, rather than the seller or the buyer or their servants. Here, if the seller is *not* bound to hand over the goods at a particular place, the risk passes 'when the goods are handed over to the first carrier for transmission to the buyer in accordance with the contract of sale. Where the seller *is* bound to hand over the goods to a carrier at a particular place, the risk does not pass to the buyer until the goods are handed over to the carrier at that place. As Nicholas (1989) explains, the policy underlying Article 67 is that risk should pass at the beginning of the agreed transit, since the buyer is usually in a better position than the seller to assess any damage which has occurred in transit and to institute claims in respect of it. (Nicholas (1989) p.238)

In (2), under Article 68, the risk passes to the buyer from the time of the 'conclusion' of the contract-in English law terms, at the time of its *formation*. The Article goes on to say that 'if the circumstances so indicate, the risk is assumed by the buyer from the time the goods were handed over to the carrier who issued the documents embodying the contract of carriage.' Following on from this, the Article inserts what English lawyers would call 'constructive notice' because it then says: 'Nevertheless, if at the time of the conclusion of the contract of sale the seller knew or ought to have known that the goods had been lost or damaged and did not disclose this to the buyer, the loss or damage is at the risk of the seller.' Thus it will depend on what the phrase 'if the circumstances so indicate' means.

Article 69 deals with cases not covered by either Articles 67 or 68 and states that in such cases:

> (1) the risk passes to the buyer when he takes over the goods or, if he does not do so in due time, from the time when the goods are placed at his disposal and he commits a breach of contract by failing to take delivery.
>
> (2) However, if the buyer is bound to take over the goods at a place other than a place of business of the seller, the risk passes when delivery is due and the buyer is aware of the fact that the goods are placed at his disposal at that place.
>
> (3) If the contract relates to goods not then identified, the goods are considered not to be placed at the disposal of the buyer until they are clearly identified to the contract.

Clearly the general idea is that the seller should bear the risk of loss so long as he has control of the goods. In paragraph (2) of Article 69, however, if the buyer is to take over the goods from a third party, usually from a warehouse, then the seller is in no better position than the buyer to protect and insure the goods or to pursue any claims which may arise. Hence the buyer should bear the risk as soon as he is in a position to collect the goods (see Nicholas (1989) p.240). There is, however a potential problem with paragraph (3) of Article 69 if a case like *Sterns* v. *Vickers* [1921] 1 KB 78 arose. In that case, although the property (or ownership) in the goods had had not passed because no appropriation had taken place, it was held that the parties must have intended the risk to pass when the delivery order was delivered, so that the buyer remained liable to pay the price.

Under Article 69(2), the intention seems to be that the risk should pass at once, yet under paragraph (3) the implication seems to be that risk would not pass until there has been some act of identification or appropriation. Nicholas believes this conflict was the result of a drafting oversight and suggests that the matter be dealt with as under Article 98(3) of the ULIS which reads: 'Where unascertained goods are of such a kind that the seller cannot set aside a part of them until the buyer takes delivery, it shall be sufficient for the seller to do all acts necessary to enable the buyer to take delivery.' (see Nicholas (1989) p.240).

iii. Validity and Passing of Property Excluded

9.5.3 Two important aspects of the contract of sale of goods have been excluded under the Convention: the validity of the contract and the passing of property. Article 4 categorically states that the Convention 'governs only the formation of the contract of sale and the rights and obligations of the seller and buyer' and that it is not concerned with (a) the validity of the contract or any of its provisions or of any usage; (b) the effect which the contract may have on the property in the goods sold.' Excluded matters will be governed by domestic law.

Passing of property proved to have too many national variations to be reconciled and, in any event, the subject extends outside the law of contract. The Convention does regulate matters such as the seller's obligation to deliver goods free of third party claims(Articles 41-43) and the passing of risk (Articles 66-70).

Exclusion of validity was also unavoidable because there is a wide spectrum of approaches in national laws on matters such as mistake and fraud and the practical problem is that national courts might adopt too varied a range of interpretations to maintain any consistency or unity in approach.

iv. Interpretation of the Convention

9.5.4   In the area of interpretation of the Convention and the filling of gaps, Article 7 states:'(1) In the interpretation of this Convention, regard is to be had to its international character and to the need to promote uniformity in its application and the observance of good faith in international trade.' The success or failure of the first part of this provision will clearly depend on the willingness of the national courts to consider the background of the Convention, relevant national caselaw of domestic tribunals and doctrinal writing. But it was the interpretation of 'good faith' that proved to be particularly controversial at the Working Committee stage of the Convention process. Basically, the common law states objected to the proposal of the Working Committee to require parties to 'observe the principles of fair dealing' and 'to act in good faith'. They argued that while the requirements were certainly desirable, the use of the terms was too uncertain and open-ended. Another proposal to adopt the German BGB formulation in paragraph 242 thereof was also considered too risky for commercial certainty. The text finally adopted represents a compromise.

The reference to the 'general principles' for the purpose of filling gaps was included in the hope of discouraging too precipitate a recourse to domestic law (see Nicholas (1989) p.210) but it surely turns on whether a court adopts a restrictive or extensive approach. Article 7 (2) requires a court to decide that there is no relevant general principle contained in the Convention before it may refer to domestic law as a source. There is a general requirement for the courts to promote uniformity in the application of the Convention.

As far as *trade usages and practices* are concerned, Article 9 (1) states that the parties are bound by 'any usage to which they have agreed and by any practices which they have established among themselves.' On the other hand, Article 9(2) suggests that

a party will be bound by a usage of which he did not know if it is one that is widely known and regularly observed in the particular branch of international trade that is involved and if the court's view is that he ought to have known of it. This resembles the English Law notion of an *implied term*, where a trade custom will be *deemed* to form part of the contract if the custom is generally accepted by those doing business in the particular trade in the particular place and so generally known that an outsider making reasonable enquiries could not fail to discover it (see *Kum* v. *Wah Tat Bank* [1971] 1 Lloyd's Rep. 439,444(Privy Council)).

On the form of a contract that would be acceptable as legally valid, there was inevitable disagreement but a compromise was reached. Article 11 preserves the right of freedom of form but Article 12 and 96 also allows a Contracting State whose legisation requires contracts of sale to be concluded in or evidenced in writing to make a declaration that any provision of the Convention that 'allows a contract of sale or its modification or termination by agreement or any offer, acceptance, or other indication of intention' to be made otherwise than in writing shall not apply where any party has his place of business in a state making the declaration. This does not mean that the formal requirements of the declaring state will automatically apply. That will occur only if under conflicts of laws principles, the declaring state's law is the applicable law.

Article 12 is the only provision that the parties are precluded from excluding under Article 6.

v. Ratifications

9.5.5   At the time of the UNCITRAL meeting in April 1988, no less than sixteen states had ratified or acceded to the Convention and these included Argentina, Australia, Austria, China, Egypt, Finland, France, Hungary, Italy, Lesotho, Mexico, Sweden, Syria, the USA, Yugoslavia and Zambia. The Federal Republic of Germany and the Netherlands were then reportedly in the process of ratification and Norway did so at the end of 1988. Since 1988, Bulgaria, Byelorussian SSR, Chile, Czechoslovakia, Denmark, Germany, Finland, Iraq, Spain, and the Ukrainian SSR have also ratified the Convention. At the end of its fifty-one-year gestation period, the Convention is by no means free from difficulties but at the very least, represents a monumental achievement of comparative law, a fusion of different traditions, flawed but fertile, providing a solid model of a truly international law.

F. COMPARATIVE OVERVIEW

9.6   Our comparative study of typically civil law and common law approaches to sales of goods reveals a great deal of similarities, partly attributable to the common heritage of the law merchant (*lex mercatoria*) or ancient mercantile law, but also attributable to the far-reaching changes wrought first by the industrial revolution, then by the impact of nationalism and codificatory tendencies, and the dawn of the technological era. It is also increasingly influenced by the unprecedented speed of technological advances which have exposed the archaic and outmoded legal structures in Western Europe and Britain. The wave of consumerism and the legal, social and political movement towards Consumer Protection begun in the 1960s and 1970s have also accelerated the need for change in transactions as fundamental as the sale of goods. Both civil law and common law systems have similar safeguards for consumers, as well as duties imposed on sellers and buyers. One key difference lies in the rules relating to risk of accidental loss or damage. Yet all three systems allow the parties free rein to decide when the passing of ownership of the goods should take place and may agree that the seller should remain owner until he receives payment. The English Sale of Goods Act, in common with French and German laws, allows contracting parties fairly generous room within which to exercise their autonomy and freedom of choice. In cases of supervening events rendering performance of the contract difficult or impossible, all three systems have a legal concept that attenpts to deal with it, the French version being the most severe. In the case of remedies, the similarities are certainly striking, although each system inevitably has its own idiosyncracies and individual nuances. German law is unique in its use of the Good Faith principle as a general clause applicable and adaptable to a wide range of diverse situations while English law with no equivalent doctrine, prefers to deal with each situation on an *ad hoc* basis, never straying from their underlying requirements of honesty and fair dealing between buyer and seller. All three systems apply variations of similar sorts of rules limiting the scope of damages to losses which are the direct consequences of a breach of contract. All three systems have statutory rules regulating the sales of goods but typically, English law statutes are consistently interpreted in the light of existing caselaw with the aim of giving effect, wherever possible, to the intention of the parties. Civil law codes are more strictly applied but there is no doubt that there is increasing reliance on caselaw. In many cases, the differences are rendered nugatory by the basic similarities in approach which often produce the same outcomes. Thus the marvel of modern European society is that quite independently, legal systems steeped in different traditions and philosophies are undoubtedly converging at certain levels and in certain spheres of activity.

This is also happening in Eastern Europe, the new Russian republics and indeed, in other parts of the developed world. A question that must now be addressed is whether the complexity of English law and its many facets of antiquity should, with other European systems, be adapted through legislation so as to adopt a more unified and 'harmonised' approach such as that of the UN Convention of Contracts for the International Sales of Goods, so that there will be greater harmonisation of the laws of sales of goods. This law is a mixture of Continental and Anglo-American law but it represents the concerted effort and combined experience of a vast number of European countries, but a number of non-European countries, such as China, Argentina and Zambia have also ratified it. The United Kingdom is yet to ratify this Convention but the United States has already done so. In the light of impending European unity in some form or other, our preceding comparative survey of the sale of goods indicates that there is far more in common than is generally appreciated or realised.   In the context of European or global unification or (at least) harmonisation of laws, the sale of goods is certainly an area in which there is far more convergence than divergence and in which an impressive measure of consensus has already been reached in the regional and international sphere.

SELECTIVE BIBLIOGRAPHY

Bewes THE ROMANCE OF THE LAW MERCHANT (1923)

Lawson 'The Passing of Property and Risk in Sale of Goods - A
    Comparative Study' (1949) 65 LQR 352

Daniels 'The German Law of Sales' (1957) Am.JCL 470

Kruse 'What does 'Transfer of Property' mean with regard to
    Chattels? A Study in Comparative Law' (1958) Am.JCL 500

Schmitthoff 'The Unification of the Law of International Trade'
    [1968] JBL 105

Cohn   MANUAL OF GERMAN LAW (1968) Vol I: section IX

Battersby & Preston (1972) 35 Mod. LR 268

Pennington (1975) ICLQ 277

Smith PROPERTY PROBLEMS IN SALE (1978)

Atiyah SALE OF GOODS (1980)

Horn, Kotz and Leser GERMAN PRIVATE AND COMMERCIAL LAW (1982)

Nicholas 'The Vienna Convention on International Sales Law'
    (1989) 105 LQR 201

Whincup   CONTRACT LAW AND PRACTICE: The English System and
    Continental Comparisons (1990)

Wheeler   RESERVATION OF TITLE CLAUSES (1991)

Maitland Hudson FRANCE: Practical Commercial Law (1991)

Bocker *et al* GERMANY: Practical Commercial Law (1992)

CHAPTER TEN

Labour Law

A. SCOPE OF ANALYSIS

10.0 This chapter examines labour law and industrial relations as they exist in common law countries such as Great Britain, and in civil law countries such as France and Germany. Primary interest will be focused on these three countries. The main comparative objective of our enquiry will be to discover how legal systems with different historical and cultural backgrounds albeit within the Western hemisphere, have responded to the needs of society at different periods in history and the nature of their employer-employee and employer-trade union relationships. As far as German labour law is concerned, the situation is particularly interesting in view of German unification in 1990 and it preliminary implications will therefore be considered *en passant*.

As with previous substantive chapters, our objective is to examine common legal issues and problems which have arisen in this area, such as the functions of collective agreements, the Legislator's Role in the development of collective bargaining, the status of collective agreements (is it a contract/statutory instrument?), and briefly, a comparison of the development of the collective agreement in common law and civil law countries.

As usual, we examine this area from legally significant and therefore selective comparative viewpoints, with an emphasis of concepts and do not, in any way, purport to undertake a comprehensive substantive survey of the particular legal topic.

B. HISTORICAL DEVELOPMENT

i. Great Britain

(i) Early Phases of Historical Development

10.1 Great Britain is the country where industrial relations originated and where the first seeds of labour law were sown. Itwas the 'workshop' of the world and in the 19th and 20th centuries, the 21 million British citizens who emigrated to America, the British Colonies and overseas dominions, brought to these other jurisdictions uniquely English attitudes about industrial relations in the workplace and a typically English common law approach to employer-employee relationships. Britain was the first country to legalise trade unions in 1824, a legislative step which was in keeping with the *laissez-faire* liberal capitalism which dominated it between 1820 and 1850. In accordance with the legalisation, the notion of *collective bargaining* developed and spread to other parts of Europe over the next seventy years or so. Not only did French and German workers visit Britain on fact-finding missions to discover how the British-style trade unions operated but British workmen's compensation schemes also served as a model to countries as far-flung as Japan.

Yet in 1852, the law dealing with labour relations was primarily concerned with the individual relationship between employer and employee, reflected in the first book published at that time being called the law of master and servant. This continued until the commencement of the Second World War. The next phase of development occurred as a result of the dramatic changes in employment practice and industrial relations which were effected during World War Two. However, *collectivism* eventually replaced *individualism*, and the law relating to trade unions and industrial action (strikes, go-slows, etc) came into its own and became known as Industrial Law.

(ii) Rights for Individual Employees

10.1.1 In 1963, Britain became the last country to introduce statutory minimum periods of notice to terminate employment, followed by a series of rights for individual employees, predominantly based on 'unfair dismissal'. In the early nineteenth century, English employment law had evolved a set of rules concerning termination which were, at bottom, founded on contract. The practical consequence was that individual contract law developed in true common law fashion, that is, when cases came to court. These usually occurred when dismissal had taken place and it became very difficult for the employee to win such cases. It was generally not financially worthwhile to even bring such cases to court. Management was therefore left largely unchallenged and unchecked until about 1972, when a statutory system of job protection was introduced, which was based on a test of 'reasonableness'. Arbitration by an industrial tribunal was offered as it had been in the past, but the system has never really been able to break free from its contractual antecedents.

After the failure of the Industrial Relations Act 1971, which appears to have miscalculated the desire of employers to use the law and trade unions to co-operate with it, the Labour Government under Harold Wilson entered into a *'social contract'* with the Trades Union Congress (1974-79) which resulted in a considerable amount of legislation which enhamnced the role of the industrial tribunals (which had been established in 1964). There was, however, an ongoing struggle to reconcile collective bargaining with incomes policies and reformist legislation. The victory of the Conservatives in May 1979 resulted in the abandonment of direct incomes policies and support for collectivism was replaced by a policy of legal restriction on trade unions and the reintroduction of market regulation and an era of market individualism. In other words, there has been an explicit attempt to restrict collective bargaining.

(iii) Content of English Labour Law

10.1.2   Since about the mid-1960s this law has been called Labour Law, a change generally attributable to the influence of the universities and Professor Otto Kahn-Freund, who apparently first used it. Lord Wedderburn (1986) described the term itself as usually including:
(i) The employment relationship between worker and employee;
(ii) The area of collective bargaining between trade unions and
     employers;
(iii)A panoply of rights for individual employees ranging from
     safety at work to rights relating to job security;equal pay;
     sex and racial discrimination and protection of wages;
(iv) Strikes, lock-outs and industrial action generally;
     interplay of parliamentary statutes and court decisions;
(v) Status of trade unions, rights of union members and the
     role of the trade union movement.
In the course of this chapter we shall compare the approaches taken by civil law countries such as France and Germany to the area of labour law and employment rights.

(iv) Current State of Labour Law: An Overview

10.1.3   English Labour law's early development was *based on contract* and this is still very much a feature of the present law. Briefly, it is the *individual's contract of employment* (and therefore its termination, and his/her redundancy) that remains the focus even in the early 1990s, *not* collective bargaining. The basis of English labour has thus been the law of contract, generally case-derived, despite legislation in the field, which has significantly influenced the development of the law of dismissal and therefore the whole of English labour law.

Whcre government intervention was clearly seen as desirable in the earlier stages of labour law's history, it is unclear at the present time how the present Conservative government intends to balance effectively the legal regulation of collective industrial relations, management of the economy and general legal control of labour relations. English labour law may, at the present time, be divided into 'contract-based rights, statutory employment protection and collective labour law'. (see Rideout (1985)). The historic fourth Tory election victory in May 1992 has appeared to seal the fate, at least for the foreseeable future, of policies such as an unrestricted 'right to strike' and the banning of secondary picketing is set not merely to continue but to become entrenched. High unemployment and relatively stagnant policies with minimal or negligible rises in social security benefits has led to a widening of the gulf between a group of secure, full-time well-paid workers and a group of people who remain on the fringe of the core labour market. It would appear that the *future of trade unionism*, not just its political power) is now in doubt with increasing State control and even de-unionisation being part of the industrial scenario in the year 2000.

We shall now turn briefly to the historical development of Germany and France, as examples of civil law countries, before undertaking a comparative overview of selected aspects of the substantive Labour Law of Britain, France and Germany.

ii. Germany

(i) Nineteenth Century Labour Law

10.1.4 The history of the labour law of a Germany which was divided into East and West after the Second World War but was reunited in October 1990, must still consider the period before the founding of the German Reich in 1871. German industrialisation started later than Great Britain so that, in 1848, for example, there was only 5.5 per cent of the population above 14 years of age who were working in factories and in the mining industry, with the remainder working in agriculture or handicrafts. The governing legal principle at that time was *freedom of contract*. The General German Workers' Association, (*Allgemeiner Deutscher Arbiterverein*), led by Lasalle, was founded in 1863, with its main objective being to promote the workers' interests by giving everybody the right to vote. However, this and similar associations more closely resembled political parties than trade unions but are now seen as the first important steps taken towards German free unions or socialist unions. Moreover, the fusion of the second German Workers' Party with the first was the birth of the *Social Democratic Party*. Even before the German Reich was founded in 1871, therefore, two competing union movements already existed. Kronstein (1952) therefore argues that 'collective bargaining has an old tradition in Germany, interrupted only by National Socialism'. In 1873, printers' unions and the association of employers in the printing business agreed that (i) union men should be employed by members of the association only on the basis of the conditions stipulated by the two organised groups; and (ii) members of unions should be given preference in employment. Kronstein (1952) also points out that from the earliest times, German employers utilised a bargaining platform based on a multi-unit basis (regional or inclusive of all industries), whereas labour bargained through craft unions combining people of similar skill and occupational background.

However, the socialist unions were seen as a danger to the system and the Government banned them in 1878. Nevertheless, not only did they survive but the Social Democratic Party grew ever stronger from election to election and the 1878 law was repealed in 1890.

Eventually various species of workers' representation groups were formed, with the intention of assisting the workers to be integrated within the enterprise structure and to serve as a foil to the socialist labour movement. These groups were recognised by law and thus was formed the dual structure mechanism typical of German collective labour law, namely (i) a two-channel representation by unions; and (ii) works councils. A third group of unions, the Christian union, was formed but in the early twentieth century, the socialist unions were certainly the most important group by a considerable margin of membership and influence.

In the late 1890s, a debate occurred within the socialist unions, wherein collectivism was rejected in favour of increased democratisation and increased participation became cornerstone concepts. By 1891, the labour movement had become more reconciled with the works' council. By the early part of the present century, employers' associations had begun to be formed as a response to the labour movement. A critical legitimating factor for the socialist movement was its cooperative attitude towards the government during the First World War which led to its legal recognition as the authentic representative of the work-force.

(ii) Impact of the Weimar Period

10.1.5   With the split in the Social Democratic party in 1917, internecine conflict within the working class appeared to take place. But under the influence of a politically and industrially active labour movement, the Weimar Republic established certain rights for workers. Thus,after the War, when the Weimar Republic was formed, Article 159 of the Weimar Constitution guaranteed *freedom of association* without limitation for the first time in German history. This basically meant the right to form trade unions and this was complemented by the enactment of the *right of equal representation* on various 'economic-political' bodies under Article 165.

During this period, the so-called Central Commission of Co-operation (*Zentralarbeitsgemeinschaft*) was formed by the main organisation of employers' associations and trade unions.

Weiss (1989) highlights three of the most fundamental developments of the time which can be seen as crucial to modern-day labour law: (i) the Act on Works Council of 1920; (ii) the creation of a specific system of labour courts in 1926 and (iii) the establishment of a system of unemployment insurance and placement service in 1927.

A nascent concept of economic democracy also started to develop which intended to give workers a greater say in the decision-making process which was unable to blossom in the wake of the 1929 global crisis. There followed a rapid decline in the system of industrial relations and unemployment was extremely high. It was no wonder that collective bargaining fell into disfavour and with increasing Governmental intervention, working standards were continually lowered.

10.1.6 Despite the fact that the Nazis dissolved trade unions and employers' associations, replacing them with an organisation designed to promote the Nazi State, the effect of the Nazi regime and the War put paid to ideological disunity, which was soon subsumed in the aftermath of the War. The labour movement managed to be re-organised and reconstructed by the allies in a such a way that it began to embrace all manner of ideological and political persuasions within the trade unions. Notions utilised by the Nazis to serve the ends of the Third Reich, and which had developed Nazi connotations, such as 'togetherness between the leader of the establishment and his work-force' (*Betriebsgemeinschaft*) and the 'duty of fidelity' as interpreted by the Nazis, took somewhat longer to practically disappear from the labour-force ethos.

The tradition of *positive rights*, however, is contained in Article 9(3) of the German (formerly FRG) Constitutional Basic Law of 1949, which declares the 'right to form associations to safeguard and improve working and economic conditions'.

(iv) Labour Law in the Former GDR

a. East German Law as Instrument of the State Plan

10.1.7 Labour law in the former German Democratic Republic (GDR)- East Germany-was utilised primarily as an instrument to implement the State Economic Plan. As with other Socialist systems, mechanisms were developed in pursuance of the objectives of certain goals of production. There was therefore no free market environment and thus no labour market in which individuals could interact in any sort of parity with their employers. Individuals were simply cogs in the wheel of the great State Plan, who simply had to conform to the needs of the Plan. Labour laws were focused on the collective needs of society, as dictated by the Marxist objectives, and not on any Western-style perspective of protection of the worker from exploitation or promotion of equal bargaining power.

b. Duality of Trade Union Functions

10.1.8 It would appear that the role of the trade union indicated a conflict of interests since, as one commentator explains, 'it was defined as the representative of the workers (as ..in western countries)' and yet 'its main task was to guarantee the performance of the economic plan and thereby execute the Party's and the government's intentions' (see Weiss (1991)). On the other hand, another commentator sees no conflict of interests in such duality of function because the interests of the Party, the government, the trade union and the workers was supposed to be identical (see Mampel *'Arbeitsverfassung und Arbeitsrecht in Mitteldeutschland'* (1966), p.75).

c. No Conflict Resolution Mechanism

10.1.9   It is important to note that any 'agreements' between government and trade unions or between government and industrial entities were not collective agreements in the Western industrial democratic sense. They were yet another means of implementing the Plan. Hence the idea of conflict was never officially recognised nor accepted as part of the labour scenario, which meant that no structures or mechanisms for conflict resolution were ever developed.

d. Minor Role of Courts

10.1.10   East German courts only played a somewhat minor role, since the only route into court for dismissal cases, for example, was with the support of the trade union and this was by no means
easy to obtain. The courts were, in any event, merely another State organ intended to promote the goals of the party. In the absence of any separation of powers, the judiciary, government and parliament were all seen as having a commonality of function.

e. Positive Rights under East German Labour Law

10.1.11   Nevertheless, the Labour Law of the GDR was not without some positive features. It enacted the 'right to get a job' (article 24: *Die Verfassung der DDR* (VERF)) whereby any individual who was willing to work was guaranteed a job. This was not without its difficulties in implementation since it required a massive administrative undertaking to organise career planning and job distribution and led to a severe surplus of staff which was simply not economically viable in an economy which had such strict market constraints. Another consequence of this statutory right is its effect on female workers. Since women could also avail themselves of this right, this meant that arrangements had to be devised whereby women could work and have a family at the same time. Many Western countries could do worse than follow this example as a positive means of helping the modern working woman.

f. Transferring the FRG Legal System to the GDR

10.1.12   In the early period of transition in 1990, there was still hope among the GDR population that unification would result in a system of real integration and not simply one which had to adapt to the FRG pattern. Labour law and social security in a unified Germany was therefore conceived to become a mixture of the better parts of both systems. Unfortunately, this was not to be and measures soon began to be implemented which made it clear that the FRG legal framework was indeed going to be imposed on the former GDR. For instance, since labour courts did not exist in the GDR, the

Treaty established the GDR's duty to provide a preliminary and temporary mechanism for resolution of legal disputes during the period in which labour courts were not yet established. (see Weiss (1991) p.6)

A new Labour Code was enacted on 22 June 1990 which introduced a number of provisions which originated from the FRG law. Weiss emphasises that some of the GDR provisions were more favourable to workers than the corresponding provisions in the original FRG such as longer annual minimum vacations, better protection of pregnant women and better minimum standards for breaks and rest periods during working time (see Weiss (1991) *ibid*).

According to Article 8 of the Treaty on Political Unification (the Treaty), all law of the original FRG, including individual labour law was extended to the territory of the former GDR. The five exceptions to this rule are: (i) where the law involved is one which applies only to specific states of the original FRG; (ii) where the Treaty itself explicitly states exceptions; (iii) where specific provisions of FRG law are either abolished or amended in the context of unification; (iv) where FRG provisions apply only in a modified version until a certain deadline in the former GDR; and (v) where the Treaty allows GDR provisions to remain valid temporarily until a certain deadline. (see Weiss (1991) p.7).

There is, moreover, an attempt to possibly strike a compromise between the GDR and FRG laws. According to Article 30, paragraph 1 of the Treaty, the Parliament of the unified Germany is supposed to codify, as soon as possible, 'the law relating to the individual employment relationship as well as the protective standards referring to working time, work on Sundays and holidays and the specific protection of women.' Paragraph 2 of this Article further extends this programme to the codification of health and safety standards.

g. Problems in Implementation

10.1.13   Several obstacles to privatisation exist and the conversion from planned economy to market economy is fraught with difficulties. Weiss (1991) highlights four problems: (i) there is uncertainty as to whether, and to what extent, existing companies can be rescued and privatised, or whether they must be closed down A 'trust agency' has been established to deal with this problem which carries out evaluation of each industrial unit. Approaval of this agency is required before the transformation of the company may take place. Being a bureaucratic organisation, this is a long and slow process which is unfortunately slowing down the restructuring through privatisation.

(ii) the infrastructure of the former GDR is in an antiquated and parlous state. As Weiss explains 'the telecommunication system is simply not functioning; the energy supply system must be totally reorganised; and air pollution and land contamination need to be reduced dramatically.' (Weiss (1991) p.9).

(iii) there is a serious problem in dealing with the loss of land ownership due to unjustified expropriation during the Communist period. The Treaty distinguishes between two periods: expropriations before and expropriations after the foundation of the GDR. Expropriations before the foundation of the GDR are considered to be irreversible, although the original owners may be entitled to compensation. The legislature has broad discretionary power to determine the amount of compensation in each case. Expropriations which occurred after the 1949 founding of the GDR are treated differently under the Treaty: original owners may claim ownership if they can present evidence that they lost property in an unjustified way. Claims have to be filed within a specified period. In the light of these problems concerning the property question, privatisation is greatly delayed and the establishment of regional branches of employers' associations will take time. In the meantime, the functions of employers' associations (as is the case with trade unions) will be performed by the headquarters in the western part of the unified country.

The fourth problem is the lack of a functioning labour court system. As things stand, the arbitration bodies set up under the Treaty only exist on paper in that it is very rare for these bodies to have been created in accordance with the legislation. Labour courts function in a very limited manner. There is tricky question of which judges should serve on such courts since any appointments or allocations in this connection could be seen as inappropriate, politically insensitive or simply another example of colonisation, if FRG judges merely replace the former GDR ones.

The treaty provides that specific committees be established by the new states of the former GDR to check the past performance of each judge in the former GDR to decide if he is eligible to continue in the new system. This system has not worked very well, and the least of their problems has been that a longer evaluation period has been needed, various GDR judges were simply encouraged to quit for a variety of reasons and there has been a great need to have judges sitting on the various courts. There has therefore been an unavoidable transfer of a significant number of judges from the former FRG.

A number of other problems bedevil the labour market. Since a job was guaranteed, in the former GDR, to anyone willing to be employed, there is now a huge problem of overstaffing in the 'new' Germany. The rate of unemployment has shot up and only temporary employment is available to these millions of people.

The German federal government has taken measures to deal with this in the form of vocational training programmes, job creation schemes and placement, as well as 'skilling companies'. These are companies which are run jointly by employers' associations and trade unions and which receive fairly large subsidies from the federal government. Unfortunately, these skilling companies did not succeed in gaining the co-operation of the employers' associations although the trade unions have pressed for their creation for some time.

The process of restructuring the economy of a united Germany in the light of the labour market in the former GDR will clearly be a long and sometimes painful process. The concept of social partnership has been strengthened and coperation between social partners and government is apparently occurring on a permanent basis. However, with the removal of the planned economy, many units of public administration have become redundant, from the secret service to departments in the universities. The Treaty on Political Unification terminates employment contracts of employees in such units. These employees will receive seventy per cent of their former net wage until a final decision is made on whether they will be re-employed elsewhere in the public sector. (see Weiss (1991) pp.13-14).

Yet another problem facing the restructuring programme is the 'dramatic'(Weiss) wage gap between the original FRG and the former GDR workers. The average wage level of a worker in the former GDR was less than half that of a worker in the western part of the country. The need to equalise wage levels is especially urgent in the public sector. A rather radical rearrangement of the wage structure must be devised before collective agreements will be of any utility so that job classification according to criteria of skill and performance should replace the pattern in the former GDR.

(v) Key Features of Contemporary German Labour Law

a. Multiplicity of Statutes

10.1.14 Contemporary German Labour Law consists of a variety of statutes. They may be grouped under the following four categories: (i) Individual employment law; (ii) Business constitution law; (iii) Collective bargaining law.

Individual employment law covers the contractual relationship between an employer and an a particular employee. It includes the law of contract, and protective laws such as the law of termination protection.

Business constitution law deals with the internal organisation of large and medium-sized firms, including the right of co-determination and internal collective agreements.

Collective bargaining law deals with strikes, the formation of trade unions, and collective bargaining agreements.

b. Operation at Different Levels of Hierarchy

10.1.15 A noteworthy feature of German labour law is that it operates at different levels so that there is a hierarchical relationship between these groups of laws. It could be envisioned as a pyramidal structure with the laws being based on the employment contract, which can be modified by collective agreements, which must comply with the rules of statutory law. They therefore operate according to the following order of priority: (i) Binding rules of statutory laws and regulations; (ii) Collective bargaining agreements; (iii) Factory agreements; (iv) Internal collective agreements; (v) Individual contract. (see Bocker *et al* (1992) p.104).

At the apex of the hierarchical structure is the Basic Law (Federal Constitution) which provides that 'the right to form associations to safeguard and improve working and economic conditions is guaranteed to everyone and to all trades, occupations and professions'(Article 9, paragraph 3 GG). This is a mandatory rule which will invalidate agreements, contracts and statutes to the extent that they breach this basic right of association. (see Horn *et al* (1982)p.311).

312

This order of priority is not adhered to in the case of the 'benefit principle' which permits agreements of a lower ranking to prevail if they are more beneficial for the employee than the collective agreement. (Bocker *et al.* ibid)

c. Further Special Statutory Regulation

10.1.16 Many special statutes have been passed dealing with different aspects of the individual contract of employment such as notice, protection against unfair dismissal, sick pay, and holiday entitlements. Other statutes deal with the protection of children and minors, expectant and recent mothers and severely disabled persons (see Horn *et al* (1982) p.311).

d. Many Specialist Courts

10.1.17 There are, of course, a number of specialist courts which deal with labour law cases: Labour Courts, Labour Appeal Courts and the Federal Labour Court.

Labour Courts deal, *inter alia*, with disputes arising out of the relationship between employer and employee or claims related to strikes and other actions by trade unions. There is a three-tiered appeal system, in every German district/region and a Federal Labour Court which determines appeals on points of law for the whole country. Parties may be represented by representatives of trade unions before all labour courts except the Federal Court, which requires the parties to be legally represented. Professional and honorary judges sit together to hear labour cases, with trade unions and employers' unions making nominations for honorary judges who are then appointed.

e. The BGB and Contracts of Service

10.1.18 The BGB also regulates contracts of service, which are contracts whereby one party 'undertakes to provide the agreed remuneration' (paragraph 611: BGB). These must normally be concluded for an indefinite period of time since fixed term contracts cannot be concluded unless special circumstances justify them. These circumstances have been specifically listed and confined by the Federal Labour Court to include only the following: (i) the need for temporary staff; (ii) the need to fulfil a specific task such as a research project; (iii) seasonal jobs; and (iv) up to eighteen months fixed term for a single contract under the employment promotion law(see Bocker *et al* (1992) p.105). Chain contracts are usually treated as contracts for an indefinite period of time.

Paragraph 618 of the BGB stipulates that a person who is entitled to demand a service pursuant to a contract of service must ensure the safety of the premises, installations and equipment with which the other party will come into contact in performing the service. However, since all employees are covered by a statutory scheme of employment which is part of the social insurance system, this provision is simply irrelevant. Employees suffering personal injuries in an accident arising in the course of his employment will obtain compensation under the statutory insurer, but *not* for pain and suffering. Entitlement does not depend upon proof of anyone's fault and is unaffected by his being at fault himself, unless he caused the accident intentionally. The injured party's survivors are bound by the same rules.

There is no disadvantage to this scheme except in the case of serious injury where the victim would be better off if he could bring a claim against his employer. In that case, he would receive a pension, obtain damages for pain and suffering and an indemnity for all his lost earnings. Separate considerations apply if a third party is responsible for the industrial accident. If he has supplied a defective tool which caused the injury or was a motorist who carelessly injured the workman on his way to or from work (which is an 'industrial accident in Germany), the workman or his survivors may sue the third party for financial loss not covered by the insurance and for pain and suffering. (see Horn *et al* (1982) p.322).

f. Organisation of Unions

10.1.19 The unions in Germany are organised as industrial unions which means that the branch of industry to which a worker belongs, rather than his own trade or skill will determine the trade union toi which a worker will belong. It is noteworthy that Article 9, paragraph 3 of the Basic Law has been used as the source of rights pertaining to union membership and union activities. The German courts have interpreted this Article to mean that 'an individual has not only the right to join a union but also the right not to join one.' (Horn *et al* (1982) p.313).

g. Operation of Collective Bargaining

10.1.20 Collective bargaining takes place 'above the plant level' in Germany (Horn *et al*(1982)p.314). Various employers in a number of industries will negotiate with a local section of the appropriate industrial union. In addition, there are consequences on two levels resulting from collective agreements between unions and employers' associations work: First, the *'normative effect'* which means that they apply directly to every individual contract of employment between any employer who is a member of the employers' association that is bound by the agreement, and any employee who is a member of the union that is similarly bound. Secondly, the *'obligational effects'* which generate duties as with any other contract, for the parties themselves, namely, between the employers' association on the one hand and the union on the other. (Horn *et al*(1982) p.315) The most important of these obligational duties is to the duty to keep the peace (*Friedenspflicht*). Basically, for the duration of the agreement, the parties must avoid taking any step which might cause industrial conflict.

If a breach of duty to keep the peace occurs, the affected employer may sue the union for an injunction and damages. As Horn points out, although it is the employers' association that is party to the collective agreement, the

314

courts treat the collective agreement as a contract for the benefit of third parties (paragraph 328 BGB). Accordingly, they allow the individual employer to sue in his own right. (see Horn *et al* (1982) p.316).

The union has a right to call a strike if collective negotiations collapse. The employer may retaliate by ordering a lockout but the legitimacy of this measure has been the subject of intense debate in Germany and the best that can be said is that the Federal Labour Court has held that it is sometimes justifiable to order a lockout in response to a strike.

h. Legality of Strikes

10.1.21   The question of whether the strike is lawful is central in Germany and the matter has been determined by caselaw. The cardinal point is that strikes can only be lawful if they are called and conducted by a trade union. The rationale is that the function of strikes is to lead to the conclusion of a collective bargain and only unions can be parties to such bargains. Hence wildcat strikes and strikes called by works councils are unlawful.

However, a strike called by a union is nevertheless unlawful if if it is called in breach of the union's duty to keep the peace; or if it is called in pursuance of an aim other than those that may be achieved by a collective agreement, namely 'the improvement of economic and working conditions' of employees (see Collective Agreements Act, article 1: Horn *et al* (1982) p.317). As far as sympathy strikes are concerned, this will only be lawful if the strike in support of which they are called is itself lawful.

Another perspective on legality of strikes has come from the Federal Labour Court which is that a strike will be unlawful if it offends against the '*principle of proportionality*'. In other words, if the harm caused to the general public by the strike, is out of all proportion to what the union stands to achieve thereby BAG (Grosser Senat) NJW 1971,1668 (Federal Labour Court).

i. The Works Council

10.1.22   The Works Council is a distinctive feature of German labour law, which refers to a body elected by *all* employees (union members and non-union members) who are eighteen years or older and is meant to represent the interests of all workers. It will participate in decisions 'at the *plant level* on social, personal, and economic matters.' (Horn *et al* (1982) p.319).

Participation at the *company level* has existed since the 1950s, wherein workers in the mining industry and (since 1977) in undertakings with more than 2,000 workers, have had the right to choose half the members of the supervisory board.

The Labour Management Relations Act 1972 ('the 1972 Act') provides detailed rules for the election of the works councils, their legal position, and their powers. The number of workers in each plant will vary with the size of the plant. Works councils have the right to enter into factory agreements with the employer on behalf of the employees. But its role is to co-operate with the employer so that it is not permissible for it to enter into a confrontational situation with the employer. Indeed, the 1972 Act expressly requires the works council and the employer 'to work together in good faith for the welfare of the workers and the factory'. (see Horn *et al* (1982) p.320)

The works council also has several statutory rights and duties. This will vary from a right to be informed or consulted to a right to be involved in some way in decisions taken by the employer. If it is a situation where the works council enjoys a right of co-determination, the employer cannot take steps without its consent, for example, in the employment of new staff, fixing the hours of a working day, including breaks, formulating general rules regarding behaviour in the plant, timing of holidays and provision of sick pay (article 87: 1972 Act). On the other hand, in the case of dismissal procedures, consultation but not consent will be required before notice can be given.

'Framework agreements' (*Manteltarif*) are nowadays entered into which contain important rules on the reciprocal rights of the parties and these often replace statutory law. Short-term collective bargaining agreements dealing with wage and salary are also entered into into many industries.

Discriminatory employment practice is prohibited by virtue of Article 3 of the German Constitution. Nobody must therefore be discriminated against as a result of his sex, race, origin, creed or religious and political views. Collective bargaining agreements and statutory law are directly bound by this principle.

The individual employer is also prohibited from discriminating against certain groups of employees. Under the doctrine of equal treatment, arbitrary differences in treatment of employees should be avoided. Article 611 (a) of the Constitution gives an action for damages against an employer who discriminates against employees because of their sex. Claims for equal treatment are sometimes initiated on other grounds. (Bocker *et al* (1992) p.113).

iii. France

(i) Early History

10.1.23 The notion of *droit du travail* in France is of recent origin. In 1701, Loyseur was still describing a 'master-servant' relationship in his compilation of manorial customs, *Les Oeuvres de Maistre Charles Loyseau*. It was really the customs and conventions of the local community which regulated the rights and obligations arising from services performed for another, rather than any formal, much less written law. The absolute authority of the *patron* reigned supreme over workers, servants, and apprentices which derived from the notion of the patriarchal head of the household, which also signified the absolute rights of parents over their children. Rights and duties outside these well-established *mores* were simply non-existent.

It was only when the ideal of a classless society led to the emergence of a working class, ignited by the flames of the French Revolution, that abolition of the *privileges* of the aristocratic class and of a stratified social structure was even contemplated. The ideals of liberty, equality and the autonomy of the individual were translated into a philosophy that freedom of contract would be the only means of adjusting individual interests in a classless society and that equality of bargaining power should be present in economic and political terms.

The Civil Code thus envisaged workers and employees being linked to *patrons* within a framework of contractual relationships. Inevitably, the popular ethos of *laissez faire* arose as a reaction against the stifling mass of economic regulation which had swamped the country, leading to the steady rise in the popularity of freedom of contract and the severe restriction of any form of mandatory legislation.

By the early nineteenth century, French labour law was merely a part of *droit civil* and assimilated into the general corpus of general rules of law. Present day French labour law can probably trace its legislative development to 1791 when the Assembly of the Revolutionary period enacted two statutes: (i) one abolishing the guilds which had exercised a monopolistic control over industry; and (ii) the other which forbade the organisation of workers. Reynard (1952) submits that both these enactments were in keeping with the individualistic spirit of the French Revolution, which placed a strong emphasis on the liberty of the individual and construed it to extend to the 'liberty to work'.

Indeed, the French Penal Code of 1810 even contained an article prohibiting any concerted action of workers aimed at the improvement of working conditions. This was subsequently repealed.

10.1.24 However, the onset of the Industrial Revolution brought a new awareness of inequality, highlighted by the organisation of large-scale industrial enterprises involving substantial numbers of workers under the control of a single, discrete management structure. The sheer speed and extent of the growth of towns and cities accentuated this new consciousness, so that by 1848, class consciousness and new working environments led to a demand by the working-class French industrial worker for special legislation which would protect him from exploitation. Labour law thus started off on the premise of *protection for the industrial worker*.

The second half of the nineteenth century saw several statutes passed for the benefit of industrial workers, and similar laws were subsequently passed to include farm workers, artisans, and employees and agents of business houses. Collective bargaining agreements, international treaties and decisions of arbitration tribunals were all made the subject of the ever-widening legislation. In 1864, a statute was enacted limiting the application of the Penal Code provision (see above) and more importantly, impliedly recognising the right of workers to organise for mutual sel-improvement for limited purposes.

In 1884, French labour was basically free to bargain collectively. In that year, penal laws which rendered trade unionism illegal were repealed and unions were recognised as legal personalities with only certain restrictions. This Act gave the courts considerable problems in a number of cases involving the recognition and enforceability of collective agreements. In 191, the French legislature adopted its first comprehensive enactment in the field of labour law which became the French Labour Code. This substantially codified the rules, which had been evolving in the courts, but also clarified and expanded on them, establishing formal requirements for collective contracts, declaring which person were to be bound by such agreements, defining the scope of permissible individual agreements, declaring the nature of the obligations that were thereby created and designating the parties who had the right to sue for the enforcement of such contracts.

Between 1919 and 1936, the date of the next legislative enactment in this area of law, two important events occurred: (i) the *Confederation Generale du Travail* (CGT), which was the most influential and largest of the French labour unions, split into two factions, the CGT and the Confederation Generale du Travail Unitaire (CGTU), as a result of political differences sparked off by the issue of Communism. In the light of this sundering of labour forces, collective bargaining experienced a very low ebb, which was not helped by the next event; (ii) the second event was the financial crisis of the early 1930s, which contributed to the depressed condition of collective bargaining. Eventually, a reunion of labour forces took place, to combine again as the CGT, which supported the Popular Front forces in the election, and swept that party into power in 1936. A series of devastating strikes followed, which then led to the Accord of Matignon.

This Accord or agreement resulted from a meeting between the leaders of French labour and industry, presided over by the new Prime Minister, Leon Blum. On behalf of the government, Mr. Blum agreed to attempt to codify and implement the terms of this Agreement in legislation. Under the Accord, both management and the unions agreed to the immediate conclusion of collective bargaining agreements, to a substantial adjustment in wages and to the establishment of grievance machinery and other procedures for collective bargaining.

These terms were essentially embodied in the Act of 1936 which represents the first instance of the French government actively promoting collective bargaining and which gave a remarkable impetus to the collective bargaining process. There were two significant features in the 1936 Act, namely (i) a specialised type of bargaining process by the most 'representative organisations' and (ii) the principle of governmentally administered extension of contracts so concluded to any outsiders who did not participate in the negotiations. However, the Act did not secure industrial peace and a wave of strikes followed, particularly when wages and prices failed to keep pace with each other. Employer resistance hardened and eventually, the government introduced compulsory arbitration in two statutes of 1936 and 1938.

During the Second World War, the free trade-union movement was completely abolished in France in 1941 but although restored in 1946, the relevant Act of 1946 bore the hallmarks of a policy that equated uncontrolled collective bargaining with uncontrolled inflation. A subsequent statute was passed, the Act of February 1950, which is substantially similar to the Act of 1936.

Clearly, the scope of labour law has changed quite radically from the original basic idea of protecting the industrial worker.

10.1.25   The simplistic notion of *patron* and worker as conceived by the Civil Code is no longer a viable working concept in modern-day France. Labour Law is now focused on the *status* of the individuals in the employment arena, so that 'status has to a large extent supplanted contract, mandatory rules of law replace contractual arrangements, and administrative regulation and adjudication play an important role' (de Vries (1975)). It also includes matters unconnected with the employer-employee nexus, such as social security legislation, administrative regulations, family allowances, tax privileges and old-age pensions.

Collective bargaining takes place at different levels. There is a hierarchical structure to the law to the effect that the national agreement constitutes an industrial code, supplemented by regional agreements which themselves supplement local agreements. Article L.132-1 of the Labour Code enumerates a list of different collective agreements arranged in a hierarchy: national agreements, local agreements and agreements limited to one or several enterprises or one or several workshops. Article 133-3 lists various items to be regulated in a collective agreement which will be subject to the extension procedure (see below), inter alia, the minimum wage for unskilled work, principles for additional pay for skilled work, additional pay for unpleasant, dangerous, or unhealthy work, periods of notice for termination and so on.

10.1.26   The Law of 1971 has been passed which again modifies certain provisions of the Labour Code and aims to strengthen the bargaining procedure, containing the rule that only the most representative unions are allowed to enter into collective agreements. It also seeks to encourage the conclusion of agreements at two extreme levels: (i) at the plant level; and (ii) at the inter-industry level. It further aims to make the 'extension procedure' simpler. The *extension procedure* is a method whereby the Ministry of Labour declares that the agreement is to be binding upon all employers and workers and workers within the area covered by it. Under certain circumstances, it may also be extended to include additional areas. If the extension procedure is implemented, all persons falling within the scope of the agreement are placed in the same position as if they were members of signatory organisations. (see Schmidt and Neal *International Encyclopedia of Comparative Law (IECL)*: vol. XV, chapter 12. p.68).

In more recent times, a new type of collective agreement has appeared-an agreement covering all industries,the 'all-embracing collective agreement'.

On the question of the effect of the collective agreement, French law adopts the German approach (see above) so that it governs all those who have signed the agreement as parties, together with those who are, or who become, members of signatory organisations.

Where an employer is bound by a collective agreement, either as a direct signatory or as a member of a signatory organisation, the provisions of that agreement will apply for all contracts of employment entered into by him

(Article L: 132-10:paragraph 2: Labour Code). The purpose of the French legislature has been to bring as many as possible within the scope of the collective agreement.

a. Ideological Pluralism and Rights

10.1.27 The Preamble to the French Constitution declares that everyone has the right to strike, the right to defend his interests by trade union action and the right 'to belong to the trade union of his choice'. The right of 'choice' between trade unions in France has been called 'ideological pluralism' because 'from its inception the modern [French] labour movement was accustomed, in both its industrial and its political wing, to speak the language of political ideology and rights' (Wedderburn (1991) p.42). For most of its history, French trade unions have been divided into groups which have been closely related in structure and in policy to the divided political parties of the left.

The *Cour de Cassation* in a 1973 case (March 21) has defined a strike as 'a concerted stoppage of work aimed at pressing ascertained demands on the employer, which he refuses to satisfy.' The right to strike must be exercised within the framework of the laws which exist to regulate it.

b. Classification of the French Collective Agreement

10.1.28 The French collective agreement has been described as 'nothing more than a declaration of ceasefire' which only lasts for the time being (Schmidt and Neal (1982) IECL,p.121). The *'peace obligation'* which is imposed depends on the meaning of the statement in the Labour Code article L 135-1, to the effect that a party is under a duty not to do anything which could prevent the faithful performance of the collective agreement. Any commitment binding a party for a long period of time would be contrary to the policy of the French unions, not to submit to restrictions upon the freedom to strike. It should be noted that no peace obligation is imposed upon the individual worker, and the constitutional right is primarily a prerogative of the individual. hence the peace obligation is of a limited character and may be regarded as nugatory.

The nature of the collective agreement in France has been the subject of considerable debate in France. The basic argument is whether it is primarily a contract or in the nature of a statutory instrument. Modern French writers take the view that it has a mixed character, composed both of contractual elements and of elements of a statutory instrument(Schimdt and Neal (1982) p.104). Schmidt and Neal, however, submit that there are several reasons why it should be classified as a statutory instrument: (i) only representative unions are permitted to be parties to a collective agreement; (ii) the collective agreement is binding upon all those who are members, or who become members, of an organisation which is a signatory to the agreement. The point is that this rule is not really relevant where the individual employee is concerned. Thus, the effect of Article L 132-10. paragraph 2, is that when negotiating a collective agreement, the union is acting as the representative of all employees-members and non-members; (iii) government takes an active part in the creation of certain collective agreements, namely those open to extension (see above on 'extension procedure'); (iv) Labour Code Article 133-3 sets out in detail the subjects to be covered by the collective agreement. (v) the collective agreement concluded after consideration by a Joint Committee which the Minister of Labour may set up, may be subjected to a special procedure and, by means of a ministerial decree, be extended to cover a certain field of application. Such an agreement will then constitute the law for all enterprises within its field. (see Schnidt and Neal (1982) p.105).

It will be seen that the legislature has acted rather like a social reformer in France, subjecting the law on the collective agreement to 'continuous revision in the light of past expereince and present needs' (Schmidt and Neal (1982) p.99. The terms of the collective agreement are made a required minimum, with an all-embracing character which invalidates private agreements with an employee but also implies that a collective agreement cannot be used as an instrument imposing duties on an employee.

In France, one also distinguishes between collective and individual disputes. A collective dispute must include 'a procedure to deal with potential collective conflicts, and must also contain procedures for revision, modification, and termination of the agreement'(Schimdt and Neal (1982) p.124). Conciliation appears to be the method most utilised to preserve the *status quo* between the parties in conflict. (Schmidt and Neal, *ibid*, p.125).

Labour law has steadily becoming more systematised and been increasingly subjected to specialised interpretation by doctrinal writers. It has acquired a unique substantive content, approach and methodology, which merits its specialist treatment.

c. The Superior Court of Arbitration

10.1.29 Separate tribunals and procedures were set up and devised to deal with labour law cases, so much so that in 1936, the Superior Court of Arbitration (*Cour superieure d'arbitrage*) was created, mainly staffed by judges who were public law jurists. This was entirely independent of the other courts, including the administrative courts, and possessed jurisdiction to issue binding judgments from which there were no rights of appeal. Although it ceased to be operational in 1939, it left a legacy to modern French labour law in its concepts and theories. In declaring itself not bound by the formal French doctrine which disallows courts from establishing precedents, it evolved a 'technique of regulatory decisions' (de Vries). This meant that courts could at least consult and refer to previous decisions where they were hearing similar cases.

Among the other remarkable facets of this Court of Arbitration were (i) the possibility of courts reviewing and revising collective bargaining agreements on the basis of changed circumstances; (ii) the shifting of the burden of proof to the employer with regard to termination of employment, limitation of disciplinary powers of management and the reinstement of employees who were found to be improperly dismissed. (see Picard (1931)).

d. The Specialist Labour Tribunals

10.1.30   The Court of Arbitration's decisions are still cited today as authority in doctrinal writing but the modern-day labour courts are primarily courts of first instance, that is, *Conseils de prud'hommes (tribunals consisting of 'men of loyalty and integrity')*, numbering over 280, at least one of which exist in each *departement*. These are 'labour conciliation tribunals' or industrial conciliation tribunals which consist of employers and employees from which there is a right of appeal to the *tribunal de grande instance*. An may be made to the *chambre sociale* (social division) of the *cour d'appel* (court of appeal) and thence to the *chambre sociale* of the *Cour de Cassation*.

There are five divisions in these tribunals, with each consisting of at least three elected representatives of employees and three of employers. There will always be an equal number of representatives from each group. These divisions may be divided into sections. These courts possess a dual function of adjudication and conciliation. Accordingly, they sit as a *conciliation panel* and *adjudication panel*. All litigants must initially appear before the conciliation panel, which comprises two assessors (one employer, one employee). The adjudication panel consists of four assessors (two employers and two employees). If there is a split decision, a judge from the district court will preside at a rehearing of the case. Urgent interlocutory applications may be heard by two assessors sitting alone and acting for all divisions. If the assessors cannot agree, a district judge will be called upon to resolve the issue.

iv. Current English Labour Law: Wedderburn's Observations

10.1.31   In a paper delivered in 1988, Lord Wedderburn highlighted five headings which illustrate the New Labour Law programme which the Tory Government appears to have created: (i) Disestablishing Collectivism; (ii) The Deregulation of Employment Law (iii) Union Control and Ballots for Individuals; (iv) Enterprise Confinement; and (v) Sanctions Without Martyrs. (Wedderburn 'Freedom of Association and Philosophies of Labour Law' (1989) 18 Industrial Law Journal 1, reproduced in Wedderburn *Employment Rights in Britain and Europe* (1991) p.198)

These headings are described in considerable detail in his paper and it is proposed here to merely deal with a few salient points thereof. Under (i), he argues that 'the government has removed most of the measures designed to support collective bargaining and to prop up collective organisation', frequently by imposing specified minimum conditions. He also points out that Wages Councils' powers have been reduced and replaced to setting one basic rate-young workers were excluded and wages inspectors were reduced by administrative means by thirty-five per cent since 1979. Further, 'privatisation and other pressures for decentralisation or 'flexibility' demand that unions today should move further towards enterprise unionism, while in some types of 'single union' agreements the identity of the bargaining union owes more to the preference of the employer granting organising rights to a union even before any workers have been hired than to any democratic choice by the workers themselves.' In his view, both law and society have conspired to deregulate the market. There is an 'absence of a legal duty to bargain with a union democratically 'representative' of the workforce.

Under (ii), he focusses on the individual employment relationship which he says has also been 'deregulated'. He mentions, *inter alia*, the 'creeping erosion of the floor of rights on employment protection, hand in hand with a gradual reduction of social security rights towards a bare floor on proof of need.' (Wedderburn (1991)p.215). This has resulted in a 'diminution of maternity rights, the removal of protection against unfair unfair deductions from wages, the alleviation of the employer's burden of proof, the extension of the employee's qualifying period to two years and similar changes in unfair dismissal law.'

Under (iii) he pinpoints 1982 as marking a watershed in the control of the union and the place of ballots. The main objective, it seems clear, was to secure the paramount rights of the non-unionist. Under the 1988 Employment Act the closed shop ballot is abolished entirely. Although formal freedom of contract is preserved by permitting UMA agreements to be lawful, all the collective pressures to make them effective are outlawed. The rationale put forward by various leading members of the British government is that individual rights must always prevail against the association or group. The trade union is seen as an obstacle to the competitive market and a threat both to individuals and to private property. Wedderburn sees this insistence on the so-called individual rights which the State now tries to ensure will prevail against the trade union, as 'the latest marker to characterise the new British labour law'.

Under (iv) he observes that the theme running through the legislation under the Tories is that if trade unions are to continue, they may need to be confined to the plant or to the enterprise. As he puts it 'the principle is that the needs of the market demand the confinement of workers' influence within each enterprise-the doctrine of enterprise confinement.' This doctrine is further refined by section 17 of the Employment Act 1988, which introduces a doctrine of 'workplace confinement' so that under it, each separate place of work must produce its own majority in a separate ballot before industrial action becomes lawful there.

Under the final heading (v)(Sanctions without Martyrs), Wedderburn turns to the law on trade unions themselves. The immunity of trade unions being limited to trade disputes has been hotly debated and in 1982, unions were again made liable in tort. In Wedderburn's view 'this is the key that makes the new system work' for it represents the substitution of union liability for the liability of officials which seeks thereby to avoid the 'martyrdom' problem. The sweeping reductions of the immunities previously enjoyed by trade unions, is predicated upon the perception of unions as an improper restraint of trade in the market and industrial action as an unlawful interference with contracts and property rights. Thus 'the exposure of union property to civil liability' under common law is the key which makes the machinery work. (Wedderburn (1991) p.224)

A few brief comments may be made on Wedderburn's points. In some ways, it must be said, it was events such as the miners' strike in the early 1980s, and the 'winter of discontent' which helped the Tories to their second consecutive election victory in 1983 that led to a backlash of feeling on trade unions and the right to strike 'gone wild'. Accordingly, Tories would maintain that their so-called 'union-bashing' is merely a response to the untrammelled privileges which trade unions have enjoyed and that the sight of 'block voting' at Labour Party conferences have also helped to fuel feelings of being 'ruled by the unions'. Nevertheless, he is very perceptive in his appraisal of the law relating to English labour law at the present time.

C. COMPARATIVE OVERVIEW

10.2 As far as collective bargaining is concerned, there are disparate means of administration. However, Schmidt and Neal see the major distinction between various common law and civil law countries as being 'between countries where entry into a collective agreement relationship represents the statement of a particular *status quo* between the bargaining parties which is to be maintained within a formalised system of administration, and...countries in which the collective agreement is viewed as a part of the continuing process of bargaining.' (Schmidt and Neal (1982) p.127).

It seems that although there are several common features in the various jurisdictions, each country is, as ever, a product of its particular history, heritage, political fortunes, culture and distinctive character. 'Rights' abound but they all exist or function within fairly well-defined or (in the English case) deregulated, parameters.

Perhaps the last comparative observations should belong to Lord Wedderburn, the *doyen* of labour law in both the national and international context. Having surveyed the labour law in a number of European countries, he found that certain values can be found constant in Western and Eastern European countries. First, there is 'the belief that the task of the law in employment...is primarily the protection of the worker whose living is obtained, in high technology or in low, by the sale of labour power in the 'work-wage bargain'. From that relationship itself springs the need and the right of workers to organise and to take action in free and effective trade unions.' As he stresses, 'The predominance of that need and that right remains, in Western and Eastern Europe.'

Secondly, he emphasises that 'an understanding of collective freedoms which are crucial for workers' self-protection, men and women, young and old, must be rekindled in the 1990s after a decade in which the values of fraternity and community have been swept aside in favour of an ideology of commercialised individualism.' Thirdly, he highlights the need for 'free research' because 'the causes of employment protection and trade union freedom are advanced not by heads buried in the sand but by liberal enquiry and free expression to which employers and trade unions contribute.'

It need only be added that labour law and the rights that have been gained through its development, is simply another manifestation of the modern-day recognition of the certain basic rights of the individual in his workplace. In an uncertain economy and time of recession, however, it is these rights that will increasingly be subjected to intense scrutiny and probable diminution.

SELECTIVE BIBLIOGRAPHY

Kronstein 'Collective Bargaining in Germany: before 1933 and After 1945' (1952) Am.JCL 199

Reynard 'Collective Bargaining and Industrial Peace in France' (1952) AmJCL 215

Kahn-Freund 'Labour Law' in LAW AND OPINION IN ENGLAND IN THE TWENTIETH CENTURY (1959) (ed. Ginsberg), P.215

Clegg THE SYSTEM OF INDUSTRIAL RELATIONS IN GREAT BRITAIN (1970)

Aaron and Wedderburn INDUSTRIAL CONFLICT (1972)

Rood et al FIFTY YEARS OF LABOUR LAW AND SOCIAL SECURITY (1978)

Schmidt & Neal COLLECTIVE AGREEMENTS AND COLLECTIVE BARGAINING (1982): Chapter 12 in International Encyclopaedia of Comparative Law: vol XV:LABOUR LAW

Whelan 'On Uses and Misuses of Comparative Labour Law: A Case Study' (1982) Mod. LR 285

Hepple and Fredman LABOUR LAW AND INDUSTRIAL RELATIONS IN BRITAIN (1986)

Rideout 'Labour Law in the United Kingdom' in COMPARATIVE LAW AND LEGAL SYSTEM (1985) (ed. Butler & Kudriavtsev)

Wedderburn THE WORKER AND THE LAW (1986)

Weiss LABOUR LAW AND INDUSTRIAL RELATIONS IN THE FEDERAL REPUBLIC OF GERMANY (1989)

Weiss 'The Transition of Labour Law and Industrial Relations: The Case of German Unification-A Preliminary Perspective' (1991) 13 Comparative Labour Law Journal 1

Maitland Hudson FRANCE: Practical Commercial Law (1991)

Blanpain LABOUR LAW AND INDUSTRIAL RELATIONS OF THE EUROPEAN COMMUNITY (1991)

Wedderburn EMPLOYMENT RIGHTS IN BRITAIN AND EUROPE (1991)

Bocker et al GERMANY: Practical Commercial Law (1992)

PART FOUR: FINAL OVERVIEW AND CONCLUSIONS

CHAPTER ELEVEN

Comparative Law and the New World Order

A. INTRODUCTION

11.0 As comparatists survey the global legal landscape of the early 1990s, and compare it to the global scenario of the 1970s or 1980s, or even further back to the nineteenth century when so much happened to influence the style, content and legal destiny of those systems, they will note the significant and sometimes dramatic and far-reaching changes which the two of the world's major countries have experienced-not least, in the last three years. Who would have thought that East and West Germany would have become a united nation again, at least in political terms, in 1989-90? Who would have envisaged that the mighty linchpin of the Communist *bloc*, the Soviet Union, would have produced a man who would strive for a new social democracy in the USSR, and who, in introducing two terms into popular usage, *perestroika* and *glasnost*, would have caused his own downfall? Even less likely, who would have imagined that the result would have been the disintegration of the USSR, into one set of Russian republics forming a Commonwealth of Independent States and another group proclaiming their independence from the new power structure and new President? In the light of the ongoing collapse of communism in Eastern Europe, the 'great Socialist tradition' must indeed be in danger of disappearing altogether, at any rate in Europe. Even if rumours of its death have been slightly exaggerated, our approach to the study of major legal tradtions, for example, has been radically altered. The Russian republics are presently engaged in returning to their civil law roots, or at any rate unshackling themselves from the main ideological trappings of Communism with the possibility of retention of some of the elements of

327

their Marxist era. If they do so, they will either be part of the civil law family once more or become a novel hybrid system with civil law and customary law co-existing together with remnants of socialist laws.

As for the common law world, it could scarcely have been expected in the 1960s that since the 1980s, the smaller courts and tribunals would account for a quarter of a million cases a year, the overwhelming proportion of overall cases that are heard in England and Wales in the 1990s. Or that legislation, so reviled in the nineteenth century by the English jurists as at best a necessary evil, would multiply and burgeon to such an extent that, in the 1970s and 1980s, it has become the major lawmaking instrument which accounts for a greater proportion of substantive law than the caselaw being laid down by the courts. Or that the one aspect of public law that has grown at a phenomenal rate in England is in the area of 'juducial review' of the administrative actions of public authorities and State-controlled organisations.

In the civil law world, it was at least predictable that France and Germany would begin to have recourse to an increasing amount of caselaw to supplement their nineteenth-century and other codes to such an extent that their caselaw has now to be considered a practical necessity and an aid to the interpretation of law. Even if not theoretically admissible, it is a very real, empirical source of law.

As 1993 approaches, and Europe lurches its way to a Single Market, scheduled to take place at the end of 1992, having combined to form a Common Market comprised of several soverign States, it becomes increasingly imperative to consider the implications of this 'new' European law, one which may well be interacting at the 'crossroads of legal traditions' (Koopmans (1991)).

The purpose of this chapter is (i) to consider the relevance of legal history, noting the agents and catalysts of change; (ii) to examine the New World Order (already labelled the 'New World Disorder' by some (see Anderson *Editorial* (1992) New Left Review, May/June), seeking some explanations for the transformation of the world scenario and consider the contemporary relevance of comparative law to this New Order; (iii) to survey the phenomenon of European convergence; (iv) review the so-called theories of convergence to consider if legal systems are indeed converging. This will include a brief consideration of the reception of American law in Europe and will reiterate the influence of legal traditions on the development of European community law, noting *en passant* the contribution of the comparative legal method (iv) to consider whether the world has possibly seen the Last Big Idea (the Fukuyama thesis)-the concept of democracy, which will lead inexorably to complete assimilation of all systems into one politically monolithic entity; (v) to assess the possibility of convergence occurring between common and civil law systems; and (vi) contemplate the dawn of a new era in world history.

B. THE SIGNIFICANCE OF LEGAL HISTORY

11.1 It seems fair to say that the greatest determinants of legal history have been Wars, Revolutions, uprisings, great philosophical, ideological, socio-economic and legal movements. Legal history is an integral paret of the comparative law enterprise. But how does one interpret it? As Karl Popper put it 'There can be no history of the 'past' as it actually did happen; there can only be historical interpretations and none of them final...the so-called 'sources' of history record only such facts as appeared sufficiently interesting to record, so that the sources will often contain only such facts as fit with preconceived theory.' (Popper *The Open Society and Its Enemies* (1973)pp.268,265).

In seeking to place any legal doctrine or principle of legal development within its historical context, it is therefore sensible to heed Popper's thoughts on the question of interpreting history. Although the history of the common law and civil law has been well-documented by eminent and fastidious researchers and historians, historical surveys must needs contain several competing theories. Theories in themselves do no harm provided they are presented as theories. As the eminent historian Collingwood points out, the historian is well aware that his only possible knowledge of the past is 'inferential' or indirect' and never empirical. He suggests that re-enactment of the past in the historian's own mind is what is required in the search for the historical significance of past events. (see Collingwood *The Idea of History* (1973) p.282)

With respect, I would suggest that it is this sort of subjective re-enactment that can often lead to a subjective, and sometimes misleading analysis which one tends to 'fit' into preconceived theories. It is therefore suggested that the Popperian method of 'conjectures and refutations' is far more intellectually viable since this enables an objective critical analysis of historical facts to be carried out. (see Popper *Conjectures and Refutations* (1972) *passim*) In essence the Popperian method involves analysing the strengths and weaknesses of a theory and after subdividing it to the full extent of its conjectural possibilities, to subject it to rigorous critical analysis. Another technique of this method is to begin with a general concept and proceed to analyse those instances where it does not apply,(that is, its exceptions), to see if they undermine it to such an extent as to deny its validity. The method is therefore more deductive than inductive.

The historical analysis would then be one of continuous reappraisal and more 'open-ended'. Conclusions may therefore be drawn but these will be deduced without falling prey to the vice of 'interpreting the past in the light of the present' (Fifoot *History and Sources of the Common Law* (1949) vii).

C. THE NEW WORLD ORDER

i. Global Wars and Civil Strife: Historical Perspectives

11.2   In a recent editorial, Benedict Anderson proferred a very brief glimpse of what he called the 'New World Disorder' and the current global condition. (see *New Left Review* (1992)). It is particularly fitting, in may view, to refer to salient features his brief survey to place the preceding pages of this book into some sort of historical perspective, and to set the scene for future comparative law research.

He begins by referring to one 'deep tectonic movement' which stretched across more than two centuries, the disintegration of the great polytechnic, polyglot and often polyreligious monarchical empires built up so painfully in medieval and early modern times.' This emphasises the influence of various Empires that subjugated by force and military might and then left their indelible imprint on the laws, cultures, ideologies and customs of the people they conquered or colonised. The 1770s saw the first nation-state born in North America, as a reaction to imperial Britain, but which had to undergo 'the bloodiest civil war of the nineteenth century' before it was able to settle into some kind of stability. Several other great wars also transpired, leading to the emergence of other nation-states. Civil wars also ensued in China in the wake of the demise of the Ch'ing Empire in 1911. Partition in British India, the Thirty Years War in Vietnam, and the civil strife in Northern ireland are all seen by Anderson as part of the same 'tectonic movement'.

In the midst of all this, another violent revolution produced Communism, with Lenin at the heart of the Soviet experiment. However, the Soviet Communist *bloc* and its latter-day Stalinist excesses was destined to become a superpower enclave which, having seen off Nazism, then proceeded to promote an era of Eastern European Communist states with national names. After this came Yugoslavia, North Korea, China, Cuba, and Vietnam, Laos and Cambodia.

In the immediate post-Second World War era, the colonial empires of Britain, France, Holland and Belgium and Portugal all went into decline and disintegrated, culminating in the late 1970s with a United Nations membership that had quadrupled the original League of Nations which had been formed fifty years before.

The People's Republic of China has emerged as a Communist superpower and remains the solitary major bulwark of Communism at a time when Communism and Socialist systems are, to all intents and purposes, turning to some form of Western democracy, with the exception of isolated countries such as Cuba. Anderson surmises that it is perfectly possible that the People's Republic of China in its present form will also disintegrate and the Tianamen Square incident certainly supports his view.

ii. Reasons for the Transformation of the World Order

(i) Mass Communications, Migrations and Ethnicity

11.2.1   Anderson (1992) emphasises that nationalism is by no means dead but is being constantly refuelled, most recently by a rise in ethnicity, and pinpoints two main reasons for these changes in the world order. First, he attributes these phenomena to mass communications and secondly, to mass migrations. 'Capitalism and especially industrial capitalism' changed the widespread illiteracy and immobility of peoples, who never moved from the country of their birthplace. The mass-oriented newpaper and the worldwide dissemination of books, the standardisation of textbooks, curricula, and examinations, which also spread to the colonies, meant that 'republicanism, liberalism and popular democracy' would reach nearly all parts of the world.

Mass migration has, in the context of this book, meant that whole communities have travelled and continue to travel to foreign lands, bringing their laws, customs, religions, cultures, languages and traditions with them. People moved not because of disasters or wars but because of commerce and the promise of economic wealth and social and political aggrandisement.

The current 'ethnicization' which has occurred throughout the globe from North America to Australia, and which has existed long before the Arab-Israeli conflict, is indicative of a form of nationalism which is almost always divisive and rarely reconcilable. One reason why the colonising powers almost always left indigenous customs practically untouched was because of the immense local pride that exists in maintaining well-established customs.

(ii) Ideas whose Time has Come?

11.2.2   There are, of course, several theories available to explain why the world is in the state it is in, such as the shift in industrial and commercial power from Europe to the United States, to the Middle East (because of oil) to Japan, and which is now slowly shifting to the Far East. However, as far as the end of the Cold War and the inexorable shift towards democratic capitalism is concerned, various writers have also speculated on the possible reasons for this. Seyom Brown (1991) offers five possible explanations: (i) 'Imperial Overstretch'-empires enlarging their sphere of influence and control to the point where their capabilities can no longer sustain their commitments; (ii) Hegemonic Peace-the presence(or absence) of a dominant great power whose security and well-being depend on the perpetuation of a peaceful international order; (iii) 'The *Geist* whose *Zeit* has come': the movement towards democratic capitalism is simply a manifestation of the spirit of the times(*Zeitgeist*) which simply cannot be contained; (iv) The Influence of Gorbachev as a 'great man of history': it is arguable that momentous events are brought about partly by great men, such as Gorbachev, who clearly opened Russia to Western influences; and the interaction of Gorbachev's policies of *glasnost* and *perestroika* combined with Zeitgeist is 'a crucial determinant of the drama of history' (Dean Keith Simonton *Genius, Creativity and Leadership: Historiomatic Inquiries* (1984) p.165). (see Brown (1991))

Brown suggests that it could well be that the explanation for the transformation of world politics is found in *all* of the above theories. He argues that 'the *interpenetrability* of (let alone simple interdependence) of the various systems that make up the world political system would seem to be a more useful premise on which to understand the kind of systemic change we have been experiencing'.(Brown (1991) p.218).

(iii) Reasons for the Fall of Communism in Eastern Europe

11.2.3   In Timothy Ash's *The Magic Lantern* (1990) and William Echikson's *Lighting the Night* (1990), two books on the fall of Communism in Eastern Europe, at least five main reasons are suggested for the demise of Communism. Echikson's reasons are (i) the economic failure of communism, which combined with (ii) the constant struggle of nations who wanted to win freedom. To these are added three further reasons by Ash: (i) Gorbachev; (ii) Helsinki; and (iii) de Tocqueville. Gorbachev, as we have already noted (see above) was a catalyst for change because of his policies of *perestroika* and *glasnost* and a clear message from Moscow that they would not provide any assistance to these countries to protect the *status quo*. Helsinki is mentioned because it stands for the financial and moral pressure from the West that prevented local communist elites, abandoned by Moscow , from suppressing the wave of change by force. De Tocqueville is also significant because he once described the most important element of a revolutionary situation as 'the ruling elite's loss of belief in its own right to rule'.

It is significant to note that the Communist party's loss of faith in its legitimate right to rule was a widespread feeling among the middle and upper level bureaucrats, and there was 'a clash of ideology with reality'. (Osiatynski (1991) p.829) There was also a loss of popular legitimacy, that is, among the local population-the left wing *intelligentsia* and the workers. The fall of Communism was precipitated by 'the emergence of a broad anti-communist coalition in Poland' (Osiatynski (1991) pp.832).

D. CONVERGENCE OF LEGAL SYSTEMS

i. Current Common Law and Civil Law Trends

11.3   From at least the time of Cicero, differences between legal systems have been regarded as inconveniences which have to be overcome. We have seen how the common law and civil law systems are clearly differentiated not just in historical heritage and derivations but also in a wide range of matters including their sources of law, the structure of their legal professions and legal education, divisions of law, their court structures and fundamental attitudes to law and legal philosophy. Yet we have also seen that there are clearly similarities in these two systems in the way that they deal with various aspects of sales of goods, contract, tortious liability, and in their forms of business organisation. We have also noted that despite a different attitude towards caselaw or judicial decisions, and legislation, both systems are 'converging' in their use of both these sources of law. In England, there has been a noticeable and fairly dramatic increase in the amount of legislation passed since the present Conservative Government first came to power in 1979, which has recently been used to enact *regulations* granting more executive power. In the practitioner's journal, the New Law Journal, in 1991, were recorded the observations of Lord Simon in a House of Lords debate which took place on 11 December 1991. Lord Simon highlighted current trends which were 'the cause of great constitutional concern', firstly, the 'aggrandisement of the Executive at the expense of both Parliament and individual rights'; secondly, the dramatic increase in *Government by regulation in place of statute*. He cited as an example, the Child Support Act 1991, which has over a hundred regulation-making powers in its fifty-eight sections, only a dozen of which were subject to the affirmative resolution procedure. Thirdly, even parliamentary control over the making of regulations was gradually being downgraded, with the use of the negative resolution procedure in preference to the affirmative procedure, increasingly accepted by both

Houses of Parliament. The point was, 'side by side with aggrandisement at the expense of Parliament was an aggrandisement of the executive at the expense of the courts.' Under the Child Support Act 1991, 'individual officials were being given the power to make decisions formerly made by courts of law, with appeals lying to administrative tribunals rather than courts'. There was also an increasing tendency to enact 'Henry VIII clauses' which were clauses containing ministerial power to amend by regulation an Act of Parliament without going through the normal parliamentary process.

The English legal system has clearly begun to make more active use of the legislative process, as they did in the nineteenth century but making far more use of *regulations*, in a civil law style very like the former Soviet Union, as a means of speedy implementing of legal reforms rather than to allow the courts to develop the law as they have been doing for several hundred years. But cases remain important and even the Child Support Act 1991 does not exclude the courts in the cases it does not cover (eg, stepchildren) and with regard to the general common law position.

On the European Continent, civil law systems are beginning to rely increasingly on caselaw, particularly in the German constitutional courts and the French administrative courts. Indeed, even in subject-areas where Codes and statutes have traditionally been the single authoritative source, the discovery of several 'gaps' in the law has meant that the judges have been given a far greater 'lawmaking role'. Is there therefore a convergence of systems? Let us first examine the phenomenon of European convergence, before considering the various theories of convergence.

ii. European Convergence

11.3.1   Since 1989, seven countries in Eastern Europe have commenced the transition from one-party rule to constitutional democracy. These are Albania, Bulgaria, Czechoslovakia, Hungary, Poland, Romania and Yugoslavia. With the exception of Hungary, whose constitution is a 'patchwork' all the others are currently rewriting their constitutions. The current wave of 'democratisation' is not unprecedented in some respects since Japan, Italy and West Germany created democratic constitutions after the Second World War. Nevertheless, as Elster points out, this is a remarkable development because (i) all these countries were once under communist rule; (ii) all of them had pre-communist constitutional traditions although only Czeschoslovakia enjoyed constitutional democracy in the period between the two World Wars; (iii) they are all undertaking simultaneous transitions from central planning to a market economy as well as political modernisation. (iv) the histories of these countries are intertwined; (vi) the developments in 1989 can now be seen as a 'snowballing process in which events in one country inspired and accelerated those in others' (Elster (1991) p.448)

It may be said, therefore, as one writer has, that 'Eastern Europe has ceased to exist'. (Osiatynski (1991)p.823) Even more stunning was the pace of events at which the fall of communism took place. There were 'six different phenomena, linked primarily by the chain of events: one revolution unleashed another, in particular after the collapse of the Berlin Wall.' (Osiatynski (1991) p.837).

Writing as a participant in a conference held in Berlin in 1989, at the European Regional Institute on Comparative Constitutionalism, Gerhard Casper relates that in all Eastern European countries other than Hungary and the former GDR, new Constitutions are being drawn up on the basis of Western European examples, since all these countries aspire to join the Council of Europe and the European Community. All these new Constitutions will, in one way or another, implement a form of democratic society and government, and although the state will still regulate many aspects of life, it will also serve as 'the ultimate guarantor of many human aspirations.' (Casper (1991)p.445). Thus the new constitutions will have comprehensive bills of rights, just as their predecessors had but the private realm will receive constitutional protection. The new constitutions will 'institutionalise judicial review' but will follow the Austrian, German and Italian model of separate constitutional courts, having their own procedures(Casper (1991) p.446).

A democratisation process appears to be taking place in Europe and indeed, at least on paper, in most of the former Soviet Russia. As these countries attempt to implement a democratic way of life, this in itself heralds a new legal order. But is is clearly an order that is dominated by a new pride in one's ethnic origins and represents a return to one's roots and perhaps a yearning for past glories. Perhaps it is true to say that the people in these countries no longer want to talk about freedom and democracy as ideals, but simply want to live as free and democratic individuals.

iii. Philosophies/Theories of Convergence

11.3.2   There are several philosophies of convergence: (i) Return to the *jus commune*; (ii) Legal evolution; (iii) The Natural Law Theories; (iv) the Marxist thesis.

(i) The Jus Commune Theory

a. The Theory

11.3.3   This theory is based on the idea that in the era before the rise of the nation-state, the entire 'civilised world' was governed by one legal system: the Roman-Canonic *jus commune*. The two essential elements of the *jus commune*, fused into a single normative system, were (i) the Roman law of Justinian's era as rediscovered and developed by the Glossators and Commentators (see Chapter 3), and then received by a large part of continental Europe as the civil law of the Holy Roman Empire (the so-called 'Roman common law'); and (ii) canon law, or the law of Roman Catholic Church , the universal Church. The *jus commune* was considered the law of Christendom, ruled by two supreme authorities, the Emperor, the temporal head and the Pope, the spiritual head. (see Cappelletti, Merryman and Perillo 'The Rise of the *Jus Commune*' in *The Italian Legal System* (1967)). Hence there was, according to this theory, a 'common law of Europe, a common literature and language of the law, and an international community of lawyers.' (Merryman and Clark (1978)p.52).

Merryman and Clark (1978) point out the flaws in this particular thesis. To begin with, the medieval *jus commune* only applied throughout Christendom, and not to large areas of the world outside it, which would have been entitled to be called 'civilised' even by modern-day standards. Further, it was not clear even within Western Europe that the *jus commune* was a normal, accepted part of the civilised world as it existed then. Hence, although it was sustained by the Church, it seems incongruous to expect nations that were never part of, nor had received nothing of, the *jus commune* to 'return' to it. England, for instance, was never part of the *jus commune*.

A final difficulty with this theory is that it argues on the basis of the disruption caused by the nation-state whereas the nation-state actually unified the many diverse laws of the towns, communes, dukedoms and principalities into one major convergence of laws within its jurisdiction. Forcing common law and civil law jurisdictions into accepting one law would offend both group and legal interests.

b. Reception of American Law in Europe

11.3.4 Another development of some considerable consequence has been taking place in Europe since World War Two-the reception of 'American Law'. (see Wiegand (1991)). An analogy may be drawn with the 'Latin Middle Ages' wherein the dissemination of the *jus commune* was a European-wide phenomenon. The American language has penetrated into everyday French and German (and incidentally, has also travelled *via* television and books, to the Far East as well). With regard to jurisprudence, nearly all fundamental and far-reaching changes in European law during the post-war era have started from America. Wiegand (1991) explains that American law has now infiltrated to such an extent in Europe that there are:(i) new business concepts, spawned from the American-based practices of leasing, factoring and franchising; (ii) new legal concepts in business and tort law and constitutional law. In the area of products liability and in 'medical malpractice law' (which has also absorbed the term 'informed consent') the American approach has been adopted in nearly all European legal systems. American approaches to consumer protection has also influenced European countries. (Wiegand (1991)pp.236-46)

As far as concepts are concerned, European systems have started to adopt the 'economic analysis of law' approach which is typically associated with American law as well as an 'interdisciplinary' approach.

Reasons for this 'reception' range from the education of European lawyers (a great many Europeans taking up postgraduate legal training in the USA),to the fact that lawyers occupy key positions in academic institutions, law firms, major banks, and private industry, which has already had a fundamental effect on European law and practice. The needs of a post-industrial era and service-dominated society have also been readily addressed by American law, so that European law has been quick to draw upon the American solutions to deal with similar needs. Switzerland, in particular, has undergone an American reception in many aspects of its legal scenario. Hence, even if America ceases to dominate European markets in the near future, the seeds have been sown for the 'Americanisation' to continue.

(ii) Legal Evolution Theory

11.3.5   This theory proceeds on the basis that legal change is a natural process which will proceed inexorably and irresistibly because it is controlled by forces beyond human power. Thus, legal systems are at different stages of development and when they converge it is because the less developed system is catching up with the more mature one. Since the civil law is much older than the common law, the logical corollary to this thesis is that the common law will gradually become more like the civil law. However, trends toward convergence may be observed in both systems.

While there is more 'codification' in common law countries, particularly in the United States, there is also the phenomenon that civil law judges are becoming more active 'lawmakers', any *jurisprudence constante* is being followed more than ever, and the rights of the defendant in civil law criminal proceedings are also becoming more like their common law counterparts. In the absence of any universally acceptable crtiteria, it is extremely difficult to say whether the common law or civil law is more 'developed.' Thus any discussion of legal evolution divorced from its socio-cultural or ideological context is otiose and too abstract to be of any practical value.

(iii) Natural Law Theory

11.3.6   This theory argues that the common nature of human beings will eventually lead to the creation of similar social structures, laws and legal systems. This common nature will therefore be observed and expressed by law. (see Merryman and Clark (1978)p.54). Unfortunately, there is no universal consensus about which common characteristics of human beings and human society determine, or ought to determine the character of the legal system. As Merryman and Clark put it 'The argument that we are all one does not take us very far if there is substantial disagreement about the nature of the one.' (Merryman and Clark (1978) p.54).

(iv) The Marxist Thesis

11.3.7   Marxist theory, which has been discussed in Chapter 6, it basically argues that law is mere superstructure. Accordingly, law is merely another instrument for the furtherance of certain economic, social and political ideals. Western bourgeois capitalist nations will all share the same fundamental core values and beliefs and their systems will have converging tendencies whereas socialist societies will have divergent legal systems which reflect the distinct nature of socialist politics, society and economics. Hence differences between socialist and Western legal systems are irreconcilable whereas the legal systems of France, Germany and England are basically reconcilable since the differences in law are purely superficial, being mere superstructure.

Of course, the events of the past three years strongly suggest that the socialist system is now in terminal decline and that Eastern Europe is well on the way to adopting a more capitalist and Westernised approach to law and

336

society. As such, although complete privatisation will take many years, perhaps even decades in the case of certain countries like Hungary and Poland, convergence in economic, political and social philosophy has already begun to take place between former socialist systems and Western capitalist ones. Of course, the West has already entered into international and regional agreements seeking international economic, social and political integration as expressed in the creation of the European Community, and the conclusion of international treaties such as the European Human Rights Convention. Convergence of the common and civil has also been set in motion, at least in the field of monetary and economic co-operation and in the field of human rights. The UN Convention on the Rights of the Child, which has received the largest number of signatories of any international treaty in modern times is indicative of the much wider convergence which exists both within and outside Europe on certain matters.

E. GLOBAL CONVERGENCE AND THE FUKUYAMA THESIS

11.4 In the summer of 1989, an article by a deputy director of the American State Department, Francis Fukuyama, entitled, 'The End of History' was published. It theme was that liberal democracy is the only ideology left in the greater part of the civilised world. This was by no means a earth-shattering or mould-breaking revelation but Fukuyama's article won notoriety and he has since written a three-hundred and sixty-page book (*The End of History and The Last Man*) which seeks to clarify to the world his ideas in the article. He explained that his title was merely an example of an idiom that has not been fashionable since the nineteenth century: Hegelianism. Several writers and philosophers have exposed the flaws in Hegelianism, culminating in a book by Karl Popper, *The Open Society and Its Enemies*, published in 1945.

It is not the purpose of this section to discuss the many interesting and sometimes provocative aspects of the book but it is relevant to the notions of convergence because it argues, *inter alia*, that in Southern Europe, Latin America, Asia and Eastern Europe, free-market economies and parliamentary democracy are, with notable exceptions, fast becoming the norm. He emphasises the victory of the principles of liberal democracy and more precisely, the liberal *idea*, rather than liberal practice. (see Fukuyama (1992) p.45). Hence, as he puts it 'for a very large part of the world, there is now no ideology with pretensions to universality that is in a position to challenge liberal democracy and no universal principle of legitimacy other than the sovereignty of the people.' (Fukuyama,*ibid*).

Though there are no longer any serious competitors to it, he raises the question of whether its own internal fissures may not gradually destroy it from within. One of Fukayama's concerns is that the rights and freedoms of liberal democracy, the safety of the person, equality before the law, and the protection of property, may not be enough to ensure its survival.

337

He therefore argues that a society needs to be free in a much wider sense so as to pursue dreams and aspirations. Tracing this idea to Plato's *thymos* ('courage'; 'public spiritedness') which Hegel develops as 'the struggle for recognition' he develops his theme that this concept helps to illuminate an understanding of the contemporary world.

Whether one agrees with Fukayama's ideas, and it should be noted that he does not, in fact, believe that history has 'ended' in any sense, he has highlighted a 'worldwide liberal revolution' while noting the exceptions-China, which will no longer serve as a model for revolutionaries around the world; Cuba, North Korea and Vietnam, Ethiopia, Angola and Mozambique. Authoritarian rulers have been forced to promise free elections in a host of other African countries. He also places the beginning of this 'revolution' as having occurred in 1974, when the Caetano regime in Portugal was ousted in an army coup the socialist Mario Soares was elected prime minister in 1976. 1974 was also the year when the Karamanlis regime was elected in Greece, which put paid to the era of the colonels who ran the country since 1967. In Asia, the overthrow of the Marcos dictatorship in the Philippines in 1986 is signficant as is the announcement in February 1980 by F.W. de Clerk in South Africa that Nelson Mandela would be released and that the African National Congress and the South African Communist party would have their ban lifted. In the 1980s, the Chinese communist leadership began permitting peasants , who constituted eighty per cent of the population, to grow and sell their own food. Thus, agriculture was 'de-collectivised' and capitalist market relationships began appearing throughout the countryside and in urban industry as well.

As far as the power of Islamic States is concerned, he concedes that Islam has defeated liberal democracy in many parts of the Islamic world, but argues that 'this religion has virtually no appeal outside those areas that were culturally Islamic to begin with.' (Fukuyama (1992) p.46) Indeed, he argues that the Islamic world would seem 'more vulnerable to liberal ideas in the long run than the reverse since such liberalism has attracted numerous and powerful Muslim adherents over the past century and a half'. No doubt Islamic adherents or historians would take issue with him on that point, but the fact remains that there appears to be a worldwide movement towards more liberal ideas and philosophies, which is traditionally associated with Western ideas of liberal democracy. As Fukuyama argues, there were thirteen liberal democracies in 1940, thirty-seven in 1960 and sixty-two in 1992. By his reckoning, there was not a single true democracy in the world until 1776, if one defines democracy as including the 'systematic protection of individual rights'.

By the end of the 1980s, therefore, China, the former Soviet Union and the countries of Eastern Europe had all 'succumbed to the economic logic of advanced industrialisation' (Fukuyama (1992) p.96). Even the Chinese leadership had accepted the need for markets and decentralised economic planning and 'the close integration into the global capitalist division of labour.'

The problem which Fukuyama poses in his final chapters is how far liberal democracy can fulfil the human need for recognition and how far it can become a permanent and stable society-the last-stage of history. That, as with many of his other concerns, will surely remain a matter for history itself to answer.

338

F. UNIFICATION OF LEGAL SYSTEMS

i. Strategies of Convergence

11.5   Three main 'strategies' or modes of convergence have been identified by Merryman and Clark (1978): (i) active programmes for the unification of law; (ii) transplantation of legal institutions; and (iii) natural convergence.

Unification of law is sought to be achieved through the use of international institutions specifically intended to promote the unification of law. Agencies such as the International Institute for the Unification of Private Law in Rome, the Hague Conference on Private International Law and the UN Commission on International Trade Law. Programmes of international organisations with broader objectives also frequently seek to generalise or standardise legal rules and practices, for example in the European Community. Other examples of agencies which include unification of law as one of their objectives are the International Labour Organisation, the European Commission on Human Rights and the Organisation of American States.

Unification of law is often attempted through supranational legislation and judicial decision binding on and applicable within individual member states, in the case of regulations of the European Community and the decisions of the European Court of Justice, provisions of treaties and multilateral conventions (for example the International Copyright Convention). Another recent example of a UN Convention which has revised an original version of a uniform law which has had global input is the UN Convention on Contracts for the International Sale of Goods. The objective of unification of law places great store on legislation and focuses on rules of law, along the lines of Savigny and Thibaut's arguments. The practical efficacy of unification will, however, be necessarily circumscribed by the legal structures, institutions and procedures existing within nations which will determine the degree of uniformity in the application and interpretation of rules. (see Merryman and Clark (1978) p.58).

ii. Legal Transplants

11.5.1   As Alan Watson puts it, 'Borrowing from another system is the most common form of legal change' (Watson *Legal Origins and Legal Change* (1991) p.73) and legal transplantation has a long history. There was the reception of Roman law in later Europe, the spread of English law through the colonies of the British Empire, even into parts of the United States which had never been under British rule, and the tremendous impact of the French Civil Code on other civil law systems in Europe and abroad, and latterly, the spread of American law to Europe, especially in places like Switzerland. The so-called hybrid or 'mixed jurisdictions' jurisidictions still show the effects of such transplantation in their unique blends of common law, civil law and local customary law.

Transplantation may occur *voluntarily* by for example, the adoption or imitation of a foreign Code; or *involuntarily* as when a country is colonised and has a foreign legal system imposed on its indigenous culture. Legal transplants across the common law-civil law boundary inevitable lead to convergence of the two systems. Tranplantations may or may not be 'successful' depending on a country's particular conditions for receptivity. While the notions of the condominium and community property system were transplanted quite easily into the United States from the civil law, the Uniform Law on Negotiable Instruments Law which was widely adopted in the United States failed in Colombia.

iii. Natural Convergence

11.5.2   This theory argues that the legal systems of societies will tend to become more alike as the societies themselves become more like each other. Thus there are similarities in constitutions in Western democracies, and a common international culture brought about by increased international communication and travel, international trade, international organisations, the internationalisation of business and technology and a growing awareness of shared global concerns (pollution, the environment, global warming and so on), student exchange programmes and scholarly exchange schemes.

There are several examples of this type of convergence of civil law and common law: safeguards for defendants in criminal proceedings, adoption of graduated income tax, legal aid schemes, uniformity in definition and protection of individual rights, the rise in judicial review (bearing in mind that this term means different things between America and England, as well as between civil law and common law systems). (see Merryman and Clark (1978) p.60).

There are several notable historically explicable differences between the legal systems of civil law and common law countries, although they have a pronounced concordance of legal principles. The point, perhaps, is that while there are many practical similarities in their legal solutions, fundamental and deep-rooted differences exist in juristic style, philosophy and substance, in court structures and sources of law and more importantly, in their judicial and administrative ethos, legal divisions and categories, and their professional structure and legal education.

Legal transplantation may, of course, affect the speed and direction of change in civil law and common law countries. So may revolutions, even if they are non-violent ones, such as the recent global movement towards the liberal idea and principles of democracy.

iv. Convergence and Divergence between Common and Civil Law

11.5.3   Since the two main Civil Codes were enacted in the early and late nineteenth century, they could not possiblty have anticipated the pace or scale or technology of the modern twentieth century. Civil law judges have therefore had to create legal rules to cope with situations which could not have been envisaged by the legislators of the Codes. French law on torts is therefore primarily found in widely published and cited decisions of the courts. Common law judges have always had a high profile and have resorted to judicial lawmaking whenever a 'gap' has appeared in the statute or in cases where the statute has been ambiguous or could produce a manifestly absurd or unjust result.

German lawyers and judges rely very heavily on the Short Commentary on the German Civil Code for daily practice, which contains thousands of cases. This again resembles common law legal practice although it should be pointed out that there is no doctrine of binding precedent as such on the Continent (see Chapter 3).

There has also been a growth in public administration which has accompanied this decline in legislative authority. Members of the public administration itself, sitting in a council of state, decide on the propriety and legality of State administrative actions. In England, there has been a dramatic increase in the use of the application for judicial review of administrative actions and most of the law is laid down by Parliament. Further, most of the non-legislative law is being created by the ever-growing network of administrative tribunals. Caselaw has tended to feature heavily in the German Constitutional court and French administrative court. However, recent cases tend to indicate that the distinction between public and private law is breaking down *both* on the Continent and in England. The recent English House of Lords case indicates that the mere assertion of a private law right entitles an individual to proceed by an ordinary action, rather than be restricted to judicial review, even though he was challenging a public law decision (see Chapter 4).

There has also been a rise in Constitutional power, in the sense that Constitutions are increasingly being treated as supreme sources of law, in civil law countries and in the United States of America. Although the actual technical basis of the constitutional review is by no means identical under civil law and American law, there are common features since in both types of jurisdiction, there is a move to promote, guarantee and if necessary, expand individual rights. This is seen by commentators such as Merryman as another example of 'decodification' since the Codes are no longer seen as fulfilling a constitutional function. (Merryman (1977) p.157). Judges have therefore acquired an enhanced status and expanded role in this context, particularly in the civil law courts.

Finally, there is the existence and growing influence of European Community law. The European Court of Justice has the power to set aside national laws that conflict with Community law so that like American Federal law, it regns supreme in certain areas of endeavour. As a result of the notion of English parliamentary sovereignty or supremacy, the UK European Communities Act 1972 has specifically accepted the supremacy of EC law so that Community law has the status of law in the British courts. However, since the 1972 Act is a UK statute which derives its authority from the British Parliament, it could always be repealed. However, the 1972 Act has created a legislative conduit which will allow EC law to be take precedence over and be part of English law, until and unless the 1972 Act is repealed. (see Chapter 5).

An analogy could be drawn between Community Law and the canon law *jus commune* since EC Law and the European Human Rights Convention could be seen as the foundation of a new *jus commune* 'based on common culture and common interests' (Merryman (1977) p.158). The current uncertainty surrounding the implementation of closer economic and monetary union through the Maastricht Treaty may not ultimately affect the development of the new *jus commune*.

G. THE DAWN OF A NEW ERA IN WORLD HISTORY

11.6   In his Shimizu lecture, Professor Markesinis laments the fact that Comparative Law is a subject in search of an audience and offers a powerful exposition of 'the value of presenting a foreign system to an unfamiliar audience primarily through its case law rather than by means of codal provision' (see Markesinis (1990) p.1). Three years hence, it would seem that the time is now ripe for lawyers, judges and students to investigate and utilise the delights of comparative law. With the impending Single Market, the convergence of European systems, the growing influence of European Community Law, the global village phenomenon, and a communality of purpose in the protection and enforcement of human rights, it behoves practitioners and international law specialists to seize the opportunity to establish more positive and imaginative programmes for inter-regional research and practice.

 While Eastern European legal systems may be gravitating towards capitalist democracies, basic changes are also taking place in Western Europe. Both the Atlantic alliance and the European Community are facing fundamental challenges. The North Atlantic Treaty Organisation is facing the cuurent wave of American isolationism, and the desires of the Europeans to give defence a 'European identity' whereas the Community itself is grappling with the Danish rejection of the Maastricht Treaty and the dilemma of how far and how fast to expand their economies-assuming there is an upturn in the current economic situation.   There is therefore a new European geopolitics which resembles the nineteenth century fluid, open system of diplomacy. The European Court of Justice has become a source of legal innovation in Europe 'not only because of its position as the Community's judicial institution, but also because of the intellectual strength of its comparative methods'. Thus, the development of European Community law appears to be the 'progressive construction' of a 'many-sided edifice' (Koopmans (1991) p.505-6). It has 'many parents and foster parents' (Koopmans (1991) p.506) so that it becomes increasingly important to know the origins or even existence of different legal doctrines and ideas so as to cope with a rapidly changing technological world.

H. CONCLUSIONS

11.7   The configuration of the law and legal systems by the end of the twentieth century will therefore depend on a number of variables and imponderables such as whether new military alliances are formed within Europe, without the United States as a partner or whether the new united Germany finds itself balancing off France and Russia, as it did in the nineteenth century. On the other hand, what of the economic power of the Japanese; and American economic fortunes? What is going to happen in the 'new Russia' in the next five years or so?

Although we might appear to have come full circle, there are many elements which will not change and have not changed. The fundamental ideological, doctrinal and religious differences that exist between countries in the Muslim world and the West, will be a very long time changing, although the last three years indicates nothing is impossible. Newly-emergent and poor nations have a greater need than ever to have the benefit of not just Western aid and technology but also Western experience and sometimes, Western legal ideas which could speed their constitutional and political development and resolve their many local problems.

Transnational companies are already on the lookout for lawyers who are conversant with more than one system of law and who have an above-average understanding of more than one legal system. The ever-increasing membership of the European Community, its supra-national legal regime and the continuing transplantation of Western ideas to countries all over the world, provide an ideal environment in which the comparative law methodology should not just be used but will be absolutely essential to an understanding and appreciation of the law. The contemporary relevance of the comparative law method is that it could help to facilitate an understanding of the differences between the old world order and the new.

Ultimately, the enduring value of the comparative law method must lie not merely in its providing a window to the world's legal systems, or in its intellectual merit, or in its provision of substantive doctrines at the international and domestic level. Surely the most valuable benefits of comparative law are that it enables us to look beyond our narrow parochial interests, illuminate our understanding of legal rules and concepts, and reminds us that despite differences in culture, history, law and language, we are all part of the larger community of mankind. In the words of Jerome (*On Getting on in the World*)(1889):

'We are so bound together that no man can labour for himself alone. Each blow he strikes on his own behalf helps to mould the universe.'

Although the current enterprise has ended, for the would-be comparatist, it is only the beginning. As a new era in world history dawns, perhaps the ethos of 1992 will herald another era-the modern era of the comparatist.

SELECTIVE BIBLIOGRAPHY

Merryman THE CIVIL LAW TRADITION (1977) Ch.20

Merryman & Clark COMPARATIVE LAW: WESTERN EUROPEAN AND LATIN
        AMERICAN LEGAL SYSTEMS (1978) pp.51-67

Eorsi COMPARATIVE CIVIL(PRIVATE) LAW (1979),Part II, Ch.8

Brady JUSTICE AND POLITICS IN PEOPLE'S CHINA (1982)

Kim 'The Modern Chinese Legal System' (1987) 31 Tul LR 1413

Markesinis 'Comparative Law-A Subject in Search of an Audience' [1990] 53 Mod.LR 1

Goodman & Segal (eds.) CHINA IN THE NINETIES (1991)

Agh 'The Transition to Democracy in Central Europe:
   A Comparative View' (1991) 133
Brown 'Explaining the Transformation of World Politics' (1991)
   International Journal 207
Casper 'European Convergence' (Editorial) [1991] 58 U.Ch.LR 441
Elster 'Constitutionalism in Eastern Europe: An Introduction' [1991] 58 U.Ch.LR 447
Osiatynski 'Revolutions in Eastern Europe' [1991] 58 U.Ch. of Chicago Law Review 823
Koopmans 'The Birth of European Law At the Crossroads of Legal
Traditions' (1991) AmJCL 493
Piotrowicz 'The Arithmetic of German Unification: One into Three Does Go' (1991) ICLQ 635
Wiegand 'The Reception of American Law in Europe'(1991) AmJCL 229
Anderson 'The New World Disorder' (Editorial) (1992) New Left
      Review 3
Bingham 'There is a World Elsewhere: The Changing Perspectives of English Law' (1992) ICLQ 513
Milband 'Fukuyama and the Socialist Alternative' (1992) New Left
      Review 108
Rustin 'No Exit from Capitalism?' (1992) New Left Review 96
Fukuyama THE END OF HISTORY AND THE LAST MAN (1992)

INDEX